Writing Your
JOURNAL
ARTICLE
in
12 WEEKS

For my parents, with respect and gratitude

Writing Your
JOURNAL ARTICLE
in
12 WEEKS

A Guide to Academic Publishing Success

Wendy Laura Belcher

Princeton University

Los Angeles • London • New Delhi • Singapore • Washington DC

For information:

 SAGE Publications, Inc.
2455 Teller Road
Thousand Oaks, California 91320
Email: order@sagepub.com

SAGE Publications India Pvt. Ltd.
B 1/I 1 Mohan Cooperative Industrial Area
Mathura Road, New Delhi 110 044
India

SAGE Publications Ltd.
1 Oliver's Yard
55 City Road
London, EC1Y 1SP
United Kingdom

SAGE Publications Asia-Pacific Pte. Ltd.
33 Pekin Street #02-01
Far East Square
Singapore 048763

Printed in the United States of America

Library of Congress Cataloging-in-Publication Data

Writing your journal article in twelve weeks : a guide to academic publishing success / Wendy Laura Belcher.
    p. cm.
  Includes bibliographical references and index.
  ISBN 978-1-4129-5701-4 (pbk.)
  1. Scholarly publishing—United States.   I. Title.
  Z471.B45 2009
  070.50973—dc22

                                    2008037599

This book is printed on acid-free paper.

09   10   11   12   13   10 9 8 7 6 5 4 3 2 1

Acquisitions Editor:	Lisa Cuevas Shaw
Editorial Assistant:	MaryAnn Vail
Production Editor:	Appingo Publishing Services
Cover Designer:	Arup Giri
Cover Photography:	Garon Kiesel
Marketing Manager:	Jennifer Reed Banando

Contents

Acknowledgments

I owe much to Assistant Vice Chancellor Jim Turner, emeriti professor and mentor extraordinaire, who incubated the writing workshop at UCLA with me; to Vice Chancellor Claudia Mitchell-Kernan, who hired me to teach the workshop for the UCLA Graduate Division for ten years; to UCLA Extension Program Writing Director Linda Venis, who hired me to teach for the first time; and to Elin Skaar, who brought me to teach the workshop in Norway.

Many thanks to my writing group, Harryette Mullen, Alice Wexler, Kathleen McHugh, Mary Bush, and Ellen Krout-Hasegawa, for reading early drafts and offering essential suggestions; to Judith Stevenson for keeping me going with daily encouragement; and to Bonnie Berry-Lamon, fellow writer, for being there since ninth grade and negotiating the contract.

For anecdotes, advice, encouragement, or invaluable assistance, thanks to Sana Abasher, Ali Behdad, D. Christopher Belcher, John H. Belcher, Zara Bennett, Erica Bochanty, Jean Arnold, Martha Banta, Haeng-ja Chung, Helen Deutsch, JaneAnn Dill, Cynthia Feliciano, Stefan Frazier, the late Guillermo E. Hernandez, Ruth E. Iskin, Meg Powers Livingston, Suzanne L'Oiseaux, Bharati Mandapati, Janice Molloy, Peter McLaren, Tammi Monsanto, Angela Nonaka, Chon A. Noriega, Paul Ong, Carrie Petrucci, Samantha Pinto, Mark Quigley, Karen Quintiliani, Sam See, Sean Silver, Vivian Sobchack, Guri Stegali, Liz Taylor, Ward Thomas, Juliet Williams, and Alayne Yonemoto. Thanks also to the wonderful folks at Sage, including its editors Lisa Cuevas Shaw and John Szilagyi; its directors Alison Mudditt, Jim Brace-Thompson, and Blaise Simqu; the book's shepherds MaryAnn Vail, Cassandra Seibel, Stephanie Adams, and Belinda Thresher; its copyeditor Belea T. Keeney; its proofreader Lisa Allen; and its compositor/designer Trice Atkinson.

For enabling me to teach the workshop in Africa, I am especially grateful to friends at the Chr. Michelsen Institute in Bergen, including Siri Gloppen, Pavla Jezkova, Lise Rakner, Elin Skaar, Gunnar M. Sørbø, Lars G. Svåsand, and Arne Tostensen, and to all the workshop participants in Sudan and Malawi, including Abdel Ghaffar Ahmed, Sana Abasher, Nandini Patel, and the late Nixon Khembo. I wish I could thank all my students by name; each one of them made this book stronger.

Most of all, I thank my parents, who taught me to love writing and books. While I wrote, they regularly showed up to take care of cooking, car maintenance, laundry, and even the bills, and devoted many long days to reading every page of this workbook with enthusiasm and care.

Introduction

Using This Workbook

GOALS OF THE WORKBOOK

The primary goals of this workbook are to aid you in revising a classroom essay, conference paper, unpublished article, chapter, or thesis and sending it to the editor of a suitable academic journal. That is, the goals are active and pragmatic. The workbook provides the instruction, exercises, structure, and deadlines needed to do an effective revision. It will help you to develop the habits of productivity that lead to confidence, the kind of confidence that it takes to send out into the world a journal article that you have written. By aiding you in taking your paper from classroom or conference quality to journal article quality, it also helps you to overcome anxiety about academic publishing.

HISTORY OF THE WORKBOOK

Nothing quite like this workbook exists. Most books on scholarly writing give advice based on the experiences of only the author, a few scholars directly in the author's field, or the author's undergraduates. This workbook is not the product of one person's experience or thought. It was not written over just a semester or a year. This version is the product of ten years of repeated experimentation with hundreds of scholarly writers. I have revised it again and again, based on the dozens of courses in which I have used this workbook to teach graduate students at UCLA and faculty members around the world. It is also based on what I learned managing a peer-reviewed journal for ten years. Every time I taught the workbook, I have asked its users how it was working for them and what would improve it. Every year, I kept in close contact with my course participants as they submitted journal articles, underwent peer review, and got published. I learned more and more about what actually succeeds in the peer review process, not what is theorized to succeed. On the basis of these participants' experiences, I wrote and rewrote this workbook to be the most helpful it could be. I will continue to do so and am always interested in hearing from readers about how it worked for them. Very few books on scholarly writing have undergone the fire of testing among hundreds of scholars across a wide range of disciplines. This one has.

PHILOSOPHY OF THE WORKBOOK

Most instruction books are prescriptive, setting up an ideal process and encouraging you to aspire to it. I don't believe in the ivory tower approach. My aim is to help graduate students and junior faculty understand the rules of the academic publishing game so that they can flourish, not perish. Thus, this workbook is based on what works. I don't tell you to write eight hours a day; that doesn't work. I don't advise you to read everything in your field; you can't. I don't describe how to write perfect papers; no one does. Publication, not perfection, is the goal here, so it is based on what students told me they actually did and what they were willing to do. This workbook is not intended for academic purists, but for those in the academic trenches who sometimes grow discouraged and who fear that they are the only ones who haven't figured it all out.

As a result, the workbook details shortcuts and even a few tricks. And it always tells the truth, however upsetting. Some journal editors don't like statements that publishing in certain types of journals will not serve you well when it comes to hiring, tenure, and promotion. Some professors don't like statements that pre-tenure scholars should prioritize certain types of articles and research. But, I state these truths anyway. The workbook's advice on query letters and argument regularly inspires debate and yet continues to help students achieve academic publishing success. I may not agree with the relentless professionalization of scholarly publishing, but I do believe everyone should know the rules and have a chance to succeed.

Over the history of writing this workbook and teaching my courses, I've noticed that a preponderance of my students were women, people of color, non-Americans, and/or first-generation academics. I would repeatedly hear from my students: "No one ever told me this" or "I had no idea!" This workbook has been responsible for helping many on the margins—racially, economically, internationally, and theoretically—to feel more confident and to frame their fascinating work in ways that would be acceptable to mainstream journals. That's why several people have said I should call this an "underground" guide to entering the profession, since it demystifies EuroAmerican academic conventions. My hope is that enabling more scholars from the periphery to publish in scholarly journals will improve (and radicalize) scholarship for the better.

PEDAGOGY OF THE WORKBOOK

Most books on academic writing assume that the most difficult part of writing is arriving at good ideas. This may be difficult for undergraduates, but it is not for graduate students or junior faculty. In my writing workshops, good ideas abound. The real problem is how many good ideas languish in unfinished, unpublished articles. What most graduate students and junior faculty need is a way to make publishable the research they have already conducted, or written up in graduate school, or taught. They know that their classroom essays, conference papers, dissertation chapters, or rejected articles are not ready for journals, but they don't know how to improve them. Thus, in my workshops, I focused on guiding students through a revision of something they had already written, an exercise many graduate students claimed never to have done before. I firmly believe that revision is the heart of good writing and that many scholars are unpublished not because they have bad ideas, but because they have never learned how to improve their drafts. This workbook focuses on revision as a key to publication.

If you think you have no draft to revise for publication, read the Week 1 section for Day 2 titled "Selecting a Paper for Revision." You may find that you do have something to revise. It doesn't matter if the draft is poor or little more than an outline, the workbook will still aid you in revising such, although you will need to allot more time for writing. You may think it is better to start from scratch, but my students have found that revising their drafts was more effective. Once they learned to diagnose and correct their erroneous tendencies in a draft, they wrote their next article from scratch much more easily. They learned more from revising their work than drafting it. If you are in the social sciences and really don't have a suitable draft, you might want to consult Anne Sigismund Huff's new book *Designing Research for Publication* (in which she addresses disciplinary fields of inquiry, scholarly conversations, and the evolution of research projects), Nicholas Walliman's *Your Research Project: A Step-by-Step Guide for the First-Time Researcher*, or Catherine Marshall and Gretchen B. Rossman's *Designing Qualitative Research*. Alternately, you can use this workbook to draft an article by reading the text, taking notes on what makes for a good article, and then starting. But, the workbook works best for those reworking a draft for publication.

Most books on academic writing are also excessively concerned with style. Half their pages are devoted to improving word choice and syntax. In my experience, this was the least of students' problems. The writing research supported my own observation that what most students need is a better grasp of the macro aspects of writing—argument, structure, and summarizing—not the micro aspects. Thus, this workbook is devoted to "deep revision," the changes that make the biggest difference to an article's quality and thus success.

I designed this workbook to help you build both skills and self-assurance. If you have neither, one, or both—welcome.

GENERAL INSTRUCTIONS

This workbook is designed to be written in. Go ahead and scribble (unless this is a library book, in which case, don't!). You may also access some of the sheets at my website, www.wendybelcher.com, so that you keep the workbook "clean."

Each week you will have five specific daily **tasks** designed to aid you in accomplishing your goal of submitting your article to a journal in twelve weeks. These tasks encourage limited but daily writing, so that the revision of your article can proceed steadily despite your other responsibilities like teaching, a full-time job, or caring for children. Although some of the week's tasks build on those of the week before, if you find that you need to switch one week with another (for instance, working on your introduction before working on your related literature review), that's fine. In some cases, you may find that you do not need to do a task because you have already done it. But if you come across a task you have not done, make sure you do it. Every task has been carefully designed to move you forward and to assist you in developing the good writing habits that will aid you in writing further articles. To arrive at the destination of publication, spend time at each station on the journey.

Although I wish it were otherwise, this workbook does not work by osmosis. You cannot just turn the pages, read the occasional text, and then magically have an article by the time you turn the last page. Reading the workbook is just a fifth of the work you must do to ready an article for a journal. The workbook makes that work easier and more straightforward, but it does not do the work for you. Rather, it provides a structure within which to perform the required tasks. If you read through the workbook just to pick up some tips, you won't learn nearly as much as you will by doing the related tasks. And you probably won't retain much. Doing is learning.

If you happen to fall behind on the daily tasks, don't give up or waste time feeling guilty. The times listed for the duration of each task are meant as minimums, each may take quite a bit longer. If you fall behind, just try to have a catch-up session or reset your twelve-week calendar accordingly. I have seen many cases where authors took twenty-four weeks (or months) rather than twelve weeks to send their article to a journal, and got published just the same. Persevering is the key.

There are four types of tasks in this book. In *workbook* tasks, you read the workbook and do the exercises. In *social* tasks, you talk about or share your writing with another student or a faculty member, or with a writing partner or writing group. Inw *writing* tasks, you write some part of your article, like an abstract, or something related to your article, such as a query letter. In *planning* tasks, you document your plans and track your success in achieving them.

USING THE WORKBOOK ACCORDING TO YOUR TEMPERAMENT

You can progress through this workbook in several ways. Early on, I observed that many of my students did not want the burden of free choice but wanted to be led, as Dostoyevsky's Grand Inquisitor put it. If you prefer a very structured approach, and like the security of detailed instructions, just follow the daily tasks and proceed through the workbook chapter by chapter. If you do this, you will have a journal article ready to go out in twelve weeks. There is a lot to be said for clear guidance.

If you hate to be told what to do, and like the freedom of making your own decisions, but still feel that you have much to learn about writing a publishable journal article, then don't follow the detailed instructions. Instead, set aside an hour every week to read a chapter of the workbook and outline its implications for your revising of your article, and set aside at least four hours a week to work on actual revising. After the first week, you can read the chapters in any order and focus each week on the main tasks outlined in that chapter, for example, improving your argument or selecting a journal. When you have completed them all, you are ready to send off your journal article. It may even be a good idea to switch the order of the chapters, since the most discussed aspect of this workbook has always been the order of advice. In the early years, I kept changing the order—moving the chapter about journals forward or back in the weekly line up, for instance—but soon found that no matter what order I picked, someone wanted another. All had excellent rationales for wanting the journal chapter in the first week or the editing chapter in the third week. I think the current order of chapters in the workbook is the best order, but you are free to construct the best order for your particular circumstances.

Two warnings about this approach. Freedom has its price—inertia. If you have a problem staying focused or have not written much in a long time, you should really try to follow the structured approach for the first three weeks. Then, if you want to follow your own path through the workbook, you will be doing it backed by the strength of habit. Two, try not to work on your article only one day a week or only on the weekend. The workbook is structured to keep you working on the article steadily, keeping you and it fresh, while you go about the rest of your life. Writing research shows that writing a little bit every day is more effective than bunching up your writing into big blocks. The Week 1 chapter explains this more thoroughly.

If you find at any point that you have moved through a week's tasks more quickly than anticipated—for instance, if you already had a strong abstract or structure—don't stop working for that week. You can either move right into the next week's tasks or you can spend the extra time reading related articles or books. Since most of us feel that we have never done enough reading, this is a good use of your extra time.

USING THE WORKBOOK ACCORDING TO YOUR DISCIPLINE

This workbook is useful for those in the humanities and social sciences. Many scholars have used this workbook to write journal articles in the humanities on literature, art, architecture, film, television, digital media, drama, and music. Others have used it to write about social constructions like gender, sexuality, philosophy, race, culture, ethnicity, nation, region, class, and religion. Still others have used it to write journal articles in such social sciences as cultural anthropology, applied linguistics, geography, archaeology, education, political science, public policy, psychology, social welfare, sociology, business management, international relations, and urban planning. Those in the natural sciences who are writing less scientific articles have also used it—such as those in bioethics, public health, medical anthropology, development studies, and sometimes, economics. Only a few have used it for legal writing.

Those writing up research in the sciences—in such fields as biology, mathematics, chemistry, engineering, computer science, and physics—will not find the workbook very helpful, as the writing process for and the structure of scientific articles varies so much from those in the humanities or social sciences. I have had some authors use this workbook in such fields, but they have had to extrapolate quite a bit from the text, so I don't recommend it. If you are in such a field and use this workbook, let me know if you found it useful.

USING THE WORKBOOK
ACCORDING TO YOUR CAREER STAGE

I wrote this workbook for graduate students and junior faculty and never thought it would be used by anybody else. Then I found out that draft copies were circulating among senior faculty. Since I think it is important not to aim at pleasing all possible audiences, I have kept this workbook oriented toward those who have rarely or never published before. Despite this, the workbook continues to appeal to those who have already published, perhaps because published authors aren't always sure what enabled their published articles to succeed or because they still feel the need for deadlines and structure to complete further articles. Perhaps most of us never stop thinking of ourselves as graduate students; certainly, learning to write well is a lifelong journey.

USING THE WORKBOOK BY YOURSELF

You can use this workbook by yourself. Some of the tasks require submitting parts of your journal article to another student or a professor for comments—but otherwise you can use this workbook independently. You should set aside about an hour a day five days a week to work through that week's readings and exercises.

USING THE WORKBOOK
WITH A WRITING PARTNER

You can also use this workbook with a writing partner. This is a wonderfully effective method for completing your journal article. Since most students' real challenge when it comes to writing is actually getting writing done, having a partner helps ensure that you persevere. Moreover, such writing partnerships can turn into lifelong working relationships. I recently helped a department's graduate students set up writing partnerships and it transformed their educational experience.

To use the workbook in this way, find another student who wants to revise an article and is willing to commit to doing so in twelve weeks. It is best to pick another student with similar academic goals and abilities, but you do not need to be in the same discipline or field. In fact, it can sometimes be helpful to work with someone unfamiliar with your content, so that you are forced to be clear about your topic. Since writing in the social sciences, the humanities, and the sciences are so different, it is best to work with someone from the same broad category, but this is not absolutely necessary. It is more important to pick a partner who is likely to persevere. It is also wise to think about what kind of person is most likely to keep you going: someone supportive or someone competitive. Ideally, your partner will be both, someone who encourages you when you feel discouraged, but whose drive pushes you to keep up.

As individuals, you should set aside about an hour a day, five days a week, to work through that week's readings and short exercises. As partners, the two of you should commit to meeting once a week to talk through that week's readings and exercises and to report on how you have completed the week's goals as stated in the workbook. This is best done in person, but can be done over the telephone or by e-mail. When the workbook task is to submit your article to someone else for review, you should submit them to each other for comments.

Since this is a serious endeavor, and will only work if both of you take it seriously, I recommend that you make a written commitment to each other to work together for twelve weeks. Although it may seem forced at first, people who make binding, formal agreements find it works to keep them on task. Either design your own agreement or copy the form on the next page. Then sign it and post it near your computer, front door, or refrigerator as a reminder.

Many people have found it useful to promise to pay a penalty for not following through on their commitment. One writing instructor required his students to write a $25 check to a political organization that they abhorred and give the check to him in an envelope addressed to the organization (Boice 1990, 75). If the student did not meet his or her commitment, the instructor promptly sent the check. He claimed that this worked as a great motivator! Other possible payments can be penance (such as grading exams for the writing partner) or public shame (such as writing about your failure to three friends).

Others prefer the carrot to the stick and like to use positive incentives rather than such negative ones. Some rewards you can give yourself for meeting your twelve-week commitment are a weekend trip, a celebratory meal with friends, or a particular concert. Of course, the best reward will be the sense of accomplishment you feel when you submit the article. There is no substitute for it!

> **Commitment to Writing Partner**
>
> I commit to meeting with _____ every week on
> [partner's name]
>
> _____ at _____. During each of the next twelve weeks, I commit
> [day]   [time]
>
> to reading the appropriate workbook chapter and completing the weekly exercises.
>
> I also commit to spending at least fifteen minutes a day, five days a week, on revis-
>
> ing my article until it is ready for submission (or for twelve weeks, whichever comes
>
> first). I commit to carefully reading and reviewing _____
> [partner's name]
>
> article during the fifth and ninth weeks. If I cannot meet any of these commitments due
>
> to a prolonged illness or a family emergency, I will inform _____
> [partner's name]
>
> immediately. If I cannot meet any of these commitments for any other reason, I will
>
> pay the following: _____. If I meet all of these commitments, I will gain the fol-
> [fee]
>
> lowing: _____.
> [benefit]
>
> _____
> [signature]

USING THE WORKBOOK IN A WRITING GROUP

You can also use this workbook with a writing group. Groups are great for helping you to stay motivated because they provide support and friendly pressure.

Find three or more people who want to revise an article and are willing to commit to doing so in twelve weeks. If your department already has a journal reading group or writing group, this may serve as a good starting ground. You do not need to be in the same discipline or field, however. In fact, it can sometimes be helpful to work with people who are unfamiliar with your content, so that you are forced to be clear about your topic.

As individuals, you should set aside about an hour a day, five days a week, to work through that week's readings and short exercises. As a group, you should commit to meeting once a week to report on how you have completed that week's goals as stated in the workbook. This is best done in person, although some extremely committed groups have succeeded in meeting by e-mail. When the workbook task is to submit your journal article to someone else for review, you should exchange articles with others in the group. If possible, you should read the article of the person who is reading yours, rather than randomly exchanging articles, so that you have an incentive to be kind and clear. Nothing encourages careful reading like knowing that you will be critiqued by the person you are critiquing.

It is also worthwhile to have one of your group do a little additional reading on that week's topic and report to the group on findings. As you know, having to teach something helps you to learn something.

If you have never participated in a writing group before, you might want to look in advance at the Week 9 chapter on giving, getting, and using feedback. You should make sure your group is a supportive environment for writing, not a graduate seminar for deconstruction. Be sure to treat all drafts and discussion as confidential since the group must be a safe place for people to bring their writing at any stage. Criticisms should be offered with care and clarity. Remember that you are working together to become productive writers, not perfectionists.

This is a serious endeavor and will only work if your group takes it seriously. I recommend that you sign a written commitment to each other to work together for twelve weeks. Although it may seem hokey or forced at first, people who make their work together intentional in this way find they are more productive. Design an agreement of your own, or make copies of the form below for each member, and have each person sign all the copies. Then consider posting your copy near your computer, front door, or refrigerator as a reminder.

Commitment to Writing Group

I commit to meeting with _____
[names of group members]

_____

every week on _____ at _____. During each of the next twelve
 [day] [time]
weeks, I commit to reading the appropriate workbook chapter and completing the

weekly exercises. I also commit to spending at least fifteen minutes a day, five days a

week, on revising my article until it is ready for submission (or for twelve weeks,

whichever comes first). I commit to carefully reading and reviewing other group mem-

bers' articles during the fifth and ninth weeks. If I cannot meet any of these commitments

due to a prolonged illness or a family emergency, I will inform the group immediately. If I

cannot meet any of these commitments for any other reason, I will pay the following:

_____. If any of us do meet all of these commitments, we will gain the following:
 [fee]

_____.
 [benefit]

_____
 [signature]

You may want to decide together what the penalty will be for not following through. For instance, you can collect $20 from each member, put it in an envelope, and split the total among those who actually send their chapter out. Alternatively, you can use the money toward a group activity when you send off your articles, such as a celebratory meal. Of course, the best reward will be your sense of accomplishment when you submit the article.

USING THE WORKBOOK WITH COAUTHORS

You can also use this workbook with coauthors. How you use it depends on your cowriting process. If your cowriting consists of working separately and then splicing your writing together into an article, you can use the workbook as outlined in the earlier "Using This Workbook with a Writing Partner" or "Using This Workbook with a Writing Group" section. If you are working more closely, practically drafting every sentence together, you may want to read the workbook together and do the exercises together as well.

USING THE WORKBOOK TO TEACH A CLASS

You can also use this workbook to teach a ten-, twelve-, or fifteen-week writing class that meets once a week for two to three hours. Most graduate schools do not provide pragmatic writing instruction, so be prepared for your class to be popular! At each class meeting, assign the next week's chapter for reading and have the students do all the assignments over the course of the week. In class, discuss the advice given that week in the workbook, particularly any conflicting advice that students may have heard. Such discussions are excellent opportunities for altering expectations according to your field and challenging students to arrive at what works best for them. Then have students report on how their daily writing proceeded and what they accomplished by doing the exercises. Encourage students to talk about their feelings about writing, both positive and negative. Any of the assignments designed for partners or groups can, and perhaps should, be done in class. Make sure to use a full class session at least once for exchanging drafts, as detailed in Week 5. Additionally, have students make individual presentations on journals they would like to publish in or on article standards in their field. For more information on using the workbook to teach a class, see my website www.wendybelcher.com.

FEEDBACK TO THE AUTHOR

I am constantly updating this workbook. If you have any thoughts on its content, please contact me with them. I always welcome corrections of any sort (e.g., where the workbook has typos or grammatical mistakes), examples from your work (e.g., how you revised a poor title into a strong one), insights on what makes a journal article publishable (e.g., how it works in your field), successful strategies for getting motivated, and exercises that helped you. To contact me, please go to my website www.wendybelcher.com.

Week 1

Designing Your Plan for Writing

Day to Do Task	Week 1 Daily Writing Tasks	Estimated Task Time
Day 1 (Monday?)	Read through page 10 and fill in the boxes on those pages	60 minutes
Day 2 (Tuesday?)	Select a previously written text to develop for publication (pages 11–18)	60 minutes
Day 3 (Wednesday?)	Choose and improve your writing site (pages 18–19)	60+ minutes
Day 4 (Thursday?)	Design a daily and weekly writing schedule for twelve weeks; anticipate obstacles and interruptions (pages 19–39)	60 minutes
Day 5 (Friday?)	Start documenting how you spend your time currently (pages 39–40)	60 minutes

Each week you will have specific tasks designed to aid you in accomplishing your goal of sending your academic article to a journal in twelve weeks. Above are the tasks for your first week, broken down day by day for five days of work and about five hours of work for the week. Some find it helpful to work on their article a bit every day of the week, to keep it fresh, in which case you should spend fifteen minutes revising the article on the sixth and seventh day. The first task, for Day 1, is to read the material below. This week has the most reading of any of the weeks.

UNDERSTANDING FEELINGS ABOUT WRITING

Writing is to academia what sex was to nineteenth-century Vienna: everybody does it and nobody talks about it. The leading researcher on academic writers found that most academics were more willing to talk about even their most personal problems, including sexual dysfunction, than about problems with writing (Boice 1990, 1).[1] The prevalent belief among academics seems to be that writing, like sex, should come naturally and should be performed in polite privacy.

Because of this silence, writing dysfunction is common in academia. A recent survey of over 40,000 U.S. faculty revealed that 26 percent of professors spent zero hours a week writing, and almost 27 percent had never published a peer-reviewed journal article (Lindholm et al. 2005). In addition,

43 percent had not published any piece of writing in the past two years. The majority, 62 percent, had never published a book. Put another way, only 25 percent of faculty spent more than eight hours every week writing and only 28 percent of faculty had produced more than two publications in the past two years. Furthermore, these statistics are self-reported and reflect the activities of only those organized enough to respond to the survey. Some scholars believe the figure is much lower, estimating productive academic writers as less than 15 percent of faculty (Moxley and Taylor 1997, Simonton 1988). Since publication is the major marker of productivity in academia, these statistics are surprising. Or are they?

You do not have to be Freud to figure out that academia's silence about writing may be repressive. Writing is, after all, a creative process and like any such process, depends on connection. If you try to create in an environment where sharing is discouraged, dysfunction is the inevitable result. Certainly, many have found that talking about their struggles with writing has been very freeing, both for them and their chosen confidant. The lesson: Learning to talk about writing is an important key to becoming a productive writer.

One of the reasons that academics do not talk about writing is that it involves talking about feelings. Academics tend to be more comfortable with the rational than the emotional. Therefore, even if we do manage to talk about writing, we are more likely to talk about content than process. In fact, many of us have feelings about writing that we rarely acknowledge in public. The first step to success is understanding your relationship to writing.

So, let's get started with a very broad question. What feelings come up when you think about writing? I recommend that you call a classmate or colleague and discuss this question with them before using the chart below to jot down your answers. Or you can compose an e-mail to a friend or family member.

My Feelings about My Experience of Writing

(If you skipped this last exercise, do go back and write down at least one feeling. The following will make more sense if you take the time to write something there.)

When I ask this question about feelings in class, usually negative feelings come up first. I have cited these verbatim from my class notes:

> I feel both terror and boredom. . . . I get depressed when I think about having to write. . . . I feel discouraged because I feel like I have never done enough research to start writing. . . . I have fun in the beginning but I really hate revising. . . . I enjoy revising, but I hate getting that first draft down. . . . My advisor is so critical that whenever I think of writing I feel inadequate. . . . I feel like there are rules that everyone knows but me. . . . I feel like procrastinating whenever I think of how much writing I have to do and how little I have done. . . . I feel ashamed of my writing skills. . . . I wish my English was better. . . . I feel that if people read my writing they will know that I'm a dumb bunny. . . . I feel like I work at writing for hours and have so little to show for it. . . . I spend so much time critiquing my students' writing that I shut down when I come to my own. . . . I get a good idea but then I feel a fog come over me. . . . When I think about the fact that my entire career depends on publication, I feel completely paralyzed. . . . I feel confident that I could do anything, if I could just get out of bed.

Guess what? You are not alone! Most writers, even accomplished writers, hear these inner negative voices that whisper their fears to them whenever they think about writing. Using this workbook will diminish those voices, but the most important step is to realize that these feelings are warranted. Writing is difficult and scary. Feeling anxious is an entirely appropriate response.

It is worthwhile to spend some time thinking about what links your negative feelings. Do they revolve around one or two anxieties, perceptions, habits? Do they point to a particular fear, such as what others will think of you? Or to a particular negative self-assessment, such as labeling yourself lazy? Use the next chart to identify these links.

Common Elements in My Negative Feelings about Writing

(You will spend time later in the chapter on how to address your negative feelings, but for now, just write them down.)

When I ask students to discuss their feelings about writing, some positive feelings usually come up, too. Students say things like:

I feel excited when I think up a good idea. . . . Sometimes I write a sentence that comes out more coherently than I expected and I feel great. . . . I feel euphoric when I realize that I have a good conclusion that ties the paper together. . . . I love the feeling of having just finished a paper. . . . When I reread something I wrote a year ago, I'm impressed and I think, did I write that!?

In order to feel better about your writing, then, remember the context in which positive feelings arose.

For instance, do you have any particularly good memories of writing? During that experience when you felt good, what was making that happen? What are the lessons you can learn from those experiences?

Lessons to Be Learned from My Positive Experiences of Writing

(You will spend time later in the chapter on how to use these lessons, but for now, just write them down.)

When I ask this question in class, students list good experiences like:

I had a deadline that forced me to sit down and do the writing. . . . I had an advisor/friend/spouse who was encouraging. . . . I was working on a paper that meant a lot to me personally. . . . My parents took my kids for a week. . . . I got into a rhythm of writing every evening after *Seinfeld*. . . . I had a part-time job that forced me to use my time more efficiently. . . . I read an article that really inspired me and got me going. . . . I asked my advisor to meet with me once a week and to expect some writing from me every time.

Interestingly, the lessons students learn from these experiences are similar. Apparently, happy writers are all alike, to paraphrase Tolstoy. Successful academic writers share similar attitudes and work habits. I call them the keys to academic writing success.

KEYS TO POSITIVE WRITING EXPERIENCES

I've designed this workbook to help you develop skills around the four keys to academic writing success. These essentials can also help you design your own program.

Successful Academic Writers Write

Samuel Eliot Morison, author of several academic classics including *The Oxford History of the American People*, had the following literary advice for young historians, "First and foremost, *get writing*!" (1953, 293).

It may sound tautological, but the main key to a positive writing experience is writing. Most students' negative experiences of writing revolve around not writing (i.e., procrastinating) and most students' positive experiences of writing revolve around actually doing it. That is, when students write, they feel a sense of accomplishment and the pleasure of communicating their ideas. In this sense, writing is the same as exercise. Although it may not be easy at first, it does get easier and more pleasurable the more you do it. As the very productive academic writer and my colleague Chon A. Noriega tells his graduate students when they embark on their dissertations, "One usually gets better at whatever one does on a regular basis. If one does *not* write on a regular basis, one will get better at *not* writing. In fact, one will develop an astonishing array of skills designed to improve and extend one's *not* writing."

Those who do not write often claim that they are "too busy." Indeed, people today are very busy. Some students have long commutes, others have full-time jobs, and still others have young children. So, here's the good news and the bad news. Lots of busy people have been productive writers. Are they just smarter? No. If you pay attention to the way you actually spend time, you will find that you may not be quite as busy as you suppose and that writing doesn't take as much time as you fear.

Robert Boice, the leading scholar on faculty productivity, proved this by finding faculty members who claimed to be "too busy" to write and then following them around for a week. With Boice staring at them all day, most had to admit that "they rarely had workdays without at least one brief period of fifteen to sixty minutes open for free use" (1997a, 21). His subjects spent this free time in activities that were neither work nor play. Boice also found that those likely to describe themselves as very "busy" or very "stressed" did not produce as much as those who were writing steadily. In other words, you are not too busy to write, you are busy because you do not write. Busy-ness is what you do to explain your not writing. (If you skimmed over those last two sentences, I recommend you go back and read them one more time. It's essential.)

No matter how busy your life is, make a plan for writing. Successful academic writers do not wait for inspiration. They do not wait until the last minute. They do not wait for big blocks of time. They make a plan for writing every day and they stick to it. Much of this workbook will be devoted to your developing writing into a habit.

Successful Academic Writers Make Writing Social

The myth that writing should be a solo activity is just that, a myth. Yet, the popular image persists of the writer as someone who works alone for months in a cold garret, subsisting on bread and cigarettes while coughing consumptively and churning out page after page of sui generis prose. It's a lonely, hard life, but that's what writing takes.[2]

Academics in the humanities persist in believing that texts spring fully formed from the mind of the writer. In the sciences, this myth is not so prevalent since most science articles are the result of a team of researchers who publish as coauthors. Students in the sciences work as secondary authors, contributing sections or data to faculty members' articles, long before they ever become primary authors. That is why the rate of writing dysfunction in the sciences is so much lower. Scholars in the sciences consistently see writing as a form of conversation. When this idea of collaboration is lost, many of the writing problems so common in the academic community arise—writer's block, anxiety over having one's ideas stolen, the obsession with originality, the fear of belatedness, difficulties with criticism, even plagiarism. All rise from the myth that writing should be private and isolated.

Just look at the host of reviewers, friends, and family members thanked in any published book. This is not just civility on the part of the author; authors are usually understating the case. Those thanked may have performed research, suggested theses, recommended resources, and actually written conclusions. This was especially true in the past, when faculty wives not only typed and edited manuscripts, but also sometimes wrote sections of their husbands' texts. The recent legal suit against the *Da Vinci Code* for copyright infringement suggests that such wives are still around. According to Dan Brown, his wife Blythe Brown did most of the research for the *Da Vinci Code*, suggested the idea of centering a book on the suppression of women in the Catholic Church, and insisted that the book include a child of Jesus Christ and Mary Magdalene (Collett-White 2006). Because the myth of originality is so strong, authors rarely give these laborers coauthor credits. This variation on the repressive silence discussed at the beginning of this chapter is the result of not recognizing that writing is collaborative labor.

A useful corrective to the myth of the solitary writer is the experience of Indonesian novelist Pramoedya Ananta Toer, who was Southeast Asia's leading contender for the Nobel Prize. Toer spent fourteen years as a political prisoner on Indonesia's infamous Buru Island. Denied paper and pen, from 1969 to 1973, Pramoedya composed oral stories for the eighteen prisoners in his isolated camp, who would whisper the latest installment to other prisoners during their only daily contact, in the showers. These stories were so rich and human that many prisoners attributed their survival to them. Pramoedya himself has called the Buru novels "my lullaby for my fellow-prisoners, to calm their fears, they who were suffering so much torture" (Belcher 1999). The prisoners, in turn, did his work and gave him their food to enable his creation. When his captors finally allowed him to write in 1975, "it was like a dam breaking." Toer wrote continuously to capture the stories from memory, sitting on the floor and writing on his prison cot. Only four of these books were smuggled out; six others were destroyed by prison guards. The first, *This Earth of Mankind,* is one of the best novels of colonialism ever written in English. The quartet of which it is a part is a defining work of this century. Is Toer's story unusual? Yes. But his experience of writing highlights a persistent truth: The best writing is created in community with a strong sense of audience.

So, work to make your writing more public and less private, more social and less solitary. Start a writing group. Take a writing class. Convince another student to cowrite an article with you. Meet a classmate at the library or a café to write for an hour. Attend conferences, participate in electronic discussion lists, join journal clubs, and introduce yourself to scholars whose work you admire. Do not get distracted into reading yet another article when a conversation with someone in your field can better help you to shape your ideas and direction. You should be spending as much time on establishing social scholarly connections as you do on writing, for the best writing happens in active interaction with your potential audience.

The more you participate, the better your experience of writing will be. This is partly because others give you ideas and language. But it is also because you must relate your ideas to others' ideas. You must know what theories professors in your discipline are debating, what their primary research questions are, and what methodologies they consider appropriate. You can only know this if you are an active member of the community.

Students usually experience several problems with making their writing more social. First, many students feel real horror at the prospect of networking. Some feel awkward or invasive attempting to contact someone they admire. Others experience deliberate attempts at befriending others as superficial or brown-nosing. Certainly, reaching out socially takes courage and tact. Yet, you will find that others are often interested in meeting you and even grateful to you for taking the first step. Many established scholars enjoy being asked for advice on the field. So, whatever your comfort zone, try to push outside it.

Second, many students are hesitant about showing their writing to anyone. The university environment can encourage students to see their colleagues as adversaries rather than advocates. Classmates and professors can appear too busy to read and comment on your work. Students can be afraid that sharing their work will reveal them as impostors and demonstrate their deep unsuitability for the academy. Fortunately, if you manage to share your work, you usually find that others are happy to help and that you are not as much of an idiot as you thought you were. Moreover, others can quickly identify omissions and logical breaks that would take you weeks to figure out. Of course, some readers will be too critical and others will give you bad advice. But an essential part of becoming a writer is learning to sift useful criticisms from useless ones. The more often you deal with others' subjective reactions to your work, the more readily you will be able to deal with peer reviewers' comments down the road.

Third, some students are good at sharing their work, but only when they consider the article complete. Avoid waiting until your manuscript is "done" before sharing it. You will be disappointed when you share it with others, expecting compliments. Instead, you will get recommendations for revision that you are little interested in addressing. The point of sharing is to improve your writing, not to convince others of your talents. So, share your writing in the early stages. Show outlines to classmates, faculty members in your discipline, or even journal editors. Exchange abstracts. Give out drafts and ask for specific comments about aspects of your writing that you suspect are weak. Learn to share your writing at all stages.

Fourth, students fear that sharing their work will lead to their ideas being stolen. Like so many of the anxieties named in this book, there is a rational reason for this fear: students' ideas are stolen. Stories are always circulating among graduate students about stolen intellectual property. But hiding your work will not solve this problem. In fact, getting your work out to a number of people will protect it. Furthermore, no one can articulate your idea like you can. You may suspect that anyone could do a better job of presenting your ideas than you could, but this workbook will help you see that's not true.

All these activities will help you counter the myth of the lonely writer. Nothing is as collaborative as good writing. All texts depend on other texts, all writers stand on the shoulders of other writers, all prose demands an editor, and all writing needs an audience. Without community, writing is inconceivable. This workbook will help you to develop social writing habits and to share your work. If you are using this workbook with a writing partner or in a group, you are making excellent progress already!

Successful Academic Writers Persist Despite Rejection

The writing life is filled with rejection. This is one of the few shared experiences of great writers and terrible writers. A quick read of *Pushcart's Complete Rotten Reviews & Rejections* offers the comfort of knowing that most canonical authors (for instance, Hermann Melville, T. S. Eliot, and Virginia Woolf) had their work rejected in the strongest possible terms (Henderson 1998). Jack London received 266 rejection slips in 1899 alone (Kershaw 1997)! The economist George Akerlof received three rejections for a journal article that later won him the Nobel Prize (Gans and Shepherd 1994). Indeed, studies of Nobel Prize winners found that editors had rejected many early versions of their award-winning work (Campanario 1995, 1996). If you write, you will be rejected. This is unavoidable. The important thing is not to let it stop you.

Although it is tempting to let others' criticism be the measure of your writing or even your own worth, don't let it be. The business of reviewing is a subjective process rife with bias and carelessness. Work rejected by one journal is often embraced by another. The only difference between much-published authors and unpublished authors is often persistence and not worthiness. Published authors just keep submitting their work. If one journal rejects their article, they send the article to another. They keep a positive attitude. A professor I know has fond memories of her dissertation advisor, who papered his office with his article rejection notices. To see him working away amidst the negative notices of a lifetime, she says, was inspiring and encouraging.

Several of my students have exemplified the usefulness of persistence. In one of my classes, Carrie Petrucci revised her wonderful article arguing for introducing the apology into the criminal justice system. She knew that resistance to her argument would be high, but felt committed to demonstrating that criminal apologies provided some real benefits for victims and perpetrators. So she was very disappointed, but not surprised, when the first journal rejected her article. Petrucci stopped everything she was doing and took two days to make changes based on the comments she had received from the editor and previous readers. She then sent it right back out again to another journal, this time to a social science journal rather than a law journal. After that second journal also rejected her article, she again devoted two days to making changes. Making writing social helped her persevere. "What kept me going through two rejections," she e-mailed me, "was the fact that I had had several people read it prior to my submitting it to any journal and a handful of those people, who had nothing to gain by it (including yourself), had given me the impression that it was strong. . . . Believe me; I clung to those comments as I got some pretty negative feedback on rounds one and two."

So, she sent it out a third time, to an interdisciplinary journal in law and social science. A few months later, she got a message from that journal accepting her article for publication and stating that the reviewers were extremely enthusiastic about the piece. "Congratulations," the editor exclaimed. "It is quite unusual to have a manuscript accepted without requiring any changes. But yours is a high quality product. Good job." Her persistence paid off. She later won the first Nathan E. Cohen Doctoral Student Award in Social Welfare in 2002 for this article and then got a job working to improve the criminal justice system (Petrucci 2002).

One of my students told us the story of a friend who was more fainthearted. When she received a response from a journal, she opened the letter with trepidation. The first paragraph included the sentence: "The reviewers' reports are in and both agree that your article is severely marred by poor writing." Upset, she flung the letter aside and spent an hour in bed ruing her decision ever to enter academia. When her husband got home, he picked the letter off the hallway floor, read it, and entered the bedroom saying, "Congratulations, honey! Why didn't you tell me your article got accepted?" Upon actually reading the letter through, she found that the editors had accepted the article pending major revisions. She hired a copyeditor to work with her on her prose and resubmitted the article. When starting out, harsh criticism can stop you in your tracks, but if you persist, you often find that things are not as bad as they seem at first.

Successful Academic Writers Pursue Their Passions

When students list positive experiences with writing, they often note genuine interest in a topic as a real engine. Successful writers do not write primarily for their professors, their classmates, or their hiring committees. Rather, they focus on the questions that fascinate them.

For example, one of my students was writing about the negative effect of welfare reform on Cambodian women. She drafted and revised her article in record time because she was so angry about the policy's consequences. A Korean student who grew up in Japan persevered despite several obstacles to publish her research showing that Koreans in Japan labor under legally imposed hardships. A student who wrote about pedigreed dogs and another who wrote about food metaphors always worked steadily because the topics were also life-long hobbies. Other students used their own experiences of ethnicity, gender, or nationality to reinterpret canonical texts, placing the traditional in a completely new light.

The lesson? The world changes quickly, so you are more likely to have positive writing experiences if you follow your deepest interests rather than passing fads. As the authors of *The Craft of Research* point out, "Nothing will contribute to the quality of your work more than your sense of its worth and your commitment to it" (Booth, Colomb, and Williams 1995, 36).

My model for this is an artist I discovered while doing research on street art in Washington, D.C. I spent a summer walking the inner city photographing everything creative I could find: murals, street games, hair weaving, garbage can musicians, fence art (Belcher 1987). I spent a lot of time in alleys looking at graffiti and I kept coming across the same thing. Huge spray paintings of women's shoes. Not just life-size, but ten feet across. All of the shoes were portrayed from one side, in profile, and all of them were pumps. I became an expert on the development of this artist whom I never met, soon able to distinguish early pump (when shoes went untitled) from later pump (when shoes appeared with titles like "Black Evening Pump" or "Leopard Skin Pump" and were signed "Ray (c) 1987"). Whenever I found a new one, in yet another out of the way place, I was delighted. Because this artist took his or her idiosyncrasy and pushed it, unafraid to paint feminine footwear across an entire urban landscape. So obsess about things, pursue your passions, do not be bullied. Whatever your pump is, paint it.

DESIGNING A PLAN FOR SUBMITTING YOUR ARTICLE IN TWELVE WEEKS

As mentioned in the Introduction, just knowing what the habits of the successful academic writer are does not automatically put them within reach. Many of us find it especially hard to pick up the most difficult key to success: making time for writing. The most important step is making a plan. When you design a plan, you set up goals and deadlines. Once tangible, these goals and deadlines can be realized. This workbook aids you in designing a plan to send an article to a journal in twelve weeks. So, let's move into the next exercise and build a plan for writing.

Day 1: Reading the Workbook

On the first day of your writing week, you should read the workbook up to this page and answer all the questions posed up to this point.

Day 2: Selecting a Text for Revision

Many students believe that in order to be published they must start from scratch. Nothing will do but to begin a brand new article on a brave new topic. This is not true. Most students have already written classroom essays, conference papers, or thesis chapters that contain the seed of a publishable journal article. Some students have drafts of coauthored articles that their professors have asked them to improve. Others have been asked to write up parts of a research study they did not conduct. Since revising is the key to publication, I recommend that students focus on reworking an already written text, however poor. The trick is to identify which text provides you with this fertilizable seed. Answer the questions below to help you identify such a text.

Considering a Text You Have Already Written

Praise. Has a professor ever suggested that you submit a text of yours for publication? If not, has a professor ever suggested that a text you wrote was particularly strong or intriguing?

Title:	

Pleasure. Are there any texts that you enjoyed writing or researching and that you still think back on with gratification?

Title:	

Relevance. Do any of your texts address some aspect of a current debate in your discipline? In your recent reading or conversations, do you find yourself thinking of something you wrote and its relevance?

Title:	

Research. Are any of your texts particularly well researched? Did you do substantial reading for one and still have all the sources?

Title:	

Findings. Do any of your texts have particularly strong or unusual findings? Do any contain an original insight that could carry a whole article?

Title:	

Conference paper. Have you ever given a conference paper? Did you get a positive response? Did you get useful comments that would help you in revising the paper for publication? (Several studies suggest that about 50 percent of conference presentations are later published as articles [e.g., Autorino et al 2007].)

Title:	

Thesis. Have you written an M.A. thesis or Ph.D. dissertation? Are parts of it worth revising for publication?

Title:	

Rejected article. Have you ever submitted an article for publication and gotten a revise and resubmit notice? If not, have you ever gotten a rejection notice?

Title:	

Texts that Offer Particular Challenges

If reading through the above brings several texts to mind, remember the following when making your final choice of which texts to work on.

General: Broad surveys. Articles surveying the field or the state of the discipline are rarely published. When they are, veterans in the field write them. The conventional wisdom is that a junior scholar hasn't been following the debates long enough to be able to weigh in on such matters. If a professor tells you that you are an exception to this rule, go for it. If a professor hasn't, why attempt to scale entrenched obstacles? You don't have to throw the work away—use the survey to write an introduction to an article.

General: Purely theoretical. Articles are rarely published that only explore the strengths and weaknesses of a particular theory without any case study or textual evidence. Junior scholars can make the mistake of assuming that an article that helped them think through something theoretical will be useful to others. Sometimes it can. Just make sure that a colleague or professor has read the article and agrees that it would be a fresh contribution. Editors will quickly reject theoretical articles on topics that they think have been exhausted or are virtually unassailable. Also, make sure that you send such an article to a journal that is open to very theoretical articles. And remember that most important theories were launched with case studies or textual evidence.

General: Dated research. If your paper is quite old, and subsequent research may have vitiated its findings, you may want to think twice about picking it for revision. Some research articles are "evergreen" as they say in the magazine business. Others address a particular academic concern that has waned or have findings that have been superseded or disproved. Such papers can be updated, but you will need to do additional research. If you are not sure where your paper stands, you may want to ask someone in your field to read it with an eye for its current relevance. It is safe to say that choosing to revise anything you wrote more than ten years ago will take a lot of extra work; something your wrote five or six years ago should be carefully reviewed for relevance.

General: Outside your discipline. It is harder than most students think to write for another discipline. Just because you took one film class and wrote a paper for it, despite being in the political science department, does not mean that you know how to write for film scholars. You might, but be sure that someone in that field has sanctioned your approach. Many times your ideas will not be new enough or clearly enough related to the field to warrant publication. One study has shown that those from outside a discipline are significantly less likely to get published in a journal within that discipline (Goodrich 1945).

General: Polemics. The world is a racist, sexist, homophobic, xenophobic, classist, and (insert your own concern here) place. However, you can't get published by simply asserting that this is the case, no matter how much the journal editor may agree with you. You must do more than declare that some institution is not working, that some particular artwork is problematic, or that some social condition is egregious. In the social sciences, you must have proof. Without proof, you are simply writing a newspaper editorial. So, if you've written a classroom essay stating that Latinas face many obstacles in graduating from college or that welfare is destroying the fabric of American society, you must have evidence other than your own casual observations and experiences. Both can be extremely helpful to you in designing a study to test your hypothesis, but without a study, you have no proof. In the humanities, you must have something more interesting to say than pointing out blatant racist or sexist statements in a famous text. To get published, you are going to have to make more developed arguments about how the text is working. For instance, you can sometimes get published by arguing against the common wisdom and asserting that a text widely thought to be racist is actually more open, or that a praised text is covertly sexist. Just be aware that simple readings will not get you into peer-reviewed journals.

General: Too similar. When you are starting out, this is not such an issue, but don't pick a paper to work on that is very similar to something else you have published. If the paper has different data (whether experimental or textual) or a different argument (or hypothesis), then it is probably fine, but if it shares both with a previous publication of yours, select something else.

General: Master's or undergraduate thesis. It is a great idea to revise your thesis for publication. Be warned, though, most students struggle with the massive amount of cutting that is required. Most theses need to be cut by two-thirds to be viable. Of the students I know who have been successful in turning a thesis into a publication, most of them read through the thesis, opened up a brand new empty electronic file, and typed up what they remembered. It may seem counter intuitive, but they found that starting over took less time than cutting. Just taking out a sentence here or there is not going to do the job. Starting from scratch sounds scary, but the students I know who did this found that much of the paper flowed for them, once they escaped the strictures of the fifty- to seventy-page draft. If you can do this, master's theses tend to do quite well in the peer review process, as they have a richness that impresses reviewers.

General: Dissertation chapter. Revising a dissertation chapter is a standard route to publication. The challenge for most, however, is that you must both shorten and lengthen the chapter. You must shorten because chapters are often twice the length of journal articles; but you must lengthen because the article must stand alone, unlike the chapter, and needs additional information. When cutting, be ruthless; when adding, be judicious. Readers often need less background information than authors assume they do, and peer reviewers easily ask for more if they need it. See below for additional information on what types of chapters to chose.

General: Unwritten dissertation. If you are in your first years of graduate school and you have a paper that you think is going to be the basis of your dissertation, or an important chapter in your dissertation, you might want to think twice about revising it for publication now. The reason is that your ideas may change radically as you write the dissertation and then you may wish you had waited to publish on the topic. If you really want to work on a prospective dissertation chapter for publication now, do not let my advice here stop you. If you are wondering, however, whether to choose future dissertation research or something that will not appear in your dissertation, I recommend the latter. Likewise, if you think you will be writing your dissertation on a particular author/place/culture and you have one paper about that author/place/culture that contains your dissertation argument and another paper on that author/place/culture that does not, pick the latter paper for revision.

General: Not in English. This workbook aids you in revising an English-language article. If you are planning to revise and submit an article in a language other than English, be aware that non-English-language journals often have quite different standards for publication than English-language ones. Therefore, you may have to extrapolate quite a bit from this workbook. If, however, you plan to revise in that other language but translate the completed article into English, the workbook can help. A perennial debate in my international workshops is whether nonnative speakers of English are best off drafting articles in their own language, and then later translating them into English, or whether they should start drafting articles from the very beginning in English. Some authors insist that they find it better to draft in their own language and then translate the article into English. They like the smoothness and logical flow this drafting process enables, although they find they spend some time rooting out the syntax and structure of the original language when doing the translation. Others say that it is easier to be analytical or argumentative in English than in other languages, so it is better to start from the beginning in English. These are some of the trade-offs that you must weigh before deciding how to proceed with an article that is not in English.

General. Too introductory or descriptive. To get published, your paper will have to go beyond introducing an object or practice, or merely summarizing the research about an object or practice. Some students have papers describing a particular geography, agricultural technique, painting style, literary movement, and so on. Without an argument, theoretical approach, or a study, such a piece of writing is more suited to an encyclopedia than a journal.

Humanities: Narrow close readings. As an undergraduate in literature, doing a close reading of a single literary text can gain you admiration and an A. Among peer-reviewed journals, it is likely to gain you a dismissal. Journal editors want to see something more than an unpacking of the various meanings of one text. Single-text journal articles are still published but most journal editors will expect the article to speak to disciplinary debates. If you have a single-text paper, make sure you can take it beyond merely unpacking your text. It helps if you are using the single text as a leaping off point for theorizing about a broader issue, or if the single text is obscure but important.

Humanities: Popular text studies. Be wary of picking a paper you have written on one widely discussed text. I know of one journal that used to reject automatically any paper that focused closely on Morrison's extraordinary novel *Beloved*, because they got dozens every year. It is not easy to know what a popular text is—especially in literary fields that focus on canonical texts—but it is safe to say that any text that is taught in every literature department in the country is in this category.

Social Sciences: Reports. Social scientists working for public agencies often have written many reports, whether for funders, internal purposes, or policymakers. While such reports can hold amazing data not available in print, reports are very different beasts than articles. A report is rarely argumentative, something an article needs to be. You will have to do a lot of work to transform a report into an article. If the data in the paper was carefully collected and supports a strong argument, then go ahead and pick it, but be prepared to do much revising.

Social Sciences: Literature reviews. Many students would like to try to publish literature reviews from their dissertations or master's theses; that is, long summaries of others' research. I discourage students investing in such essays. Most journals are interested in original research, not in a re-presentation of others' ideas. Editors spot plain literature reviews a mile away and usually send them right back without doing more than skimming them (unless written by a very well-known scholar). If you have read almost everything on a topic for which there is no published literature review, and if you really think you have something original to offer—a new and useful critical take on what has already been written—then proceed, but be sure to ask people in your field first. You also might consider submitting it to a journal as a review essay. This does not "count" as much a journal article, but it is a very good publication to have on your curriculum vitae.

Social Sciences: Teaching experiences. At some point in their careers, everyone wants to write an article about their experience of teaching a particular class. Some of these articles are excellent, some are poor. The problem for both is finding a place to publish. Short articles on the topic are perfect for the *Chronicle of Higher Education*; most peer-reviewed journals won't be interested in publishing such pieces. If you really want to publish such an article, search hard for a journal that has a record of publishing them.

Social Sciences: Small sample size. If you have based your paper on a qualitative study with just two subjects, even qualitative journals may reject it. Most social science fields are so quantitative now that the sample size of even qualitative studies has become an issue. Speaking to others in your field can be helpful in identifying an adequate sample size in your field, but anything under five is probably too small.

Social Sciences: No study. In some social science fields, it is perfectly acceptable to theorize and conjecture without a quantitative or qualitative study; in many, it is not acceptable. If you have a paper in which you speculate on the causes of social conditions or the motivations of individuals without a study to back up your speculations, find out if your field is one that accepts such work. A journal will want to see evidence showing that, for instance, racism is the cause of student failure, sexism is preventing male nurses from doing their jobs adequately, or parents would be willing to pay for their children to attend better public schools. You will need interviews with or surveys of such students, nurses, or parents to back up your claims.

Prioritizing Among Several Paper Choices

If the questions above have brought to mind a good paper, great! I recommend that you revisit that paper and consider reworking it for publication. If several papers rose to mind, and you are unsure which one to pick, you have several options.

If a professor has recommended that you think about publishing a paper, you should definitely consider this paper. One professor told me that he had given up recommending publication to students. Although he had several times offered to meet with students to talk about revising their papers and choosing a journal venue, no student had ever taken him up on the offer. I have since heard other professors comment on how rarely students take advantage of such an offer to help. If you have such an offer, take advantage! Although it can be scary to work this closely with someone, a more advanced scholar can get you to publication so much more quickly than you could by yourself—by recommending sources, identifying debates, and contacting editors.

If you are sitting on a revise and resubmit notice, you should definitely consider this article. It always surprises me how many students are sitting on articles that journals have asked them to revise. Many students read revise and resubmit notices as rejections, but they are not. It is better to think of them as an editing stage in the publication process. Even if your article was rejected, you may want to consider it for revision, especially if the reviewers gave you solid recommendations for revision.

If none of these situations is the case, you can pick the one that you think requires the least amount of work to get ready for publication, or you can pick the one you feel most excited about working on. For those just embarking on a publication career, it is wise to choose a paper that will provide you with the energy to remain motivated. Keeping all this in mind, use the chart below to identify the paper you will revise. Feel free to talk this over with others first.

My Chosen Title			
Class/Conference	**Professor/Moderator**	**Date/Semester**	**Length**

Day 3: Choosing Your Writing Site

Having a customary writing site is part of forming the habit of writing regularly. It is worthwhile to spend a few minutes thinking about which study site has worked best for your writing. Many graduate students have a variety of writing sites, including library stacks, reading rooms, coffee shops, bedrooms, and kitchen tables. (One prolific professor I know could only write while lying on a futon on his left side while using a red pen on a yellow legal pad. Now he can only write in a coffee shop.) Since you will be writing every day (more on this below), will it still be feasible to work at the library, for instance, where you do not have access to your computer? What changes will you make to your writing site to ensure that it is comfortable, convenient, and nondistracting? Can you use your day-job office when you cannot get to your usual writing spot?

If feeling lonely while writing is a problem, you might want to think about writing at a nearby café. You could also write in a university common room, but you will have to be firm with friends who want to sit down and chat. If distraction in a busy household is a problem, you might want to buy earphones. If you work at a computer, be sure to have a proper chair and to place your keyboard at the proper height. If you have been thinking about getting an ergonomic chair, I recommend you do it now. It's a great way to reward and encourage your decision to complete an article.

Some students tell me that they are itinerant writers. Fixing on one writing spot doesn't work because, after working in a space for a week or two, the place becomes tainted for them. As you become a better writer, you may find that this phenomenon fades. Otherwise, notice when a place is no longer working for you, and move on to the next. May you live in a town with many coffee shops!

The point of writing regularly is to develop a habit of writing, and part of that is having a habitual writing spot. Use the chart below to indicate your writing sites.

	Mon.	Tues.	Wed.	Thurs.	Fri.	Sat.	Sun.
Regular Writing Site							
Backup Writing Site							

Use the chart below to indicate what improvements you will have to make to these writing sites to ensure that they are comfortable and nondistracting.

Regular Writing Site Improvements	
Backup Writing Site Improvements	

It's interesting to note that some students have a site that they use to get themselves in a positive writing mood before moving to their writing spot. One student would enter the bathroom, close the door, and sit on the floor while wearing a particular hat. In that odd sanctuary, she thought through her writing plan for the day and initiated her writing mindset. Another student with a long commute would talk aloud to herself in the car. Speaking the words helped her to gain focus and to argue with potential critics. Use the chart below to note anything you do to start writing.

Preparatory Writing Activity	

Day 4: Designing Your Writing Schedule

Many students believe that in order to write they must have long, uninterrupted stretches of time. Nothing will do but to be at their desks eight hours a day, all night, or six days a week. Only then will they be able to concentrate. Such stretches are elusive, however, so they wait for the weekend, and then for the break between classes, and then for the summer. Waiting becomes a permanent state, with writing something that you will do after, for instance, your qualifying exams or your first year teaching.

Others forcefully create blocks of time. As one of my students put it, "If I wait until the night before to write my paper, I will only be miserable for eight hours!" Such students believe that containing the process will reduce the painfulness of the experience. What they don't understand is that this irregular practice is producing the painfulness. Imagine deciding that "Running marathons is painful, so I'm never going to run except on the day of the marathon." Of course, the marathon is then an extremely painful experience you never want to repeat. By contrast, people who run a mile or two every day really enjoy running and often feel lost without it.

Study after study shows that you do not need big blocks of time to write.[3] In fact, writers who write a little bit every day produce more manuscripts than those who alternate weeks/months without writing with extended writing sessions. Writing just thirty minutes a day can make you one of those unusual writers who publishes several journal articles a year.

> Those who write in regular, unemotional sessions of moderate length completed more pages, enjoyed more editorial acceptance, were less depressed and more creative than those authors who wrote in emotionally charged binges. (Boice 1997, 435)

When I make this assertion in class about how little time it can take to be productive, most students look at me skeptically. It is by far the most controversial idea that I introduce in my course—simultaneously the most contested and the most embraced. Not surprisingly, many immediately voice their disbelief. "No way," I hear. "That's impossible." When I ask why, this is what students tell me:

> I need whole days to write; otherwise I forget what I'm working on. . . . I lose track. If I don't stay in one mental space for an entire week, my ideas don't cohere. . . . I need to get up a head of steam and just keep on going because if I stop, I'll never get started again.

I listen to the students' objections, but then ask them to indulge me. "Just as an experiment," I say, "try writing fifteen minutes a day for the next week." I remind them that we all manage to get to work, use a microwave, and answer e-mail without having to do it for ten hours at a stretch. "But writing is different," they argue. "It's intellectual; it's about ideas." Just indulge me, I reply.

The next week, the student who protested the most is usually the first to volunteer that, wow, it really does work. One student told me that he had reorganized his entire life into fifteen-minute chunks arranged around work and childcare. "Not only did I do fifteen minutes of writing a day, I did fifteen minutes of gardening, fifteen minutes of cooking, and fifteen minutes of reading!" Another student told me she had solved an important revision problem while standing in line at the Department of Motor Vehicles. Yet another student set herself the goal of writing a 2,000-word essay for a trade magazine in her field without ever writing more than fifteen minutes a day. In two weeks, she had submitted the essay.

One student explained it like this: "I'm usually an environmental perfectionist when it comes to writing, I have to be at my computer, it has to be silent, I must have coffee. But I was stuck waiting at the airport for a flight to a conference, and I thought about what you said. So I decided to try writing for fifteen minutes. It worked fine. Then I worried about having to take the time to type up my penciled notes, but I found that in transcribing them I revised them as well, so it wasn't wasted time. A busy airport would still not be my writing site of choice, but I can see how, by being flexible, I can ensure that I write a little bit everyday and keep my ideas fresh."

Another person told me that, "I can't do the fifteen-minute thing. But I believe in the concept of writing daily so the way that I've interpreted that concept for myself is that I always have whatever journal article I am working on open on my computer. It's the first thing I open when I turn on my computer and the last thing I close. That means that every day at some point I do something to the article—I add a citation, change the spaces in the table, cut a few words from the methods and so on. It keeps it fresh."

Almost all of my students who actually do the exercise admit that they get a useful amount of work done in fifteen minutes and that they have no problem remembering where they are or what they are doing when they start up the next day. Writing every day keeps the article in the forefront, so that you think about it while driving or doing the dishes, instead of forgetting about it. Furthermore, if you write in the morning you feel so productive that the rest of the day seems much more manageable.

For many of us, writing more than fifteen minutes is preferable and given the choice, we will set aside one to four hours for writing. If you have financial support and no other obligations, you can ratchet your hours as high as you can stand it. But what if you don't? What if you are a new professor teaching three new courses? Or a new father who isn't getting much sleep? Large blocks of time don't exist. The good news is that you can get some writing done in the few minutes that do open up and they will be effective. It means if you suddenly spend half-an-hour writing, you can be pleasantly surprised and not disappointed that it was not a full day. You can rearrange your thinking to value any and all writing opportunities. Writing in short daily bursts is especially helpful if you only have one block of time a week. That is, your Saturday afternoon of writing will be much more productive if you spent fifteen minutes of writing each of the four previous days. You are limbered up and don't need much warm-up time. Some find that the short sessions are best for revising and the long sessions for drafting—discover what works for you. Some consider that writing time includes writing up their notes on reading. Whatever works for you is fine with me.

The moral? Writing daily works. Writing in painful binges does not. The problem with binge writing—where you don't write for weeks and then stay up all night (or the whole weekend) writing—is that the less you write, the harder it becomes to write. Part of the reason students feel they need big blocks of time is because it takes them so long to silence their inner critic. In the absence of the small but satisfying successes of daily writing, that critic becomes harsher and louder. If you have been writing every day, you don't have this problem. The more of a habit that writing becomes, the more likely you are to complete writing projects and to enjoy writing.

Therefore, I can guarantee you dramatic improvement as a writer if you commit to being at your writing site and writing five days a week, for fifteen to thirty to sixty minutes. The key is to establish a regular, reasonable writing schedule and then discipline yourself to maintain it.

Few graduate students, in my experience, have good writing schedules that they discipline themselves to maintain. In this, they are little different from most faculty members, as you learned at the beginning of this chapter. One study of new faculty followed them over the course of the first two years of their tenure-track appointment. The new faculty had estimated that they would spend at least ten hours a week writing and would produce at least two articles. But, over that period, they spent an average of only thirty minutes a week on writing and produced only a third of one manuscript rather than two (Boice 1997, 24). Clearly, making time to write is a widespread problem. So, let's focus on setting up a reasonable schedule. This next section is long, so be sure to allot enough time to do all the tasks.

Establishing a Firm Deadline

I designed this workbook to aid you in sending an article to a journal in twelve weeks. I recommend that you consider this current week as Week 1 and eleven weeks later as your deadline for sending the journal article. Alternately, you can identify external deadlines that will keep you disciplined, such as the conference date when you must present the article. Once this firm completion date is set, you can plan your time accordingly.

If you do not feel this is a good week to begin, choose next week. You could even choose the week after or set the book aside for next summer, but I do not recommend this. Then you are falling into the trap of thinking you can only write with large, uninterrupted chunks of time. If you think this way, you will start by waiting for the break between classes to write, and then for the summer, and then for sabbatical, and then for retirement. And then, let's be frank, you will be dead!

There is no time like the present. If you've read this far in the workbook, you are definitely prepared to undertake this task. Since I designed this workbook to accommodate writing to your life, rather than the other way around, you can reach your goal of sending your article out even if this is a busy time for you. In the next session, I am going to address the writing anxieties that may prevent you from starting *right now*, but before that, please set your final deadline by using the twelve-week calendar on page 24.

Weeks. Under each of the twelve week boxes, fill in the exact dates between now and your firm completion date.

Setting a Realistic Writing Goal

This workbook sets a goal of writing and submitting a journal article in twelve weeks. To do this, you must write between fifteen minutes and one hour a day, five days a week. It is unlikely that you will need more time than this (fifteen to sixty hours) to complete your article. If you very rarely write now, it is best to start small and set a goal of writing fifteen minutes a day. If you have developed some good writing habits, you should set a goal of writing one to three hours a day on this article. If you are on fellowship or your sabbatical, with no other responsibilities, you may write for more than that, but recognize that there often are diminishing returns after three or four hours. Short and steady sessions will also win the race.

Make sure your goal is realistic rather than ambitious. For instance, recent research suggests that being a morning or evening person has deep psychological roots that you ignore to your detriment (Diaz-Morales 2007). If you are not a morning person, do not determine to get up every morning and write at 5:00 a.m. This is not realistic. Pick a time of day when you are most alert and energetic. If you work full time Monday through Friday, don't determine to write every evening for four hours or to set aside your entire weekend. This is not a realistic goal and will only discourage you. Aim instead to write fifteen minutes a day during the week and for several hours on Sunday afternoon, for example. This will keep your ideas fresh during the week so that your weekend session is productive. If your schedule is to write one hour Monday, Wednesday, and Friday, still try to get in fifteen minutes on Tuesday and Thursday so that you don't grind your gears on fuller writing days.

The most unrealistic writing schedule is none at all. Don't believe that somehow, miraculously, your article will get written in the next couple of months simply because you need it to be submitted.

You may have to adjust your goal as you go along, but for now, you should focus on what is doable given your obligations and work habits.

> With but a few exceptions, writers who remained in a schedule requiring an hour or less a weekday of writing mastered a sequence of strategies for remaining truly productive over long periods of time. (Boice 1990, 3)

Weeks. Under each of the weeks in the twelve-week calendar on page 24, note the days and weeks when it will be especially difficult to find time for writing. For instance, perhaps certain days of the week regularly fill up with childcare or teaching. Perhaps you or someone in your family is scheduled for surgery. Perhaps relatives are coming to visit for a week. Perhaps you have a deadline for another piece of writing. Use the calendar to anticipate packed schedules. You may want to skip a particular week in your twelve-week writing plan, if that week is harried, and stretch the plan to thirteen weeks.

Days. Under each of the seven days in the weekly calendar on page 24, cross out the times unavailable for writing in the next week, such as when you have classes, work, appointments, meals, sleep, and so on. Fill in the exact times when you plan to do your daily writing. If you can schedule the writing for the same time every day, all the better. If you cannot, still try to come up with a regular pattern. Don't forget to schedule two hours each week to go through the workbook. Here are some samples:

- Sample: Monday–Friday, 15 minutes when I wake up in the morning.
- Sample: Wednesday–Sunday, 8:00–8:30 a.m.

- Sample: Monday, Wednesday, Friday, 10:00–11:00 p.m., Thursday and Saturday, 11:00–12:00 a.m.

- Sample: Wednesday and Friday, 12:00–1:00 p.m., Monday, Tuesday, Thursday, 15 minutes after supper.

Minutes. At the bottom of the calendar, fill in the total number of minutes that you plan to spend writing that day.

- Sample: 15 minutes, 1.5 hours, 3 hours

Tasks. At the bottom of the calendar, write down the tasks you would like to have completed by the end of the week.

- Sample: Finish reviewing paper and marking it for needed revisions and additions.

Twelve-Week Calendar for Planning Article Writing Schedule									
Week	**Task**	**Mon.**	**Tues.**	**Wed.**	**Thurs.**	**Fri.**	**Sat.**	**Sun.**	**Total Hours**
Week 1	Designing Your Plan for Writing								
Week 2	Starting Your Article								
Week 3	Advancing Your Argument								
Week 4	Selecting a Journal								
Week 5	Reviewing the Related Literature								
Week 6	Strengthening Your Structure								
Week 7	Presenting Your Evidence								
Week 8	Opening and Concluding Your Article								
Week 9	Giving, Getting, and Using Others' Feedback								
Week 10	Editing Your Sentences								
Week 11	Wrapping Up Your Article								
Week 12	Sending Your Article!								

Time	Monday	Tuesday	Wednesday	Thursday	Friday	Saturday	Sunday
Weekly Calendar for Planning Article Writing Schedule							
5:00 a.m.							
6:00							
7:00							
8:00							
9:00							
10:00							
11:00							
12:00 p.m.							
1:00							
2:00							
3:00							
4:00							
5:00							
6:00							
7:00							
8:00							
9:00							
10:00							
11:00							
12:00 a.m.							
1:00							
2:00							
3:00							
4:00							
Total Minutes Plan to Work							
Tasks Aim to Complete							

Day 4 (continued): Anticipating Writing Obstacles

The best laid plans oft go awry. The key to following through on the plan you just made is to anticipate the kinds of interruptions and excuses that are going to arise. In my classes, students have named entire mine-fields of writing obstacles. I have listed the most common below and some of the solutions.

Obstacle No. 1: I really am too busy! If you really are too busy to fit in fifteen minutes of writing a day, then this workbook cannot help you. I recommend that you plan, in the very near future, a weekend away from it all where you can really think about your life. If taking this time off means you cannot meet some obligations, do it anyway. Serious thinking about the quality and direction of your life is in order.

Obstacle No. 2: Teaching preparation takes up all my extra time. A common complaint of graduate students (and faculty) is that teaching preparation takes up the time they had hoped to use for writing. Certainly, preparing for class can devour time, especially if you have rarely taught before and want to avoid appearing like an idiot in front of thirty undergraduates. There is always more preparation and reading you can do for any class. Teaching assistants in the humanities can easily spend a forty-hour workweek just on meeting with students and grading.

The best solution for this very real problem is to set limits on your preparation time. You should learn to do this if you plan a career in academia since preparation will be an ongoing reality. Schedule your writing time before your teaching prep time. For instance, do not start to prepare for class until you have done half an hour of writing. That way, teaching preparation cannot spill over into your writing time. Now that you know that writing does not have to take hours and hours, and can be done daily, you should be able to fit writing in before other tasks.

Finally, if you are dedicated to being a good teacher, you should know that, among untenured faculty, having a commitment to your students correlates positively with higher rates of writing productivity (Sax, Hagedorn, Arredondo, Dicrisi 2002). Being well-rounded matters!

Obstacle No. 3: I will write just as soon as (fill in the blank). Many students explain to me that they will get to writing just as soon as some more important task is completed. This list is varied and fascinating; that is, as soon as the apartment is clean, my lecture notes are organized, exams are over, the divorce is final, my advisor comes back from sabbatical, my medication kicks in, and so on. Only you can tell if these situations really do demand a break from writing. I suggest to you, however, that if you have not been writing regularly, none of these is an adequate excuse for not writing fifteen minutes a day.

Oddly enough, the most common "important task" of this sort is cleaning the house. Apparently, it is a common fact that many people simply cannot write if the house is dirty. My advice to you: Clean your house! In fact, if the way you get yourself in the writing mood is to spend fifteen minutes of cleaning before you spend fifteen minutes of writing, I'm all for it. Many of these same people feel that once they start cleaning they cannot stop, however. If so, I recommend that you reverse the order and do your fifteen minutes of writing first.

In other words, you don't have to "clear the decks" before you can get started on a writing project. Writing seems to thrive on messy decks.

Obstacle No. 4: I'm too depressed to write. This is a very real problem and should not be underestimated. Depression among graduate students and faculty members is a common reason for underproductivity. Depression is variously defined, but some causes are useful for academics to remember.

Depression is an emotional disorder usually triggered by environment. Some researchers believe that continuous stress over a long period tricks the brain into responding to all events as stressful, which in turn triggers depression (Blackburn-Munro and Blackburn-Munro 2001). Since there may be no better description of graduate school than operating continuously in stress mode, it is not surprising that depression is such a common problem in academia. Although the trigger is environmental, the effect is chemical—an imbalance in the neurotransmitters called dopamine, norepinephrine, and serotonin. Low levels of these natural brain chemicals prevent the nerve cells in the brain from transmitting signals normally. This slow down makes people feel that performing daily activities is like struggling to walk through mud.

The terrible curse of depression is that it impairs the very faculty you need to solve that problem. So, if you suspect that you are depressed, go to your campus clinic and ask for an appointment with a doctor. If you don't have such access, e-mail a few people for references and make an appointment with a doctor. This is the easiest step I know of to start moving beyond depression. The doctor can then refer you to a counselor, whose services are often provided free for graduate students, or can recommend an antidepressant. Taking any medication is a serious step, but antidepressants aren't designed to make you feel euphoric or to take away your blue feelings. They are designed to help you get up in the morning and complete tasks. They are about escaping that feeling of moving through mud; they are not about escaping your life. The doctor may also recommend exercise, which has been found a good antidote to mild depression.

If you are depressed, I know how hard it can be to take the steps to take care of yourself, but you simply must. Your academic future and maybe your life depend on it.

Obstacle No. 5: I'm going to make writing my number one goal in life. This may seem counterintuitive, but focusing all your energy on writing will not result in more productivity. In fact, research shows that whatever goal you make your highest priority you most likely will not attain. That's because "the most valued activity" always "carries demands for time and perfection that encourage its avoidance" (Boice 1997, 23). Writers who make writing a modest, realistic priority are more productive.

Do not establish self-defeating writing goals that relegate everything else in your life to mere backdrop. Aiming for a forty-hour writing week will only make you feel guilty, not productive. Furthermore, the feeling that you should always be working will haunt every pleasurable moment. You do not resolve desires by suppressing them entirely. Make time to go to the beach, meet a friend for dinner, or play basketball. A well-balanced life—with time allotted for friends and family, games and sports, movies and light reading, as well as writing, research, and teaching—is the best ground for productive writing.

Making writing your last goal won't work well either. In some cases, you may need to think long and hard about what your real goals are. You may need to work on seeing your number one goal as completing your dissertation, not perfecting it.

Obstacle No. 6: I couldn't get to my writing site. "Living in limbo" is the graduate student's theme song. One is always standing in some line, stuck in some meeting, stranded in traffic, lingering for delayed public transportation, or sitting around until someone shows up for an appointment. Whole days can be frittered away in waiting. If you find these times useful for planning your day or just relaxing, then all power to you. Most people, however, waste this time on feeling frustrated. It can be useful to carry a draft of your article everywhere. You can review the draft and make notes to yourself on improvements or do line editing. Many students I have worked with get their fifteen minutes a day done during these down times. There is nothing like doing two things at once to give you a marvelous feeling of efficiency!

Obstacle No. 7: I have to read just one more book. Many of us tend to bog down in research. We find it difficult to get to writing because we are lured into the forest of no return, otherwise known as the library. Each article leads to another and then another, especially online. We wander deeper and deeper into this forest, rarely finding a path out. Why do we do this? While we remain in the forest, we are safe from the perils of writing. The idea that just one more article is going to give us mastery is an illusion. If such a thing as mastery is possible, it comes from writing not reading.

The best way I know to get out of the research bog is to do your writing and research at the same time. Do not take endless notes and underline huge sections of books, and then feel overwhelmed because you have to go back through all of those notes and texts. Read and then write an actual paragraph, however loose, about what you have read.

The point here is that you do not have to "finish" research before you start writing. You do not have to complete your literature search or finalize your data analysis or even read your advisor's book. You do not have to know everything on the subject. Start writing and find out what you must know. As Boice puts it, "Writers who learn to leave holes in manuscripts to be filled later master valuable skills in writing: they learn to proceed amid ambiguity and uncertainty" (1997, 29). I know a graduate student who claims that she finished her dissertation by posting this quote on her computer and looking at it every time she wanted to reach for another book.

Erich Auerbach's masterpiece *Mimesis: The Representation of Reality in Western Literature* is a good example of this principle of research. Discharged from his university position in Germany by the Nazi government, Auerbach emigrated to Turkey, where he wrote *Mimesis* from 1942 to 1945. In his epilogue, Auerbach explains that the book lacks footnotes and may assert things that "modern research has disproved or modified" because the libraries in Istanbul were "not well equipped for European studies." Then he adds a fascinating note. "It is quite possible that the book owes its existence to just this lack of a rich and specialized library. If it had been possible for me to acquaint myself with all the work that has been done on so many subjects, I might never have reached the point of writing" (1953, 557).

Don't feel bad about not having done enough research. In the twenty-first century, it is no longer possible to be comprehensive. As knowledge expands and ways to communicate that knowledge explode, accelerating ignorance is an inevitable state. The best future researcher will be someone who learns to make a path through this immensity without getting overwhelmed.

Obstacle No. 8: I just can't get started. Many students find sitting down at the computer and starting to write to be the most difficult challenge facing them. Indeed, the horror of the blank page is a frequent theme of literature. The literary scholar Richard D. Altick talked about "First Paragraph Block" (1963, 190). Francoise Sagan described writing as "having a sheet of paper, a pen and . . . not an idea of what you're going to say" (Brussell 1988, 618). Getting started is painful. One of the reasons for this, as one of my students put it so well, is that "if I never start, then I never fail."

An excellent way of dealing with the difficulty of getting started is to make a preferred task contingent on a nonpreferred task, as the behavior management experts put it. In this case, writing is the nonpreferred task you have to complete before you get to something you prefer. For instance, do not allow yourself to read the morning newspaper or check your e-mail before you write for thirty minutes. Tell yourself that you will call a friend or watch a favorite television program after writing for an hour. Most students flip this and tell themselves "I'll watch TV for an hour and then write." But it is better to make the pleasurable activity a reward. Turn your procrastination tactics into productivity tools.

One warning on this tool. A friend of mine, when invited to socialize, always told us that she couldn't get together because she had to write. When we called her the next day, however, she usually admitted that she had just watched bad television. It's better to feel guilty about really enjoying something than to feel guilty about misspending your time *and* not writing. Denying yourself a real pleasure in order to force writing rarely works. Delaying a pleasure does.

Another method is to start by writing something else. Some students begin by typing a quote from their reading. Others write a plan for what they would like to do in that writing session. If you really feel shut down, it is useful to start by writing down the thoughts of your inner critic. You know, "It's hubris for me even to pick up a pen, I haven't a prayer of actually finishing this article in time," etc., etc., etc. When you get bored with this inner critic and think, "Oh come on, things aren't that bad," then you can start writing your article. Eventually you get bored with this voice. It's not very good company and writing becomes preferable to whining.

Another method is to focus on writing badly. If you can't get started because your first sentence has to be perfect, this method can be useful. For fifteen minutes, write down every thought you have about your article without stopping to edit. Just let it all hang out. This is writing what Ann Lamott has celebrated as "a shitty first draft." I could use the more alliterative word fecal, but shitty gets at the real feelings of shame and revulsion many have about writing. If you set out deliberately to write something horrible, this roadblock is erased. Again, eventually you write a sentence or have an idea that, despite your best efforts at producing ghastly work, sounds pretty good. And then you are on your way.

Still another method is to have a phone or e-mail partner. Arrange with another prospective author to agree to write at the same time. Check in by phone or e-mail when you are supposed to start, encourage each other, and then get started writing, knowing that someone else is going through the same horrible suffering, I mean, wonderful process that you are. Lots of my students have found this really helpful. It seems to be more helpful than the plan of meeting at someone's house to write together, which often ends up being a talking session rather than a writing session.

A final method is to plan the agenda for your next writing session at the end of the last one. That way you will know what to do when you sit down to write. This will also help you stay focused on your article as a series of small tasks. Some authors even recommend that you always stop in the middle of a sentence, so that you have somewhere to pick up. I prefer to recommend pushing a bit into the next section.

Obstacle No. 9: I'm afraid of writing because my idea is very controversial or emotional. Again, this is a very real concern. As one of my students put it, "sometimes I'm afraid my idea will come back and bite me." One student had done a study on earnings and ethnicity, hypothesizing that salaries would be lower for a minority group in a certain profession. Her analysis of the data revealed that there was no significant difference. This finding went against her own experience and was disturbing to her advisor. Whenever she thought about writing, she felt shut down. Even if her initial findings were true, were they what she wanted to associate her name with? She felt an obligation to the truth, but also to justice and her career. How could she write when she was caught between such hard places?

As is so often the case, she found her way out through writing. She used the discussion and conclusion section of her article to suggest some alternative approaches to understanding the findings. She then used them as a platform for extending her future research to incorporate a more detailed investigation of earnings by adding qualitative in-depth interviews to her previous quantitative approach. In other words, she used an obstacle to become a better scholar. If you find yourself in a similar position, talking and writing can be the cure.

Obstacle No. 10: I'm afraid of writing because publication is so permanent. This fear is one that professors often aid and abet. Graduate students in the humanities are often warned not to publish until they are completely ready and in absolute control of their topic. Professors caution that early articles can come back to haunt and embarrass the author. Nevertheless, the benefits of publication outweigh its dangers.

The argument for waiting to publish goes something like the following story, told to me by a friend who is a professor. An assistant professor in the department was up for tenure when hostile committee members dug up the professor's first article. They proceeded to lambaste the professor with it, calling it a "vulgar tract." In this case, my friend pointed out, publication had hurt rather than helped.

I asked my friend two simple questions. First, had the professor gotten tenure? My friend had to admit that the professor had. Perhaps the professor told the committee that the article was early work, and that if the later work could develop so far beyond the first article, this boded well for the trajectory of the professor's career. Apparently, whatever the defense, it won the day. No one expects that scholars are going to have the same theoretical or ideological approach over the course of a lifetime

My second question was, had the professor published the article in a peer-reviewed journal? In fact, the professor had not. The article had been published in a collection of conference papers, where the papers were not properly vetted. That's why I emphasize that students send their work to peer-reviewed journals only. The review process, however faulty, provides a safety net. If a peer-reviewed journal accepts your article, it probably won't embarrass you later.

Other professors are more to the point than my friend. "There's enough bad writing out there, why increase it?" one said. "Most graduate students have nothing worth publishing." All I can say in response to such critics is that they have not read my students' articles. Students' first drafts for the classroom can be rough, but those students willing to do real revisions often produce fascinating, cutting-edge work that many professors would be proud to publish. Certainly, if quality were the only criteria for publication, many a faculty member dedicated to the obtuse would have to recuse him or herself from this debate.

Obstacle No. 11: I'm not in the right mood to write. Many people believe you have to be emotionally ready to write. If you are not in the right mood, they argue, don't even try getting started because it's not going to work. Yet, many can testify that it is possible to get in the writing mood. Behavior modification theory shows us that emotion follows action, not the other way around. If you don't feel like doing something, then start doing it and usually your feelings will follow.

Individuals who procrastinate frequently confuse motivation and action. You foolishly wait until you feel in the mood to do something. Since you don't feel like doing it, you automatically put it off. Your error is your belief that motivation comes first, and then leads to activation and success. But it is usually the other way around; action must come first, and the motivation comes later on. (Burns 1999, 125)

David D. Burns's book *Feeling Good* describes many techniques for thinking positively about your life and work so that you can overcome perfectionism and guilty feelings.

You can also use ritual to overcome feeling unready. You can jumpstart the mood for writing by lighting a certain candle, playing a certain song, or doing certain stretches. When someone I know was writing her first book, she started every writing morning by reading a section from the King James Version of the Old Testament. The beauty of the passages always called up a writing response in her. Even on those days when she didn't much feel like writing, she responded to the ritual. If Pavlov's dogs can do it, so can you.

So, don't wait until your feelings catch up with your goals. Just make a plan and follow it.

Obstacle No. 12: My childcare responsibilities are preventing me from writing. Interestingly, students with children are often the best practitioners of the tenets of this chapter. Caregivers simply do not have big blocks of time, so they get used to working in time-bound segments of one to four hours. They cannot make writing their number one priority, so they do not fixate. They cannot stay up all night binge writing and then take care of the baby the next day, so they plan ahead. For those of you who don't have kids, no, I'm not recommending that you adopt. But if you have friends who are caregivers as well as students, you might want to study how they get it all done. You can learn good lessons from them.

If you are not getting writing done due to childcare responsibilities, you already know the answer: getting others to care for your children several hours a week. Many students would love to have such help, but are far from family and cannot afford to pay someone. Perhaps you might look into a shared childcare arrangement. Find another student who is a caregiver and arrange to trade baby-sitting so that each of you gets a full morning for writing. Or, if what you really need is some sleep or to run errands, exchange for that as well. Just remember to get fifteen minutes of writing done in that time. If none of this is possible, focus on working with the small amounts of time that crop up. Write for half an hour after you put the kids to sleep and before you start cleaning up.

If it's any comfort, studies differ as to the effect of marriage and dependents on faculty productivity. One study found that female faculty with children have lower tenure and promotion rates, while male faculty with children have higher tenure and promotion rates (National Science Foundation 2004). Another study found that family has little effect on the actual productivity of either female or male faculty (Sax, Hagedorn, Arredondo, Dicrisi 2002). These scholars speculate that the gender gap in publication rates, which has steadily been closing, is not explained by the weight of domestic responsibilities. Rather, this slightly lower rate seems to have more to do with women's prioritizing of "social change" over advancement and field recognition. This isn't to imply that male and female faculty experience family responsibilities in the same way. Among men and women with the same publication rates, female faculty did more work around the home and spent fewer hours per week on writing and research than male faculty (ibid.). That is, women were more efficient, producing the same amount of writing in less time.

Obstacle No. 13: I really can't move forward on this writing project. Sometimes, through no fault of your own, you cannot write. Perhaps you must wait for a result or further funding or your advisor's response. If the way is blocked on one project, turn to another. Success correlates with authors who are not monomaniacal but have several writing projects going at once. If bored or frustrated with one, you can switch to the other. Do not fall into the trap of thinking that only full-time dedication to a single project will result in success. If you're brought to a standstill, work on a grant application, revise an old article, or draft ideas for another article. You should always be moving forward on some front.

Obstacle No. 14: I can't write because my idea sucks. Many students do not trust the composing process. They dismiss their initial ideas as derivative or silly and stop writing in the hope that better ideas will somehow show up. As one of my students said, "I feel like writing should be perfect and easy the first time. If it's not perfect, I feel I need more time to think before I start."

But writing and thinking are a loop: thinking leads to writing, which leads back to thinking. I often write in order to find out what I think. Certainly, one need not have a fabulous, publishable idea to start writing. Writing generates its own answers.

So, to have positive writing experiences, allow yourself to develop ideas without immediately critiquing them. Spend a page or two fleshing out an idea and then call a classmate to develop it. If you encourage yourself in this way, you will find ideas flowing more readily and quickly. By ignoring your inner critic when developing a project, you encourage your mind to be a fertile ground for new growth.

Obstacle No 15: My thesis advisor is more of an obstacle than an aid. A student once volunteered that he was having trouble writing because "my advisor is the anti-Christ." For some odd reason, of all the negative feelings about writing that students have voiced in all of my classes, this one got the biggest laugh. Perhaps it was nervous laughter rather than sympathetic laughter, but the truth remains that a hypercritical mentor is a real obstacle. This is especially the case if you must work closely with him or her on the article you are revising for this workbook.

If you are in this situation, you have three choices. First, try telling your advisor that research shows that when drafting an article it is a good idea to focus on what is working rather than what is not working. Add that you would like the space to develop your project without too much detailed feedback and that when you are done with a second draft you will welcome all of your advisor's comments, negative and positive. If your advisor argues that he or she is just trying to head you off at the pass, before you dedicate too much work to an errant direction, state that you are happy to revise when the time comes and to throw out sections if need be. This technique is risky, because your advisor may be even more critical if he or she has not had the opportunity to be so early on. But, since you will have had more time to develop your ideas, and defend them on paper, your direction may seem more palatable than it would have in an early draft. Professors can describe as wrong or untenable those ideas that you simply have not yet fully defended. Once you marshal more proofs, their objection fades.

If this sort of rational conversation is not possible, you might want to consider switching advisors. There is nothing wrong with letting an advisor know that you think you would both be happier working with others. There is no need to say specifically why or to offer the professor a critique of his or her advising style. Just focus on moving on. Make sure you have found another professor who is willing to be your advisor before you take this step.

If neither of these approaches are options, make sure to have some arena where you go for responses that are more positive. I recommend a writing group that focuses on offering support and encouragement. Feel free to tell the group that you are getting all the negative feedback you can handle and you would be grateful if they would focus on the positive.

Obstacle No. 16: I can't sit still. Some energetic people find it hard to stay in one place. As one student put it, "I was writing when I suddenly found myself sweeping the kitchen. I have no idea how I got there!" Aiming to write no more than fifteen minutes at a stretch can be very helpful for this problem. It's easier to sit still if you know it's not for hours and hours. One student would set a kitchen timer for fifteen minutes. "When the alarm went off, it reminded me that I was supposed to be writing. I would often find myself doing something else and the alarm would help me refocus." I know one professor who belts himself into his chair. He pulls his belt out of some loops, threads it through the back of his work chair, and then belts it back up. That way, if he gets distracted, he is quickly reminded to stay seated! This technique seems extreme to me, but he swears by it.

Obstacle No. 17: I feel guilty about not writing. It's ironic that the very tool most of us use to spur ourselves into action also prevents us from acting. Guilt can be a useful goad, but it can also be a terrible obstacle. Most graduate students feel too much guilt about not writing. Some feel so guilty that it actually prevents them from writing. My unauthorized theory of why feeling guilty doesn't work is this: If you already feel guilty about not writing, you do what you can to avoid feeling even more guilty. The longer you go without writing, the less guilty you have to feel, because writing is clearly an impossible task. Following the exercises in this workbook and its model of a slow and steady pace should help overcome this feeling.

Obstacle No 18: I write so slowly that I never seem to get much done. Remember that it is extremely rare for a writer to churn out perfect first drafts. Even those who are famous for composing quickly may not have been so quick. The prolific eighteenth-century writer Samuel Johnson once wrote an essay in about half-an-hour while the printer's runner was at the door. When a friend asked if he could read it, Johnson handed the essay to the runner and told the friend, "Sir, you shall not do more than I have done myself" (Boswell 1793). These are the kinds of stories that people use to make themselves feel bad about their pace of writing. But these stories are mythical in several significant ways. First, Johnson composed much of his writing in his head and then wrote it down in a short space of time. Second, he was not writing for academic publication. If he had been, editors would have regularly rejected his articles for plagiarism and inaccurate quoting of sources (which he did from memory). You are working under different constraints! So, don't torture yourself with these examples. While some people who have been writing steadily for more than a decade can quickly write good first drafts, they are still the exception rather than the rule. Most people plod along, deleting one sentence for every three sentences they write and having to repeatedly read and revise their work to get it right. This does not make you a bad writer, it makes you a good writer. Over time, you will get faster. For now, applaud the amount of time you spend on writing instead of bemoaning your low output.

Obstacle No. 19: If I have a long, productive writing day, somehow it is harder to get started the next day, rather than easier. Boice observed this phenomenon during his research—that it was possible to have too much of a good thing. His advice is to limit the amount of time that you write (Boice 2000). While this can seem counterintuitive (What?! You want me to stop writing when I am really moving along?!), I have heard from those who tend to "overwrite" that the advice is sound. One student told me that his writing got better, smoother, and quicker when he started to limit the amount of time he spent writing. He tended to spend many hours a day writing, not due to any deadline but just by nature, and so limiting the amount of time he spent writing prevented him from "fussing with it." Others simply can't avoid spending long days writing; for instance, those whose first job depends on their finishing their dissertations in several months. If that is you, don't let me stop you. But there is a cost. I have noticed that those who had to binge write their dissertations often struggle later with post-traumatic dissertation syndrome. The feelings associated with writing for so long were exhaustion and anxiety so they recoil when faced with writing now. Avoid the marathon session.

Obstacle No. 20: I know my writing habits are bad, but that's just who I am and I can't/don't want to change. Only you can tell if the way that you write is fundamental to your being or just an accident of your life experiences and education. If you feel strong resistance to any of my adages, you should pay attention to that. Believe your resistance, as they say. Not every tactic works for everyone. But do pay attention to whether you are feeling resistance or fear. Resistance is positive, the sense that something just isn't for you. Fear is negative, the false sense that you just can't do something. So, watch what's happening because of "who you are." If who you are is preventing you from attaining the goals that are valuable to you, you may have to think hard about how you can turn that character trait into a positive or whether you want to go on being yourself. Behavior modification asserts that you are not a Russian doll, with layers of wooden selves to your very core. Rather, you are a protean being who does not take advantage of half your potential, skills, or smarts. Be wary of labeling some dysfunction as your essence. Sometimes you have to choose being productive over being unique.

Obstacle No. 21: I am eager to write but I don't have the material or scholarly resources. In some circumstances, you may not have access to a computer or to research publications. Maybe you are no longer at a university or your university doesn't have these resources. One Sri Lankan scholar tells the story of having to choose between writing his article submission by hand or on an ancient typewriter with a threadbare ribbon (Canagarajah 2002). He had paper only because he had bribed someone for it. EuroAmerican editors are rarely aware of the deep challenges facing scholars from countries outside of Europe and North America. Faced with a handwritten submission, editors may automatically return it. What can you do to improve your odds? This workbook is one attempt to level the playing field by giving you some solid knowledge of what U.S. journal editors expect.

I have two other recommendations. Plan now on sending your submission with an explanation of your circumstances. If material conditions limited your research, not your own thought, it is important that the editors know that. Few U.S. editors will know what you face. If they know, they can be more helpful. Many journal editors wish that they received more submissions from outside the United States and say that they would be willing to work with foreign authors who asked for some assistance. The key to inspiring such help is your data. Since you don't have access to the secondary literature (and so can't relate your research to the field), you will have to depend heavily on possessing exceptional data. Fortunately, scholars from outside the United States often have unique data and texts to offer U.S. journal editors; for example, a quantitative study never done in your nation or an epic poem undiscussed in a European language. You are more likely to get a EuroAmerican editor's assistance for a data-rich article than a theoretical one, unfortunately. Find a way to keep going.

Obstacle No. 22: I have to make progress on several writing projects at the same time, and I am in a panic. The writing research shows that those scholars with more than one writing project going at a time do better than those with only one (Boice 2000). Perhaps this is because you can switch from one to the other when you get stuck. Whatever the reason, having more than one writing project is a plus, not a minus. You probably have to prioritize one, but make a plan for working on both.

Obstacle No. 23: I would love to ask someone to read and comment on my work but everyone seems so busy and I don't want to bother them. It can be tough to ask people to spend their precious time reading your work. One way to make it easier for others to do this is to make that reading social. That is, instead of handing over your prose and asking your reader to get back to you when they have had a chance to read it on their own, read each other's work together. Schedule some time at a café or someone's home and read the work right there, then comment on it. It can be easier to read work when someone else is keeping you company and when you know that it is an exchange. Exchanging writing is often more effective anyway, as your reviewer knows he or she is about to be reviewed and will take care to be kind.

Obstacle No. 24: I'm beginning to wonder if being a professor is really the career for me, so what's the point of writing? I probably won't get a job anyway. It is easy to get discouraged when you have to keep doing something you don't feel good at. Being a professor depends on developing skills in teaching, writing, research, socializing, organizing, and discipline. Few jobs require so many different skills. It's a really difficult job! In fact, it is so difficult that most people spend decades figuring it all out, often after they have gotten their first jobs. So, be nice to yourself. In this workbook, you are going to work on one facet of being a professor—writing. Fortunately, learning to write well is a skill that will serve you in any profession so it is not a waste of time even if you don't plan to be a professor. When you are done with this workbook, you may feel better about your skills and may be more willing to spend the time to develop them. Or, you may feel more clearly that being a professor isn't for you. If that's what you decide, be kind to yourself about that too.

Obstacle No. 25: I'm not smart enough to do this kind of work. Sometimes, the most comforting response to our feelings of insecurity is to allow them. Maybe you are not smart enough to do statistics, learn several languages, understand complex theory, lecture without notes, or write without agony. For me, though, that's not the right question. The right question is not "Am I smart enough to do this work?" but "Am I passionate enough?" Do you love your topic or project? Do you believe it can make a real contribution? Sometimes it is easier to believe in the project than in yourself, and that's okay. Many average people have accomplished extraordinary things through their commitment and passion. Through hard work, they develop skills that were not innate. Maybe you are smart enough, or maybe you aren't. But if you care deeply about what you are doing, it may not matter. In the timeless words of that great sage Professor

Albus Dumbledore, "It is our choices, Harry, that show what we truly are, far more than our abilities" (Rowling 1997).

Obstacle No. 26: I get distracted by web surfing, e-mailing, and text messaging. As more than one scholar has argued, our communication technologies have "become both utterly integral and a major source of exhaustion and disquiet . . . E-mail must rank as one of the most time-devouring timesavers of all time. Too often it makes nothing happen—fast" (Nixon 2000). A student of mine resorted to working in a nearby fast food restaurant undergoing renovation because it had no wifi and the noise was so loud that she couldn't hear her cell phone ring. I hope that you find an easier method than this to cut down on your connectivity. Try closing your e-mail software or web browser while writing. Try checking e-mail only in the evening—or whenever you have the least energy. Don't make the mistake of thinking that you will get started after some quick web browsing. Try to do writing first, not second.

Obstacle No. 27: It is so difficult to write in English! My sympathies! Writing in English when it isn't your native tongue is difficult. Whole books have been written about the bizarre spelling, pronunciation, grammar, and syntax of this crazy language. If you are fairly good, hiring a copyeditor may be useful. If you have a long way to go in improving your English, read academic works in English. Then read some more and then read some more! Reading helps you absorb the structure of the language at an intuitive level so the more you do of it, the better. Finally, support journals in your own language, if possible. I know universities in many countries now prioritize publishing in English-language journals, but it is extremely important to keep research going in native languages.

Obstacle No. 28: I need big blocks of time to write, and my schedule doesn't allow such blocks. I addressed this topic earlier, in Designing Your Writing Schedule, but let me repeat. The first question I like to ask people who make such claims is: Have you ever tried it any other way? Many students believe that in order to write they must have long, uninterrupted stretches of time and yet they have never tried it any other way! It is unscientific to have such firm beliefs without having tested them. According to actual writing tests, there are two problems with this big block of time theory. One, such stretches are elusive, and virtually nonexistent once you become a professor. Two, people who use only big blocks of time to write are less productive and more unhappy than those who write daily. They have problems getting started and they often don't feel good about their writing. Study after study shows that you do not need big blocks of time to write. In fact, writers who write a little bit every day produce more manuscripts than those who alternate extended writing sessions with weeks/months of not writing. Writing just thirty minutes a day can make you one of those unusual writers who publishes several journal articles a year.

Day 4 (continued): Overturning Writing Obstacles

Use the chart below to note each of the major obstacles in the way of your writing goals—whether mentioned above or not. Also, note whether its interference level is high, medium, or low.

Estimated Interference	Writing Interruptions and Obstacles

So, what do you intend to do to interrupt your interruptions and overcome your obstacles to writing? If need be, review the interruptions and solutions listed above and return to the lessons you learned from noticing your feelings about writing earlier in this chapter.

Solutions to My Writing Interruptions and Obstacles

Day 5: Documenting How You Spent Your Time

On the weekly plan given earlier, you graphed out what time you would like to spend writing. Now, I would like you to spend some time every day this week filling out the weekly plan on the next page with how much time you actually spent writing and what you did with the rest of your time. List everything: watching television, attending class, commuting, sleeping, caring for family members, performing household tasks (e.g., cleaning, laundry, cooking), etc. This is an excellent exercise for finding out where your time goes and a useful tool for identifying how you to use your time more efficiently.

Week 1 Calendar

Time	Monday	Tuesday	Wednesday	Thursday	Friday	Saturday	Sunday
5:00 a.m.							
6:00							
7:00							
8:00							
9:00							
10:00							
11:00							
12:00 p.m.							
1:00							
2:00							
3:00							
4:00							
5:00							
6:00							
7:00							
8:00							
9:00							
10:00							
11:00							
12:00 a.m.							
1:00							
2:00							
3:00							
4:00							
Total Minutes Actually Worked							
Tasks Completed							

At the end of the week, look back at this record and consider your accomplishments. Even if you did not get as much done as you hoped, you have gained understanding of your patterns and are poised to do better next week. Remember, feeling too much guilt is counterproductive!

Week 2

Starting Your Article

Day to Do Task	Week 2 Daily Writing Tasks	Estimated Task Time
Day 1 (Monday?)	Read through page 60; discuss your article topic with a writing partner; start documenting your time (page 65)	60 minutes
Day 2 (Tuesday?)	Print out and reread your chosen paper, discuss it, then make a list of revision tasks (pages 60–61)	60 minutes
Day 3 (Wednesday?)	Draft an abstract and get a review of it (pages 61–62)	60 minutes
Day 4 (Thursday?)	Find and read a model article in your field (pages 62–63)	90 minutes
Day 5 (Friday?)	Revise abstract according to review (page 64)	30 minutes

Above are the tasks for your second week, which add up to about five hours of work. If you want to keep up your momentum, you can spread the tasks out over seven days, so that you are writing daily. In such a seven-day schedule, it's wise to limit writing on two of the days (e.g., to fifteen minutes each on Saturday and Sunday). Make sure to start this week by scheduling when you will write and then tracking the time that you actually spend writing. Documenting how you spend your time increases your effectiveness.

FIRST WEEK IN REVIEW

One of the lessons you learned last week was the importance of moving beyond solitary writing habits and into more communal writing practices. Several of the tasks for this week depend on you having a writing partner or advisor. If you are proceeding through this workbook with a writing partner or writing group, you have already accomplished this task. If you are working alone, have you thought about whom you will ask to provide occasional feedback? He or she does not have to be in your discipline; in fact, it may be better if the person is not. It just needs to be someone in the humanities if you are in the humanities, someone in the social sciences if you are in the social sciences. Also, it must be someone who is willing to meet with you for an hour, two or three times over the course of the next twelve weeks.

Another important lesson you learned last week was that you do not need big blocks of time to write. Instead, writing a bit every day is a much more effective writing practice than saving up your writing for the weekend, spring break, the summer, your sabbatical, or retirement. That's why this workbook breaks down, into manageable chunks, the tasks involved in revising an article for publication. You can do many tasks in an hour or less. If you manage to get some writing done every day for twelve weeks, you will have done more than submit an article to a journal—you will have developed writing habits that will carry you for a lifetime. Professors will always need to teach classes and serve on committees. Learning to juggle teaching, service, and writing is a strength that will stand you in excellent stead. If you think of your days as regularly involving all three (e.g., one hour of writing, one hour of reading, one hour of service, one hour of grading and meeting with students, two hours of teaching prep, two hours of class time), you will be well on your way.

TYPES OF ACADEMIC ARTICLES

At this point in the workbook, you should already have chosen what article you would like to revise, but you will find it useful to see what type your article seems to be. Knowing this can help you determine how to proceed in revising, especially since not all journals publish all types of articles. I have listed the following types from those that have the least weight with a hiring committee to those that have the most weight.

Annotated Bibliography. These articles list texts with two or three sentences describing each. Few journals publish this kind of "article"—they are more frequently part of books—so I wouldn't recommend this type to you. If you have enough material to do an annotated bibliography, develop it into a review article instead (see below).

Book Review. These articles critique one recently published book. Many book reviews are now published by graduate students, perhaps since they count for so little on your curriculum vitae. You have to publish six to ten book reviews (depending on your discipline) before you have something equivalent in weight to a research article. In some places, it never adds up, counting for nothing. If you can produce book reviews quickly, it can be in your interest to pursue such writing, since it helps you write your dissertation literature review and get in the habit of briefly summarizing and critiquing books. Or, if you have devoted ten pages of your article to discussing a recent book and now realize that section needs to be cut, perhaps you can shape the pages into a stand-alone book review. But never substitute writing book reviews for writing a research article. Indeed, some professors warn graduate students not to publish book reviews, since the authors you review may turn up on hiring committees. I wouldn't go that far, but I would say that you should only review books that you think are a significant contribution to the field. Don't do reviews of bad books; most aren't worth your writing time. Further, unless the author is deceased or famous, you don't really want to go on record lambasting him or her before you have tenure. Before writing a book review, always ask an editor at a suitable journal if he or she would be interested. They may have already assigned the book for review to somebody else.

Trade/Professional Article. These articles are for a nonacademic audience. In order to get the word out, academics sometimes write articles for newspapers, popular magazines, trade journals, or practitioner newsletters. They do so to shape policy, change community practices, advance causes, or decry injustices. Some authors regularly publish distilled versions of their academic articles in such journals, efficiently getting two publications out of one idea. Such articles can do a great job of getting your name out there and changing the world we live in, but they do not weigh much with hiring committees. This is so, even though popular magazines or newspaper opinion pages can be much harder to get published in than any academic journal. If you can produce such articles quickly and would like your research to have a real-world impact, publish such articles for your own satisfaction. Just don't let them become a substitute for a research article or so close to one that a peer-reviewed journal wouldn't view a related submission as original.

Notes. These short articles document a small finding. Notes are usually around 500 words, and are, typically, a case history, a methodological innovation, one observation about a particular text, and so on. Notes are good for offloading interesting but brief passages that you cannot fit into any of your research articles without digressing. If the observation is more directly related to your research, consider developing it into a research article. Articles published in note sections will not "count" for as much in a job or tenure review, although they frequently count for more than a book review or trade article. Many disciplines do not have note journals.

Interviews. These are a brief introduction to and transcript of an interview with another scholar, political figure, or artist. Interviews can be a good way to get a publication under your belt and develop a relationship with someone you admire, but they require some care and planning. First, you must design pointed questions focused around a topic of interest to other scholars and the audience of a particular journal. Interviews in which figures simply report on the events of their life or their general intellectual development don't tend to get published. Like an article, interviews need to be focused. Second, you must tape the interview and then transcribe it, a painful process if you are not an extremely fast typist. In general, transcribing takes about three hours for every hour of tape. Third, your interviewee must provide provocative answers to your questions, a feat which is not within your control. Frequently, the aim of a journal in publishing an interview is to make a scholar's ideas more accessible and vivid. If the interviewee is not clear or says nothing new, you may have spent a lot of time on something that is unpublishable. If you feel you have an interesting topic and interviewee, however, it can be a good experience. You will be seen as someone who cares about other people's ideas and is committed to the development of the field. Before starting, always ask an editor at a suitable journal if he or she would be interested in considering the interview for publication.

Translation. These articles are translations, of a journal article or creative piece by someone else, into English from another language. Again, this is a lot of work for a publication with not much weight. Still, if it gets you familiar with another's work or introduces an important work to a new audience, then proceed for your own satisfaction. After all, Gayatri Spivak did make her name translating Jacques Derrida. You can also translate articles from English into your own language to aid your students. This can be tremendously helpful, but may not count for much with faculty committees.

Response Article. These articles respond to a previously published article and are published in the same journal (Parker and Riley 1995, 65). A response article is usually shorter than a research article and easier to write, since it addresses only one article rather than a whole literature. It is like a long letter to the editor. It is also easier to get published, as most journal editors want to spark debate and increase attention to their publications. The drawback is that such an article, precisely because it is easier to write, is less prestigious and counts for less. Still, it counts for more than the previously listed types and can be valuable in spreading your name. If you read a recently published article that sparks your interest, and you can confirm, contradict, or expand on the author's argument, it can be worthwhile to write a response and send it to the editor of the journal in which the article appeared. Just be careful, as a junior scholar, not to use this as an opportunity to firebomb another author. Tenure exists for a reason; it protects the honest from the sensitive.

Review Article. These articles review the literature on a particular topic. A leading scholar in the field usually writes articles of this type, although junior scholars, especially in the social sciences, sometimes publish reviews of a new literature or a sub-field. To be published, such an article cannot be just a summary or synthesis of relevant articles and books. It must also provide some kind of critical perspective, pointing out contradictions, gaps, and enigmas in the literature, and suggesting directions for future research. The ordinary dissertation literature review is not sufficient. Despite the amount of work review articles represent, they often do not have as much weight as a research article. Most journals are interested in original research.

Theoretical Article. These articles review and advance theory. Such an article traces the development of a certain theory and then goes on to propose a new theory, lambaste errors in the old theory, or suggest that one theory is better than another. It rarely has any concrete evidence. Again, advanced scholars usually write such articles. The weight of a theoretical article depends on the era, hiring committee, and field. In some times and places, a theoretical article can have tremendous weight. In others, it can be dismissed as too rarefied. I mention this possible drawback only because so many students feel they must write theoretical articles. You don't have to. But, if you have a strong, original contribution to make to theory building, by all means, do so and damn the caveats.

Social Science Research Article. An article reporting on data collected about human behavior. Such articles are the standard in the disciplines of anthropology, sociology, psychology, political science, economics, geography, education, and sometimes history and law. They aim at conjecturing the general rule from the particular case and usually include a literature review, description of methods, and discussion of the results. There are three main kinds of social science research articles: quantitative (which use statistics to analyze data), qualitative (which use observation to analyze data), and interpretive (which uses secondary sources). Scholars conduct quantitative research primarily to find the amount or incidence of a particular variable; they conduct qualitative research to find out what those variables should be.

Quantitative Research Article. An article reporting on data collected using a scientific experiment (whether yours or others). Since the 1950s, this counts as the most prestigious kind of article to publish. A quantitative article has a very strict structure, rigorous statistical analysis of the data gathered during the experiment, and tables and charts.

Qualitative Research Article. An article reporting on data collected using ethnographic research. Qualitative research is growing in respectability and impact, but some scholars and journals will always see it as less serious or reliable than quantitative research. Its methods are lengthy open-ended interviews with a small sample or participant observation.

Interpretive Research Article. Some social science research articles are not based on experimental studies, either qualitative or quantitative. This is particularly the case in the "soft" social sciences, where authors may take approaches to their topics that are more speculative. If yours is such an article, it may be more useful to follow the humanities models in this workbook.

Humanities Research Article. An article presenting original analysis of human expression. Such articles are the standard in the disciplines of language and literature, art history, architecture, film, television, digital media, theater, musicology, religion, philosophy, and sometimes history. Humanities articles have widely varied structures and objectives, largely because they are devoted to valuing the particular over the general.

Natural Science Research Article. An article reporting on data collected about the physical world. This workbook does not address articles in the sciences—such as biology, mathematics, chemistry, physics, astronomy—which have very particular structures and are often coauthored.

What type of article is yours? Is it a research article, the kind of article for which you get the most credit? If it is not a research article, will it be possible or right to remake it into one?

What is my article's type?	

If my article's type is not recommended, should I convert it into a research article?	

MYTHS ABOUT PUBLISHABLE JOURNAL ARTICLES

The review of article types above suggests that your best bet is to focus on publishing a research article. But what exactly does this mean? What are the essential ingredients for a publishable research article? Most students know that their classroom papers are not yet publishable, but they are not entirely sure why. Let's deal with the good news first and debunk some common myths about what makes an article publishable. Then we can turn to what really does make an article publishable.

Myth 1: Only those articles that are heavily theoretical with sweeping implications will get published.

Most students have an exaggerated idea of what publishable quality is because they rarely read the average journal article. For instance, many students are surprised to hear that most published scholarship is narrow in claims and context. Since graduate seminar readings tend to concentrate around the four or five leading thinkers in the field (e.g., Keynes, Skinner, Chomsky, Jameson, Said, Kristeva) plus a few articles the professor considers groundbreaking, the characteristics of the great majority of scholarship is something with which students seldom acquaint themselves. Even if you are doing revolutionary research, it is still important to get a sense for the journal article norm. As mentioned, the average journal article is not a broad survey of the field or a philosophical manifesto bent on theory building or broad argument. When first starting to publish, you do not need to write such articles.

Myth 2: Only those articles with lots of interesting ideas will get published.

Most students think that interesting ideas make an article publishable. Although it is to be hoped that any article has interesting ideas, their sheer accumulation is not what makes an article publishable. This perception about ideas probably comes from classroom grading, where so many checks in the margin equal a B and so many more equal an A. In the classroom, you can win praise for the simple generation of ideas, the more the better, no matter how disconnected. But journal articles are a different story. In fact, a focus on simply spraying ideas can be detrimental to publication. Articles get published not for the number of ideas presented but for being carefully organized around a single significant idea.

Myth 3: Only those articles that are entirely original will get published.

Most students have an exaggerated idea of what makes something original, thinking that only unique work gets published. When students find upon doing a literature search that "someone has written my article," they feel discouraged. Yet almost all published scholarship is not the first on the subject and is openly derivative or imitative. Even in sixth century BC, writers were noting that "there is nothing new under the sun. Is there a thing of which it is said, 'See, this is new'? It has been already in the ages before us. . . . Of making many books there is no end" (Ecclesiastics 1:9–10, 12:12). Today the idea of originality still inspires cynicism, with authors frequently redefining it as "undetected plagiarism," "the art of concealing your source," and "nothing but judicious imitation" (quoted in Brussell 1988).[1] Scholarship shows that many of the most famous ideas of supposedly original thinkers were not their own. The "unconscious," for instance, is not a Freudian idea, but predates him, and the juxtaposition of profiles was not invented by Picasso, but borrowed from African arts.[2]

If originality is so elusive, why do those in academia always harp on its importance? Because it remains true that you must do something "new" to be published. In order to get a better sense for this point, let's take a closer look at the difference.

WHAT GETS PUBLISHED AND WHY

Research articles get published because they say something new about something old. A publishable article is organized around a single significant new idea that is demonstrably related to what has come before. If your idea is interesting but not new, your article will not be published. If your idea is new but not related to the old (usually previous research), your article will not be published. If your ideas are new but disconnected from each other, your article will not be published. As some scholars put it, "Tell me something I don't know so I can understand better what I do know" (Booth et al. 1995, 18).

Note that I did not use the word "original." In contrast to "original," the strict meaning of "new" is not "the first" or "previously nonexistent," but something that has been seen, used, or known for only a short time. For instance, if you write an article about Vietnamese women's reproductive strategies, some of which have existed for centuries, your information will not be "original," but knowledge of it may be "new" to the field of medical anthropology. To bring attention to something can be sufficiently original to get an article published.

Something new can also be a variation. For instance, if you write an article about schizophrenia using statistics collected by someone else but correlating variables he or she did not correlate, or interpreting the correlation differently, you will have done something new. To write a variation on scholarship that already exists can be sufficiently original to get an article published.

Do not get hung up on the idea of originality. Make your material, whether ancient or just invented, fresh and you will be published. How do you do that? And what is considered new for the purposes of publication? Three types of newness mark publishable articles. To understand these categories, let's take a closer look at the kinds of journal articles that get published.

Publishable Article 1:
Approaches new evidence in an old way.

This is the most typical publishable student article. In such an article you do not create a new approach, but rather present new evidence to support an existing approach (in the social sciences and sciences, this is often a theory your advisor developed). This new evidence can result from your laboratory experiments, field observations, or archival research. It can also be evidence recently created by someone else, such as a new film or painting (anything produced in the past ten years is considered new in the humanities, where articles can take five years from inception to publication). Since students are usually more in touch with new cultural trends and practices, they can often make real contributions to the literature by writing this kind of article. Graduate students from countries outside the West or those who have grown up in transnational or subcultural contexts also have an advantage in collecting such data.

Unfortunately, just having new evidence will not suffice. It is not enough simply to introduce a new text, draw attention to a movement little discussed, detail the events of a religious ritual, add a note to a historical figure, announce your experiment's results, or fill in the details on a little-known cultural practice. While this is important work (and, I think, sadly underappreciated in academia as an end in itself), it is not the kind of research that tends to get published. You have simply written a report, a paper typical of the classroom but uncommon in journals. To be published, you must relate the new to the old. "Because new ideas must be situated in relation to assimilated disciplinary knowledge, the most influential new ideas are often those that most closely follow the old ones" (Hyland 2004, 31).

For instance, say that you have written an article about the cultural practices that developed among the embattled citizenry during the siege of Sarajevo. If you simply describe where the poetry readings were, who painted what kind of paintings, and how the lyrics of various popular songs of the day related to current events, you probably will not get published. This is so even if you are providing new data that few have collected or presented in scholarly journals. If, however, you describe this new evidence and employ it to theorize (as just one example among many) how citizens use culture to recast national identity, then you are on your way to a publishable article. That is, since the development of nationalism and national identity has been a wide-ranging theoretical concern of the twentieth century you will have provided new evidence for the theory that human beings use culture to construct identity. If you simply report on cultural production in Sarajevo, you can publish your article in a newspaper or magazine, but you can't publish it in an academic journal because you did not present your evidence in the context of ongoing academic concerns. You did not approach the new in an old way.

This requirement to combine the new with the old is part of the reason for the paucity of published research on non-Western cultures by non-Western scholars. Although scholars in Ethiopia and Ghana, for instance, are producing a tremendous amount of fascinating new data, little of it is published in the West. This is largely because African scholars have limited access to Western journals and books and so cannot relate their findings to Western approaches, and partly because these alien approaches infrequently explain their findings. Thus, the requirement that articles be related to Western thought does result in the exclusion of wonderful research.[3]

Your new evidence does not have to support the old approach; you can use it instead to disprove standing approaches. Of course, this is more risky since readers tend to accept evidence for things they believe in and to be critical of evidence against things they believe in. If you decide to contradict existing approaches, you must have very strong evidence. An example of an article that would provide new evidence to contradict an old approach would be if you found that low self-esteem was not correlated with eating disorders. That is, although almost every researcher on the topic has found a strong correlation among low self-esteem, depression, and eating disorders, your test administered to undergraduate women did not find a strong correlation. You would be using new evidence to undermine an existing theory.

Publishable Article 2: Approaches old evidence in a new way.

This is not a typical student article since it requires the author to have an excellent grasp of existing theories and methodologies, something graduate students are often still trying to attain. In such an article, the author does not introduce new data, but rather develops a new way of explaining or approaching old data. This new way can be a new method of criticism, a new method of data gathering or analysis, a new research design, or a new theory.

Again, just having a new approach will not suffice. It is not enough simply to claim that a new theory has explanatory power or that a new methodology will be more useful than an old one. Rather, you must apply the new approach to something that already exists. If the possible error in writing publishable article 1 (based on new evidence) is that the article is too bound to concrete data, the possible error in writing publishable article 2 (based on a new theory) is that the article is too high in the theoretical stratosphere. The new theory must be related to old evidence.

For instance, say that several years ago you had written an article about critical race theory, a theory not many scholars had published on at that point. If you stated that this new theory combined various approaches and would aid younger scholars in better understanding complex phenomena, and then stopped there, you probably would not get published. You introduced and defined a new theory, but you had not applied it to anything. If, however, you detailed how the theory successfully explained the quantifiable failure of existing techniques of teaching bilingual students of color and how it aided some teaching assistants in creating new techniques, then you are on your way to publication. You brought something new to an old problem in education. Your article used a new approach to existing evidence.

Another example is an article comparing how governments respond to human rights atrocities perpetrated by previous governments. If you merely document that some governments respond to the atrocities by holding truth commissions (which do not have the power to punish victimizers) while others respond by holding tribunals (which can and do punish victimizers), you probably won't get published. This is old evidence, data you can collect from the *New York Times.* If, however, you argue that more stable governments with strong public pressure tend toward tribunals while unstable governments with weak public pressure tend toward truth commissions, you are on your way to publication.[4] You have approached this old evidence in a new way, with a new explanation.

Publishable Article 3:
Pairs old evidence with old approaches in a new way.

This is another typical publishable student article. It presents neither new evidence nor a new approach; it merely links evidence and approaches that have not been linked before. Since very little in the world is really new, you can create newness by bringing together things that have not been brought together before. "The originality of a subject is in its treatment" (Disraeli 1870, 142). Those with strengths in several disciplines are most able to make these kinds of links.

For example, say that you have written an article about the problems of racism and sexism in the Hollywood film. If you simply note that many

Hollywood films are racist and sexist, you will have done nothing new. Many scholars have now noted this problem, usually through analyzing representations of race and gender in various genres, during various eras, and by various directors and writers. Likewise, if you have written an article detailing Federal Communications Commission (FCC) board policies during the 1960s and 1970s, you probably will not get published. Neither article includes new evidence or a new approach. If, however, you link the two, documenting how FCC policy shaped film production away from inclusion, you are on your way to getting published because you have paired an old approach, analyzing FCC policies, with old evidence, films' racism and sexism, in a new way.[5] That is, instead of focusing on representation, you looked at the policy context that enabled these racist and sexist representations. You brought existing data and approaches together to create a new understanding.

Another way to think about this type of article is to see it as weighing in on a debate. That is, do you think that existing approaches explain the existing evidence well? For instance, say that you have written an article about the role of white women in the south during the Civil War. If there is a debate about women's role—with many theorists arguing that the Civil War widened the scope of women's work and a few theorists arguing that it narrowed women's options—you can weigh in on the debate by arguing that the war reinforced women's gender roles, using as evidence an examination of *The Diary of Miss Emma Holmes*. That is, both the approach and the evidence are old, but no one has brought the diary to bear on the question of white women's freedom during the Civil War. You have done something new.

Whether they contain new evidence, or a new approach, or they include an old critical approach to old evidence that no one has investigated in this way, the above publishable articles all contain something new. We live in a modern age: newness is the mark of value.

What is new about my article?	

If you must pair the new with the old to get published, what do you need to do to your article to make it more publishable?

What revisions do I need to make to my article to link the old to the new?	

ABSTRACTS AS A TOOL FOR SUCCESS

One of the best ways to get started on a revision of your journal article is to write an abstract—something that describes your article's topic and argument. Unfortunately, many scholars see writing an abstract as the last step to publication. In the humanities, writers may never have to write one. But writing an abstract, regardless of whether journals in your field require it or not, is an important step in revising your article, not mere paperwork. More than one authority has noted that "a well-prepared abstract can be the most important paragraph in your article" (APA 1994, 8). Why is writing an abstract so important?

Solving problems. Writing an abstract helps you clarify in your own mind what your article is about, a real aid in drafting and revising. It helps you solve the problems you will have to solve in the article as a whole. Since an abstract is a miniature version of your article—less than 250 words in the humanities and less than 120 in the social sciences—it provides you with the opportunity to distill your ideas and identify the most important. It also serves you as a diagnostic tool: If you cannot write a brief abstract of your article, then your article may lack focus.

Connecting with editors. Having an abstract provides a way for editors to connect with your work without reading your entire article, a real aid in finding an appropriate journal, as we will find in Week 4. With it, editors can encourage potential peer reviewers to review your article. Since getting reviewers can sometimes be troublesome, this is an important effect of a good abstract.

Getting found. If your abstract is published—and abstracts have grown more common even in humanities journals—you provide a way for scholars to find your work and read it. Keywords and proper nouns embedded in the abstract provide an important path to your article for researchers who would not find your work based on your title alone.

Getting read. Your abstract is essential in convincing scholars to decide to read your article. It communicates the article's importance and demonstrates whether reading it will add to a researcher's knowledge. It helps potential readers decide if your methodology is adequate or your approach is fresh.

Getting cited. Many readers will never go on to read your article, so the most-read piece of your work after the title will be your abstract. In fact, more than one person may cite your article based on reading your abstract alone. And, odd as it sounds, you want to provide an abstract so good that someone could cite your article with accuracy based on your abstract. Although this may seem shocking, there are instances where scholars do this kind of citing. For instance, a scholar writing an article about the efficacy of the women's environmental movement in Senegal may want to state in passing that scholars have published many more articles about the efficacy of the women's environmental movement in Kenya. If your article is about such Kenyan movements, you want that scholar to be able to add your article to the endnote listing such works even if the scholar has only had access to your abstract online.

INGREDIENTS OF A GOOD ABSTRACT

An abstract is a condensed version of your article, a distillation of the most important information. Several common problems plague even published abstracts. Be sure to avoid the following.

- Don't just introduce your topic; that's what your introduction is for.
- Don't have an abstract that reads like a plan. It shouldn't include statements like "we hope to prove" or "this article tries to analyze" or "this study seeks to." These are okay in grant proposals or conference paper proposals but not in a research article. An article abstract is a report on what you did do, not what you hope to do.
- Don't give a barrage of data without an argument or a conclusion; an abstract should tell (or at least hint at) a story.
- Don't include footnotes or citations (some journals allow exceptions, but this is the general rule).
- Don't include quotations; paraphrase instead.
- Don't include abbreviations, symbols, or acronyms, instead spell out all terms (some journals allow exceptions, but this is the general rule).

Be sure to include as many relevant keywords as possible, since many search engines search by abstract and title alone. Finally, include nothing in the abstract that you need the article to understand.

Good Social Science Abstracts

The basic ingredients of a solid abstract in the social sciences are the following. Indeed, if you can include one sentence on each, you have written a solid and brief abstract.

- State why you embarked on the project—often some reference to a gap or debate in the literature or a persistent social problem.
- State what your project/study was about, the topic of the article.
- State how you did the project, your methodology.
- State what you found through the project, your findings.
- State what conclusions you draw from the project, your argument.
- Some abstracts include recommendations, although this isn't necessary.

Let's look at a real student social science abstract to get a better sense of what's required.

> Feliciano, Cynthia. 1999. The Benefits of Biculturalism: Exposure to Immigrant Culture and School Drop Outs among Asian and Latino Youths.
>
> Conventional assimilation theory, which holds that immigrant children enjoy greater educational achievement as they "become American," has begun to be disputed for the children of recent immigrants. *This study* uses data from the 1990 Public Use Microdata Samples *to examine how* retaining an immigrant culture lowers school drop out rates among eight of the largest Asian and Latino groups in the United States: Vietnamese, Koreans, Chinese, Filipinos, Japanese, Mexicans, Puerto Ricans, and Cubans. Language use, household language, and presence of immigrants in the household are used as measures of exposure to immigrant culture. Overall, *the study found* that these measures have similar effects on these diverse groups: bilingual students are less likely to drop out than those who speak only English, students in bilingual households are less likely to drop out than those in English-dominant or English-limited households, and students in immigrant households are less likely to drop out than those without immigrants in their households. *These findings suggest that*, contrary to straight-line assimilation theory, those who enjoy the greatest educational success are not those who have abandoned their ethnic cultures and are most acculturated. Rather, bicultural youths who can draw resources from both the immigrant community and mainstream society appear to be best situated to enjoy educational success. (italics added)

Note how skillfully the student writes this abstract. She summarizes the literature in one sentence. In that sentence, she manages not only to explain why she is doing the study, but also to give a definition of the theory that her research works against. She summarizes her study in two sentences, describing the methods and the population. She carefully details all three of the study's findings. Finally, she states her conclusions (and argument) elegantly and convincingly. (Note that her regular use of the passive voice has not weakened the abstract.) Since the abstract is a bit long for many journals (at 209 words), it was shortened upon publication (to 150 words).[6]

Here is another good social science abstract, one that a journal published.

> Simon, Patrick. 2003. "France and the Unknown Second Generation: Preliminary Results on Social Mobility." *International Migration Review* 37, no. 4 (Winter): 1091–1120.
>
> The growing concern about the future of the offspring of immigrants in France has prompted the rise of a "second generation question." Access of "new second generations" (i.e., those born

from the waves of immigration of the 1950s and 1960s) to the job market and their visibility in social and cultural life have challenged the "French model of integration." Moreover, the ebbing of social mobility in the France of the 1970s led to a process of social downgrading which may affect significantly the second generation due to their social background and the persistence of ethnic and racial discrimination. It is thus important to investigate what kind of social mobility is actually experienced by people of immigrant ancestry, and what could hinder their mobility. This article uses the data from a new survey, the Enquete Histoire Familiale (family history survey) conducted in 1999 and based on 380,000 individuals, which analyzes the positions of second generations of Turkish, Moroccan and Portuguese origin. We argue that they follow different paths: a reproduction of the positions of the first generation; a successful social mobility through education; or a mobility hindered by discrimination.

The above abstract gives a full sense for the article and doesn't withhold information.

Some social science abstracts proceed slightly differently than the one above. They start with one or two sentences giving the topic, another sentence giving the argument, and two or three sentences providing the results or proofs. Whatever their order, these ingredients are essential.

Good Humanities Abstracts

Humanities journals are less likely to publish abstracts, but they are still a useful tool in thinking through your article and getting it through the peer review process. In the humanities, published abstracts often tend to omit information on the methodology or findings. The order of information also tends to be looser than in social science abstracts. The basic ingredients of a solid abstract in the humanities can include the following.

- Context—that is, information on the historical period, the geographic region, the social conditions surrounding the human creations being investigated
- Subject—the literary or artistic works being discussed, their creators and dates
- Claim for significance—announcement about the uniqueness of the subject or your approach to it
- Theoretical framework—often more suggested than stated, the theory you are using to discuss the subject, such as feminist or psychoanalytic approaches
- Argument—what your analysis of the subject revealed about the subject, current approaches to the subject, or society
- Proofs—your evidence for your argument about the subject, or the elements of the subject that you analyze (such as textual passages)

Below is a version of a humanities abstract that appeared in the journal I managed.

Berg, Charles Ramírez. 2003. "Colonialism and Movies in Southern California, 1910–1934." *Aztlán: A Journal of Chicano Studies* 28, no. 1 (spring): 75–96.

Once the film industry moved to Los Angeles from the East Coast in the 1910s, Hollywood became the source of the negative stereotyping of Latinos in mainstream American cinema. This article argues that the anti-Mexican American discourse in Southern California during the motion picture industry's formative years provided the impetus for those derogatory film images. In doing so, the essay synthesizes two bodies of literature that rarely comment on one another: early Hollywood studio history and works treating the Mexican American experience in Southern California. Three main Southern California social elements that shaped the anti-Mexican American discourse in films are discussed: (a) the ostracizing of Mexican Americans to East Los Angeles at the same time that the movie companies were flocking to the opposite side of town; (b) the social, economic, and political climate that resulted in anti-Mexicano attitudes; and (c) the view of Mexico as a playground for the United States.

These are just a few examples of some good abstracts in the social sciences and the humanities. Many others exist, and it is a good idea to study published abstracts to get a sense for how they work in your field.

Later in the week, you will get a chance to draft and revise your own abstract.

GETTING STARTED ON YOUR ARTICLE REVISION

Day 1: Hammering Out Your Topic

On the first day of your writing week, you should read the workbook up to this page and answer all the questions posed in the workbook up to this point. You should also use the daily writing chart to schedule your writing time in advance and then start tracking when you actually wrote.

Then your task is to refine the topic of your article. You should have picked a paper by now, but if you are still debating between two, pick both for this assignment. Going over them with another person will help you to pick the right one.

Since this is a social assignment, you will need someone to work with. If you are working through the workbook on your own, pick up the telephone and call an academic friend. You will need to talk out loud with someone to complete this task.

Describe. Tell your chosen confidant about your article. Start with, "My article is about" or "I am writing . . ." and then follow with a description of your work. Try to give the other person a real sense for your topic, approach, findings, and argument. When you have finished describing the article, ask him or her if what you said was clear, and if he or she has any questions.

Summarize. Once the person has given you comments, try to give your description in a more succinct form. Distill your article into no more than two or three sentences, as if you were doing a brief presentation of your work during an introduction at a conference or in the elevator to a professor you just met. Then ask him or her to repeat back what you said, to make sure that it is clear.

Write. Once you've done this, pick up a pen and use the chart below to write one sentence starting "My article is about" or "I am writing . . ." (If you are on the telephone, don't wait to hang up. Do it right then while you are still on the telephone. If you want, you can ask your interlocutor to write down one sentence about your article as well.)

My Article Is About . . .	

Were you able to do this exercise? How did it make you feel to say what you are doing aloud? Did your statement change? How?

What I Learned by Doing This Exercise

What did you just do? You wrote a first draft and then revised what you wrote. By interacting with another person, you got clarity on your topic and started to frame that on paper. The point of this exercise is to get you started writing and to show that both writing and editing are completely natural.

By making writing social and brief, you just did it. Writing is as natural as this exercise. And with a little attention can become as straightforward.

Day 2: Rereading Your Paper

Getting reacquainted with your paper is the next step of the process.

Locate your paper on your computer. Print out a hard copy. Make sure you locate the very latest version. There is little more frustrating than starting work on a paper only to realize that you are working on an old version. If you cannot find an electronic copy, but only a hard copy, you may find it more useful to edit the hard copy and then type it in yourself. This gives you an easy chance to edit as you go along.

Reread the hard copy once without touching it. Sometimes it will seem better than you remember: congratulations! Other times it will seem dreadful. Be of good courage. As they say in theater, the worse the dress rehearsal, the better the opening night. Good writing is all in the rewriting.

Reread the hard copy with pen in hand. In the margins, note what you need to do to each paragraph to get it ready for publication. Be kind to yourself; keep these notes clinical and not insulting. For instance, some notes might be:

- find page reference
- fix logical break
- provide transition
- state relevance or delete
- delete redundancy
- provide citation
- find additional source
- move paragraph to first section
- beef up evidence
- rewrite introduction
- add conclusion

Make a list of revision tasks. Identify what you need to do to prepare your paper for publication. This workbook takes you through a step-by-step revision of your paper, but each case is specific and you should identify independently what you think you need to do. You can then assign the tasks to the relevant week. So, on the next page, jot down a few notes below about what you think you must do to revise the paper into a publishable article. The aim is to identify quickly some of the tasks ahead of you, such as doing additional research, rewriting or cutting sections, completing your literature review, providing an argument, adding proofs, finding exact sources, restructuring the paper, and so on. Identify where you are in the writing process. Do not get discouraged if it seems like you have a lot of work ahead of you. At least you are not starting from scratch but from a draft.

Estimated Time	Revising Tasks

Day 3: Drafting Your Abstract

Draft. Follow the directions in the earlier part of this chapter for writing your abstract. Make sure your abstract includes all the necessary information and can stand on its own. When you are done with the draft, you can paste a copy on this page if you like.

My Abstract

Share. Your next step is to share your abstract with someone else to get suggestions for revision. It is best if you can do this with a writing partner. Exchange abstracts so that each person gets a chance to review and be reviewed. This keeps everyone kind.

If you cannot do an exchange, try to meet with your reader and do the review in person. That is, hand a hard copy of your abstract to your reviewer and have them respond right there and then. You can also send the abstract to someone for review by e-mail, but the chance to discuss it in person will work the best for you. It is part of making writing social. In person, someone can work with you to improve the abstract, rather than just critiquing it. You have a chance to explain what you were trying to say and to better formulate it right then.

When you are done with this exchange, write down a few notes about what your reviewer suggested would improve your abstract. You can revise the abstract now, or you can let the comments sit for a day and revise it on the fifth day of this writing week.

Reviewer's Comments on My Abstract

Day 4: Reading a Model Article

Search for an article that can serve you as a model in writing your own. To be a good writer of journal articles, you must read journal articles. It is a common misconception that great writers are uniquely talented; they are more often prolific readers who have intuited many of the principles of writing for their field by reading widely in it. Part of the purpose of this workbook is to get you in the habit of reading journal articles that relate to your work.

When reading journal articles, read them not just for their content but also for how the author presents that content. Today the workbook will lead you through a structured reading exercise.

Do an online search for articles. Look for articles written recently in your field. They do not have to be on your topic, just in your field. Then skim those you find to see if any are solid articles that you would enjoy reading. If it is from one of the journals you would like to publish your work in, all the better.

Do a shelf search for articles. If you have a chance to go to the library and skim articles in recent copies of relevant journals, do so. It can often be easier to skim many articles at the university library's periodical shelves than to skim articles online. Hard to believe, but true! Journals can organize materials in more relevant ways than huge online databases. Again, see if you can find an article that can serve as a model for you in its presentation.

Pick a model for your article. Having done both of these searches, you should have found several possible articles that could serve as a model for how scholars in your field are writing. This model does not have to be similar in content; rather it should provide a sound structure and solutions to some of your writing dilemmas. In fact, it can be best if the article is not on your topic, so that the content doesn't distract you. For instance, if you have written a paper on *Don Quixote*, it may be better to pick a single-text study on another literary classic than to pick a multiple-text study that includes *Don Quixote*. If you have written a qualitative paper, don't pick a quantitative article. If you have written a short, focused paper, don't pick a lengthy, rambling one. Try to find an article that approaches material in the way that you hope to.

Avoid picking certain kinds of articles. Try to pick an article that was published in the past year, not ten years ago. Journal styles change. Try not to pick an article by a very famous person—they tend to be unusual, both much better or much worse than the general article. Don't pick a bibliographic article, a literature review, or a broad survey if that's not what you are doing.

Get a hard copy of your model article. If you find any suitable articles, print them out or photocopy them.

Study your model article. Carefully examine how the article's author presents information. Look at the first few paragraphs. Can you describe what the author is doing in the article's first paragraphs? That is, how is it presenting content? What does the article start with? What kind of information does the author give you, the reader? If you walked away after reading nothing but the first paragraph, what would you know about the article? This is an exercise in thinking about how people set up their article vis-à-vis the audience.

Look at the other sections of the article. If you are in the experimental social sciences, study how the author has written the methodology section, results, and discussion. What information has the author relegated to tables? If you are in the humanities, study how the analysis proceeds. What comes first? How has the author organized the material? Getting a grasp for how others organize content will help you organize yours.

Make some notes. Jot down two or three things you want to learn from your model article. You may find that, on closer reading, the article is not as good as you thought. Jot down what you want to imitate and what you want to improve upon. These notes don't have to be long, just something to remind you later what you thought on reading the model.

What I Learned by Reading the Model Article

Day 5: Revising Your Abstract

Revisit your abstract and revise it. You can do this with your reviewer's comments in mind, or with various models in mind. This abstract is going to serve you in multiple ways, so be sure to do this exercise. You can revise it again later as well, as you proceed with your revision process, but it will be easier to revise then if you have something solid now.

For those in the humanities, keep the abstract short. It's true that conferences will let submitted abstracts balloon up to 200 or 250 words, but it is better to get in the habit of writing shorter abstracts, around 150 words. Shorter abstracts are more useful to editors, more compelling to peer reviewers, and less likely to have problems.

My Abstract

DOCUMENTING YOUR WRITING TIME AND TASKS

On the following weekly plan, please graph when you expect to write and what tasks you hope to accomplish this second week. Then keep track of what you actually did. Remember, you are to allot fifteen minutes to one hour every day to writing. At the end of the week, take pride in your accomplishments and evaluate whether any patterns need changing.

Time	Monday	Tuesday	Wednesday	Thursday	Friday	Saturday	Sunday
Week 2 Calendar							
5:00 a.m.							
6:00							
7:00							
8:00							
9:00							
10:00							
11:00							
12:00 p.m.							
1:00							
2:00							
3:00							
4:00							
5:00							
6:00							
7:00							
8:00							
9:00							
10:00							
11:00							
12:00 a.m.							
1:00							
2:00							
3:00							
4:00							
Total Minutes Actually Worked							
Tasks Completed							

Week 3

Advancing Your Argument

Day to Do Task	Week 3 Daily Writing Tasks	Estimated Task Time
Day 1 (Monday?)	Read through page 92 and fill in the boxes on those pages; start documenting your time (page 97)	60 minutes
Day 2 (Tuesday?)	Draft a statement of your argument and discuss it with several others, both in your field and outside, then revise it (pages 93–94)	60 minutes
Day 3 (Wednesday?)	Review your article and note where your argument is disappearing and should appear (pages 94–96)	60 minutes
Day 4 (Thursday?)	Revise your article around your argument (page 96)	60+ minutes
Day 5 (Friday?)	Revise your article around your argument (page 96)	60+ minutes

Above are the tasks for your third week. You can add two additional days of writing if you want. Since many students read the information in this chapter and find, to their dismay, that their article does not have an argument, you may have to spend extra time writing this week to stay on deadline. Make sure to start this week by scheduling when you will write and then tracking the time that you actually spend writing.

SECOND WEEK IN REVIEW

If you didn't get as much writing done last week as you hoped, join the club. Very few scholars ever feel that they have done enough. Whether you spent long hours working and don't have much to show for it, or procrastinated when you had every plan of getting a lot done, avoid feeling guilty and start this new week afresh. After all, you have twelve weeks to get it right. If you managed to fit in fifteen minutes to an hour of writing most days, congratulations! You are on your way to making writing a habit.

Either way, take a minute to write in the chart below what you learned this week about making time for writing. What aided or hindered your writing goals? What were the challenges? What worked? Did you find any solutions? What could you continue to do or start doing this week to make time for writing? Was your writing plan for last week realistic or unrealistic? Don't hesitate to make this social. You can call a colleague and do this exercise aloud or write an e-mail to a friend.

Lessons to Be Learned from Week's Writing Experiences

If you are not happy with what you produced last week, remember that your goal in using this workbook is productivity, not perfection. It does not matter if what you wrote last week was genius or schlock. Spending regular time writing is one of the most important things you can do to improve the quality of your writing. Therefore, a focus on producing will get you to the goal of publication. Continue to aim for writing at least fifteen minutes a day.

The first week you identified feelings about writing. You learned what makes for a successful academic writer. You designed a work plan. The second week you studied the various forms of academic articles, learned the myths about what it takes to get published, and the reality about what makes a research article publishable. You then hammered out your topic and worked on an abstract. In other words, you established where you are and how to get where you want to go. This week you are going to identify what makes an article publishable and learn the main key to a successful revision.

COMMON REASONS WHY
JOURNALS REJECT ARTICLES

Last week you looked at what makes an article publishable, so let's turn this week to what makes an article unpublishable. In many cases, an accretion of small problems causes peer reviewers and journal editors to return an article, rather than some huge theoretical problem. Editors immediately reject between 10 and 15 percent of submitted articles, without even sending them through the peer review process, for problems that have nothing to do with the originality of the piece. If the journal has recently published an article on the same topic, even if it wasn't as brilliant as yours, the editor really can't accept your article. Likewise, if the editor is working to ensure that a variety of topics or fields is covered, the editor may not be able to accept your article on an overrepresented topic. Some editors admit that they don't have space in their journal pages for all the good articles that they receive (Weller 2001, 52). Finally, an editor may not be able to accept an article if it is no longer timely. See Week 4 (journals) for advice on how to prevent these types of rejection.

If you can learn to avoid being rejected for the following reasons, you will vastly improve your chances of getting into print. I have arranged these mistakes in the order of the workbook itself (not in order of importance). It's a lot to absorb in one session, so don't try. Rather, get to know the general categories of article problems. Then, in each week, you will work on overcoming one or more of these problems.

Too Narrow or Too Broad

Editors reject articles for problems with focus. A narrow article is one that editors think will not interest enough readers; a broad article is one that will seem unnecessary to readers. The words that reviewers and editors may use to identify this problem include calling the article "too superficial," "too speculative," "too esoteric," "too preliminary," or "too technical." Some signs that an article has focus problems are a failure to do the following: state what is important about the (narrow) research, provide enough examples, estimate the audience's level of knowledge correctly, or match length to topic (e.g., submitting a long article on a narrow topic, or a short article on a broad or deep topic). Fortunately, there are some straightforward solutions.

Contextualize. To avoid having your article dismissed as too narrow, make sure to set your article in a broader context. If you are addressing a narrow problem, describe how it relates to larger problems. Explain the historical background or relation to other debates. With proper contextualization, nothing has a limited purpose and audience.

Aim at a broad audience. To avoid having your article dismissed as too narrow, direct your article to a broad academic audience. Articles written for the classroom often assume a reader more knowledgeable than the author; that is, the professor. You must assume the exact opposite for a journal article. In general, journal readers will have less knowledge about your specific approach or topic than your instructor or advisor. Journals have different types of readers, some of whom may not be familiar with the particular problem, text, or object you address. Make sure to introduce your topic as if the reader was intelligent but hasn't read anything on the topic lately.

Aim at a smart audience. To avoid having your article dismissed as too broad, however, don't give pages and pages of information about the country, conflict, or culture. A little bit of topical information goes a long way. Be efficient. With easy internet access to encyclopedias, journal editors are cutting more and more background information.

Give pertinent examples. To avoid having your article dismissed as too broad, don't devote too much of your article to the big picture or the theoretical frame. Make sure you give specific examples to support your argument. In the social sciences, if you don't have many findings or have few findings that support your argument, your research may be too preliminary to be published. See Week 6 (about evidence) for more advice.

Relate examples to the argument. If you spend too much of your article at the micro level, presenting strings of data without analyzing it or failing to describe how your close reading supports your argument, your article can be rejected for being "too technical" or "too narrow."

Watch length. If the journal prefers short articles, and you send a long one, editors can easily dismiss it as too broad. Likewise, if the journal prefers forty-page articles and you send a thirteen-page article, editors can dismiss it as too narrow. Study the page requirements of the journal to which you intend to send your work. See Week 4 (about journals) for more advice.

Select an appropriate journal. What may be "too technical" or "too narrow" for one journal may be just right for another. Study journals before submitting your work to them—they can vary quite a bit in what they publish. See Week 4 (journals) for advice.

Does my article have problems with focus? If so, how am I going to revise it?	

Off Topic

Editors will reject articles without even sending them to peer reviewers if the articles don't seem relevant to the mandate of the journal. They may declare that the article has "inappropriate subject matter," is on "an unsuitable subject," or falls "outside of the scope of this journal." Rejection in this case has nothing to do with the quality of the article, just its aptness. Those who work outside the journal's discipline are more likely to receive this judgment since they will be less knowledgeable about its conventions.

It is not always possible to tell what an editor will think is appropriate. If you write about Koreans in Japan, it is possible that the editor of a journal on Japan will consider your article off topic. That's why you must spend time studying journals to which you want to submit your work. It is also a good idea to contact the editor.

Is my article appropriate for the journal I have selected?	

Not Scholarly

Editors and reviewers rejecting an article for not being scholarly enough may say that the article is "sloppy," "rudimentary," "basic," "colloquial," or "obvious." Among the leading causes for this kind of rejection are the absence of references to literature in your field, many dated citations, errors in documentation, or simplistic language. Although these seem like very serious errors, there are some solutions. Indeed, editors generally see such problems as correctable (Weller 2001, 52).

Be meticulous about documentation. When editors and reviewers see problems with documentation—much missing information in the bibliography, numerous misspelled author names, mismatching publication dates, and many typos or grammatical errors in quoted material—it raises a red flag. If you are not a careful documenter, they suspect your scholarship may be shoddy in other ways as well. Perhaps you are unintentionally plagiarizing or mixing up references. Or maybe your research itself is suspect.

It is easy to fall into bad habits about documentation. You assume that you will go back later to fill in citations' sources, so you fail to write down the full source when taking notes or you just list an author's name after a quote in text. Later you have no idea where the quote came from or in which of the author's texts the quote appeared. It can be very hard to unlearn these bad habits, but learning to document your sources properly is one of the most important things you can do to make your route to publication smoother and your sanity more secure. I recommend that you never quote or paraphrase anything in a text without immediately inserting a footnote and listing the full reference, even if you listed it just a sentence before. This is easy to do with electronic footnoting, copying, and pasting. That way, if you shift sections around and a citation is separated from the rest, you will still know where the quote came from. Always try to type exact quotations from the source itself, rather than from your notes or someone else's article. If you simply do not have a reference at hand and can't get it immediately, still put in a footnote (e.g., such as "read this at library in book by big author on Alzheimer's, appeared on top of a left page"). Fortunately, with the advent of Google Books and Google Scholar, it is much easier than it used to be to find the source or page number of quotes.

Cite recent literature. If you are writing in the social sciences and many of your citations are more than three to five years old, the reviewers may state that the article is not up-to-date. In the humanities, you can cite older material, but most editors and reviewers will still expect to see some citations from material published in the last three years. If the only relevant citations are old, you will probably need to explain this. Primary sources can be from any period.

Cite multiple sources. Editors and reviewers grow concerned if your article seems to rely too heavily on one article or book. Make sure to cite a variety of sources, at least ten to twenty.

Cite relevant literature. As mentioned earlier, it is vital to link the new to the old. This means acknowledging those who wrote before you. You can write a poem or novel without doing so, but a journal article is not scholarly until you discuss the ideas of those who have written about your topic. An article is like the Academy Awards; no artist leaves the stage until each thanks those who helped realize the work. You don't have to mention everyone—in most cases this would be impossible—but you must cite and discuss at least some of them, preferably those who had the most influence on your thought and those who strongly agree or disagree with your argument. Paraphrase, don't quote them; group and summarize authors in the introduction; concentrate on those authors with theoretical contributions. If you don't cite everyone relevant, that should not be a reason for rejection. Many editors and reviewers see literature reviews with some shortcomings as a reason that an article should be revised, not rejected (Weller 2001, 52).

Reference debates in the field. As a corollary of the previous point, be sure to reference not just particular authors, but particular discussions. That is, instead of analyzing each author individually, you can group authors by which side of a debate they appear on. For instance, to borrow from the work of Fong and Yung (1996), discuss the differences between those who see interracial marriage as a simple product of assimilation and those who see it as a complex product of raced and gendered power relations. By doing such encapsulating, you advance the field, not only acknowledging the shoulders you stand on but also interpreting those predecessors for others. Just be sure that the debates you are citing are recent (unless your argument is that returning to an old debate helps us better understand a new debate).

Use discipline-related expertise. Each discipline has practices that editors and reviewers of disciplinary journals may expect to see alluded to in articles. Thus, a history article that does not mention "archival research" may appear insubstantial to a history editor or reviewer. Likewise, an anthropology article that doesn't mention the author's field research, an education article that doesn't mention the author's classroom observation, a psychology article that doesn't mention the author's clinical or laboratory experience, or a geography article without maps may seem odd to an editor or reviewer. If you are submitting your article to an interdisciplinary journal, they will not expect to see discipline-related expertise. If you are submitting your article to the large association journals of a discipline, they might.

Provide a critical framework. You must also present your ideas within a critical framework. You do not necessarily need to name this framework, but editors and reviewers want to have some sense for your approach to your topic—new historicist, Marxist, structuralist, behaviorist, econometric, Foucauldian, post-feminist, rational choice, and so on. If your work is critically eclectic, you may have to address this question in the editors' or reviewers' minds.

Provide evidence. You cannot simply assert that some argument is true; you must prove it with evidence. A journal article is not a political speech, it is more like a court case.

Does my article have problems with scholarliness? If so, how am I going to revise it?	

Too Defensive

The mark that most distinguishes the classroom paper from a journal article is defensiveness. Students seldom have the experience to be confident as writers, and so they tend to overemphasize their apparatus (e.g., the materials for critical study) and underemphasize their content. Editors and reviewers notice this almost intuitively and will sometimes even say that the article "reads like a classroom paper." This problem of confidence naturally resolves itself the more you write and publish. Learn to write for the field, not to prove that you have done your homework, are intelligent, or read widely. Some solutions are the following:

Avoid extensive quotations. Reduce the number of quotations and abridge most of those remaining. You can tell a classroom paper almost by flipping through. It is the one with lots of block quotations set apart from the text, a remnant of trying to get the page count up or trying to signal to the professor that you did all the reading. Of course, if you are doing a textual analysis, you must quote from it; but even then, you should avoid long quotations that you leave the reader to interpret. Reading research shows that readers tend to skip quotes.[1]

Avoid the famous for fame's sake. Do not quote famous authors just for the sake of having their names appear in your article. Nothing marks an article as written for the classroom more than a not-very-apt quote from Aristotle or Habermas or Marx. It's okay to quote the heavy hitters, but only if the quote is eloquent and completely related to your research. Likewise, don't state the banal and attribute it to someone famous (e.g., "power is important, says Foucault").

Avoid excessive documenting. Cite only relevant studies. Do not prove that you have neglected no source. Again, classroom papers are the ones with long bibliographies designed to impress rather than document.

Avoid monotonous synopses of others' work. Keep reviews of previous scholarship brief. Some student papers devote half of their length to simply reprising the ideas of others. But editors do not publish articles to teach readers about what has already been written. Articles are not instructional tools. Editors publish articles to advance the field and to forward new ways of thinking among professors, not to teach newcomers.

Avoid jargon. In the 1990s, academia favored the creation of unique terms to communicate new ideas in cultural studies. Now the trend is away from this, so be especially careful about jargon. Run a spelling check and consider replacing correctly spelled but unrecognized words that pop up (except for proper nouns).

Avoid provenance labels. Some students seem to think that leaving the name of the class and professor or conference on the title page of their article will lend it stature. The exact opposite is true. No editor likes to receive an unrevised classroom or conference paper. Many may actually feel insulted by clear indications that you have not massaged the article for his or her journal. Delete all references to former incarnations on the title page. If need be, you can mention in the notes that the articles is "a revised version" of an article presented at such and such a conference but I wouldn't say it was "started" in such and such a helpful class.

Avoid dogmatism. Always include some evidence that seems to contradict your thesis. You do not need to have an airtight case to convince your reader. Indeed, a willingness to acknowledge arguments against your position shows confidence and scholarly rigor.

Does my article have problems with defensiveness? If so, how am I going to revise it?	

Not Sufficiently Original

One of the most common reasons that editors give for rejecting an article, according to their own report, is that it adds "no new knowledge" (Weller 2001, 50). They describe an article's novelty as a big part of its appeal, especially if it is on a hot or timely topic (Weller 2001, 92–94). Several problems can cause editors or reviewers to dismiss your article as unoriginal. These include duplicating already published articles, rehashing others' ideas, addressing a topic or text that holds little interest to their readers, constructing an opposing position that doesn't really exist, and failing to announce originality. Again, there are some straightforward solutions.

Read in your field. It's difficult to know if you are replicating others' work if you are not reading peer-reviewed journals in your field. At a minimum, receive journal tables of contents by e-mail or RSS feed, so that you can know what topics your colleagues are covering.

Focus on the new. After addressing others' ideas in the introduction or a background/history section, move on firmly to your ideas and data. You must introduce your topic properly, giving background and context, but do not, after the article is underway, spend much time defining common terms, describing the theories of famous authors, or rehashing disciplinary knowledge.

Argue the real. Do not attack straw men; that is, do not cobble together an opposing argument without real advocates and then deconstruct that argument. Be sure you are debating a real force in the world.

Articulate originality. Tell the reader what is new about your evidence, methodology, analysis, or theories. Underline what's different about your work. What will scholars find out that they did not already know? Students often fail to announce such matters. They tell me that by the time they are completing their articles, their "new" argument seems entirely obvious. That's just because you have been working on it for a long time. Ask colleagues what they think is new about your article if you can't remember.

Claim your ideas. I have often found that students will unwittingly present their own ideas as if they were common knowledge or even the work of other people. Women are especially prone to this error. Make sure you make statements such as, "I argue that" or "The thesis of this paper is" or "My term for this is." Otherwise, you may present your best work as ownerless observations randomly picked up.

Develop a voice. The most difficult task of any writer is to develop a voice that can be heard above the babble of cited authors. Although there are many components to having a writing voice, the easiest move you can make is to embrace the personal pronoun. When you work to excise yourself from your research, your writing loses its flavor. In some fields, such as law, it simply isn't done to refer to "I" or "my," but you can still work toward a more personal, direct tone. Avoid passive voice when you can and eschew false attempts to appear objective. Never moralize, but find ways to express your passion for the topic and sometimes allow humor, enthusiasm, loathing, or sadness to color what you write. The key is to remember that a little personalizing goes a long way, especially in the social sciences.

Does my article have problems with originality? If so, how am I going to revise it?	

Poor Structure

Editors and reviewers perceive an article as poorly structured if it lacks organization or has a very muddled one. They may not mention "structure" as a problem, but remarks about "poor writing," "poor presentation," or "poor organization" often have to do with structure. Signs of structural faults are many unlinked insights, irrelevant or redundant sections, no introduction, no conclusion, or withheld findings. In the U.S. classroom and in non-U.S. academic cultures, you can get away with writing an article that meanders through various colorful observations without any clear destination. You can start right in on your observations without introducing them, and you can conclude without summarizing them. You can digress at length and only announce your findings in the final paragraph. Indeed, one hundred years ago, you could have published such an article. Now you cannot. Your article must have a clear beginning, middle, and end. Each section must proceed with a firm sense of purpose and a clear relationship to the other sections. If your article has structural problems, your article will have a tough time surviving the peer review process. Be sure to complete Week 6 of this workbook, where you will learn how to improve the structure of your article. One of the most helpful techniques is the post-outline, in which you outline your article after you've written a draft.

Surface your structure. Sometimes your article has a structure but it is submerged. Just because you know where the article is going doesn't necessarily mean we, the readers, do. So, help us out. The old saw that you should "tell them what you are going to say, tell them, and then tell them what you just said" is still right. Use summary paragraphs, subheads, and transition sentences to announce the direction of your article. Do not assume that because something is clear to you that it will be clear to the reader. Visible cues to structure are particularly helpful in getting reviewers to look on your article favorably. That is, even if you haven't succeeded in doing what you set out to do, your general project comes across more clearly, and they can push you to do what you promised rather than reject-ing you. Some stylebooks advise against obvious "signposting" (or, in a memorable phrase, "outside plumbing") but I think the benefits at the peer review stage outweigh the costs. You can always delete such material in copyediting, after it has served its purpose.

Stick to your point. Remember what your article is not. It is not a book, which has 300 pages to explore many ideas. Instead, an article is only twenty to forty pages. Your article is also not a chapter of a book, which depends on the chapters before and after it. Instead, an article must stand alone. Your article must be carefully organized around a single significant idea. Align your insights around your main point.

Delete the redundant or irrelevant. Review your article with an eye for material said once, twice, or twenty times and for material not directly related to your single significant idea. A friend can often do this more effec-tively and quickly than you can, since you are overly familiar with all the points. If you or your reader find such material, get rid of it, no matter how fascinating. You don't have to delete this material from the world forever, just from this article. Indeed, such excised sections are often the germ of your next article and should be saved as the valuable material they are.

Subordinate the concrete. Many problems with structure arise from the author's failure to relate the particular, usually evidence or proofs, to the general, usually the theory or argument. The reader should learn no fact without knowing why that fact is important to your single significant idea. If you carefully make such links, your article will automatically begin to gain a structure.

Relinquish your findings. Many students love the mystery format. For some reason, students believe that readers will stop reading if they get the goods too early. So students withhold their article's purpose, import, significance, or argument until the end of the article. I have one word for you: don't. The sooner you can tell readers your single significant idea, the better. Indeed, scholars are far more likely to read your article if they get this information early.

Does my article have problems with structure? If so, how am I going to revise it?	

Not Significant

Editors and reviewers reject an article as "insignificant," "unimportant," "of little merit," or "not applicable" if the author does not answer the eternal question "So what?" What difference does your research make, and why should we the readers care about it? Of course, if your article really has no functional value, you cannot avoid rejection. Weak findings, statistically insignificant results, or little supporting data are not truly salvageable problems. Most of the time, however, a real lack of significance is not the problem. The problem lies in the author assuming that the significance will be clear to the reader.

Articulate significance. Articulate your work's significance or impact. For some reason, many students frequently do not state the significance of their work. They fail to say that no one else has written on this topic or that the last research done on the topic is twenty years old. They fail to say that their analysis may provide a solution to some problem or open up a new path for the field. They fail to say that another prominent scholar called for the research to be done or that the research fills a gap in that scholar's work. Of course, you do want to be careful in your claim for significance (avoid coming across as if you think your research is the equivalent of discovering the wheel) but you must state it clearly. If you are not sure what the significance of your work is, ask someone in the field. They can be helpful in identifying to which field concern your work relates. See Week 8 (about openings) for more advice.

Select the right journal. What is old news to one field may be exciting news to another. The absence of certain kinds of data or case histories may matter to one journal and not to another.

Does my article have problems with significance? If so, how am I going to revise it?	

Theoretically or Methodologically Flawed

The most damning comment to get back from an editor or reviewer is that he or she found your article's approach or evidence problematic. In the social sciences, they may say that the article has a poor conceptual design, an argument not supported by the data, insufficient data, inaccurately calculated statistics, faulty laboratory procedures, improperly taken samples or case histories, undocumented results, methodological problems, poorly interpreted results, or an inadequate research base. In fact, "inadequate theory" and "methodological problems" are among the most frequent reasons given for rejection in the social sciences (Weller 2001, 50, 52). In the humanities, the editor or reviewer may say that the article is undertheorized, not adequately conceptualized, or poorly analyzed. They may disagree with the thrust of the close reading. They may say that the article is racist, classist, sexist, imperialist, etc. Such an article has little chance of surviving a resubmission, even with a heavy rewrite. Once an editor has decided any of these are true of your article, you have little recourse but to send the article to another journal. Editors don't generally see such problems as being correctable (Weller 2001, 52–53). It's best, then, to work hard not to get a judgment of "hopelessly flawed" from an editor or reviewer.

Let me just note, however, that they may not be right. Two graduate students did fascinating interviews with leading economists asking them "to describe instances in which journals rejected their papers" (Gans and Shepherd 1994). The students' survey revealed that "many papers that have become classics were rejected initially by at least one journal—and often by more than one." Rejections of articles that went on to be cited in thousands of other articles were often rejected for theoretical reasons, that is, "too general" a hypothesis, "preposterous" predictions, "uninteresting" conclusions, "inappropriate" models, and "trivial" substance. Editors can fail to recognize an advance in the field and mislabel it erroneous.

Peer review before submission. It is always a good idea to ask professors in the field to review and comment on your article. They can help you strengthen your theoretical base or point out ways of convincing readers that your new method is sound.

Detail your methodology. Again, it is not always that your method is wrong, but that you haven't done enough to convince reviewers of its applicability. One easy way of doing this is to recognize potential problems and pitfalls. Acknowledge alternative approaches to the material and explain why you did not choose them. Be careful not to appear enamored of a particular method at the expense of your hypothesis. Cite studies defending the methodology.

Avoid imbalance. Be careful to balance your article between the theoretical and the concrete. Theory comes alive through concrete particulars just as the concrete becomes significant through explanatory theory.

Cite opposing views. Use your endnotes to indicate that you are aware of and have considered scholars who differ in opinion from you.

Review your analysis. If you have not carefully analyzed your data or interpreted your findings, be sure to revise your paper to do so. This is a correctable problem, although editors may not say so when rejecting you for this reason. It's best to correct this before it gets to editors and reviewers, since "poor analysis" or "inadequate interpretation" are frequent reasons for rejection (Weller 2001, 53).

Does my article have problems with theory? If so, how am I going to revise it?	

Too Many Misspellings and Grammatical Errors

Errors in spelling and grammar are rarely the sole reason for rejection, but if they are numerous they can provide the coup de grace. Editors or reviewers may reject your article as "sloppy," "badly written," "hastily written," "nonnative," or "poorly presented" if your article has frequent typing errors, misspellings of ordinary words, numerous problems with verb tense and agreement, twisted sentence structures, common words used incorrectly, pronouns with unclear referents, and excessive use of adjectives. Students usually know if they have such writing problems, perhaps because some professor told them so or because they lack writing experience, are a nonnative speaker of English, or have dyslexia. Whatever the cause, if you know that you need to improve your writing skills, there are some solutions. The following are the easiest.

Complete Week 10. Be sure to do the exercises in Week 10 of this workbook, where you will have a chance to work on improving your grammar and clarity. Besides this workbook, other texts can instruct you in improving your writing. See Recommended Reading at the end of this book.

Run a spelling check. Always run an electronic spelling check as your last task before submitting an article. Make sure you spell-check the footnotes, as programs often do not do this automatically. Make sure you spell-check the bibliography even though it has many proper names. Many spelling errors creep into bibliographies because authors never bother to spell-check them.

If your article has many proper nouns, especially author names, it can be a good idea to spell-check in a particular way. Create a custom dictionary for the article (in Word this is under Tools, Options, and Spelling & Grammar). When you spell-check, add all proper nouns to the dictionary. Then review the words in the dictionary (Tools, Options, Spelling & Grammar, Dictionaries, Edit). You will often find that you have spelled an author's name differently in different places (e.g., Richardson in the text and Richardsen in the bibliography). It is unlikely that an editor or reviewer will notice such errors in proper nouns (unless they are famous authors), but such sloppiness can begin to register at a subconscious level, adding to the reader's sense that your article is not careful.

Run a grammar check. Run an electronic grammar check before sending an article out. Many students find the Microsoft Word grammar check frustrating because a writer's grasp of grammar must be strong to use it. Certainly, many of the program's suggestions will be wrong so you must carefully evaluate all suggested corrections. If you are not sure whether the suggestion is correct, the program's Help feature can aid you in making the correct choice. Nevertheless, although it takes a little effort, a grammar check can help anyone identify misused words, sentence fragments, punctuation errors (especially commas and semicolons), passive voice, overuse of prepositional phrases, capitalization problems, and subject-verb agreement.

If you run a grammar check for passive voice and subject-verb agreement alone, it will prove useful.

Hire an editor. Everyone can benefit from someone reviewing his or her writing right before submission to a journal. Even excellent writers make mistakes. Some universities have writing labs, where you can work one-on-one with an editor or writing instructor. If your university does not have this, consider hiring a copyeditor. Although a professional copyeditor can be expensive (charging anywhere from $5 to $25 per page), it can be well worth the expense. If you get an article published and then get an academic appointment with an annual salary because you published that article, spending even $1,000, if you have it, will have been an excellent investment in your future earnings.

Follow the submission guidelines. Editors are used to seeing articles in the standard format of their journal, so if you don't follow the submission guidelines, editors may instinctively feel that the article doesn't belong in the journal.

Does my article have problems with spelling or grammar? If so, how am I going to revise it?	

This long list is somewhat overwhelming. Fortunately, many of these problems are connected to the same root, the main reason why editors and reviewers reject articles, which is the focus of much of this workbook and the following section.

MAIN REASON JOURNAL
ARTICLES ARE REJECTED: NO ARGUMENT

I believe that the main reason why editors and reviewers reject articles is because authors do not have an argument or do not state it early and clearly. You will dramatically increase your chances of publication if you craft the argument of your article. When you center your article on a single persuasive idea, you are a giant leap closer to publication.

> Editors . . . agree that one of the most common and frustrating problems with submitted articles is a failure on the part of authors to express their thesis clearly and early in the article. . . . Perhaps the single most important thing you can do to increase the receptivity of your scholarly article is to ensure that . . . your thesis is clearly stated. (Olson 1997, 59, 61)

Editors or reviewers may not mention the lack of an argument as a reason for rejection. They may instead state that the article is not original or significant, that it is disorganized, that it suffers from poor analysis, or that it "reads like a student paper." But the solution for all these problems lies in having an argument, stating it early and clearly, and then structuring your article around that argument.

MAKING A GOOD ARGUMENT

But what exactly is an argument? Is it the same as a thesis or hypothesis or conclusion or findings? How is it different from a topic? And how do you go about making one? Part of the reason that unclear arguments are so common in academia is because of the failure to teach what an argument is. Freshman composition courses address it and then students rarely come across the concept again. There is a reason for this: Argument is notoriously difficult to teach. One book, jammed with various techniques for teaching students how to write an argument, carefully acknowledges that post-course surveys revealed that each technique for teaching argument made little or no difference in student papers (Fulkerson 1996). So, if you feel confused about what an argument is or how to make it, you are in excellent company. Let's dare to figure it out anyway.

What Is an Argument?

Succinctly, an argument is a discourse intended to persuade. You persuade someone by engaging their doubts and providing evidence to overcome those doubts. A journal article, then, is a piece of writing that attempts to persuade a reader to believe in something. It expresses a point of view intended to influence.

Although this subjective language may scare social scientists, in fact, a hypothesis is part of an argument. A social science article sets out to persuade the reader that the hypothesis is true or false. In such articles, what I am calling an argument is often described as the conclusion. The method and manner of persuasion may be different from that in the humanities, but it is a persuasion nonetheless. If the hypothesis is "does x affect y?" the argument is "x affects y when z is present."

More technically, an argument is a coherent series of statements in which the author leads the reader from certain premises to a particular conclusion. Thus, an argument always has at least two parts: a claim and evidence for that claim. A statement that is being supported is called the conclusion, hypothesis, or claim. A statement being offered as a support to another is called a premise, proof, or evidence. Whatever your argument (or thesis or conclusion) you must provide proof (or premises).

How to test if you have an argument. One of the easiest ways to distinguish whether a statement is an argument is if it consists of statements to which you can coherently respond "I agree" or "I disagree" (Lunsford and Ruszkiewicz 2003). For instance, the statement that "Charlotte Gilman was a great writer" is one with which you can agree or disagree. The statement that "Charlotte Gilman was a writer" is not. It is a fact. The evaluation of "great writer" requires proofs in order to persuade the reader, the actuality "writer" does not. Likewise, the statement that "many California school children are bilingual" is not an argument. It is a fact. The statement that "bilingual children do better in school than monolingual children" is an argument. Many would disagree with this argument or making such a conclusion from the data.

Students interested in critical theory will have already begun to question this. Isn't all discourse an argument? Aren't all texts meant to persuade? Can we know for sure that Charlotte Gilman was a writer? Indeed, this is part of what makes argument so difficult to teach. Definitions begin to blur; meaning begins to slip.

Since my interest here is pedagogical not theoretical—I merely want to provide some useful ways of thinking about writing that enable you to get your work published—I won't go further into the thorny thickets of argument theory. I will just say that in this workbook, I use the term "argument" as shorthand for your article's single significant idea, an idea you must support with proofs to persuade the reader that your point of view has validity.

If you are interested in the topic of argument more broadly, I recommend that you consider the books I've listed in the Recommended Reading section at the end of this book. I won't spend more time here explaining what an argument is since I have found through teaching argument that it isn't that useful. The most useful way to learn to construct a journal article argument is to study examples.

How to avoid being dogmatic. When some people hear the word "argument," they think of two people yelling, neither person listening to the other or conceding legitimate points. This is exactly the kind of argument you do not want in your article. To have a successful argument, you do not need to annihilate scholarly opponents or bulletproof your position. An argument is a dialectic between opposing positions that results in a decision. It is about the search for answers through exchange. This means that you do not need to have an unassailable argument, just an interesting one. A difficult truth is that those issues most worth arguing over almost never have all the evidence on one side or the other. Both sides have compelling proofs. If you have taken up an argument that has no compelling evidence against it, you have probably not chosen a publishable argument. To persuade readers, they must first have doubts, or believe that others have doubts that your argument is right. So, to construct a sound argument, build in a consideration of opposing voices. This is a mark of the best academic writers.

For instance, one of the articles published in the academic journal I managed, *Aztlán: A Journal of Chicano Studies,* is an excellent example of a confident article with a clear argument that does not silence all opposition. Eric Avila's article analyzes Chicana/o literature for what it reveals about the Chicana/o community's view of the Los Angeles freeway. His argument is that, in contrast to the typical Anglo perspective, Chicana/os view the freeways as destructive rather than constructive, for entire Chicana/o neighborhoods were destroyed to construct them. To demonstrate the positive Anglo perspective, he cites city documents and newspapers. To demonstrate the negative Chicana/o perspective, he cites literary texts about Los Angeles written by Chicana/os. He makes a compelling argument for the two groups' widely differing views. In the final section, however, he openly admits that one group of Chicana/os did not view the freeway as negative: gay Chicano writers. Their literature about Los Angeles reveals a view of the freeway as libratory, a way out of the perceived patriarchy of the barrio. This final section is what makes his article great, he shows where his argument breaks down in an interesting way, thus making this article even stronger.

I always cite this example when students ask me, "Why would I want to include arguments that weaken my own position?" First, if you ignore research that conflicts with your claims, you must assume that the reader will not know of that research, a risky assumption at best. Second, your argument is less persuasive if you don't address possible rebuttals. Addressing likely opposing arguments shows you have thought about the alternatives. The point of argumentation and research is not simply to look for material that supports conclusions you already believe in, but to explore for answers. It is a good writer's job to show that opposing arguments are understood and credited, but need not vitiate the claim. Good reasons exist on both sides of any important argument; your purpose is to present them and reach the best conclusion possible.

In the social sciences, such openness often shows in the authors' description of the limitations of the study. The authors analyze their data as supporting their hypotheses, but admit that variations in sample or variables might have delivered a different conclusion.

How to avoid making topics rather than arguments. An argument is not a topic. Confusing the two is a major problem in student papers. In other words, many student papers range around a topic rather than having a clear argument. Indeed, when I ask students to tell me their argument, they frequently present topics to me. For this reason, let's go through some statements and identify if they are working as arguments.

- I want to tell you about a new book I'm reading. (This is not yet a topic or an argument about a topic.)

- The purpose of this paper is to analyze Jamaica Kincaid's novel *Annie John*. (This is a statement of a project, but it is not a topic or an argument about a topic.)

- This paper uncovers what we can learn about the postcolonial experience from Jamaica Kincaid's novel *Annie John*. (This is a statement of a topic, but it is not an argument about a topic.)

- Jamaica Kincaid's novel *Annie John* is helpful to our understanding of the postcolonial experience. (This is an argument but an extremely vague one.)

- Jamaica Kincaid's novel *Annie John* aids our understanding of the postcolonial experience by detailing how Annie John's British education increasingly alienates her from her mother. (This is a strong argument with a pair of proofs [Annie is British educated, she is alienated from her mother] and a pair of claims [British education causes familial alienation, this alienation is postcolonial] supporting the argument that the book aids our understanding of the postcolonial experience.)

As you can see from these examples, an argument is about establishing a position through rational support. It is about saying something that someone else could argue with, often a scary proposition for writers starting out. That's why they so often stick with topics; it is easier to declare the arena your article moves in. But you must have an argument to be successful.

Let's look at some more statements to continue to get a better idea of what an argument is. Which one of the following statements is an argument? I have taken the pair from the original and revised abstract of the same student article by Haeng-ja Chung.

- In this article, I give an overview of the issues of Koreans in Japan from the Japanese colonial period (1910–1945) to the present.

- This article asserts that the lower social position of Koreans in Japan from the Japanese colonial period (1910–1945) to the present was shaped by the decolonization process, the division of South and North Korea, and the contradictory policies of the Japanese government toward Koreans in Japan.

The first statement is not an argument. You can tell because you can't really agree or disagree with it. It has no specific claim. The second statement is an argument. You can tell because you immediately wonder if the statement is true or not. It also gives real detail rather than vaguely claiming that some factors shaped Korean assimilation.

Let's look at another pair from a published article.

- This article reviews factors that facilitate or hinder successful coping with HIV, including preexisting psychological functioning, medical health status, quality and adequacy of social support, stress and coping style, and perceived expected benefits of treatment.

- This article contends that group psychotherapy aimed at developing a positive self-identity is valuable for those individuals coping with the challenges posed by their HIV-positive serostatus.[2]

At first, it may seem like the first statement is an argument. It isn't vague and it lists variables. Nevertheless, it doesn't pass the "agree or disagree" test. Which aspect of these factors facilitates, which hinders? The author has not presented the readers with a real idea, just a list of categories to be examined. The second statement really is an argument, identifying a variable and arguing that it has an effect in the world.

A frequent mistake that students make is setting out a project instead of presenting an argument. Another mistake is believing that an argument is only a statement that your subject is important, overlooked, or worth more study. Such statements are claims for significance, not article-sustaining arguments.

- The development of democracy in Malawi over the 1990s illuminates the struggles that states face in democratizing when a significant proportion of the population is illiterate.

- This study of 1990s Malawian elections reveals that lack of literacy is a major obstacle to democratization.

Both statements are arguments, but the first is only an argument of significance. The second could sustain an article, but could be improved by addressing what exact obstacles illiteracy poses to democracy.

How to Write an Argument-Driven Article

Once you have an argument, you are not done. A problem that many unpublished articles have is that they are driven by the data and not the argument. The article has an argument, but it is unconnected to what is actually going on in the article. The article has data and evidence, but they are unconnected to the argument. Don't fall into the trap of letting your data organize your article rather than your argument.

Tim Stowell of the UCLA Linguistics Department tells his doctoral students that when writing a journal article they should not write like a detective collecting data but like a lawyer arguing a case. A detective's report states that several items were found at the crime scene, that dozens of persons were interviewed and made various statements, and that John Doe was arrested. A lawyer's brief states that John Doe committed the murder because item x was found at the crime scene and eyewitness y saw him do it. The report is data-driven, the brief is argument-driven. If your article presents all the data you went through to get to your conclusion, you have written a report, not a publishable article. Think like a lawyer and present evidence that supports your case, cross-examine the evidence that doesn't support your case, ignore evidence that neither contradicts nor supports your case, and make sure that the jury always knows whom you are accusing of what and why. Then you will have an argument-driven article.

Let's look at an example of an argumentative problem. The following abstract drafts describing the same article appear in the excellent Swales and Feak textbook on academic writing (1994). Which abstract is better?

Abstract Version A

A count of sentence connectors in 12 academic papers produced 70 different connectors. These varied in frequency from 62 tokens (*however*) to single occurrences. Seventy-five percent of the 467 examples appeared in sentence-initial position. However, individual connectors varied considerably in position reference. Some (e.g., *in addition*) always occurred initially; in other cases (e.g., *for example, therefore*), they were placed after the subject more than 50% of the time. These findings suggest that a search for general rules for connector position may not be fruitful.

Abstract Version B

Although sentence connectors are a well-recognized feature of academic writing, little research has been undertaken on their positioning. In this study, we analyze the position of 467 connectors found in a sample of 12 research papers. Seventy-five percent of the connectors occurred at the beginning of sentences. However, individual connectors varied greatly in positional preference. Some, such as *in addition*, only occurred initially; others, such as *therefore*, occurred initially in only 40% of the cases. These preliminary findings suggest that general rules for connector position may prove elusive.

It was probably easy for you to identify version B as stronger. It is well organized, announcing its topic and significance in the first sentence, its method in the second sentence, its findings in the three following sentences, and concludes with the argument that sentence connectors likely do not have general rules. The first abstract is not well organized—providing no context, unexplained data, and an unconnected argument. It is a data-driven abstract. Unorganized data overwhelms the argument. Both have arguments, but only one is argument-driven.

How to Avoid a Data-Driven Article

People doing textual analysis and field studies are particularly likely to fall prey to the problem of writing data-driven articles. Usually this is because the data is more real to you than your analysis of it. If you admire a canonical author, you may spend much of your article just summarizing the text and its beauties. If you spent a year in a village with four hundred people, it seems incredibly reductive to pick some argument and force your data to fit that tiny glass slipper. You have dozens of hours of tape, two thousand hours of observation, and more insights than it would take a lifetime to communicate. There is a desire to represent this richness. In fact, I often hear students say, "But you have to understand. I have to represent so-an-so or such-and-such. I want the reader to appreciate all the extraordinary things that are happening in this novel, this village, this case study." My advice: Don't represent. If you find yourself starting to represent your subject, resist. Publishable articles are argumentative, not representative. Don't just present all the information you have collected and let the reader make the links. If you catch yourself thinking, "Well, this section has a lot of detail and I'm not sure how it specifically relates to my argument but . . ." stop and revise. A thirty-page journal article is not the place to represent. That's what books are for. An article is for using data to make an argument. Data must be subordinated.

People who work for government agencies or nonprofit organizations have a similar problem. They are used to writing reports. The aim of a report is to present a huge swath of data about a particular problem or concern in a specific place. For example, a report may lay out all the problems facing an underfunded local teaching hospital. But the author of the report has not organized the data with any one argument; rather he or she usually states that the causes of the problem are more complex than previously imagined and that any solution will have to take dozens of variables into account. The author often concludes with pages of advice to the agency funding the report. The aim of a journal article is quite different from that of a report. An article's purpose is to argue not advise. You are not telling the reader what to *do* about the problem, you are telling the reader what to *think* about the problem.

When I make this point about not writing data-driven articles, students sometimes counter with the anthropologist Clifford Geertz's insistence on "thick description." The student will say, "I'm in anthropology/education/sociology and in our field it is okay to give a lot of description in an academic paper." I always counter by saying, fine, bring me one published in the last year. It's difficult to find such articles. I also tell a story about hearing Geertz speak at UCLA in the early 1990s. Many of us are great admirers of his work, and there were at least 500 people in the audience to witness Geertz launch into an hour-long thick description of recent Indonesian politics. It was the most painful lecture I have ever been to and if the fidgeting around me was any indication, I was not alone in my opinion. It's excruciating to listen to, or read, a continuous stream of names and dates without any generalizations. Few can absorb it. Fortunately, for those of us who continue to admire him, Geertz actually warns against this very problem in his article on thick description.

The claim to attention of an ethnographic account does not rest on its authors' ability to capture primitive facts in faraway places and carry them home like a mask or a carving, but on the degree to which he is able to clarify what goes on in such places, to reduce the puzzlement—what manner of men are these? . . . It is not worth it, as Thoreau said, to go round the world to count the cats in Zanzibar. (Geertz 1973)

So, don't count the cats in Zanzibar. Don't have streams of data without any argument. Make sure that your ideas about the data are organizing the article, not the organization of the data itself. If you have divided your article into sections that mirror the chapters of your literary subject, or the chronology of related events, or the order in which you came across the information, stop and revise. You should arrange and group the data according to what you want to argue about it.

One Argument Formula

If you still aren't sure you know what an argument is or how to make one, take some advice from Steven Posusta. After teaching in a UCLA composition tutoring lab as an English major, Posusta wrote a hilarious sixty-two-page book for undergraduates titled *Don't Panic: The Procrastinator's Guide to Writing an Effective Term Paper (You Know Who You Are)* (1996). The aim of the book is to provide the "cool tricks" and "fast fixes" that can enable a student to read Posusta's book tonight "and still hand in your paper tomorrow." As you can imagine, this book has inspired horror in some corners (Davis and Shadle 2000), and admiration in others (I know some teaching assistants who have used it in composition classes after learning about it from me). One tool Posusta provides is something I find helpful in teaching students about argument. This tool is his Instant Thesis Maker (1996, 12). It goes like this:

The Instant Thesis
#1. Although _____
     (general statement, opposite opinion)
#2. nevertheless _____
     (thesis, your idea)
#3. because _____
     (examples, evidence, #1, #2, #3, etc.)

To put the tool to immediate use: Although Posusta's Instant Thesis Maker is reductive and pedagogically problematic, nevertheless it distills the requirements of academic discourse to an easily understood essence that can be useful to students struggling with their articles because it forces the students to engage in a debate and to provide proofs in one sentence. If you are unsure what your argument is, or are having trouble articulating it, try using the Instant Thesis Maker above to get yourself started.

One caveat. Posusta's thesis maker works better when you are contesting current theories, rather than confirming theories. If you are confirming, you can try using "Many scholars argue that [argument] and I agree because [evidence]." Or, "Through my study of [topic] I found that [evidence] which suggests that [your idea]."

Since thesis makers can limit thought, some find that mapping their article is more helpful. That is, draw your article by using arrows and circled words to indicate what the relationships are between various theories, topics, and texts.

Arguments Against Argument

Sometimes students will tell me that authors in their field do not need to have an argument. Rather, they can explore a series of questions without favoring any particular answers.

It is true that in the social sciences some articles do not state an argument in the introduction. Such articles usually are borrowing from the scientific practice of posing one or two questions (hypotheses) in the introduction, and then withholding the answers until the discussion or conclusion. This does not mean that the articles have no argument. First, almost all social science articles now state the hypothesis and findings in the abstract. Since abstracts are now de facto introductions, accompanying all published social science articles, in fact, the authors are providing their argument extremely early and clearly. Second, just because an argument is stated as a hypothesis doesn't mean it isn't an argument. Often, the phrasing of the question is argumentative, and it is clear from the outset what the answer is likely to be. For instance, let's say the question posed in an article's introduction is "Do U.S. students who retain their immigrant culture have lower school leaving rates?" The positive words "retain" and "lower" do some signaling of the argument. That a variable has an affect is the argument. Third, just because an argument has not been stated doesn't mean it isn't driving the article. In the last case, if the literature review describes a series of recent articles attacking pro-assimilation theory, if the findings include a series of statistics demonstrating that such students do have lower school leaving rates, and if the conclusion argues that immigrant status is beneficial, then the argument is organizing the article. Finally, imagine a poor article on this topic: one that mentions various unlinked theories of immigration, proceeds to some random statistics about immigrant students and their self-esteem, grades, and sports interests, and concludes by noting that the impact of immigration on education is so complex as to be unmeasurable. Such an article is not argumentative and is probably not going to be published. It represents a detective's notes, not a lawyer's case.

For the humanities, it can get a bit trickier. In heavily theoretical fields, a premium is placed on asking questions and opening up possibilities rather than tying them off neatly with definitive answers. This openness doesn't mean that such articles do not have an argument. Many questions are simply masked arguments. Second, insisting that some particular text or moment cannot be reduced is often the argument. Third, the most well-known articles in the humanities, whether theoretical or not, have vigorous arguments. In her most famous article, Gayatri Spivak may have framed her argument as a question, "Can the subaltern speak?" and left it unanswered through the article, but in the conclusion she definitely answers it: "no." Although she is famous for imagining the question, she is more famous for her answer. Even if you prefer a synaptic style (see Week 6), providing a summary of your larger argument in the introduction can improve your chances of surviving peer review. Fourth, a few journals do not require an argument. They also don't require citations, a description of the study, or even data. Yes, you can get published in these journals with a descriptive article that adds nothing new and has no argument, but these are reports not articles. The rule doesn't change.

If an article is published without a clear statement of the argument in the abstract or introduction, or if it even withholds the actual statement of the argument to the end, then it is usually because that unstated argument is still driving the article throughout. No research article, even if it *is* published, succeeds without an argument. Published articles without arguments tend not to get cited.

Some Typical Arguments by Discipline

Space does not allow a full detailing of how each discipline proceeds argumentatively, but the examples below will give you a sense for a few types of arguments.

Literature. Most articles in such disciplines as English make arguments about what a literary text "means or how it should be read" (Stevens and Stewart 1987, 102). Most such arguments are along the lines of "No one has noticed that text x is really about y" or "Everyone thinks that text x is about y but it is actually about z." That is, they challenge common assumptions about the text, insisting that a different interpretation is better.

Since the rise of cultural studies and new historicism, another common argument is that a text reveals the mores, concerns, trends, identities, or prejudices of its time. The scholar Eaglestone has a useful chart in his book *Doing English* (2000) that summarizes the differences between analyzing a text as a text (intrinsic or formalist analysis) and analyzing a text as a window onto its context (extrinsic or historical analysis). Other common arguments rise from comparing and contrasting texts (or their characters, plots, or themes) to reveal that they are more similar than previously thought, less similar, or that one influenced the other. Finally, there are meta-arguments, in which the author argues that certain types of texts can be interpreted in certain types of ways or that certain types of interpretations are problematic.

Some literature arguments that used to be popular are now frowned upon as old-fashioned, including arguing that a text has a particular "message or moral," that an entire text represents one idea (rather than being contradictory and complex), or that a text reveals its author's conscious intentions.[3]

Education. Many articles in this discipline make arguments about which factors improve learning or teaching and which don't. Do low rates of unemployment increase the chances that students will drop out of high school? Do faculty benefit from mentoring graduate students? Does mainstreaming students with disabilities hinder their education? Debates focus on which practices stigmatize students, how public policies shape the educational system, and what enables schools to be better learning environments—safer, more inclusive, more stimulating.

Cultural Anthropology. Many articles in this discipline have arguments about how human social behavior is to be interpreted. Some argue that an exploration of a particular culture, system, or group reveals that human beings are challenging certain social structures, constructing relationships for some purpose, or reinventing their cultures in order to resist or preserve them. A classic article form in anthropology avoids conclusive argumentation: it announces a human puzzle, provides a narrative of that puzzle, and then states that resolution is not really possible.

Political Science. Many articles in the discipline of political science argue that statistical analysis of data collected on human behavior reveals that people tend to behave in certain ways politically. Some articles argue that research shows that a region or nation has certain political characteristics, that a policy has certain impacts, that a conflict has certain causes, that an institution has a certain purpose, or that a political system has a certain process. Other articles argue that a political issue is at stake in a certain academic field, political process, or place; that some variable is causing the rise of a certain political tendency; that some policy would mitigate some social problem; that a body of political science research changes our understanding of politics; or that the field of political science is shifting in its understanding of power, politics, or theories. Quite a few make arguments about how human rights, gender, and globalization vary across nations, parties, disciplines, or philosophies.

ORGANIZING YOUR ARTICLE AROUND YOUR ARGUMENT

Having an argument and stating it early and clearly is essential. So, how do you ensure that you have one?

Day 1: Reading the Workbook

On the first day of your writing week, you should read the workbook up to this page and answer all the questions posed in the workbook up to this point.

Day 2: Drafting Your Argument

Draft. Write a statement of the argument of your article, as you currently understand it. Feel free to do so below. Make sure it passes the agree or disagree test. If you are having trouble, try out Posusta's Instant Thesis Maker (page 89) to get you started.

My Argument
In this article, I argue that

Now, thinking like a lawyer not a detective, write a short list of your evidence. It doesn't have to be detailed, just list what you are bringing to bear to prove your argument.

My Evidence

Revise. Revisit your abstract. Does it state your argument? If not, rewrite your abstract with your argument in mind.

Share. Your next step is to share your argument with three other people to get suggestions for revision. Some should be people in your field; some should be outside of it. You can do this by e-mail or in person, in writing or orally. It can help to share your entire abstract with your reviewers, so that they have a sense for the whole. Ask your reviewers to underline the argument as they see it. If they don't find it clearly, ask them to write the argument as they understand it at the bottom of the page.

Don't be worried if your reviewers write back to you stating all the evidence against your argument. That's a good sign! If people immediately begin debating you, it means you have an argument. Congratulations! If your reviewers say that someone else has already made your argument, ask them for a specific citation. It is not all that common to make the exact same argument as someone else. Professors in particular can be dismissive, stating that something has "been done to death" or "nobody wants to hear about that anymore." If you get such a response, be sure to get a second opinion. It is often only that professor's opinion, not the vetting policy of journals.

Reviewer's Comments on My Abstract

Day 3: Reviewing Your Article for Argument

The biggest problem for authors is not having an argument-driven article. You need to make sure that your article is more like a legal brief than a detective's report. Print out a hard copy of your article. Then go through it and answer the following questions:

Early and clearly. Do I state my argument and early? It should appear within the first three to five pages. If not, how am I going to revise my article so that I can state my argument early and clearly? Will I have to add a paragraph? Will I have to move up my argument from where it appears later in the article? Use the box below to list these revision tasks.

Revision Tasks	

Introduction. Have I organized my introduction around my argument or does my introduction deal at unnecessary length with the text or the context? If so, how am I going to organize my introduction around my argument? Am I going to have to cut parts of the introduction as irrelevant to my argument?

Revision Tasks	

Body. Have I organized the body of my article around my argument? If not, as is often the case, how am I going to organize it around my argument? Am I going to have change sections? Move sections? Drop sections? Rewrite sections? Carefully evaluate every paragraph for relevance to your argument. Don't invent far-fetched links. It must be clear to your reader, not just you, how it connects.

Revision Tasks	

Evidence. Have I presented evidence related to my argument? If not, am I going to have to find new evidence or a new argument?

Revision Tasks	

Conclusion. Do I restate my argument in the conclusion or does it disappear?

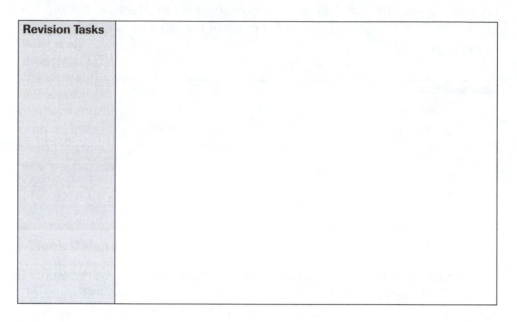

Sometimes it can be difficult to see the answers to these questions on your own. Feel free to share your article with another writer and ask her or him to identify where the argument appears or fades.

Days 4 and 5: Revising Your Article Around Your Argument

Once you've identified the problem areas, revise your article around your argument. This can take some real time but don't grow discouraged. It's vital work. You can work on this a bit every week if necessary.

DOCUMENTING YOUR WRITING TIME AND TASKS

On the following weekly plan, please graph when you expect to write and what tasks you hope to accomplish this week. Then keep track of what you actually did. Remember, you are to allot fifteen minutes to one hour every day to writing. At the end of the week, take pride in your accomplishments and evaluate whether any patterns need changing.

Time	Monday	Tuesday	Wednesday	Thursday	Friday	Saturday	Sunday
5:00 a.m.							
6:00							
7:00							
8:00							
9:00							
10:00							
11:00							
12:00 p.m.							
1:00							
2:00							
3:00							
4:00							
5:00							
6:00							
7:00							
8:00							
9:00							
10:00							
11:00							
12:00 a.m.							
1:00							
2:00							
3:00							
4:00							
Total Minutes Actually Worked							
Tasks Completed							

Week 4

Selecting a Journal

Day to Do Task	Week 4 Daily Writing Tasks	Estimated Task Time
Day 1 (Monday?)	Read through page 112 and fill in the boxes on those pages; start documenting your time (page 137)	60 minutes
Day 2 (Tuesday?)	Search for journals in your field (pages 112–118)	60 minutes
Day 3 (Wednesday?)	Evaluate the journals found and match your article to them (pages 118–127)	60 minutes
Day 4 (Thursday?)	Read relevant articles in the three most suitable journals (page 128)	60+ minutes
Day 5 (Friday?)	Draft a query letter to the editors and send it. Make a decision about which journal (pages 128–136)	30 minutes

Above are the tasks for your fourth week. Make sure to start this week by scheduling when you will write and then tracking the time that you actually spend writing. This week involves a trip to the university library, so make sure you allot an afternoon or evening to do that.

THIRD WEEK IN REVIEW

You have now spent three weeks working on your article. You have worked on setting up better work habits, on writing an abstract, and on clarifying your argument. If you find that the previous two sentences accurately reflect your recent activities, congratulations, you can move on to the section below.

If, however, they do not reflect your circumstances—if, for instance, you have been reading the workbook and just thinking about working on your article, or if you have been neither reading nor writing—stop here for a minute. While your procrastination is perfectly normal and (a special note for those of you raised in religious homes) does not make you an evil human being, it is not going to help you send a finished article to a journal at the end of twelve weeks. Unfortunately, the method has yet to be invented where you only read and think and still become a published author. So, how did you get here and what are you going to do about it?

You could close this workbook, set it aside, and determine to work on your article later, at a "better time," but the point of this workbook is to make writing a part of daily life, not a special activity you reserve for some indefinite later. If you really feel you cannot work on your article right now, at least write down a projected date for when you will do so. Write this in a date book, on a post-it on the back of your front door, in an electronic calendar, or register with an e-mail reminder service, to make sure that you actually do think about this matter again on a particular date. I also recommend that you return to Week 1 to reread the list of obstacles and the suggestions on overcoming them. It may be that you have overlooked some solution to your current inaction.

If you are not ready to give up the ghost of your article yet, well done! Some diagnosis is in order. Why aren't you working on your article and what can you do to insure that you do work on it?

Lessons I Learned from This Week's Writing Experiences

If you do not have a writing partner yet, I recommend you choose one. Find somebody to work with you through the workbook. Social support is one of the most effective ways of overcoming procrastination. E-mail at least one person right now, asking if he or she would be interested in dedicating some time to revising an article for publication. See, right here, this is the moment to stop reading, put down the workbook, walk over to your computer, and e-mail a possible writing partner or, gasp, even spend fifteen minutes writing. The great thing about this workbook is that it will always be here when you return. But, you did not read that last sentence because you are already busy at your computer, right?

Welcome back. Last week you learned about why journal articles are rejected and how to address those problems in your work. Most of all, you focused on what an argument is and why it is so essential to your success as an academic writer. Finally, you worked on revising your abstract, identifying a model article, and making a list of revision tasks. In other words, you are well on your way. This week you will learn how to select journals and will select one for your article.

GOOD NEWS ABOUT JOURNALS

Although you might be surprised to learn this, many journals need you more than you need them. Why? There are hundreds of academic journals in every discipline. Worldwide, there are nearly 250,000 periodicals. Of those, according to some sources, over 38,000 are active academic journals and over 22,000 are active peer-reviewed academic journals.[1] More academic journals are being published today than ever before. Although the increasing number of journals has been paired with an increasing number of productive faculty, the great secret of journal publishing is how often journals go begging for articles. According to one survey, only 35 percent of journals receive more than 100 submissions a year and only 5 percent have rejection rates of 90 percent or higher (ALPSP 2000). Faculty may discourage graduate students by citing the sky-high rejection rates of leading journals, but such rates are not the norm. In confidential conversations with managing editors at humanities journals, I have found that leading journals in their fields (not in their disciplines, but in their fields) can get as few as twenty unsolicited submissions a year. One small annual journal recently admitted to a student of mine that they get six to eight submissions a year. Indeed, some simple calculations with the number of peer-reviewed journals and the number of productive scholars gives ample evidence for the theory that many journals do not have 90 percent rejection rates,[2] especially in the humanities and social sciences. A 60 percent rejection rate is probably more accurate, a rate that hasn't changed much over the past three decades.[3] Frankly, these odds are much better than your odds for a professorial position or most fellowships.

In other words, your chances of getting a solid article published have never been higher.

THE IMPORTANCE OF
PICKING THE RIGHT JOURNAL

Given these facts, why does everyone have the impression that publishing a scholarly article is so hard to do? If we are desperate to publish our articles and they are desperate to publish articles, why aren't we all published? Well, there are some important caveats. As pointed out in the introduction, you can't get published if you don't submit your article to a journal. Last week you learned the most important thing you can do to improve your chances of publication upon sending: stating your argument early and clearly. This week you will work on the second most important thing you can do: picking the right journal. The costs of choosing the wrong journal are quite high. I have placed selecting an appropriate journal early in this workbook because you want to make this decision early on and revise your article with a specific journal in mind. Many professors don't even write an article until they have decided to which journal they will send it (Silverman and Collins 1975).

One of the most frequent reasons an article is rejected is that it did not meet that particular journal's requirements. Even well-written articles will go unpublished if submitted to journals that have recently published similar articles on the same topic, have large backlogs of other articles, or have a theoretical emphasis the article lacks. The rejection letter will rarely say this clearly, but many times there was nothing intrinsically wrong with the article, it simply did not fit the journal's mandate. The editor may couch this in any number of ways—this wasn't for us, or it was too long or too short, too qualitative or too quantitative, too narrow or too broad, too theoretical or too concrete, and so on and so forth—but all these comments really mean the same thing: We don't publish articles like this. Frequently, other journals specialize in publishing articles exactly like it. That is why it is so important to study actual peer-reviewed journals so that you will not cast your hard work before unappreciative editors or reviewers. It's also why the most frequently given advice to graduate students about picking a journal—submit to whichever journal is "the best"—is not good advice.

Rejection is not the only cost of picking the wrong journal. Many students are unaware that <u>you cannot submit your article to more than one journal at a time</u>. In magazine publishing, you can simultaneously submit your article to dozens of outlets, but in the academic world this is almost always forbidden. Since you must wait until you get a decision from the first journal before you can submit it to another journal, and since the review process can take three to twelve months, picking the wrong journal can significantly delay publication, perhaps even past the article's topical relevance. I've known several people who have had to abandon articles after rejections from two or three journals in a row caused the article to become too dated to salvage. Therefore, indiscriminately sending articles to the major journal in your discipline without researching your options is not a good strategy for those starting out in their academic careers. (While some are working to overturn the single submission rule, I do not recommend that junior scholars lead the revolution. Let the tenured professors do it.)[4]

Furthermore, although many students think that a journal is a journal is a journal, in fact, there are many different kinds of journals. Most universities reward only those articles that appear in "refereed" academic journals. Not all academic journals are refereed, that is, not all use the quality control mechanism of "peer review" in which manuscripts are sent for vetting to scholars in the field, usually anonymously. This process is sometimes known as anonymous or blind review (if the author does not know the reviewer but the reviewer knows the author) or double blind review (if neither knows the other). Getting your work published in conference proceedings, anthologies, or other collections often does not meet this refereed criterion and is a frequent error of younger scholars.

So, how do you go about picking the right journal from among 22,000? Let's start by looking at the types of places where you can publish an article. I recommend that you write down any journals you have been thinking about as possible publication outlets. Then you can keep them in mind as you read the following.

Journals I Know of That Might Be Suitable for My Article

Think about what your aims are in publishing this article. Since you are at an early stage of your career and publication is the key to getting your first job, your main aim may be publishing good work in a journal that hiring or tenuring committees will respect. Or, perhaps an article represents work you are no longer interested in or can't imagine doing further research on. You know you have some good insights, but it's not the main thrust of your research anymore. In such a case, you may want the "points" for publishing in a peer-reviewed journal, but it doesn't need to be in a first-rate journal. Alternately, perhaps you are trying to communicate an idea to a particular audience, such as practitioners or people outside your discipline. Some students have done research that has policy implications and prefer to publish their work in the kind of peer-reviewed journal that policymakers read rather than a leading journal in their field. Finally, some students have a particularly timely idea and want to get into print quickly, before someone else beats them to the punch. You may want to pick a related journal with a quick decision-time. Your purpose in going into print should shape what journal you select.

TYPES OF ACADEMIC JOURNALS

Some people define a journal as anything that is not a book or a newspaper but a better term is the word "periodical." A periodical is "a serial appearing or intended to appear indefinitely at regular intervals, generally more frequently than annually, each issue of which is numbered or dated consecutively and normally contains separate articles, stories, or other writings" (American Library Association 1983). Among these, academic journals are periodicals that publish collections of scholarly articles in the humanities, social sciences, or sciences.

Academic journals evolved from handwritten correspondence during the seventeenth century, when some intellectuals sent missives synthesizing the findings of the day to dozens of other scholars.[5] When such correspondence could no longer keep pace with the scientific developments of the era, serials appeared in the 1660s; the German monthly *Erbauliche Monaths-Unterredungen* in 1663, the French *Journal des Sçavans*, the English *Philosophical Transactions of the Royal Society* in 1665, and the Italian *Giornale de' letterati* in 1668. By the end of the 1700s, journals had become more specialized, and by the end of the 1800s, illustrations, references, methodologies, and peer review had become standard practice. This origin of journals in letter writing still shapes the form: academic journals are records of scholarly conversations and current concerns. It is wise to remember this origin when writing. To submit an article to an academic journal is to begin a correspondence.

Given the tremendous variation in periodicals, it is wise to learn the different types of journals out there. Knowing something about journal variations can help you determine the best journal for your work (and career) and can aid you in revising your article. Below are some of the standard types of publishing outlets for articles, divided into journals you should not publish in, journals you should think twice about publishing in, and journals you should prefer.

Nonrecommended Publishing Outlets

If you are someone with few or no published research articles and you intend to get a professorial position in the United States, I do not recommend that you initially publish in any of the following outlets. They will not lend you the status you need.

Newspapers and magazines. For our purposes, a newspaper or magazine is any popular periodical that never publishes articles with citations. Newspapers disseminate news on a broad range of topics, magazines on more specific topics. As mentioned in the last chapter, articles in newspapers, magazines, or newsletters can do a great job of getting your name out there and changing the world we live in, but do not weigh much with hiring committees. This is so even though magazines like the *New Yorker* or the *Times Literary Supplement* and newspapers like the *Wall Street Journal* or *Le Monde* can be much harder to get published in than any academic journal. The academic judgment against newspapers and magazines—despite the undoubted prestige and exclusivity of some of them—is based on the perception that many journalists do not have credentials in the field about which they are writing (and so cite information second or third hand). Articles in such venues are seen as too short to do justice to the complexity of the issue and have conclusions that are too simple or sweeping. Of course, the antipathy is mutual; newspapers and magazines will find full research articles too long and complex for their audiences. Finally, since newspapers and magazines depend almost entirely on advertisements to stay in business, academics question their impartiality. In short, their authority and legitimacy are not sufficient for your purposes.

News and information journals. These periodicals publish news articles and announcements for a particular academic field or profession.

Their content may include updates on trends in the field, opinion pieces, review articles, conference reports, book reviews, abstracts of peer-reviewed literature, job announcements, and grant deadlines. They may publish excerpts from forthcoming books (which is useful to remember), but such journals do not publish research articles and are not peer-reviewed. The *Chronicle of Higher Education*, for instance, provides news to university faculty and administrators every week. Such journals are often written by staff writers and so are rarely looking for submissions by academics. You should not consider such a journal for your article.

Trade and professional journals. These periodicals publish articles on the technical or practical aspects of performing in a particular field or profession. Because of this technical bent, they tend to be more common in scientific or professional fields such as engineering, medicine, business, or architecture, but can also be found in any discipline with practical elements, such as education, design, film, or archaeology. The articles are not peer-reviewed, have no references, and are written in an informal, more accessible style for practitioners. These journals, or practitioner newsletters, often include many field-related announcements regarding conferences, calls for papers, jobs, new technology, and so on. For instance, *Communication Arts* is the leading trade journal for visual communication and showcases design work, features profiles on artists, gives advice on the business of design, and reviews relevant conferences and books. It does not, however, publish peer-reviewed articles. Unless you are writing an article intended to instruct others in your field about how to do something well—such as how to record good oral histories or restore water-damaged paintings—such journals are not for you. Occasionally, however, peer-reviewed journals are miscategorized as trade journals, so if you find a trade journal you like, don't dismiss it before checking to see if it is actually an academic journal. For instance, *College Composition and Communication* is a trade journal that publishes peer-reviewed articles on writing pedagogy.

Society and conference proceedings. These annual periodicals publish papers presented at a conference. Such proceedings usually are not peer reviewed and frequently are not even copyedited. Studies show that the work published in their pages is not as sound as that published in peer-reviewed journals (Rochon, Gurwitz, Cheung, Hayes & Chalmers 1994). Furthermore, despite the best-laid plans, many collections never make it into print. Although it can seem like a compliment to be invited to submit your article to such an annual after you have presented a paper at a conference, resist. Some scholars have been embarrassed later by unedited, unfinished articles they published in such proceedings. If you have gone so far as to present an article and even receive praise for it, far better to focus on revising and submitting it to an academic journal where it can go through a serious vetting process. If a peer-reviewed journal accepts your work, it is unlikely that you will be embarrassed by it later—at least two reviewers thought it was sound. As a junior scholar starting out, you want to get as much mileage out of your work as you can. If you are certain that the proceedings will be peer reviewed, copyedited, and published, please read the next section about chapters in edited volumes.

Questionable Publishing Outlets

I recommend that scholars with few or no published research articles think carefully before choosing to publish their revised research article in any of the following types of outlets. If the journal you are considering falls into one of these categories, be certain it has some extra quality that negates the low status of its type.

Chapters in edited volumes. These are collections of articles published as a book. Do not let the resemblance to a journal fool you into thinking that publishing in an edited volume is equivalent to publishing in a peer-reviewed academic journal. It is not. I recommend you eschew such outlets. You should consider it only if the editor has a signed book contract with a strong university press and is a well-organized individual with a good reputation as a scholar. The draw to edited volumes for many students—particularly if they have not published before—is that it can be quite easy to get into them. Perhaps your advisor or colleague is editing the volume and guaranteeing you a place in it. Perhaps someone approached you at a conference and invited you to submit your article because your topic is on target. While flattering, you run some serious risks if you agree to submit it. Many edited volumes remain little more than a twinkle in the editor's eye. Scholars underestimate how much effort it takes to put one together and grind to a halt somewhere before actual publication. Faculty editors are not trained copyeditors and sometimes will rewrite and publish your article, often for the worse, without even asking your permission. Finally, far fewer people read the average academic book than read an average issue of a journal. Book chapters are harder to find electronically than journal articles. Edited volumes are best reserved to reprint articles that have already appeared in peer-reviewed journals. In some cases, they can be appropriate for articles that are unlikely to be accepted by peer-reviewed journals because they are too narrow or descriptive. Your task in this workbook, however, is to revise your article for a peer-reviewed journal.

Non-peer-reviewed academic journals. These scholarly periodicals publish scholarly articles but are not peer reviewed. At such a journal, only the editor (or two or three staff members) reads the submissions and determines whether each should be published in the journal. There is no editorial board or review committee whose opinion the editor takes into account; no other scholars review and rate the submissions. Since a review by peers remains the sine qua non of quality in academic publishing, you should not consider such a journal. Some non-peer-reviewed academic journals have quite high reputations within a field; *Harvard Business Review* does not have an anonymous review process or external reviewers and has an excellent reputation. These are the exceptions that prove the rule. I do not recommend non-peer-reviewed journals for junior scholars. Since it is not always clear whether a journal is peer reviewed, I will cover this later in the chapter.

Graduate student journals. These scholarly periodicals are produced and reviewed by graduate students. (UCLA, for instance, has approximately thirty student-run journals, many established in the late 1960s.) Unfortunately, the fortunes of graduate student journals fluctuate wildly, along with their unpaid, overworked editors' lives.[6] The peer review process is often spotty, with editors frequently taking on the work of ostensibly active editorial boards, and their subscription base is shaky or nonexistent. Due to lack of money and training, the editing and production values of such journals can be poor. Of course, some graduate students do a far better job of reviewing articles carefully and giving detailed responses than mainstream journals. Their lower ranking, therefore, is not always a fair assessment. In most cases, however, graduate student journals do not have solid reputations and you should act accordingly. Exceptions exist; for example, although an editorial board of doctoral students runs the journal, the *Harvard Educational Review* is one of the most prestigious journals in education and has been since 1930, with a paid circulation of over 10,000. Usually, such an editorial board would lower its rank, but in this case, probably because it is Harvard, it doesn't.

Note journals. These scholarly periodicals publish very short articles, usually less than three published pages. Scholars publish notes when they have an insight too slight for an entire article or when they do not wish to spend the time to develop an idea (perhaps because it is not related to the rest of their research). Examples of such a journal would be *Notes on Contemporary Literature, The Explicator, ANQ: A Quarterly Journal of Short Articles, Notes and Reviews,* or *Economics Letters*. I recommend that you not devote time to developing notes for such journals, but only send them notes that you have already written (say, because it was cut from an article). A note will definitely count for less with a hiring committee.

Review journals. These scholarly periodicals publish only literature reviews. Some are devoted to individual book reviews; others publish reviews that take a critical approach in appraising a whole body of literature or discussing new research findings. An example is the online scholarly review journal *H-Net Reviews in the Humanities and Social Sciences*. As noted in the last chapter, research articles count for more than review articles, so by definition, the appearance of your article in such a journal will count for less.

Local journals. These scholarly periodicals publish only local scholars for a local area. For instance, some universities have journals that publish only their own professors, and some small associations have journals that publish only their own members. An example is *Anthropology UCLA*. Such journals may not always announce themselves as such, but a look at the editorial board and recently published authors may show them to be limited.

New journals. These scholarly, peer-reviewed periodicals are planning a first issue or have only come out once. Unfortunately, the statistics on journal start-ups are dismal. A high percentage of journal start-ups never publish more than one issue, and many never publish more than three. If a new journal is being sponsored by a reputable university press, edited by a leading scholar, and has funding and a staff from a university, it may not be a terrible bet, but in general, stick with journals that have published issues for at least three years.

Electronic journals. These scholarly, peer-reviewed periodicals are disseminated only on the web or through e-mail. (A print journal that later posts its contents on the web is not an electronic journal.) Journals that appear solely online have almost achieved parity with journals that appear primarily on paper, but not quite. Nevertheless, there has been an explosion in electronic journals since the late 1980s—the Association of Research Libraries Directory listed seven peer-reviewed academic online journals in 1990 and 3,915 by 2000 (Association of Research Libraries 2000).[7] Electronic journals do have real advantages in communicating ideas quickly, enabling interactive dialogue, and providing immediate viewing of music and film clips so they will undoubtedly achieve parity some time soon. Some e-journals already have quite good reputations, such as *Postmodern Culture*, which was started online in 1990. But, depending on your field, be careful about submitting your work to journals that appear solely online, especially if you are in the humanities.

Non-U.S. journals. These scholarly, peer-reviewed periodicals are edited outside of the United States (where they are actually produced is irrelevant). In general, U.S. scholars get less credit for placing their articles in non-U.S.-based journals. Likewise, scholars outside of the United States are often given extra credit for placing articles in a journal edited in the United States. Since the United States is the world's largest and wealthiest producer of scholarly knowledge, it tends to dominate the journal market.[8] Although I do not applaud this ethnocentric reality, U.S. students should be careful about aiming for journals edited outside the United States, with the possible exceptions of Canada and Britain, and even then, only if the journal is well funded. First, even if the journal is a good one, the distance involved can sometimes make your relationship with them difficult. Despite e-mail, correspondence may be delayed and copyediting stages may be skipped. Some of this sloppiness may not be foreign journals' standard practice, but due to harried editors feeling less responsible to outside submissions. Second, non-U.S. journals do not always follow rigorous peer-review procedures. While many U.S. journals do not either, the perception is that this is truer for non-U.S. journals, which lowers their reputations in the United States. Finally, foreign journals are often built around different standards for academic writing and scholarship. In Japan, a journal on primates may publish articles on the personalities of famous apes (Asquith 1996). In Britain, journals may publish less-structured articles. (A U.S. professor of literature told me that a British journal had rejected his article with a letter to the effect that "we are familiar with this American business of getting straight to the point, but we do not care for it.") Of course, many prophets only find honor outside their hometowns so you may search for a more sympathetic audience abroad, but the journal still will not weigh as much with most hiring committees. Unfortunately, for those students doing case studies on non-U.S. countries, finding a U.S. journal willing to publish your work can be difficult. Still, it is best to try publishing in the United States before turning to outside journals.

Preferred Publishing Outlets

I recommend that you concentrate on the following outlets. They all fit the gold standard of academic publishing: they are peer reviewed and feature authors who have a deep knowledge of their field, cite their sources, and detail their methodologies so that others can replicate or check the research. Fortunately, journals in these categories still represent a range of competitiveness and quality, and therefore, are not out of reach. I have arranged these types loosely from least prestigious to most.

Regional journals. These scholarly, peer-reviewed periodicals publish articles from or about a particular locale (e.g., metropolis, province, cluster of provinces, nation). If the region is very large (e.g., the Middle East or Asia), such journals can be extremely competitive, but the smaller regions generally are not. Because of their narrower focus, and assumed smaller readership, journals devoted to a region are not rated quite as highly as other peer-reviewed journals. But they can be a good break-in journal for a first-time author if your work falls within their mandate. Some examples are *Western American Literature, Southwest Journal of Linguistics, Scandinavian Political Studies,* or *Norwegian Journal of Anthropology.* Of course, journals devoted to small regions are sometimes quite prestigious; for instance, the historical *New England Quarterly.*

A regional journal perhaps appropriate for my article is:	

Newer journals. These scholarly, peer-reviewed periodicals are three to seven years old. While brand-new journals are a bad bet, newer journals are often a good bet. Since newer journals have fewer submissions and less of a backlog, they are often actively searching for submissions, and you have a better chance of getting published quickly in their pages. They also may be more willing to work with junior scholars in shaping their work. You can tell the age of the journal by the volume number, which usually proceeds by years; thus, a journal on volume 8 is eight years old.

A newer journal that might be appropriate for my article is:	

Interdisciplinary journals. These scholarly, peer-reviewed periodicals publish work informed by more than one discipline. Interdisciplinary journals have been keeping pace with the explosion of interdisciplinary work in academia. It is now common to find journals that pair two disciplines (e.g., *Philosophy and Literature*) or that do not fit directly in any one discipline (e.g., *Human Rights Quarterly*). The problem with the reputation of such journals, as with interdisciplinary work in general, is that they tend to be less impressive to hiring or promotion committees (who work strictly within the disciplines). That is, if you write an article about metaphor in the founding legal texts of the United States, frequently neither the legal scholars nor the literature scholars will be happy with your methodology. Since this is the problem of all interdisciplinary work, it should not stop you, particularly since disciplinary journals can be quite hostile to boundary-crossing work. Just be aware that interdisciplinary journals can be viewed as less prestigious by hiring committees at research universities. One solution may be to stockpile some statistics about the journal to cite in interviews, such as its subscription level or rejection rate (if they are high) and the names of important scholars who have published in the journal. Another is to ask any prospective department about how they weight publications in interdisciplinary journals. You can use that information to predict whether you and your interdisciplinary work would do well there.

An interdisciplinary journal that might be appropriate for my article is:	

Field journals. These scholarly, peer-reviewed periodicals publish work in a particular field of a particular discipline. Field journals represent the vast majority of academic journals. Many people use the word field and discipline interchangeably, but I use the term "field" to mean a subcategory of a discipline. For instance, within the discipline of English literature, field journals are focused on regions (e.g., *African Literature Today*), cultures (e.g., *Bengali Literature*), periods (e.g., *AMS Studies in Nineteenth Century Literature and Culture*), genres (e.g., *Poetry*), ethnicities (e.g., *Amerasia*), theories (e.g., *Postcolonial Studies*), methodologies (e.g., *Feminist Studies*), themes (e.g., *Literature and Medicine*), or authors (e.g., *Chaucer Review*). Some field journals are devoted to tiny subfields (e.g., *Harvard Journal of African American Public Policy*), others to enormous fields that resemble disciplines (e.g., *Econometrica*). Field journals are the best for junior scholars submitting their work. You are publishing within your discipline and so will keep hiring committees happy. Some advise graduate students to publish only in those fields in which they plan to apply for tenure-track positions. A peer-reviewed journal article publication can't hurt you, but you may want to rethink your strategy if you have published several times in other fields and never in the field you would like to get hired in.

A field journal that might be appropriate for my article is:	

Disciplinary journals. These scholarly, peer-reviewed periodicals publish work in a particular discipline (of which there are only about twenty). Some examples are *Publication of the Modern Language Association (PMLA)*, the *American Sociological Review*, the *American Political Science Review*, *American Anthropologist*, and so on. There often are more than one such journal in each discipline; economics has the *American Economic Review*, the *Journal of Economic Theory*, and the *Journal of Economic Perspectives*, to list a few. Such journals are extremely difficult to get published in. First, the number of scholars in any discipline is much larger than in any field, thus the number of submissions received at any disciplinary journal is very high, as is their rejection rate. For instance, *PMLA* receives about 250 submissions a year and publishes only about fifteen (a 94 percent rejection rate).[9] *American Political Science Review* has a rejection rate of 91 percent on initial submissions (Sigelman 2005). Research has shown that most disciplinary journals have higher rejection rates than most field journals (Shelley and Schuh 2001). Second, disciplinary journals are, by definition, more general than field journals and thus must publish work that appeals to a diverse audience. This means that their articles tend to be broad statements of the big picture, with more complex forms of writing (Shelley and Schuh 2001). Third, such journals often have a reputation as stodgy or actively hostile to new ideas (Miller 1999). Junior scholars often complain about the difficulty of getting their new work published in disciplinary journals. For this reason, I recommend that you not focus on submitting work to disciplinary journals unless you have been encouraged to do so by an advisor who thinks you have a real chance of success.

A disciplinary journal that might be appropriate for my article is:	

FINDING SUITABLE ACADEMIC JOURNALS

As this review of types of academic journals makes clear, identifying an appropriate journal for submission is essential. But, since there are so many journals out there, how do you even begin to *find* journals to study? I recommend several approaches, keeping in mind the preferred types of publishing outlets mentioned above.

Day 1: Reading the Workbook

On the first day of your writing week, you should read the workbook up to this page and answer all the questions posed in the workbook up to this point.

Day 2: Searching for Journals

Below I offer a sequence of methods for finding a suitable peer-reviewed journal for your article.

Ask your advisor and colleagues. Students' most common method of identifying suitable journals is asking people in the field, who will often have a good sense for the major journals. Since there are so many journals to choose from, and sorting through them can be difficult, getting recommendations can be extremely efficient. Furthermore, this is a very easy question to ask in conversation or by e-mail: What do you consider the best journals in our discipline and in our field? In fact, it is a good idea to spend a moment now planning whom you will ask this question and then sending a couple of e-mails! The more people you ask, the better.

I plan to contact the following people about suitable journals:	

Suitable Journals that Colleagues Recommended

Unfortunately, people in your field are not always great sources. If they rarely publish themselves, always publish in the same journals, always publish articles unlike yours, or rarely read journals, they may not be helpful.

Also, people within a field may not know the interdisciplinary journals well. It is always wise to do some exploring beyond colleagues' advice.

Do an old-fashioned shelf search. If you have access to a good research library, sometimes the quickest search is to visit the library and peruse the journals in your field. Libraries usually have a section for recent issues of periodicals, which is a good place to start. First, look up the call number of a journal that you think might be suitable. Then find that journal on the shelf and start looking around it at the other journals that are catalogued in the same area. This can be an excellent way to find additional journals on your topic. Furthermore, you know that they are respectable, active journals because your library is subscribing to them. We live in an increasingly electronic world, but the shelf-search still can't be beat for speed and accuracy. Keywords searches are always going to miss some journals that a shelf search will reveal. If you decide to do this, be sure to look first at the other tasks this week that require a trip to the library so you can do them together.

Suitable Journals I Found through Shelf Searches

Check your citations and their bibliographies. One of the best ways to find the most suitable journals for your article is to look at the articles you cite yourself. Where were they published? Do those journals sound like possibilities for you? This helps you find journals that regularly publish work on your topic or from your angle. If you don't find much through your own citations, pull out the actual articles you cited and review their bibliographies. What articles do they cite and where were they published? Do any of them sound suitable? Finally, you can do electronic searches for full-text articles on your general topic (through such databases as Google Scholar or PubMed or directly at the publishers' websites), and then look at their bibliographies for more journal articles.

Suitable Journals that Turned up in My Citations

Join an association. Many associations will send you information about journals that are relevant to your discipline or field. Pick an association that is most closely related to your writing and join it. Associations are especially useful for finding out about new journals or special issues.

Associations are also beneficial for make writing social. Participating in their annual conferences can give you a much better idea of what the editors of its journals are looking for. Journal editors often speak at annual conferences and will often describe what kinds of articles they are tired of seeing and what kinds of articles they would like to see more of. If you present your paper at the annual conference, you can also get a sense for how people in the field respond to your paper and then shape it accordingly. You increase your chances of successfully targeting association journals by attending and presenting at their conferences.

Joining the following associations could prove useful to my writing:	

Search electronic databases. Students' second most common method of identifying suitable journals is searching for them by keyword in electronic databases. Your university library should provide you with a variety of online databases through which to search for journals. If you don't know how to access them, make a visit to your library and find out. If you do not have access through a library, I have listed some free databases below. Some of the most useful electronic databases are the following:

Ulrich's International Periodicals Directory at www.ulrichsweb.com. This database can only be accessed by paid subscribers, but it provides the most comprehensive list of periodicals available, including over 42,000 academic journals published throughout the world. Almost all of your journal searching can be done here as it has a very powerful "advanced search" engine. It is particularly useful because it gives a lot of information about each journal, including whether it is still publishing, how often it is published, who the editor is, how to contact the journal, what subjects it covers, and whether it is peer reviewed. Furthermore, all of these categories can be searched, you can link to the journal's home page to learn more, and reviews of each journal are provided. The latter is particularly useful in getting a sense for the journal's reputation. The information in Ulrich's is generally correct, except for the peer-reviewed status of the journal. That is, if it says a scholarly journal is peer-reviewed, it is; but if it says it is not, it can be incorrect. For instance, *Callaloo: A Journal of African-American and African Arts and Letters* was not listed as a peer-reviewed journal even though it is.

Genamics JournalSeek at www.genamics.com. If you do not have access to Ulrich's through your library, JournalSeek is a free online service providing information on over 93,500 journals. It includes a subject search and links to the journals' home pages. You can also search web directories at Google and Yahoo, although you will have to sift the results much more thoroughly. In the past, some authors published books that indexed journals within a discipline, which were useful because they articulated general perceptions of a journal's rank, but with the advent of the internet, such books have waned.

Electronic archives. One of the best ways to find a suitable journal is to look at actual journals online. A number of electronic archives now exist, including the Project Muse at John Hopkins University at muse.jhu.edu/journals; JSTORE at www.jstor.org; Ingenta at www.ingentaconnect.com; Informaworld at www.informaworld.com/journals; or Google Scholar at scholar.google.com. They provide access through your library to the actual text of journals. Do a search for your topic in an article index database like Infotrac's Expanded Academic ASAP to identify journals that publish work like yours.

Journal databases. Searching the websites of large academic publishers can also be a good way to find out about journals. First, they have fewer journals and so are not as overwhelming as Ulrich's: their relative smallness makes it easier to search by disciplinary category. Second, almost all of their journals are peer reviewed. Third, since these are commercial presses, their journals must be going concerns and so are good bets for you. Finally, the publishers give full descriptions of each of their journals, unlike Ulrich's. An ancillary benefit of searching such websites is that you can register to receive journals' tables of contents to stay abreast of developments in your field. Some of the largest academic journal publishers in the humanities and social sciences are the following:

- **Cambridge University Press** at www.cup.org. Over 230 journals.
- **Oxford University Press** at www.oup.com. Over 200 journals.
- **Sage** at www.sagepub.com. Over 470 journals.
- **Elsevier Science** at www.elsevier.com. Over 250 journals in the humanities or social sciences (over 2,000 total).
- **Wiley-Blackwell** at www.wiley.com. Over 150 journals in the humanities or social sciences (over 1,000 total).
- **Taylor & Francis** at taylorandfrancisgroup.com. Over 150 journals in the humanities or social sciences (over 1,000 total).
- **Springer** at www.springer.com. Over 175 journals in the humanities or social sciences (over 1,700 total).

Some websites provide helpful indexes of academic publishers by discipline, such as the political science website at www.apsanet.org/section_194.cfm.

Electronic Searching Tips

When searching, remember to use many different keywords. Start with a search on your narrow topic, then on your general subject, and then with keywords reflecting your theoretical approach, your methodology, or your discipline. The latter will reveal journals that are not devoted to your subject but that might be interested in publishing your article. In other words, topic is not your only way into a journal. Slight variations in keywords can make a difference in finding suitable journals. Two student searches illustrate this point.

One student was looking for a suitable journal for her article about representations of the independence struggle in a Congolese film. She started with Ulrich's quick keyword search by searching narrowly with the paired keywords "Congo film" and "Congo cinema." As she expected, no journals showed up. She then searched for "Africa cinema" and got four journals, but two were no longer active, and the other two were not peer reviewed. Next she searched for "African cinema" and this slight variation from "Africa" to "African" returned four entirely different journals. Three were not scholarly, but one was: a cinema, television, and video journal published in French and English called *Ecrans d'Afrique*. Since the film she was discussing was in French, she thought that the journal might be suitable, although it was published in Italy by an association, the Panafrican Federation of Film Makers, rather than an academic publisher. She noted the journal to research further. Next she searched for "Africa film" and got seventy-five journals to plow through. Most of these journals were not peer-reviewed, or addressed African American film only rather than continental African film, but three were suitable, including *African Arts*, *Research in African Literatures*, and *Literary Griot: International Journal of Black Expressive Culture Studies*. She had never heard of *Literary Griot*, so she clicked Ulrich's review button and found that the journal had recently been praised by *Magazines for Libraries* so she added it to her list. Finally, she did a search for "African film" and got seventy journals, mostly the same ones. She looked briefly at *Cultural Critique: An International Journal of Cultural Studies*, thinking it might be suitable, but then realized they did only literary criticism, not film criticism.

Next, since she was in the French department and thought it might be better to publish in a journal closer to her discipline than the African studies journals that had showed up thus far, she then did a search using "francophone," which turned up seventy-eight journals, including the *Bulletin of Francophone Studies*, the *International Journal of Francophone Studies*, and *L'Esprit Createur: A Critical Quarterly of French Literature*. Unfortunately, the first two were by small British publishers and the latter did only special issues. Since the upcoming topics were not relevant to her article, it was out. A fourth journal was *Presence Africaine*, a famous, refereed francophone journal publishing articles in both French and English, which she promptly added to her list.

Finally, just to see if there was anything she had missed, she did a quick search on "cultural studies" and turned up too many to review: 1,376 journals. Therefore, she limited her search by doing an advanced keyword search on active, refereed, "cultural studies" journals. This turned up fifty-two journals, including several that seemed worth further research: the *Journal of African Cultural Studies*, *Cultural Critique*, and *Cultural Studies*.

Another student had written an article on conversation analysis and biosemiotics and was feeling discouraged because he knew of only three suitable journals, two of which were pretty obscure, the last of which was very competitive: *Journal of Consciousness Studies, Cybernetics and Human Knowing,* and *Semiotica.* Since he was in the philosophy department, he really wanted his article placed in a philosophy journal, not a linguistics journal, so he didn't bother doing searches for "conversation analysis." But, doing an advanced keyword search on Ulrich's for active, refereed, "philosophy" journals returned 167 refereed journals. So, he narrowed his search to "semiotics." This turned up *Applied Semiotics* (which was a web-based online journal), *Social Semiotics* (which seemed to publish more social activist articles than his), and *American Journal of Semiotics* (which had two or three scholars on the editorial board whom he knew). So he was able to add the last journal to his list. Then he accidentally came across a journal called *Social Epistemology,* which publishes articles about the social production of knowledge. He had not really thought about his article as epistemological, but it was definitely about the social production of knowledge and so he started doing keyword searches with "epistemology" and "knowledge" and found another thirty journals to look at.

If you don't spend an hour doing an electronic search for suitable journals, you will have missed an opportunity not only to increase your chances of publication, but also to expand your research. Make sure you take this essential step.

Suitable Journals I Found through Electronic Searching

Sometimes students will come to me and insist that there are no more than one or two journals in their field. I used to believe them; now I don't. If you haven't found at least a dozen journals that might be suitable for your article, you simply haven't searched hard enough. A student recently told me that she could only find two journals to publish her cinema article in: *Cinema Journal* (perhaps the leading journal in the field) and *Film Quarterly.*

While it is true that there is a dearth of peer-reviewed cinema journals, when I did a search on "cinema," "film," or "visual studies," I found quite a few journals. Some were brand new, some were published abroad, but several were real possibilities. Don't give up. Even if you don't send your article to any of the journals you find, knowing what journals are out there can help you when you start your next article.

Day 3: Evaluating Academic Journals

This step is best done by taking this workbook to your university library and spending an hour in the periodical section. It is tempting to do this kind of research online, but I highly recommend going to the library to look at print copies. This will be most informative and efficient.

If you use all these search techniques, you are bound to find more journals than you know what to do with. From the section on journal types you know that your best bet is to focus on publishing in a U.S.-based, peer-reviewed journal that has been around for at least three years, appears in print, and publishes research articles in a particular field rather than discipline. But what if these requirements hardly narrow your choices? What if you are still left with dozens of journals? One approach is to rank the journals you have found. That is, how will a potential employer or dean weigh the importance of the peer-reviewed journal where your article appeared?

In the humanities, journals are ranked qualitatively; that is, through general observation and opinion. The intangible of reputation counts for a good deal. Do academics in your field speak well of the journal? Do they refer to it as a "leading journal" or a "first-tier" journal? Do they comment on the quality of the articles or how well run the journal is? Do you ever hear academics outside your field or discipline talk admiringly of the journal? These are all qualitative signs that the journal has a good reputation. Good reputations in the humanities tend to depend on the prestige of the editor, editorial board, and authors, as well as the past, present, and perceived future impact of the journal on the field.

In the sciences, and sometimes in the social sciences, journals are ranked quantitatively; that is, by rigorously collecting and analyzing data about the influence of the journal. The major source for information on journal ranking is *Journal Citation Reports*, which reports on a journal's rank and impact factor.[10] Rank is calculated from dividing the number of citations a journal's articles received in one year by articles the journal published in the two previous years. Impact is calculated from how often a journal's articles are cited in the literature and for how long its articles are cited after they are published. So, for instance, the *New England Journal of Medicine* is often ranked first or second of all journals, having an impact factor of 51.296 in 2006. More than half of all journals have a rank of under 1. Likewise, the *Journal of Biological Chemistry* was cited an astounding 410,903 times in 2006, although its impact factor was 5.8. In contrast, the *Australian Veterinary Practitioner* journal was cited 88 times in 2006 and has an impact factor of 0.171. Of course, the very fact that the journal is listed in *Journal Citation Reports* is a sign that the journal is in the preferred publishing outlet category. Some scholarly associations also publish journal rankings; for instance, the American Political Science Association did so in a 2003 bulletin. You can find these journal rankings posted online.

Many other factors can figure into ranking a journal. For instance, the higher the number of subscribers, the better the ranking of the journal. In the humanities, journals with more than 500 institutional and individual subscribers are respectable. Journals having a readership of over 1,000 are considered strong. Journals can have tens of thousands of subscribers, however, especially if they are automatically sent to all the members of an association. Other factors in ranking a journal are the journal's funding, publisher, age, authors, board, and so on.

Remember that picking a journal with a very high rank may not be the best decision, as mentioned earlier. Many faculty tell their graduate students what was told to them—send your article to "the leading journal." If it gets rejected, send it to the second leading journal; if it gets rejected again, send it to the third; and so on. You may be eighty before you get published, but at least you started at the top. The vagueness of the term "leading journal" is part of the problem. In which field? In which discipline? Even where there is agreement on what constitutes a "leading journal,"[11] junior scholars may have trouble getting in their pages. The *Chronicle of Higher Education* regularly reports on internecine wars over the content of flagship journals.[12] Finally, despite the widespread perception that articles in more selective journals (that is, journals with high rejection rates) are better reviewed, better copyedited, and better written, the research does not support this (Weller 2001; Shelley and Schuh 2001).

The status of the journal you publish your article in may matter more to job committees than your article's content, but there is no point sending your work to a journal that doesn't publish that type of work. For instance, the leading feminist journal *Signs* rarely publishes feminist analyses of single texts. When they do, it is because the analysis is so original or so global that they make an exception. Yet, year after year they receive such articles, solid but narrower work than they usually publish, because the authors are "starting at the top." Such articles might go straight to publication somewhere else, but at *Signs* they won't even go through peer review. With 250 submissions a year, the editors are looking for something broader. If you do careful research on a leading journal, establish that they publish work like yours, and decide to send your article there, you will have my full support, but I don't want you to send your article to a journal just because someone told you it was a leading one. This path will not ensure you early success.

Finally, while I advise eschewing the general advice to aim for the top journal in your field, I have noticed that some of my students—particularly women, nonnative speakers of English, and American minorities—aim too low. Since having less confidence is often marked by gender and ethnicity, if you tend to undersell yourself, don't. Make sure you pick a peer-reviewed journal, not conference proceedings; a newer journal, not a brand new one, and so on.

Evaluation Process for Potential Journals

So, if you are not going to send your article to the highest ranking journal you can find, what are you going to do? If you took the search process seriously, you will have three to ten journals that look like good places for your work. Now go the library, gather together several years of the journals, and physically examine them. You should never send your article to a journal that you have not read or closely examined. Since you can only send your work to one journal, this final step will help you decide which one journal will be best for your article.

This evaluation process is what I would like to turn to now. Using the form on page 127 (or from my website), answer all the questions on the following pages. Use a different form for each one of the journals you found. On the form, square check boxes indicate positive or neutral journal characteristics, round check boxes indicate negative ones. When you are done with your ranking, take home three or four issues of the journals. You will need them for Day 4. If you prefer, you can combine this day's tasks with the next day's tasks and just spend a long afternoon or evening at the library reading.

On the form, you should have a yes answer to all of the following questions:

Is the journal peer reviewed? Oddly enough, finding out whether a scholarly journal is peer reviewed can be one of the most difficult tasks. This essential information about whether the editor sends submissions to referees for anonymous review is often not directly stated in the actual journal. If it is, it will generally be found on the first page or on the inside of the back cover, where the journals' guidelines or mandate are stated. If the journal does not give this information directly, you can check their website for it. If you still can't find this information, you can often guess from other information in the journal. The presence of an "editorial board" usually indicates a peer-review process. If the journal submission guidelines request that three or more hard copies be submitted without the author's name, this is a sign that the article is undergoing a peer-review process. Likewise, if the notes of articles in the journal thank anonymous reviewers, you can assume that the journal is peer reviewed. Again, this is important to check because you want to make sure that you are submitting your work to only those journals that are peer reviewed. If it looks like the journal is not peer reviewed, set it aside and start collecting this information for the next journal on your list. Using the form on page 127, indicate the journal's refereed status.

Is the journal in the recommended publishing outlet category? With extremely rare exceptions, you should not be looking at trade journals or conference proceedings. With some exceptions, you should not be looking at edited volumes, graduate student journals, or brand-new journals either. Rather, you should be looking at journals with a U.S.-based editorial office, national base, print version, and a solid reputation. On the form, check off the box next to the type of journal. Also, indicate where the editorial office is.

Does the journal have a solid reputation? When you asked others about journals in your field, was this journal mentioned? Have you heard it discussed in favorable terms? On the form, check off the box next to the level of the journal's reputation.

Does the journal have a reputable publisher? In general, journals that are published by a large university or commercial press are more stable than those edited and published by micro presses—by a particular scholar, department, or center. Although journal editing is often done out of a university department, the actual publishing is often done separately by a large press or association. Since most academics are not trained in running businesses, and the bureaucracy of most academic departments is anathema to business efficiency, micro-published journals tend to run into financial and organizational problems fairly quickly. Thus, publication by a university press (particularly at one of the large public universities or an Ivy League university), or by a large association (such as the Modern Language Association), is a sign that the journal is around to stay. Commercial presses are also good, although the prestige associated with them is slightly less than that of a university press. On the form, write down the name of the publisher (to be found on the copyright page) and whether it is large or small.

Has the journal been around for a while? As noted before, the longer a journal has been around, the more stable it is. If the journal has been published for more than ten years you can assume that it is well organized enough to survive the vicissitudes of publishing. If it has been around for more than thirty years, you can assume that the journal is on a topic of long-term interest to academia. This information may be gathered from the copyright page or from the number of volumes, which correspond with calendar years. On the form, write down the date the journal started, what volume number it is on, and how long the journal has been around.

Is the journal carefully produced? U.S. journals with lots of typos and design problems are in danger of collapse. Either the journal is not professionally run or it is underfinanced. Journals that have many smudges, photocopy-quality photographs, mismatched fonts, skewed text, insufficient publication information, thin paper, or otherwise show signs of neglect are usually not well respected. In general, the more solvent a journal is, the better it looks. Unfortunately, journals in most sub-fields and fields are not self-sufficient and no journal is self-sufficient when starting out. The annual cost of running a biannual U.S. journal is at least $60,000, and many journals do not have enough subscriptions to cover these costs regularly. Without university support, they do not survive the lean years. Therefore, journals for which a university provides office space and paid staff dedicated to the journal alone are generally more stable and of a better quality. Very large associations can also provide such support. Of course, some journals charge such high subscription prices or have such massive numbers of subscriptions that they do not need financial support—they are successful businesses. Outside the sciences, however, this is not the norm. The average price for a chemistry journal in 2007 was $3,429, in anthropology $534, and in art history $198 (Van Orsdel and Born 2007). Finally, some social science journals have instituted a submission fee, ostensibly so that they can pay reviewers, but this practice is still frowned upon. On the form, write down whether the journal looks professionally produced.

Does the journal come out on time? A journal that does not come out on time is a journal in danger of collapse. You do not want to send your work to a journal that may fold in the next year or two. If the journal is supposed to come out in the spring and fall, and it comes out in the summer and winter, this is not so bad. If the journal is regularly two or three years behind, that is a bad sign. How can you tell if a journal is struggling? If it is supposed to come out twice a year and instead it publishes a "double-issue" at the end of the year, or the journal sports a date on the cover (say 2007) that is two or more years behind the actual date of publication (2009) listed on the copyright page. On the form, write down whether the latest issue at the library is from the current year. If it isn't in the library, do check online as sometimes libraries are behind, not the journals. Remember to use the date on the copyright page not the cover.

Are the authors published in its pages diverse? First, compare the names on the editorial board with the names in the table of contents. Are the names frequently the same? That is, does the journal ever publish anyone who is not on the editorial board? Go through several back issues to check if people other than those on the board publish articles and whether it is always the same people. Some journals are very insular, designed to publish the work of a select few.[13] Do not focus on sending articles to journals that publish almost entirely work by their own board. Second, if the authors and board members are not always the same, review the status of those who publish in the journal. Does the journal ever publish anyone below full professor? Are the authors all from research universities? Alternately, are quite a few of the authors graduate students? Journals that publish mostly famous scholars may be hard to break into; journals that publish only graduate students may be too low in status. On the form, check off whether the journal is insular or open to new writers, and the rank of those it publishes.

Does the journal publish more than five or six articles a year? Although they may seem like small details, journal sizes and publication schedules have implications for your chances of success. The more often a journal is published and the more articles it publishes a year, the bigger its demand for articles. This can mean that a more frequently published journal is a better bet. Journals that publish only one issue a year can be very competitive; journals that publish more may not be. On the form, write down how many issues and articles the journal publishes in a year. Do not count book reviews or nonscholarly articles without endnotes.

Is the journal online or indexed electronically and where? Since electronic access to your work is so important to increasing your reputation, seriously consider publishing in only those journals that are electronically indexed in the large databases. Some scholars won't publish in any journal that doesn't have the full content of the articles online as well. This is probably a wise decision. On the form, check off whether the journal is electronically indexed.

Does it take a long time to get published once you submit your manuscript? It is an unfortunate truth of academic journal publishing that articles are frequently published two or three years after submission and thus five or six years after conception. This gestational period is even longer than that of elephants! This is due to journals' turnaround times and backlogs. Turnaround is the time between submission and decision; backlog is the time between decision and publication. That is, many journals have accepted articles for several issues in advance. Once accepted, your article must wait in the pipeline until those previously accepted articles are published. This can mean delays of one to three or even four years, depending on the journal. This delay between acceptance and publication is usually not a problem to writers since a letter of acceptance from a journal will carry the same weight as actual publication with hiring committees. Nevertheless, the longer the article takes to get published, the more likely it is that someone else will publish similar work. You can get an idea of how long journals take to evaluate and publish articles by checking dates in the published articles' bibliographies. If the articles in the journal never have any citations from the current or previous year, it's a sign that the journal has a large backlog. Sometimes those in the field can know which journals have backlogs, but be careful because sometimes their information is out of date. On the form, check off whether the journal appears to have a large backlog.

Is the journal going through a transition? If you ever hear that a journal is "going through a transition," avoid sending your article there. New editors, new editorial offices, new mandates, new titles, and new publishers are potential signs of trouble. A student of mine had submitted an article to a journal and received it back in proof form (as it looks when it is going to be printed) but heard nothing else. She assumed that it had not been published. When I pushed her, she contacted the journal to find out what had happened. The journal admitted that in the transition from one university to another, several manuscripts were lost without them realizing it. Fortunately, they promised to publish her article if she could provide them with an acceptance letter! She did and soon saw her article published. She was lucky; you may not be. On the form, write down any signals that the journal is going through or about to go through a transition.

Who reads the journal? Whom do you want to read your work? If you would like professors in your own country to read it, then pick a journal published in your country. If you would like practitioners rather than professors to read it, pick a journal that practitioners read. If you would like a particular department to hire you, think about picking a journal that departmental members help edit. You want to get your work in front of those who can most benefit from it and who can most benefit you.

Day 3 (continued): Matching Your Article to Suitable Journals

Once you've decided that you have some suitable journals that are peer reviewed, published by a reputable press, have been around for a while, are carefully produced, and come out on time, you are ready to learn what you would need to do to send your article to each journal.

Does the journal have an upcoming theme or special issue on your topic? Some journals do special issues (an additional issue on a particular topic) or theme issues (a regular issue on one topic). Special or theme issues are wonderful opportunities that many students overlook. A survey found that almost one-third of the articles in a set of fifty journals were related to designated themes (Henson 1995). Such issues are almost always much less competitive than a usual issue of the journal. Since journals receive, on average, only a third as many manuscripts for their announced theme issues as for their general issues, submitting work for a theme issue reduces your competition by two-thirds. Even if the guest editor has a full roster of authors he or she wants to include, people are always dropping out at the last moment by not submitting their final manuscript, thus creating a place for you.

Many of my students have gone straight into print by carefully looking for such issues and then contacting the editor, even after the deadline has passed. This strategy really works. In fact, one student had an interesting experience after submitting an article to *PMLA* for a special issue. The journal accepted the article but discovered that they had not received enough submissions to produce the special issue. To honor their letter of acceptance, they moved her article into one of the main issues. Although she knew that she had gotten in through the backdoor, as it were, no one else did. Since the readership of the special issue would have been smaller, this was a nice bonus for her.

Special or theme issues are often announced in previous issues of a journal, but may also be found through e-mail announcement services, online bulletin boards of calls for papers (often organized by discipline), or online announcements of special issues at journal websites. On the form on page 127, check off if the journal does special or theme issues. If yes, what are the upcoming issues? Do any of them suit your article?

One caveat about special or theme issues. Thriving journals may have special issues but they tend not to have theme issues. The problem with regularly publishing theme issues is that it reduces the number of submissions a journal receives. Authors discover the upcoming theme issues, ascertain that their article does not fit, and send their work elsewhere. In turn, journals with declining submissions start doing theme issues as a way of soliciting articles from authors. It can be a vicious cycle. You should use special or theme issues to get into a better journal, not a declining one. If you find a theme or special issue at a journal you think of highly, go for it.

Does the journal have word or page length limits you can meet? Some journals never publish articles longer than twelve final pages; others will happily publish sixty-page articles. If you have written an article shorter than twenty-five manuscript pages or longer than thirty-five, you want to look carefully at the manuscript length guidelines in the journal. If your article is long and they prefer short, your article may not do well there. Since article length can be hard to estimate—due to notes, bibliographies, images, tables, charts, graphs, and varying type sizes—most journals now give word limits. If they give the page limit in "manuscript pages," this means double-spaced text with one-inch margins and twelve-point font, usually containing about 250 words. Thus, 5,000 words are 20 manuscript pages; 9,000 words are 36 manuscript pages. This translates variously into final journal pages, which vary from 300 to 500 words per page. The trend in journal publishing is toward shorter and shorter articles, even in the humanities (Pullinger 1996). If your article is long, you must do careful research on page limits. (You may also want to think about cutting because there seems to be an inverse relation between length and acceptance. The longer the article is, the more the peer reviewers can find to quibble with [Henson 1995].) On the form, write down any statement the journal makes about page limits and the length of the shortest and longest articles in the issues you are looking at.

Does the style of your article match the journal's style? You can tell a lot about how your article is going to do at a journal by studying the journal's style. Is the journal formal or informal, conservative or progressive, playful or serious? For instance, go through the back issues and examine their article titles. Do they seem to be in the same style as your title? If not, you may want to think about another journal or changing your title. Likewise, does the journal tend toward long endnotes and references or short? Will you need to alter your documentation if you submit your work to the journal? Are the block quotations frequent or absent? Do the article introductions start with stories or statistics? Would you have to change your voice or approach to get your article into the journal? Are the articles straightforward and clear? Do they have conclusions? Some journals are divided up into sections. If so, where would your article fit best? Are there subheadings? On the form, note this.

Do you know any of the journal's editors? It is always a good idea to study the masthead to find out if you know anyone on the staff or editorial board. Students are often surprised to find their graduate or undergraduate advisors on the editorial board of journals they are interested in. Sometimes such insiders can be helpful to you. You can e-mail them to ask if they think that the journal would welcome an article like yours.

Two caveats about writing such an e-mail. Editorial board members are not always well-informed about journal mandates and the extent of their involvement may be reading one or two manuscripts a year. If their experience of the journal is limited, their advice will be as well. Furthermore, if the editorial board member you know does research similar to yours, he or she may be selected by the editor to review your article, should you submit it. Asking their advice in advance may deny you a sympathetic reader, then, since some scholars recuse themselves from reviewing an article if they know the author.

For these reasons, I recommend that you contact people on editorial boards only if you know them quite well, well enough to have a frank conversation about all these issues. In my experience as an editor, more than one graduate student has gotten a first publication through advisors ignoring conflict of interest rules and giving favorable reviews. On the form, write down the names on the staff or editorial board of people you know and whether you think it is advisable to contact them.

How does this journal require articles be submitted? Journals often have quite strict rules about how articles should be submitted. Most social science journals require you to submit your article electronically. Many humanities journals require you to submit three print copies and make sure that your name appears nowhere in the submission. A few outdated journals may even want you to include a self-addressed stamped envelope so that they can return a decision to you. Others want you to submit articles with the documentation already standardized according to the *Chicago Manual of Style*, the *American Psychological Association Manual*, or the *Modern Language Association*. On the form, note any special requirements for submitting articles.

Making a Decision about Which Journal

Once you have filled out all the information on the forms, review each. Which journal looks like your best bet? Remember that the check boxes on the form are coded: square check boxes indicate positive or neutral journal characteristics, round check boxes indicate negative ones. If you have checked three or more round check boxes, you should think twice about sending your work to that journal.

If you have several suitable journals, that's great! If the first journal rejects your article, you can send it to the next journal on your list. Now you have a plan that enables you to respond positively to rejection.

Before you make a final decision about which journal you intend to send your work to, it's wise to send a query letter. Therefore, think about completing the tasks of Day 5 before making a final decision about which is your first choice journal.

Suitable Journals in Order of Submission

Journal Review Form

Journal title   _____

Editor's name/e-mail   _____

Managing editor's name/e-mail   _____

Editorial office addres   _____

Journal web address   _____

Peer reviewed	❑ Yes	○ No	○ Not sure (find out)
Type of journal	○ Disciplinary	❑ Field-based	❑ Interdisciplinary
	○ Trade/ practitioner	○ Conf. proceeding	○ Edited vol.
Electronic AND print	❑ Yes	○ No	
US-based ed. office	❑ Yes	○ No, based in _____	
Reputation	❑ Solid	❑ Medium	○ High ○ Low
Publisher type	❑ Large (e.g., univ., commercial, assoc.)	○ Small	

Publisher name   _____

Longevity	○ <2 years	❑ <8 years	❑ <15 years
Production	❑ Carefully produced	○ Sloppy	
Punctuality	❑ Issue on time	○ >1 year delay	○ >2 year delay
Contributors	❑ Open (often outsiders)	○ Insular (mostly insiders)	
	❑ Mixed	○ High (profs.)	○ Low (mostly grad students)
No. of articles a year	○ <8 articles	❑ >12 articles	❑ >20 articles
Indexed electronically	○ No	❑ Yes, on _____	
Backlog (guess)	❑ Articles' latest cites dated this year or last	○ Older cites _____	
Themed/special issues	❑ No	❑ Yes, on _____	
Word limits	❑ <5,000	❑ <9,000	❑ No limit ❑ Not stated
Page limits	_____ pages of shortest article	_____ pages of longest article	

Board members I know   _____

Rejection rate	❑ <40%	❑ <60%	❑ <80% ○ Over 80%
Turnaround time	❑ <1 month	❑ <3 months	○ <9 months ○ Over 9 months
Backlog	❑ <6 months	❑ <1 year	○ <2 years ○ Over 2 years

Submission Guidelines

Style manual	❑ Chicago	❑ MLA	❑ APA	❑ Other _____
Documentation style	❑ Cite in text	❑ Cite in notes		❑ Other _____
Hard copies to submit	❑ 0	○ 1	○ 3	❑ Other _____
Electronic copies	○ No	❑ Yes	❑ Send by e-mail?	
Include SASE envelope	○ Yes	❑ No		

Day 4: Reading Relevant Journals

Spend at least an hour skimming recent issues of the suitable journals you identified. If you see any articles that relate to your work, stop and spend some time reading them. If you find any relevant bibliographic articles, definitely read them. As you will remember from last week, part of getting published is citing the relevant literature. Although it is not necessary to flatter editors by randomly citing articles from the journals you intend to send your article to, it is necessary to cite directly related articles. Editors want to inspire dialogues in their pages; it helps if you clearly indicate that you are listening to that dialogue, not just speaking to it.

Look carefully at a journal's content. First, is there a trend to the articles? Has it become the journal for some debate, around which all articles now revolve? Is it getting away from its mandate? Sometimes journals have an editor's column or introduction, and this can give you good information about the direction of the journal. Second, what is the journal thin on? Does your article fill some gap? Sometimes a journal is avoiding publishing certain work, but sometimes it just hasn't gotten any good articles on the topic. Third, what articles cover ground similar to yours? How is yours different? If a similar article was published in the past three years, this may harm your chances of getting into the journal. On the other hand, if their article is older and different, the journal may feel that the issue needs to be revisited, particularly if you reference their earlier publications in your article. On the back of the form, write down whether the content of the journal matches its title and how many articles it has published in the past five years like yours.

You can also list anything else you noticed, like the length of bibliographies or notes.

Day 5: Writing a Query Letter to Editors

Some information about a journal cannot be collected by looking at the journal. Copyright pages, online submission guidelines, and electronic directories like Ulrich's will only carry you so far. Some of the most important information can only be had from the staff of the journal. This is why I recommend that you e-mail the editors of the two or three journals you are most interested in and ask them some questions. Some types of questions you should ask of the managing editor, others of the faculty editor. Although it can seem like hubris to write to one of these figures, I assure you they do not live on Olympian heights. It is their job to work with authors, and you have the right to ask a few questions before sending your hard work to them, especially since they get to publish your article for free! I have seen this step of writing to the editor(s) work to the author's advantage time and again. The only caveat is that the larger the journal, the less likely they are to respond helpfully to queries. Journals that receive more than 200 submissions a year may not respond at all, but I have had students receive helpful replies from very large journals, so I recommend trying.

So, your task today is to draft two e-mails to the editors of the journals you are most interested in. You will need a revised abstract to complete this step. After drafting the letters, you can send them whenever you are ready. Some people wait until their article is final, but I don't recommend that you wait. Knowing which journal you intend to submit your article to can shape your writing process. If you do send a query letter, use the journal log form on page 283 to keep track of what you have sent where.

What to Ask the Managing Editor

A managing editor (sometimes called the production editor or assistant editor) is the staff person in charge of the production of the journal. In small journals, one person may be playing almost all the roles; in larger journals, the roles will be spread among many. The managing editor is usually the most knowledgeable about the journal's schedule. For this reason, I recommend that you think about asking him or her three questions.

How many submissions a year does your journal receive? Like many aspects of academia, the more rejecting a journal is, the higher its prestige. A journal's rejection rate is the number of articles it publishes a year divided by the number of articles it receives a year. That is, if a journal receives thirty submissions annually and publishes only ten, it has a rejection rate of 66 percent—it returns two out of three submissions. Rejection rates at journals vary, but a rejection rate of 40 to 60 percent is standard and a rejection rate of 90 percent or higher is rare. As noted before, only 35 percent of journals have more than 100 submissions a year and only 5 percent have rejection rates of 90 percent or higher (ALPSP 2000). Because editors know that a rejection rate of 90 percent or higher is prestigious, I don't recommend asking an editor straight out what their rejection rate is. They are all invested in saying that it's high. I recommend instead that you ask how many submissions the journal receives a year. Then you can calculate the rejection rate on your own by dividing the number of articles published in the last year by the number received. The lower the rejection rate, the wider your window of opportunity. If you are just starting out, consider not submitting your manuscripts to journals with very high rejection rates.

What is your journal's turnaround time? Many peer-reviewed journals are extremely slow in making decisions about whether to accept or reject manuscripts (turnaround time). Some journals are fairly fast, in academic terms, and get back to you within three months. Others can take up to a year, and some are even longer. In all fairness, this is not usually the editors' fault, but the peer reviewers. Most of an editor's job is nagging peer reviewers to do the job they agreed to do and return a recommendation to the editor. As you can imagine, getting busy professors to do reviews is often extremely difficult. Since managing editors find it hard to be truly honest with authors about the wait, you may not get a straight answer, but it is worth asking.

What is your journal's backlog? As noted earlier, the delay between acceptance and publication is not a problem for writers with timeless articles. But sending your work to journals that are slow to publish manuscripts can be damaging if your idea is no longer novel. I recommend that you ask managing editors what their backlog is, and think twice about a journal that has a backlog of two or more years. Fortunately, most managing editors are quite forthcoming with this information.

If you are not sure how to ask these three questions, you can use the formula below.

Sample E-mail to a Managing Editor

Dear [first name, last name]:

I would like to submit an article to your journal, and I wonder if you could give me some information. How many submissions do you receive a year? How long does it take you to get back to authors with a decision about their manuscript? What kind of backlog do you have? Will you have any special or theme issues coming up? Also, I was not able to find out what your word limit was: do you have a maximum?

[If you are still concerned about bothering them, you can add a sentence or two like: I know you are very busy, but this information would be very helpful to me.]

Sincerely,

[your first and last name]

[university affiliation, department]

[city, state/country]

[No need to note student status.]

If you know the managing editor personally and can speak frankly with him or her, you can also ask several other questions: Is now a good time to submit an article? Is the editor open to student work or dismissive? What are the editor's research interests or pet peeves?

What to Ask the Editor

The editor (sometimes called the executive editor or editor-in-chief) is the faculty member in charge of the content of the journal. This person is usually the most knowledgeable about what articles are most likely to be accepted. Unless he or she is editing a journal that you know receives hundreds of submissions a year, I recommend that you write to him or her to see if you can get a mini-peer review in advance. Your letter is called a *query letter*. Sending query letters is standard practice in newspaper and magazine publishing, but uncommon in journal publishing. For this very reason it can be a dynamite tactic for you. Let me explain.

E-mailing the editors of your three top choices for journals is one of the most effective things you can do to increase your chances of publication in a good journal. As the only legitimate way around the single submission rule, it can prevent you from sending your work to a journal that will only reject your article and can aid you in finding a journal that will most likely accept your article. Why wait three to twelve months just to get rejected if you can figure this out in advance?

Writing a query letter gets you one of four types of editorial responses. If you have done your journal research carefully and written a good query letter, most editors will write back saying "send it along." No editor will make a commitment to publish your article sight unseen, no matter how good your query letter. For many students, however, even this much encouragement is helpful, creating a kind of deadline or expectation that keeps you going. Many students have told me that just knowing that an editor had their work in mind aided them in completing their article and sending it. By the way, you are under no obligation to send the article to that journal just because you sent the query letter.

Most editors will say little more than "send it along," but some editors will communicate their excitement about your project. Comments like "this is just the kind of article we are looking for" or "in intellectual terms, your manuscript sounds very interesting" or "you don't have to be a 'big' name to publish with us—we are looking for promising young researchers" (direct quotes from e-mails some of my students have received) are very encouraging. More important, some editors will write back with extremely useful information, such as, "It's so interesting that you wrote to me today because we just had an article drop out of a special issue on x and your article sounds like it might fit. Can you send the article immediately?" That is, writing a query letter to editors can gain you access to information you need to make the best decision. I have had several students who were rushed into print because they happened to write a query letter to an editor just when that editor was looking for an article on their topic.

Some editors will even give you a mini–peer review by sending you a response such as, "Your article sounds very interesting, although we usually only publish quantitative articles" or "It sounds like your article would be suitable for our journal, although your sample size might be a problem." This kind of response is money in the bank, and you should thank the editor for giving you such a helpful answer. You may be able to make small changes to your article that will dramatically increase your chances of acceptance. Or you can send it to another journal less likely to have that problem.

One student received three such helpful responses to his article on Chinese political economy. All three editors liked his abstract, but each one had a different suggestion about what might be done to the article to make it more suitable for his journal. The first noted that the student's article was a single-country study, and the journal tended to publish articles with "a broad comparative (cross-national) content"; the second said the same but recommended that the student include a section on the relevance of his case to other transitional economies; and the third recommended that the student make sure to cite their recent articles on the topic. The student, having received these wonderful mini-reviews, could then decide what kinds of changes he was most interested in making and submit his article accordingly.

The most useful editors of all are those who take the time to be negative. This may sound counter-intuitive, but getting your query letter rejected is part of what you are trying to do. Why go through the lengthy peer-review process when you can get it over with in an e-mail exchange? Be grateful for the editor who heads you off at the pass. Editors can tell you that they are no longer interested in publishing articles on your topic, that they never publish articles with your methodological approach, that they already have an upcoming article on your topic, or that they will not be able to publish any new submissions for several years. Such an editor has saved you not only months of time but also the heartbreak of wholesale rejection. It is much easier to accept rejection of your query letter than of your article. You are far more likely to pick yourself up and move on from the first rejection than the second.

One student received a very direct and helpful response from an editor, who said, "I would not encourage you to send this along to us. We are moving more and more in macro [omitted] directions, and consequently publish less and less in more purely [omitted]. In general we shy away from narrowly [omitted]—especially ones involving very small numbers of subjects. Your work sounds intriguing and I am sure you will be able to place it elsewhere without much difficulty. Indeed, you might think of trying a 'sister' journal of ours, [omitted]." In one day, the student got a peer review that usually would have taken three months. She quickly sent an e-mail to the journal the editor had recommended and moved on.

Finally, some editors will not respond. Although there can be many reasons for not responding—including being away from e-mail or the large volume of queries—it is not a good sign about the functionality of the journal. If you have written to both the managing editor and the editor and have heard from neither within two weeks, you should think twice before sending your article to that journal. Chances are that they will not be efficient about getting back to you with a peer review either.

Elements of the Query Letter

When drafting a query letter to an editor, make sure to keep it short: no longer than one page. Remember the following:

- Address the editor by name in the salutation.
- Mention any human connections to the editor that you have, such as your advisor (e.g., so-and-so recommended that I write to you).
- State briefly why the editor and the journal readers should be interested in your article (e.g., it will fill gaps, aid understanding, inspire debate, fit their theme, is fresh and different from specific articles and/or books already in print, and so on).
- Display a knowledge of the journal (e.g., mention any of their recent articles in the journal on your topic).

- Give the title of your article and your abstract (first make sure that both give a sense for your article's argument and style).
- Give your article's length in double-spaced pages or words, and note whether this includes footnotes, references, or tables.
- State that you have not published this article before, nor submitted it to any other journal.
- Name grants or awards that you received for the research.
- Always include a question that will tease out your article's chances of rejection. For instance, "I foresee one potential obstacle to the publication of my article in your journal: I note that my qualitative approach would deviate from the method used in most of the articles in your journal. Please let me know if this is a problem." Or, "The reason that I am sending you this e-mail, rather than simply sending my article along, is that I am concerned that the regional focus of my article will not quite fit the mandate of your journal. If you have any comments that could help me decide whether to submit my article to your publication, I would appreciate hearing them."
- Thank the editor.

Sample Query Letter to an Editor

Dear Dr. [first name, last name]:

I got your e-mail address from Professor [name], and I hope you don't mind my e-mailing you. I am considering submitting my article titled [title] for possible publication in your journal [name]. I notice that your journal has published articles on [your general topic] (I am thinking in particular of [title] published last year). Since there are few published studies on [your specific topic], my article may fill this gap and contribute to the understanding of [your argument].

My article argues that [abstract here].

My article is about [number] double-spaced pages long, including footnotes, references, and tables. I have never published this article, nor have I submitted it to any other journal. Grants from the [name of funders] funded the collection of data for this project.

Would such an article interest you? Please let me know if you feel that my broader focus, on [your topic], would pose a problem for acceptance in your journal. As my section on [sub-topic] is quite strong, I could recast the article to focus entirely on this [sub-topic]. Thank you very much. I am looking forward to hearing from you.

[Name without any title]

[University] [Department]

[City] [State/country]

An Example of What Query Letters Can Do for You

Below is one student's real-life journal selection experience in the student's own words:

> My dissertation director recommended three journals, but I ended up going with one he had not mentioned, though ultimately he was very pleased when the article was accepted there. Here is the process I went through with my article [title omitted].
>
> I started with the three journals he mentioned: *Renaissance Drama* (RD), *Studies in Philology* (SP), and *Studies in Bibliography* (SB). I had some reservations about these journals for various reasons. I already had an article under submission to SB and they were about three months overdue in getting back to me, and I felt SP and especially RD were probably above my reach (despite the fact that my director is on the editorial board for RD). I read all these journals and use them regularly in my own research, so I know that big names publish there, plus SB and RD are a little inbred (publishing the same names, often editorial board members, over and over). SP is less clannish but still a major marquee for big name scholars. In addition, RD and SB are annuals and each publishes only about eight to ten articles a year, sometimes as few as six. SP is quarterly but only publishes three or four articles each quarter. The numbers just weren't very encouraging.
>
> To these journals, I added two more: *Medieval and Renaissance Drama in England* (MaRDiE) and *Studies in English Literature, 1500–1800* (SEL). I also read and use these journals regularly in my own work, especially MaRDiE. Both journals publish a mix of established and young scholars. Sadly, both are only annuals (SEL is technically a quarterly journal, but each quarter is specialized and my specialty is only covered once a year, in the spring issue), but both usually publish sixteen or so articles, putting them on par with a lot of quarterlies.
>
> I did some of the basic research you recommended, checking the MLA directory of periodicals and other sources, including the internet (all of the journals I was considering have their own websites). I found out that RD was planning special topics for the next two annual issues, and the submission deadline for the topic I found more interesting had already passed. I wasn't interested in the other topic (pretty far outside my current research interests), so I eliminated RD from the list. I also decided to eliminate SB because I already had one article under submission to them that was pretty similar to the one I was working up.
>
> I was now left with SP, MaRDiE, and SEL, and I sent inquiry e-mails to their editors asking specifically about time to decision and time to publication, because I was very interested in getting something into print quickly for job-market purposes. All three responded promptly. SEL said their time to decision was forty-five

to sixty days but they had a publication backlog of three years. SP was polite but rather lukewarm in their response to my abstract, and they admitted that their time to decision is usually six to nine months. MaRDiE's response was very enthusiastic, their time to decision was thirty to forty-five days, and the time to publication was only eighteen months if I could meet a rapidly approaching submission deadline.

My gut reaction was to go with MaRDiE—they seemed enthusiastic and I like the journal quite a lot. It just felt like a good fit. By publishing there, I felt I could contribute to some ongoing scholarship and discussions in my field as well as get into print for the job search.

I probably should mention that I never considered two of the top journals in my field—*Shakespeare Quarterly* and *Shakespeare Studies*. I read those journals regularly, enough to know that they usually don't print scholarship on playwrights other than Shakespeare (with the occasional exceptions of Jonson and Marlowe) unless the article somehow connects the author to Shakespeare. I am not working on Shakespeare right now, and I didn't feel like manufacturing a connection just so I could submit to those journals. RD is THE top journal for scholars working on Renaissance playwrights other than Shakespeare, mostly because it is so exclusive, but MaRDiE actually publishes most of the non-Shakespearean dramatic scholarship around today and is also widely read and cited. My director was very happy when MaRDiE accepted my article, and he told me he was impressed that I checked out and thought out all the variables for myself and came to my own decision, even if it differed from his original recommendation.

My gut instinct paid off—I got the acceptance note just a few days before we had our workshop celebration dinner, about thirty days after I sent the article in. Couldn't have worked out better! I have since met the journal's current editor at a conference, and he was very encouraging and asked to see more of my work.

Once I file my thesis in early September, I'm going to take two weeks to beat another article into shape for submission. Now that I have something forthcoming, I'm willing to take more of a risk by submitting this next article to one of the prestige journals. This article will be less about a particular playwright and more about Renaissance drama in general and will therefore be a better fit for SP or even for *Shakespeare Quarterly*. Wish me luck!

Making a Final Decision about Which Journal

By the end of this week, you should have picked the journal you wish to submit your article to first. If you need to wait to hear back from journal editors, you can wait until then, but don't wait longer. Knowing what journal you are going to send your work to makes a big difference—it will help you shape the article when you know what conversation you are joining.

Which journal is my best bet for getting this article published?	

Now you need to list what implications this choice has for the further writing of your article. The most important issue at this point is the journal's word limits. If your article doesn't meet those limits, you must start aiming for those limits or choose another journal. I am surprised by how often students tell me that they are aiming for journals with page length requirements that do not remotely relate to their article. Don't make this mistake of not paying attention to word lengths.

What are the journal's page or word limits and what length is my article currently?	

There are other implications that the journal has for your revision process. If the journal requires that you list all documentation in the notes, not the text, and you've done the opposite, you may have to switch your article over. If the journal has a special issue that you are aiming for, you will have to take note of the date and work toward it. If the journal favors more historical work, you will need to beef up that part of your article.

What are the other writing implications of choosing this journal for this article?	

DOCUMENTING YOUR WRITING TIME AND TASKS

On the following weekly plan, please graph when you expect to write and what tasks you hope to accomplish this week. Then keep track of what you actually did. Remember, you are to allot fifteen minutes to one hour every day to writing. At the end of the week, take pride in your accomplishments and evaluate whether any patterns need changing.

Time	Monday	Tuesday	Wednesday	Thursday	Friday	Saturday	Sunday
5:00 a.m.							
6:00							
7:00							
8:00							
9:00							
10:00							
11:00							
12:00 p.m.							
1:00							
2:00							
3:00							
4:00							
5:00							
6:00							
7:00							
8:00							
9:00							
10:00							
11:00							
12:00 a.m.							
1:00							
2:00							
3:00							
4:00							
Total Minutes Actually Worked							
Tasks Completed							

Week 5

Reviewing the Related Literature

Day to Do Task	Week 5 Daily Writing Tasks	Estimated Task Time
Day 1 (Monday?)	Read through page 163 and fill in the boxes on those pages; start documenting your time (page 169)	60 minutes
Day 2 (Tuesday?)	Evaluate your current citations (pages 163–164)	60 minutes
Day 3 (Wednesday?)	Identify and read the related literature (pages 164–167)	8 hours
Day 4 (Thursday?)	Evaluate the related literature (pages 167–168)	60+ minutes
Day 5 (Friday?)	Write or revise your related literature review (page 168)	120+ minutes

Above are the tasks for your fifth week. Make sure to start this week by scheduling when you will write and then tracking the time that you actually spend writing. This week involves a lot of reading, so make sure you allot enough time to do the tasks.

FOURTH WEEK IN REVIEW

You have now spent four weeks working on your article. You have worked on designing a writing plan, finalizing your abstract, developing your argument and threading it throughout your article, and identifying appropriate journals for publication. If you have been writing at least fifteen minutes a day, you are doing great!

If you are still not writing regularly or getting around to all the tasks you had hoped to do—don't feel guilty! Guilt about the past prevents you from action in the present. When you feel bad, it is difficult to get motivated. As a friend once said, you can't hate yourself into changing. Accept that developing good writing habits often takes longer than four weeks. Then shake off those negative feelings and just focus on today. Today is just as good a day to get started as yesterday, and if you are rereading this tomorrow or in a month or a year, today is still a good day to get started. Since this workbook breaks revising an article down into small steps, you have help in setting reachable goals.

No matter what you did this last week, take a minute to write in the chart below a positive message to yourself about writing. In it, be kind to yourself and be hopeful. If this makes you uneasy, remember what Samuel Johnson wisely said, that intellectuals often believe that an "unwillingness to be pleased" is the proof of intelligence. It is "much easier to find reasons for rejecting than embracing," he points out (Johnson 1751). So let the embrace be a triumph over the quotidian. In academia, we tend to deify the hostile and the negative. Dare to be positive! You can also phone or e-mail a friend to do this exercise in dialogue.

Positive Message to Myself about Writing

Last week you learned that many journals need you more than you need them. You studied the various types of academic journals and which types were best for your article. Then you worked on reviewing several journals, both to evaluate their rank and to determine if they would be a good match for the article you are revising. These steps will help you in revising your article for a particular journal. You then worked on a query letter to the editor of prospective journals. If the editors respond, you can determine which journal would be most receptive to your article. This week you will focus on improving your literature review.

READING THE SCHOLARLY LITERATURE

As mentioned, you must relate your research to the previous research in order to be published. Yet, when most scholars think about reading in their field, a wave of anxiety sweeps over them. There is so much to read! With at least 200,000 journal articles published annually, and over 275,000 new books published every year in the United States alone (Bowker 2008),[1] it is impossible to keep up. Even a good reader, someone who manages to read five books a week, week in and week out, will only read 250 books a year or about 10,000 books over a career. Since most read more like one book a week, or 2,000 books total, our ability to read even a fraction of what is published in our discipline is limited. I was in a conference room in the early 1990s when an older professor said he could remember when it was possible to read everything published in his field. A sigh of longing went around the room.

It is essential then to abandon the hope of being comprehensive in your reading. No one is reading everything in his or her discipline. If you stop feeling guilty about what you are not reading, you can start a plan for reading what you can.

When I was a graduate student, I had the great good fortune of landing a job as an abstractor. I worked on a bibliographic project in my field in which I was required to read books and articles and write an abstract about them. Over a three-year period, I abstracted over 2,000 books and articles. I was expected to read each piece and write an abstract about it in twenty minutes. When I started the job, this requirement seemed absolutely insane. Twenty minutes! To "read" a 300-page book? I had taken a speed-reading course in high school, and the job still seemed impossible. By the end of my first year, twenty minutes still seemed too little time, but I now thought thirty minutes would do the job. What changed my mind? I learned what to look for.

When you start graduate school, reading takes a long time. You're lucky to get through a twenty-page article in two hours. Then, when you look at your reading assignments for class, much less for your own research, you can feel discouraged. When you are starting out, you must read slowly because you are still trying to get an understanding of basic concepts and approaches. Fortunately, the more you read, the easier it gets.

As you go along, you should be able to read more and more quickly. Then you will learn to skim. That's what I learned to do as an abstractor. The more I read, the more I learned not to read for elegant language or general information. I learned that what I needed to know from any piece was the same: the topic, the approach, and the argument. That's it. To learn that, I could read the back of the book or jacket flap and the first few pages of the introduction. With an article, I could read the abstract and introduction. Then I could make an informed choice about what to read more thoroughly.

Skimming is easier to do in some fields than others. The structure of science and social science articles are designed for skimming. Humanities articles that announce their project on page ten are not. Still, once you learn the conventions of your field, you can learn to skim almost anything. Once you have skimming skills, you still have a lot to read and absorb. How do you do that?

TYPES OF SCHOLARLY LITERATURE

All published journal articles cite other written materials, loosely known as "the literature." These citations of the literature fall into distinct categories. Knowing these categories can help you think about how to go about reading and citing this literature.

Original literature. These creative or documentary texts are rarely based on other texts; they are sometimes called "primary sources." If you are writing about fiction, novels and poetry would serve as your original literature or primary source; if you are writing about the visual arts, the images; about music, the scores; about architecture, the buildings. For instance, if you are a historian, you usually have many primary sources, from diaries and letters to newspapers and pamphlets. In the social sciences, if you are doing ethnographic or qualitative studies, the original literature consists of the words of your subjects. If you are writing about how women make economic decisions, their own words from interviews or focus groups would be your primary source. If you are analyzing government statistics, the government documents would be your primary sources. Much of what I say in this chapter doesn't apply to reading and writing about original literature. That's because you must engage with your original literature at a deep level; there are no shortcuts.

What is my original or primary literature for this article?	

Derivative literature. These texts for the general public are based on secondary sources (and thus are sometimes called "tertiary literature"). This is the type of literature that tends to fill classroom papers and should *not* be used for journal articles. As an undergraduate, you are expected to list all your sources and so your bibliography will often include general websites, encyclopedia entries, popular magazine articles, almanacs, and textbooks. By the time you are writing for publication, these kinds of citations make up no part of your bibliography. You do not need to include citations of where you found basic information such as the size of a country, the date of a text, the name of a particular year's Nobel-prize winner, the general meaning of a term, and so on. The rule is that if the information appears in many sources, and you are not quoting it directly, you do not need to cite where you found it. Of course, it is always wise to footnote the source of absolutely everything when you are writing, in case any questions arise. You can delete many of these later when submitting for publication (so long as you haven't quoted the derivative source directly). (One note: If you tend to get sucked into the internet looking for basic information like correct spellings or when a person died, it is better to buy and load an electronic encyclopedia onto your hard drive. It is much easier to find information quickly in such sources than on the internet. The *Encyclopedia Britannica* is my favorite.)

One common mistake that students make is citing derivative literature when they should be citing scholarly literature. For instance, you cannot cite *Newsweek* as a source on inflammation and disease, or cite a classroom website as a source for a quote from Julius Wilson. The real source of the information is not in the magazine or website, they are themselves quoting from articles in journals or published books. Derivative literature is never an adequate source for original quotes from scholars or for experimental data. Learn to use the right body of literature for the right purpose.

Contextual literature. These texts have background information on your topic. Students can spend infinite amounts of time on this category of literature. Try to avoid tracking down obscure information about the historical, epochal, geographical, economic, demographic, aesthetic, or political context of your subject. If you are writing an article about Frances Burney's *Evelina*, you may not need to read an entire book about eighteenth-century London. If you are writing an article about risky traditional practices associated with HIV transmission, you may not need to read a book about the biology of disease transmission. Only you can decide what is relevant; just be careful to limit this kind of reading so that you can actually finish your article.

How can I limit my reading of the contextual literature for this article?	

Methodological literature. These texts attack or defend the methodology you are using. If you know your methodology has its challengers, address this upfront by citing scholarly literature that addresses the methodology's shortcomings or strengths. If your methodology is common and accepted, you may not need to read this body of literature. Citations to methodological literature often appear in published articles because peer reviewers questioned the method and the author had to find support for it.

Do I need to cite methodological literature in this article?	

Theoretical literature. These texts supply you with conceptual approaches to your topic (e.g., feminist or queer theory, critical pedagogy, behavioral approaches). Scholars often read this category of literature long before writing any particular article. Your coursework as a graduate student should have introduced you to various theoretical approaches in your field. This early reading often has shaped your general thinking and may have inspired your argument in its first form. Citing these "classics," as they are sometimes called, signals your scholarly camp.

What is my theoretical literature for this article?	

Related literature. These texts are the prior research on your exact topic. As discussed in Week 2, to get published, your research must be demonstrably related to what has been written before on the topic. This is the "related literature." For many students, this point—that they must cite the related literature—is one of the most difficult concepts to grasp. Perhaps this is because a student can write a number of classroom papers without ever being asked to comment on what has already been written on the topic, especially in the humanities. Students know that they are supposed to reference various theories and theoreticians (like Giorgio Agamben, Theodor W. Adorno, or Judith Butler), but they don't always know that they are expected to cite those ordinary beings like themselves who have written on the topic itself. For instance, if you are writing about Stendahl's *Le Rouge et le noir* or the semiconductor industry, you must articulate how your article relates to the arguments of previous scholarly research on that book or industry. If you are writing about the causes of a social problem, you must discuss the research of those who have previously claimed to identify its causes. If you are challenging the premises of a particular policy, you must analyze the previous research on that policy. This week's tasks help you to focus on writing about related literature.

STRATEGIES FOR GETTING READING DONE

If scholars rarely talk about the process of writing, they almost never talk about their process of reading. It seems useful to share some strategies.

Reading Theoretical Literature

If you are in the humanities or interpretive social sciences, don't decide that you are one of those students who "doesn't do theory." Everything is theoretical. Everything you write is influenced by some theory, whether you know it or not. As John Maynard Keynes said some time ago, "Practical men, who believe themselves to be quite exempt from any intellectual influences, are usually the slave of some defunct economist. Madmen in authority, who hear voices in the air, are distilling their frenzy from some academic scribbler of a few years back" (Keynes 1936). So, don't get intimidated. Trust your instinct that quite a bit of theorizing is a case of the emperor's new clothes. Your article doesn't have to be packed with theoretical references; you just need to articulate your theoretical approach to your topic and to display a grasp of that approach. To get this grasp, try the following.

Take theory courses. If you have not read much theory, it is easier to learn the basics orally than to read such texts on your own. Although such courses can seem intimidating and frustrating, try to use the class to focus on what theories would be helpful to you in thinking about your interests.

Read with an expert. Ask to do an independent study with a professor in your field. That way you can read the seminal theoretical works and then discuss them with someone knowledgeable. This will further your understanding of their import.

Read book reviews. Reading book reviews is a great way to keep abreast of your field, theoretical approaches, and the related literature. As one author put it, "book reviews, not books, [are] the principal engines of change in the history of thought." Precisely because they reduce and summarize, they contribute the "distortions" that are essential to the "forward flow" of scholarship (Baker 1991, 64). If you don't have the money to subscribe to periodicals with book reviews, check out the free online book reviews at the H-Net website www.h-net.msu.edu. Many book reviews also appear in online databases as well.

Read biographies of theoreticians. It can be easier to grasp a thinker's ideas in the context of his or her life. Excellent biographies have been written about a number of the important twentieth-century thinkers. Many of them had fascinating lives, so such books can be more leisurely reading, something you dip into as a break from other reading.

Buy and use reference books. Always have on hand some books that summarize important concepts, theories, and terms. Some excellent sources in the humanities are the *Oxford Companion to Philosophy*, *The Norton Anthology of Theory and Criticism*, *Critical Theory Since Plato*, *A Dictionary of Cultural and Critical Theory*, *Critical Terms for Literary Study*, *A Glossary of Literary Terms*, *How to Do Theory*, or *Post-Colonial Studies: The Key Concepts*. Such books have brief, extremely helpful descriptions of important theories. These summaries help you identify theoreticians whose thoughts would be useful to your argument. When you turn to the theoretician's actual work, having read the summaries helps you to understand the original better and more quickly. It is often more important to know what scholars now think about, for example, Durkheim, then what Durkheim actually said or, realistically, what you think Durkheim said. (Unless Durkheim's thought is your whole subject.) The reference books may enable you to go straight to the most relevant pages in the theoretician's work. As a famous theoretician recently admitted, "I'm going to say this officially, so you can use it. I don't care. . . . Do you know that I have not seen a lot of the films that I write about? For example in *Enjoy Your Symptom* there is a long chapter on Rossellini. I haven't seen the films. I tried to, but they are so boring. They're so boring! . . . Now, I will reveal something [else] to you: often I don't have time to read the books about which I write. I will not tell you which ones. More and more (My God! This is a horrible thing to say!) I rely on summaries like *Cliffs Notes*" (Žižek 2003). Believe me, he is not the only one. I'm not holding him up as a model (except of scholarly courage) but as a reminder that we live in the real world, not the ideal one. All professions have Faustian bargains—for many scholars the deal they must strike is between reading and writing.

Subscribe to public intellectual newspapers. One of the best ways to learn theory is to subscribe to newspapers that publish the work of intellectuals. In such forums, scholars often present their theories in shorter form and in language that is more accessible. They also tend to be more open about their feuds with other scholars. Finally, this kind of reading tends to be a lot more fun than most peer-reviewed journals.

One of the best is the *Times Literary Supplement,* a famous British weekly, often called the *TLS*, which reviews important scholarly books. Leading figures in the field usually do its reviews, contextualizing the book theoretically and helping you get a better sense for the placement of the book in the scholarly firmament. A comparable U.S. publication is the *New York Review of Books* (not to be confused with the *New York Times Book Review*), although it tends to have a narrower range of interpretation than *TLS*. Depending on your field or interests, periodicals like *The Nation, The New Yorker, The Atlantic,* or *The New Republic* also have useful book reviews and articles.

An outstanding publication is the *Chronicle of Higher Education,* a weekly newspaper about universities. It includes articles about the business of academia, a list of scholarly books published that week, short articles by scholars about their work, and excerpts from forthcoming books. It also has many first-person articles about the joys and frustrations of being a scholar, often quite funny or moving. You can get an excellent sense for major trends by reading this newspaper. I think it is the most interesting periodical being published in the United States today. If you plan to become a professor, you should consider subscribing or at least read the online version.

Reading Related Literature

Reading the related literature requires slightly different skills than reading the theoretical literature. It usually consists of reading peer-reviewed journals. Here are some tips for doing so.

Set up your bibliographic software. It is a hassle to set up reference management software like Endnote but if you haven't done it yet, you need to do it now. The most frustrating aspect of setting up Endnote is making it actually work with your word processing software. For instance, you must still go into Microsoft Word tools to set up the link to Endnote. If you need help, see if you can get IT support to run a group session helping people in your department load the software on their laptops. Once it is up and running, it will save you time for the rest of your career.

Winnow your reading list. It is easy to drown in the related research. Your article is not your last statement on the subject and should not be comprehensive. Many articles are published that reference just five to ten related articles. Read only those materials that aid you in filling a real gap in your article over those materials that take you in a new and fascinating direction. Using your argument to guide your choices is important. Have a winnowing strategy by eliminating certain categories of materials. Some limiters that scholars use are to set aside those materials written:

- some time ago (e.g., read nothing written over ten years ago, or five or two, depending on your field)

- in another language (e.g., read articles in English and French not Spanish)

- in questionable or nonrecommended publishing outlets (e.g., don't read conference proceedings)

- for journals outside your discipline (e.g., read anthropology journals not sociology journals)

- by certain kinds of authors (e.g., read well-known authors not graduate students)

- on a different geographical area (e.g., read articles on West Africa not Southern Africa)

- on a different context (e.g., read articles on public hospitals not private hospitals)

- or a different time period (e.g., read articles about the nineteenth century not the eighteenth century)

- about different kinds of experiments (e.g., read quantitative studies not qualitative studies)

- about different kinds of participants (e.g., read studies of the elderly not teenagers)

- using different variables (e.g., read studies of age and gender, not age and race)

- without your keyword in the title or abstract (e.g., read only those articles with your keyword)

- in nonelectronic formats (e.g., read only those articles electronically accessible in full from your home computer)

I am not insisting that you use any of these particular methods of winnowing (the last one in particular is problematic). Many a scholar has gotten famous by ignoring such limits and deciding to review a category of related literature that no one else had looked at closely, like that in other languages or in dissertations. So, the choice is up to you. Just acknowledge from the outset that you cannot read everything. Have a strategy for reading rather than embarking on reading 300 articles and books in the next week and then reading only the first three on the list, which may not be relevant.

Make reading social. Start a journal club that meets once a week or once a month, and have each person report on an article that he or she read. That way you share the work. Often, you will learn more from the discussion of the article than you would by just reading it.

Schedule library reading. In scientific disciplines, graduate students were regularly given the advice to spend Friday afternoons in the periodical section of their university library. Building journal reading into your weekly schedule is an excellent idea regardless of your discipline. It keeps you up-to-date on trends and names and enables you to hold fruitful conversations with others in your field. Concentrate on those issues with articles of direct interest.

Get tables of contents by e-mail. Sign up to receive the publishers' announcements of the contents of relevant journals by e-mail or RSS feed so you can easily find relevant articles.

Subscribe to peer-reviewed journals. If you can afford it, subscribe to the main journals in your field. They will be there in your house with you, ready in handy form. While many of the articles may not be directly relevant, knowing what scholars in your field are addressing is important. If you plan to submit your article to a particular journal, it is useful to subscribe to it first. One or two apt references to articles published in the journal recently can be helpful in tilting the editor's decision toward you (the reviewers will not notice). Leading journals often have great book reviews as well.

Read the newest material first. It is frustrating to read several older books on a topic and then read the most recent book, because the most recent book often summarizes the previous ones, reviews them, and offers the best way forward. You can always go back to the older books, but it's best to start with the newest so that you don't waste time taking notes on ideas that have been dismissed or improved upon.

Limit note taking. When students start out, they find themselves using their notes to reproduce the articles they read. That's because everything about the article seems relevant, not to mention intimidatingly smart and well-thought-out. You copy down every sentence that seems particularly well put. By the time you are done taking notes, you could give a conference presentation on each article. At most, you will have space in your 5,000- to 15,000-word article for a quote or two, or maybe just one reference, from this source. Most of those words need to be your own words. Having dozens of great quotes can be an obstacle to writing an article about what you think. So, remember, when reading you aren't looking for quotes, you are looking for debates and arguments.

Don't wait to write. A student once confessed in my class that she had spent a year reading intensively, hours every day, and taking copious notes. At the end of the year, she sat down to write, picking up the notes from her first text. Unfortunately, she could not make heads or tails of her notes. She had put exclamation marks next to quotes she no longer understood the import of, and her self-admonitions were now nonsense to her (e.g., "I have no idea what I meant by my note 'make sure to address agency in this context'"). "I wish," she said, "that I had started writing at the beginning and inserted material where it seemed relevant. If I had written up just a paragraph on each text, something about what I found important about the text and how it related to my argument I would be a farther ahead. I have enough for ten books here." It is best to try to read a bit, write up what is relevant, and then read some more and write some more.

Some Famous Reading Habits

It is interesting to learn about the reading habits of productive scholars.

Henry A. Giroux is famous for forwarding critical pedagogy and writing synthesizing articles in the discipline of education. In an interview, he described his reading process. "When I first started writing, I used to put everything down on cards, file them, and then go over them when trying to write. This method failed miserably for me because by the time I finished my research I could barely remember what I had read initially, and simply rereading a number of cards loaded with various ideas just did not prove useful to me. The method I developed over thirty years ago and still use today seemed to solve the problem of working with a short memory and trying to engage a great deal of information and sources in order to do justice to any particular topic. Here's how it works. Whenever I read something, I mark off in the text those paragraphs that contain important organizing ideas. I might circle a paragraph and write an organizing idea in the margins. When I finish the piece, I copy it and go through a cut-and-paste procedure in which I type out the source on the top of a piece of paper, type in the organizing ideas from the piece (article, chapter, and so on), and place the paragraph underneath its respective organizing idea. Hence I may read a twenty-page piece by, let's say, Fred Jameson. In that piece, I may find fifteen sections that I have marked as important. I then reference the piece, type out the organizing ideas starting with the order in which I read the piece. I then paste the respective paragraphs under the typed heading. In the end, I may end up with a four-page cut-out of Jameson's piece. I then duplicate it so I can have a clean copy and I file the original. When my research is done, I read all of the cut-and-paste articles, one by one, and I write next to each paragraph in each article an organizing idea. I then type out a cover sheet listing all of the organizing ideas for each working article. I then paste all of the cover sheets on artist boards and try to figure out from reading the sheets how I might develop my arguments. The method really works for me. Moreover, I file everything that I cut and paste, and when necessary I can go back and read my notes and familiarize myself with any number of issues, traditions, or theoretical concerns in a short period of time. I must say, though, that after using this method for over twenty-five years, I have more notes than I can possibly ever read" (Giroux 2003, 102–103). His former student Peter McLaren well remembers Giroux's process of reading, writing comments in the margin, typing, cutting sources to just one page each, and then posting those pages around his writing station to read while he wrote.

Edward O. Wilson is a Pulitzer-prize winning Harvard sociobiologist and public intellectual famous for trying to integrate the sciences and the humanities. He has a publication list of over twenty books, including *The Ants* (1990) and *The Future of Life* (2002), and over four-hundred journal articles, many of which have each been cited in thousands of other journals and books. His reading method is that he subscribes to sixty journals, from the *New York Review of Books* to *Proceedings of the Entomological Society of Belgium*. He spends his mornings reading whichever journals arrived the previous day and taking notes. He then goes to one of his favorite restaurants for lunch and spends two hours writing at one of the tables. Since he is retired, he now takes the afternoons off (Ringle 1998).

Klaus Herding is a now retired German art historian who spent some time doing research at the Getty Museum in Los Angeles. An art history graduate student I know remembers Herding reading five books every morning. He arrived at work at 7:00 a.m. and read until about 10:30 a.m. That's about forty-five minutes per book. He did this to keep up with the literature and to find valuable references for his own work. He claimed that the routine of it was so familiar that he could actually read quite a bit and retain much of it. Perhaps it is not surprising that over his career he published more than 250 scholarly articles and books.

Even if you never read as much as these three successful scholars, you can learn from their principles of reading: reduce articles to their essence, read and write in the same day, subscribe to journals, and learn to skim.

IDENTIFYING YOUR RELATIONSHIP TO THE RELATED LITERATURE

Once you have embarked on reading the related literature, then what? How do you cite prior scholarship? You need to start by identifying your general relationship to the related literature and then continue by evaluating that literature. Establishing your relationship to previous arguments in the related literature doesn't have to take much space—in your introduction it can be just a sentence or paragraph.

What's Your Entry Point?

Two scholars usefully call your argument's relationship to previous arguments your "entry point," your way into the ongoing scholarly conversation on a topic (Parker and Riley 1995). If you imagine your article as entering into a conversation, it makes perfect sense that you wouldn't just walk into a room and start talking about your own ideas. If there were people already in the room, you would listen to them for a while first. If you decided to speak, you would do so because you agreed or disagreed with something someone else said. If the conversation went on for a long time without addressing some topic dear to you, you might say, "I notice that we haven't talked about such and such yet." In all cases, you would acknowledge the conversation and then make your point.

A useful aspect of this conversation analogy is that it focuses your mind on argument. You wouldn't walk into a room and portentously announce descriptive information (e.g., *Midnight's Children* was published in 1981 or South African elections were held in 1994). Everyone in the room already knows this basic information. Such statements aren't argumentative. Remember, an argument is something you can coherently respond to by saying, "I agree" or "I disagree." You enter into the conversation by supporting an argument, debating an argument, or announcing that an argument needs to be made. Therefore, your entry point is where your argument enters the debate occurring in the previous research on the topic.

Let's look at some examples in published articles of authors announcing their relationship to previous research, their entry point.

- Specialists in communication have called for additional research into traditionally accepted rhetorical strategies. [*Extending past research is a traditional entry point.*] We do research on Grice's theory of indirection. [*You are providing that additional research.*] We conclude Grice's theory of indirection is adequate for explaining how bad news is delivered and understood.[2] [*Your Argument.*]

- [The capital asset pricing model is] still the preferred model for classroom use in MBA and other managerial finance courses. [*Questioning a policy or practice is a traditional entry point.*] [While] econometricians have empirically rejected its predictions and financial theorists have criticized its restrictive assumptions, . . . no one to our knowledge has studied [the capital asset pricing model] in an evolutionary framework.[3] [*Filling a gap in the literature is a traditional entry point.*]

- Textbooks warn writers to avoid the passive voice, but actual scientific texts commonly feature such discourse. [*Addressing a contradiction is a traditional entry point.*] We have conducted a study on when scientific writers chose the passive voice in order to provide guidance for other writers.[4] [*You are solving the contradiction.*]

- Conventional assimilation theory has begun to be disputed for the children of recent immigrants. [*Weighing in one side of a debate is a traditional entry point.*] We look at how retaining an immigrant culture affects education. [*You are providing data for the question of whether conventional assimilation theory should be disputed.*] Retaining an immigrant culture, rather than assimilating into the dominant one, increases educational success.[5] [*Argument.*]

- Although educational attainment levels have improved somewhat, Latino students continue to enter school later, leave school earlier, and receive proportionately fewer high school diplomas and college degrees than other Americans. [*Addressing a social failure is a traditional entry point.*] We are interested in showing how changing social relationships, activities, and structures within the high school and university could raise Latino students' eligibility for UC admission.[6] [*You are offering a solution to the problem of low Latino educational attainment.*]

All of these entry points can be reduced to three traditional positions you can have regarding the previous research:

- finding it inadequate or nonexistent and filling the gap,

- finding it sound and extending it, and

- finding it unsound and correcting it.

Since articles often depend on several bodies of research, sometimes all three of these positions coexist in the same article. Let's look at these three positions more closely.

Addressing a gap in previous research. Identifying a gap (or more than one) in the literature and setting out to fill it is one of the most common endeavors of journal articles. It is also a strong claim for significance. Just be sure that your claim is correct if you say that very few scholars have addressed your topic, or no scholar has addressed your topic in quite your way. I have seen peer reviewers send more than one submission back to an author with the literature gap claim crossed through and a list of published works penned next to it. Also, if no one has written on the topic before, or in quite your way, you may have to prove to the reader that the topic or approach is important. That is, the reader may suspect that the gap is there for a reason. Below are some examples in published articles of author positioning based on a gap in the literature.

Humanities:

- Little attention has been paid to those texts that do not circulate primarily within identified feminist circles or feminist cultures, but which are located at the point of feminism's perceived entry into the public written discourse of the mainstream or of those in power. . . . Paying attention to such texts . . . has profound consequences.[7]

Social Sciences:

- A key to sustainable resource planning is effective implementation of management plans. Despite its obvious significance, planning implementation remains a relatively neglected area of planning research . . . The purpose of this article is to help address this gap in the literature by reporting results of a case study evaluation of a regional land and resource management plan in British Columbia, Canada.[8]

Extending previous research. Approving of and using other scholars' theories to analyze new subjects is also a common scholarly position. Thus, naming authors or articles you find useful is part of positioning yourself vis-à-vis the previous research. This can be as simple as identifying the school, movement, or tradition your research participates in. For instance, stating that your work is "psychoanalytic," or using the word "postcolonial," positions you as part of a stream of research. Below are some examples of authors positioning themselves positively vis-à-vis previous research.

Humanities:

- What I propose is a theory of interpretation based on what I refer to as the 'simultaneity of discourse,' a term inspired by Barbara Smith's seminal work on black feminist criticism.[9]

- In my search for a methodological device for a critical inquiry into Third World films, I have drawn upon the historical works of this ardent proponent of liberation [Frantz Fanon], whose analysis of the steps of the genealogy of Third World culture can also be used as a critical framework for the study of Third World films.[10]

- I situate my own reading of the rape in *A Passage to India* within the current effort of feminist theory to account for the heterogeneous text of women's history.[11]

Social Sciences:

- If it is taken seriously, this result confirms the theory of Li and Lui (2004) that a [state-owned enterprise] SOE with comparatively worse performance than an average private firm is more likely to privatize, lending supports to the efficiency hypothesis. However, since the significance level is low and the regression for privately controlled firms does not provide a significant result, this conclusion should be accepted with care.[12]

- The paper examines the impact of financial sector liberalization (FSL) policies on the financial management of small and medium-sized enterprises (SME) in Ghana, using six case studies. Its findings, which confirm and extend the conclusions of previous studies, are integrated into a framework that explains the impact of FSL and the factors at work.[13]

Correcting previous research. Another traditional position is stating that scholarly approaches to a subject are erroneous and that your article will overturn such misconceptions. For graduate students, this is often the most tempting position. And it can even be the right one. Just be sure to give credit where credit is due, to keep your tone collegial, and to acknowledge how others' work enables your work. Note the careful way in which the authors below announce their intentions vis-à-vis the previous research. They often speak about offering a contrasting or alternate opinion rather than an outright rebuttal.

Humanities:

- I hope to be able to interrogate some of the impressive claims made for [Rudyard Kipling's] *Kim* . . . In doing so, I am aware that I am reading somewhat against the critical consensus on *Kim*.[14]

- Spanish American literature has been studied mostly through the thematic or biographical approach . . . However interesting these approaches may be . . . they have not been very helpful, for instance, in evaluating the intrinsically aesthetic merits of a work.[15]

Social Sciences:

- Although many argue that conflict is a result of group solidarity, psychological research finds strikingly little evidence that this is true. Some research even finds that more cohesive groups are more likely to employ cooperative strategies in prisoners' dilemma situations . . . Overall, the preponderance of evidence suggests that, as argued here, situations of intergroup conflict can promote the cohesion of the groups involved, though not in all situations.[16]

What's my entry point? Do I state it clearly? Do I show how my argument relates to previous arguments?	

It can be that you have multiple entry points—you are addressing a gap in one body of literature, correcting some assumptions of another body of literature, and agreeing with a third body of literature.

What Is a Related Literature Review?

Above, I asserted the importance of positioning your article vis-à-vis the previous research, of articulating your entry point into the scholarly conversation. This can sometimes be done quite briefly; for instance, by stating something as simple as "no research has been done on Chicana labor in Boyle Heights factories; this article fills that gap." But what if there is a lot of literature on your topic? Or what if you disagree with what little has been written? Or what if you think that another body of research entirely can help us think about your topic? Then you must write what's called a related literature review.

For many students, the related literature review is one of the most difficult parts of the article to write. It is easy to air one's own ideas; it is not always easy to summarize and evaluate others' usefully. Related literature reviews vary so much from published article to published article that it can be difficult to determine what the common elements to such reviews are. Sometimes a literature review makes up the entire content of the article, sometimes just a paragraph.

A related literature review is an evaluation of the existing scholarship on your topic or significant to your topic. If your entry point is stating how your argument relates to previous arguments, a related literature review is an evaluative summary of those previous arguments. The literature review notes the previous research's relationships, limitations, problematic interpretations, inadequate approaches, and so on. The literature review is used to establish the significance and origin of your argument, to defend your approach or methodology, and to show your relationship to what has come before. It is a typical part of many articles' introductions.

One of the best ways to think about writing a related literature review is to imagine yourself telling a colleague about a debate you overheard. You report who participated in the debate (and sometimes who didn't), who took what side, who was most convincing to you, who the least. Then you note what would make an argument more convincing, points that weren't made, or points that could be better made with other evidence. If you hope to keep your colleague interested, you will not give a he-said, she-said version of the debate. It is not useful to anyone to reproduce verbatim all the statements made in the debate. What is useful is to summarize and evaluate it.

In a book, and especially in a dissertation, the related literature review is often exhaustive. No related book is left unturned. In an article, however, you must be more efficient. You cannot individually summarize every article and book written on the topic. You also can't list all the information to be gleaned from them. At the same time, you cannot just provide a list of titles and call it a related literature review. In writing a related literature review for an article, you must focus on evaluating the existing literature with your argument firmly in mind. This allows you to select and group the related research into sides of a debate and then review each side rather than working your way through each piece.

So, for instance, if you are writing about race and *Wuthering Heights*, you would note which of the most famous texts on *Wuthering Heights* do not address race, and then summarize the strengths and weaknesses of the racial analysis of those that did. You might divide the later into two groups, those that address gender as well and those that don't. This is one example of how a related literature review would go. It can be very helpful for you to study the related literature reviews in your field.

Many articles require more than one related literature review, as they are efforts to integrate information from various fields. For instance, if you are writing about Vietnamese immigration to the United States, you may need to review political science research about Vietnamese national politics, history research about U.S. immigration policy, and anthropological research about the living situation of Vietnamese immigrants in the United States. If you are writing about Latino educational attainment in Los Angeles, you might review the research explaining attainment and the research on Latinos in Los Angeles.

Of course, much of your analysis of this research might appear throughout the article and not just in the introduction, but the introduction is a good point to give a broad overview. In the humanities, you are not required to cite the related literature as much as in the social sciences. But, published articles are always based on a knowledge about what other scholars say, whether the articles actually cite other literature on the topic or don't.

An example of a literature review in the humanities is a review of the scholarship about Samuel Johnson's first play, *Irene*.

> Almost two hundred years later, D. Nichol Smith and E. L. McAdam kindled critical interest with their 1941 edition of Johnson's poetry. Though Smith's introduction to *Irene* is uncritical, his blanket dismissal of literary indebtedness sparked Betrand Bronson's 1944 essay, "Johnson's 'Irene.'" Comparing the play to other dramatic versions, Bronson says that Johnson robbed Irene of tragic appeal and made Aspasia the heroine: "The exigencies of the dramatist are irreconcilable with the requirements of the Christian moralist." Likewise Leopold Damrosch concludes: "Johnson the moralist has overwhelmed Johnson the tragedian."
>
> Some bold critics, however, have attempted to rescue the play from naïve and uninteresting dramatics. Philip Clayton argues its success as a neoclassic drama, and Marshall Waingrow insists that the moral question is not simple. In his enthusiasm to find Johnson always a shrewd and compassionate moralist, Waingrow contends that the play focuses on an issue larger and more subtle than apostasy: the inextricable link between vice and virtue. Thus, he can maintain that Irene is the legitimate heroine who betters Aspasia's advice. Waingrow misses the mark. He strains the evidence to claim complexity for what is an unseasoned Johnson's biased and unimaginative moral lesson.[17]

Below is an example of the type of very short related literature review one often sees in humanities articles.

> A work of *Gyn/Ecology's* scope and passionate intensity can hardly fail to generate controversy. Mary Daly has been criticized for promoting a racist rhetoric, for abrogating the right of third world

women to determine the analysis of their own culture and their own oppression, and for minimizing the material conditions of women's lives. I agree with those criticisms, but my concern in this article is a much more limited one. I want to discuss some aspects of Mary Daly's poetics (her theory and practice as a writer); take up the connection made by Laleen Jayamanne between the politics of Daly's writing and her relationship to romanticism; and then make a couple of comparisons between *Gyn/Ecology* and the work of Luce Irigaray, another feminist for whom work in and with language is of prime political importance.[18]

An example of a literature review in the interpretive social sciences appears in an article about how couples view images of romance and marriage in film. The literature review is organized by the scholarly debate.

Such questions go to the heart of a continuing debate about whether global media and culture industries deny opportunities for those who constitute "the masses" to experience "authentic" emotions and culture. For some theorists, the very existence of modern information technologies has resulted in an ordering of social relations that denies alternatives to the ruling-class hegemony, and "technology and technological consciousness have themselves produced a new phenomenon in the shape of a uniform and debased 'mass culture' which aborts and silences criticism" (Bottomore in Jenks, 1993: 109). For others, the media are instead viewed as vehicles for "reinforcing" prior dispositions, not cultivating "escapism" or passivity, but capable of satisfying a great diversity of "uses and gratifications"; not instruments of a levelling of culture, but of its democratization (Morley, 1995: 299) . . .

At issue here is the conceptualization of 'domination' or 'influence' on the one hand, and 'resistance' on the other. Yet on both sides of the debate, there is a continuing assumption that media texts—at least potentially—have a direct effect on their audiences, and that audiences have direct relationships with those texts. I intend to propose an alternative means of understanding the audience-text relationship . . . Rather than assuming that media texts influence their audiences, or that audiences resist the messages of media texts, is it possible to consider the case that both audiences and texts are subject to the influence of a cultural logic of the 'romantic'?[19]

An example of an efficient related literature review appears in a qualitative article about educational achievement. It is not organized according to a scholarly debate, but to expose a gap in the literature.

The success of high achieving Black undergraduates often draws great praise; however, research on Black collegians has focused primarily on those who experience academic difficulty. Although it is critical to comprehend the experience of Black students who struggle academically, it is also imperative to gain an understanding of the within-group differences between Black students. Black high achievers are typical college students in many ways; yet, the issues of Black students and gifted students can come together to shape their experiences in unique ways (Fries-Britt, 1997, 2000; Lindstrom & Van Sant, 1986; Noldon & Sedlacek, 1996, 1998; Smedley, Myers, & Harrell, 1993). The existing literature on Black high achievers reveals that they often face such challenges as subtle and overt racism; reconciling their racial, ethnic, cultural, and gifted identities; and social isolation (e.g., Cooley, Cornell, & Lee, 1991; Fries-Britt, 1997, 1998, 2000; Fries-Britt & Turner, 2001; Person & Christensen, 1996; Solorzano, Allen, & Carroll, 2002; Steele, 1999). These experiences can limit these students' achievement and diminish their motivation. Scholars have discussed the important role that social support structures, such as engagement with other Black students, mentoring, and interactions with faculty, play in helping students overcome negative experiences and obstacles to success (Bonner, 2001; Fries-Britt, 1997, 1998; Freeman, 1999; Noldon & Sedlacek). However, although the literature discusses barriers that Black high achievers face and the role that social support plays in mitigating the impact of these factors, there is less understanding of what pushes these students to continue to strive for academic excellence and pursue their goals despite these challenges.[20]

These four examples from published articles reveal much about what makes for strong related literature reviews. Study your field for examples of how literature review is done in your field.

Common Mistakes in Citing the Literature

Don't cite one source too much. If you cite one article or book throughout your article, or repeatedly in reference to your argument, peer reviewers may suspect that your work is derivative. Don't depend on one secondary source for more than one or two paragraphs at most. Most published articles have twenty to a hundred citations to contextual, methodological, theoretical, and related literature. For instance, a scholar studying disciplinary variation found that the average sociology article included 104 citations while the average philosophy article included 85 (Hyland 2004, 24). If a particular text is your original literature, or the primary source you are studying, you can, of course, reference it repeatedly, but if you cite any other kind of text repeatedly, you will need to make clear that you are not depending on it for the majority of your data or argument.

Don't cite irrelevant literature. If you cite literature that isn't directly related to your topic, peer reviewers can dismiss your article as digressive. For instance, if you are analyzing an educational experiment in which undergraduates do real field research, do not spend half the article discussing various theories of field research.

Don't overcite definitions. Classroom essays can devote pages to scholars' definition of various terms. Publishable articles don't. It takes a sentence and maybe a footnote to define most terms. Few articles are published that simply dispute other scholars' definitions.

Don't misattribute. If you attribute general beliefs or entire systems of thought to one person, peer reviewers can dismiss your article as unscholarly. For instance, you cannot state in passing that "Howard Winant discovered that race is a socially constructed phenomenon." Thousands have argued for the social construction of identity. At most you could write, "Sociologists since Durkheim have argued that social interaction makes reality; Howard Winant was instrumental in calling attention to the constructed nature of race."

Don't cite the citation. If you cite a scholar's articulation of another scholar's idea, peer reviewers can dismiss your article as unscholarly. That is, don't state, "I am using John Doe's definition of globalization" when Doe is using Arjun Appadurai's definition of globalization. Take the time to find the original definition or articulation of an idea and cite it. Likewise, if Brian Edwards (2007) discusses "what Edward Said called 'traveling theory,'" don't cite Edwards on "traveling theory," cite Said. Just because you found out in Edwards' article that this idea belongs to Said, doesn't mean you have to cite Edwards. It means you must read and cite Said.

Don't cite asides. If you cite as related literature those articles that don't fully address the debate you are engaging in, peer reviewers can dismiss your article as unscholarly. For instance, several articles have been written about "the age of circulation." Don't cite an article for this theory that has only a sentence or two on "the age of circulation." Students who have only read assigned reading for the classroom often make the mistake of using only what has been assigned. Take the time to find articles and books that are devoted to the topic.

Don't cite the derivative. If you cite websites or newspapers as the source of your information about important scholarly arguments and debates, peer reviewers can dismiss your article as unscholarly. For instance, don't base your article on a definition of modernism from an online site about an exhibit at the Tate Gallery in London, even if it is a really good quote. (It can serve as a primary source, just not a secondary source. That is, you can discuss the exhibit definition if you are studying exhibitions or curators.) Don't cite U.S. demographic data from any source but the census (it's easy to find online). Use scholarly sources.

Don't quote too much. Your job is to summarize and evaluate the related literature, not reproduce it. If you have too many quotes, especially block quotes, you are probably not digesting the related literature enough.[21] The literature review should not take up half of your article.

Don't omit citations. If you use the phrases "scholars argue that" or "research shows that," you should always include citations to those scholars' publications or that research. Most editors will not accept vague references to scholarly trends without citations of actual publications.

Note to Periphery Scholars

What can you do as a scholar if you don't have access to the related literature? Scholars in many parts of Africa, Asia, and Latin America do not have access to good libraries or online archives. You have some available tactics, however. First, I have found that scholars often have better access than they think they do. If you have access to the internet, be sure to use Google Scholar and other free services to search for related literature. If you find something that looks interesting, you can often find the author's e-mail address online as well, and e-mail him or her to request a copy of their article. This may even start a helpful conversation, and they may be able to provide other materials. They may be able to identify for you some of the current debates as well. It is the obligation of those scholars in resource-rich environments to aid those who are not. Second, address your limited access directly in cover letters to the editor. Tell the editors that you think you have good data, but you don't have access to the related literature. If the editors like the article, they may also be helpful. Some editors are aware of the difficulties periphery scholars labor under and sometimes want to help. Just do your best to cite at least two articles published in the previous two years.

AVOIDING PLAGIARISM

It can often be difficult to find other scholars with whom you can have frank conversations about plagiarism. The topic is so hot that most professors avoid discussing it except in warnings to their undergraduates. Unfortunately, the blanket advice given to undergraduates cannot always guide you as a person embarking on publication.

Before turning to better advice, let me give the usual warning. We are entering a brave new world where all the documents ever published are going to be available for crosschecking, and the day is coming when many published authors are going to be exposed for their borrowing of others' work. Some of this has already started happening; see the special report on the topic in the *Chronicle of Higher Education* (Bartlett and Smallwood 2004). New websites like Turnitin.com make it possible to check any article for plagiarism in seconds. Plagiarizing is no longer a lottery game where it is unlikely that your name will ever be picked. It is now an absolute that you will be caught. So, it is extremely important to get in the habit of citing others with care.

If you think that you will be able to defend your borrowing practice, be warned that deans and the general public are not impressed with the following defenses: "I have an excellent memory; I had no idea that I was repeating that work verbatim" or "I feel so bad; I'm such a sloppy note-taker!" or "The pastiche approach is an acceptable postmodern methodology" or "In my culture, this is accepted practice." The issue is so charged that little you say will be seen as anything but an expression of guilt. You may not lose your job or student status, but rumors may follow you for the rest of your career.

If you are a conscientious scholar, all these warnings will make you anxious. They make me anxious! I wrote this workbook over ten years—what if something I incorrectly copied eight years ago comes back to haunt me? But, such anxiety isn't really helpful. The very fact that you bought this book and have worked hard enough to reach this chapter is an excellent sign that you are unlikely to commit plagiarism with any deliberateness. Still, you may wonder, am I unknowingly committing some academic sin? It is easy to remain uncertain about where citation ends and plagiarism begins. Most students know the basic rules.

- Never take another's entire article (published or unpublished) and represent it as your own.

- Never take an entire article and vary every fourth or fifth word and claim it as your own.

- Never take an entire article and follow the structure and argument of the piece, exactly paralleling the author's train of thought but not quite in his or her language.

- Never take an article, translate it into another language, and claim it as your own.

- Never lift a page or section word for word from another's piece and place it in your own.

- Never lift various paragraphs word for word from another piece and sprinkle them throughout your own.

- Never lift a paragraph or a sentence word for word from another's piece and place it in your own unless you put quote marks around it and add a citation to the original.

If you avoid all of the above, you will never lose a job or your reputation due to accusations of plagiarism.

However, there remains a gray area that is often not emphasized in undergraduate courses: be careful when paraphrasing. Some types of paraphrasing are also considered plagiarism. It is not always enough to paraphrase someone else's work and cite the original. If your wording is too close to their wording, it may be problematic, despite the citation. If you stay too close to one paragraph from one source in one article, you are unlikely to be chased out of the profession. If you do this repeatedly from the same source, you are definitely plagiarizing and can be called to account.

This issue of paraphrase plagiarism is covered in the excellent undergraduate text *The Craft of Research*. The authors give a paragraph verbatim and then show various examples of paraphrasing it that are problematic. Whenever I show their "borderline plagiarism" example to graduate students, half the class exclaims, "Oh my God! I've plagiarized."

Here are the examples, taken directly from *The Craft of Research* (Booth, Colomb, and Williams 1995, 169):

Original Sentence: It is trickier to define plagiarism when you summarize and paraphrase. They are not the same, but they blend so seamlessly that you may not even be aware when you are drifting from summary into paraphrase, then across the line into plagiarism. No matter your intention, close paraphrase may count as plagiarism, even when you cite the source.

Plagiarized Version: It is harder to describe plagiarism when summary and paraphrase are involved, because they differ, their boundaries blur, and a writer may not know that she has crossed the boundary from summary to paraphrase and from paraphrase to plagiarism. Regardless of intention, a close paraphrase is plagiarism, even when the source is cited. This paragraph, for instance, would count as plagiarism of that one (Booth, Colomb, and Williams, 169).

Borderline Plagiarized Version: Because it is difficult to distinguish the border between summary and paraphrase, a writer can drift dangerously close to plagiarism without knowing it, even when the writer cites a source and never meant to plagiarize. Many might consider this paragraph a paraphrase that crosses the line (Booth, Colomb, and Williams, 169).

Correctly Summarized Version: According to Booth, Colomb, and Williams, writers sometimes plagiarize unconsciously because they think they are summarizing, when in fact they are closely paraphrasing, an act that counts as plagiarism, even when done unintentionally and sources are cited (169).

Although it is a common practice for students to do what is done above—take a couple sentences from someone else's work, then cut them a bit, vary a few of the words so there is no need for quote marks, and then put a footnote citing the original—this is borderline plagiarizing. If you are doing this repeatedly throughout your article, stop and revise. If you are just doing it occasionally from different sources, I wouldn't obsess about it. Just remember that you want to use your own language as much as possible. As the professor of health sciences Dr. David Hayes-Bautista always says, never do anything that you wouldn't want broadcast on the front page of your local newspaper.

To avoid plagiarizing, here are some helpful tips.

- When reading something useful in another text, try setting that text down and typing what you remember it to have said. Taking notes from memory like this can be a good way to avoid putting things exactly as they did. If you have an excellent memory, this may not work—be sure to check your notes against the original and confirm that they are not too close.

- Take notes in such a way that it is always clear which are your comments on the text and which are quotes or paraphrases from the text. Some have the habit, when taking notes, of always putting their own thoughts or commentary in brackets. I know someone who, when typing notes, uses all capitals for his own thoughts. That way, you know exactly what is taken directly from the text, whether paraphrased or in quote marks.

- Always revise. Any author who is carefully going over every sentence in his or her piece—seeking for ways to improve diction, sentence structure, clarity, and flow—is unlikely to have chunks of others' work remain. Even if a paragraph entered the article wholesale from somewhere else, its integrity won't survive a real revision process. Whenever I see cases of an author getting in trouble for publishing an article that includes word for word paragraphs from others' work, I always find it striking because they clearly aren't revising their work. What kind of author leaves whole paragraphs of their work untouched? The problem with such an author is deeper than merely borrowing.

WRITING ABOUT OTHERS' RESEARCH

Many of us have been reading and writing about research for a number of years. It is still possible to learn a few new techniques for doing this thoroughly and efficiently, however.

Day 1: Reading the Workbook

On the first day of your writing week, you should read the workbook up to this page and answer all the questions posed in the workbook up to this point.

Day 2: Evaluating Your Current Citations

Your first step in identifying how much reading you have left to do is evaluating your existing citations. Use the form below to evaluate whether your article has enough citations of the right type.

	Number of Citations?	More (or less) Citations Needed?	Topics that Need More Citations
Original Literature			
Derivative Literature			
Contextual Literature			
Methodological Literature			
Theoretical Literature			
Related Literature			
What percentage of my article is the literature review? Is it too long? Is it too short?			

After filling out this form, ask yourself some hard questions. How much derivative literature do you cite? (It should be zero or close to zero.) Do you cite any related literature? Is your contextual literature or methodological literature taking over the article? What kinds of citations do you need more of? Usually, you need to increase the number of related literature citations.

Day 3: Identifying and Reading the Related Literature

If you have already read the related literature, congratulations! This week is going to be a lot easier. If you haven't, as is often the case, you have some work to do. Your main aim with this article is to attempt to be thorough without bogging down. You are not trying to be comprehensive. Many of us find that starting to read articles is like entering the forest of no return. We just keep going deeper and deeper and getting more and more lost and eventually forgetting the destination we were trying to reach in the first place. I have constructed the following steps to help you in dipping into the related literature but not getting lost in it.

It is extremely important to be realistic about how much you can read. Even if you can read (and understand) a page a minute, that is 60 pages an hour or 240 pages in an afternoon or evening. You can still only read ten books in a packed forty-hour week. Very few people are reading forty hours a week or a page per minute. In the following exercise, you are going to work on skimming materials, rather than reading them, but you should still end up with a manageable final reading list of only about a dozen materials.

Ask. Ask those in your field what they recommend you read on the topic. What do they consider essential reading and what can be safely skipped? You can also ask a reference librarian for assistance in this task. Many librarians wish more scholars asked them for assistance in finding references, so don't be shy.

Search. First, you need to identify what has been published on your topic. In doing so, you follow much the same techniques as you used to find a suitable journal. Do an electronic search of several article and book databases, do a shelf search, and check the bibliographies of the books and articles you used most in writing your article. Since material is always being added to databases, you might want to do an electronic search using the keywords most closely related to your article even if you did one just six months ago.

Draft a reading list. Once you have done these tasks, collate a list of materials that you intend to skim for their usefulness. Do not spend a lot of time typing this list up, organizing it alphabetically, or otherwise massaging it. It is only a step, not a destination.

How many articles and books did I find on my topic?	

Winnow your reading list. Examine your list of unread references and start doing triage, based on the title and, if you have it, the abstract. Since you cannot read all of the materials you have identified, you must decide which ones you are going to read. See the earlier section on winnowing lists.

How do I intend to winnow my reading list?	

Be especially careful to vet the texts recommended by colleagues. When asked for reading recommendations, some scholars seem to treat this as a memory game in which the more titles they remember, the higher their score. You are more interested in relevance than their recall. If you examine lists of oral recommendations, they are not always closely related to your research. Also, colleagues often insist that you read books that they enjoyed reading, however off topic, "just for general insight." Feel free to read such works; just don't put them on your list of related literature. They are not related. If you end up with a list of more than ten articles and five books, review your list closely. Also, although professors are usually in the business of telling you to read more, more, more, they can sometimes respond well to the request for help in limiting article topics and research. If you started by asking the professor what to read, you might also ask the professor to prioritize that list.

Finalize your reading list. Once you have winnowed the list down, you should prioritize those remaining. You should organize the reading list in order from the most important to least important, so that if you are interrupted, you have been reading to effect. For instance, you may want to prioritize bibliographic articles by reading them first. Dissertations often have great reviews of the related literature. You should end up with no more than two dozen materials on your list. Even if you can read (and understand) a page a minute, reading twenty-four articles of about twenty pages each is eight hours of work.

What materials remain on my reading list?	(On a separate page, print out a list by author and date. Include library call numbers where relevant.)

Skim the identified materials. Since most of us can do research until the cows come home, try to limit this task. It's good to do this task under slightly uncomfortable circumstances. This keeps you focused on skimming, not reading. For instance, do this skimming at the library rather than in the comfort of your own home. One technique I find very effective is to skim articles while standing up in the stacks where I find the journal. In this position, you simply cannot fall into actually reading the article. If you take a pen and note cards, you can write down the citation and its main argument right there, standing. Another technique is to use the book index to focus on the most relevant pages. Remember, you are in the library merely to learn if the materials you have chosen to review are going to be helpful. Since most of us read articles online now, it can be very difficult to limit this type of reading effectively.

Do not, I repeat, *do not* get involved in skimming for future articles or research. Do not get distracted into thinking up completely new directions for your article. You have one purpose in being at the library: to find materials that are going to speed you on your way to sending your article to a journal in twelve weeks.

If, while skimming, you find some articles or books that are going to be helpful to you in revising the article, download the article or photocopy the relevant sections and take them home. Always make sure to photocopy the copyright page so you have all the bibliographic data. Again, don't download or photocopy more than five to ten such articles. If you have more, you won't read them.

You can read the few related sources you have selected in several ways.

Take notes sparingly. Do not seek to "represent" the sources in your notes. You do not have to write a book report on the book or article. You just need to identify the article's argument and which side of various debates it is on. If you can use your note-taking to start writing up your related literature review, all the better. That is, start writing up sentences about the source: "This article argues that . . . The author takes the side of . . . A weakness of this article is . . ." If you can do miniature book reviews of the book, evaluating not summarizing, that can also help.

Highlight. If the source is your own copy or book, you can read it and put pencil check marks in the margin next to useful material. You can put one check mark next to material that you find interesting, two check marks next to material that would be useful, and three check marks next to material you absolutely must include in your article. When you are done reading the book and placing your checkmarks, sit down at your computer and take notes on the material where you put three check marks. I find that, when I am reading, all sorts of things interest me and get check marks, but when I go back through, only the three check marks really matter, and a review of the two check marks shows only some of them are relevant. It's a way of tricking my perfectionist impulses. If you do this, be sure to type up your notes within a day or two of reading the material so you can remember why you checkmarked what you did.

Read and insert. Another technique is to sit down at your computer with your photocopies or electronic sources and open an electronic version of your article. Start reading the related literature, and when you come to entirely relevant material—such as the argument or a review of a scholarly debate—immediately turn to your article and add a sentence in the paragraph to which it relates. Be sure to include the reference. If you are not exactly sure how to incorporate the material into your article at a certain point, put it in a footnote. It may become clearer later how you can move this information up into the text. Most of the time, you end up deleting such material so don't add too much. The concept here is that note taking can involve you too much in the other person's thought and not enough in your own. If you have to figure out immediately where in your article the information fits, then you are forced to evaluate it realistically.

Day 4: Evaluating the Related Literature

Now that you have read the related literature, what have you found about the relationships between various articles and scholars? How are previous scholars justifying their arguments, claiming novelty, acknowledging debts, displaying allegiances, and signaling disciplinary communities? How are their arguments similar? Where do they differ? What is known and what remains to be known? What variables have been established as important, and which haven't been explored yet? How are key concepts or theories getting defined or used? What are the limitations or blind spots of this literature? Is there a narrative? Using these questions, start grouping the texts by argument and debate.

Day 5: Writing or Revising Your Related Literature Review

The best way to start thinking about writing or revising a related literature review is to read those that other scholars have written. Since you have spent this week reading articles, go back and study one or two of their related literature reviews. How did they organize it? How many articles did they cite? What proportion of the article is devoted to the literature review? Such study will guide you as you are writing your own. Some like to organize their literature review chronologically—here is what we used to think, now we think differently. Some like to organize alphabetically—by author's last name. It is best, however, to organize the literature review by the debate. That will help you avoid just summarizing instead of evaluating. As Howard Becker (1986) warns in his chapter titled "Terrorized by the Literature" (still one of the best works on citing scholarly literature), "Use the literature, don't let it use you." You can also consult the undergraduate text *They Say, I Say*, which gives detailed examples of how to relate your ideas to others (Graff and Birkenstein 2005). Just remember that your argument should be organizing your related literature review; don't let the literature take over. Spend this day writing or revising your related literature review. When done, you can ask a friend of colleague to read it and let you know if you have been clear about the debate, the related literature, and your entry point.

DOCUMENTING YOUR WRITING TIME AND TASKS

On the following weekly plan, please graph when you expect to write and what tasks you hope to accomplish this week. Then keep track of what you actually did. Remember, you are to allot fifteen minutes to one hour every day to writing. At the end of the week, take pride in your accomplishments and evaluate whether any patterns need changing.

Time	Monday	Tuesday	Wednesday	Thursday	Friday	Saturday	Sunday
5:00 a.m.							
6:00							
7:00							
8:00							
9:00							
10:00							
11:00							
12:00 p.m.							
1:00							
2:00							
3:00							
4:00							
5:00							
6:00							
7:00							
8:00							
9:00							
10:00							
11:00							
12:00 a.m.							
1:00							
2:00							
3:00							
4:00							
Total Minutes Actually Worked							
Tasks Completed							

Week 6

Strengthening Your Structure

Day to Do Task	Week 6 Daily Writing Tasks	Estimated Task Time
Day 1 (Monday?)	Read through page 185 and fill in the boxes on those pages; start documenting your time (page 187)	30 minutes
Day 2 (Tuesday?)	Outline a model article (page 185)	60 minutes
Day 3 (Wednesday?)	Outline your article (page 186)	60 minutes
Day 4 (Thursday?)	Restructure your article (page 186)	60 minutes
Day 5 (Friday?)	Restructure your article (page 186)	60 minutes

Above are the tasks for your sixth week. Some articles need a lot of restructuring; other articles will be fine. Start this week by scheduling when you will write and then tracking the time that you actually spend writing.

FIFTH WEEK IN REVIEW

You have now spent five weeks working on establishing a writing schedule, revising your argument, selecting the right journal, and reviewing the related literature. By this week, you should be in the groove, writing away, making progress, getting closer to done. But, that may not be happening. Instead, you may be wondering about your ability to convert my writing advice into better writing. Maybe the problem isn't you! Maybe the problem is that this workbook divides an organic process up into steps. The workbook posits a rigid structure, unlike real writing.

As Peter Elbow puts it, writing is not a "two-step process" where you get ideas and then write them down and then are done. Rather "writing is an organic, developmental process" (Elbow 1973, 15). You can't really start with argument and move to structure. And you can't write one right word and then another right word and then another right word. Rather you have to feel your way forward. As Elbow comments,

> The common model of writing I grew up with preaches control. It tells me to think first, make up my mind what I really mean, figure out ahead of time where I am going, have a plan, an outline, don't dither, don't be ambiguous, be stern with myself, don't let things get out of hand. As I begin to try to follow this advice, I experience a sense of satisfaction and control: 'I'm going to be in charge of this thing and keep out of any swamps!' Yet almost always my main experience ends up one of *not* being in control, feeling stuck, feeling lost, trying to write something and never succeeding. Helplessness and passivity. The developmental model, on the other hand, preaches, in a sense, *lack* of control: don't worry about knowing what you mean or what you intend ahead of time; you don't need a plan or an outline, let things get out of hand, let things wander and digress. Though this approach makes for initial panic, my overall experience with it is increased control. (Elbow 1973, 32–33)

If the rigidity of the workbook order is throwing you off, try revisiting some of the previous chapters, opening up the electronic file of your article, and working on whatever attracts your attention given that review of the previous chapters. On the other hand, if the workbook order is helping you, keep going! This week, you'll focus on improving the overall structure of your article.

ON THE IMPORTANCE OF STRUCTURE

Structure is the organization of your argument and the evidence for your argument. When each part of your article leads logically to the next part, you have a coherent structure.

You can think of structure as the skeleton of your article: invisible but essential. Without a skeleton, you have a collapsed biomass. With a skeleton, you have a living, breathing, moving entity. With a structure, your article can support the weight of its own ideas.

A strong article structure is important to both you and your readers. Since regular patterns aid readability, readers can more easily grasp the ideas in a structured article than a disorganized one. The research shows that people read a structured article faster and remember more of it (Meyer 2003). Regular patterns also aid *your* thought. Organizing your ideas helps you to understand them better and their connections to each other. Yet, revising your article for structure can be the most difficult revision you do.

> My experience, particularly with long projects, is that how well the middle works depends on the structure. Beginnings often go smoothly because of the initial inspiration and enthusiasm. Endings may exist as a goal to work toward. But the middle of a long work needs strong structural elements to support its weight.

The deepest level of revision is to make or discover the structure, the central order of a work, and this often cannot be done until the work is well underway. (Willis 1993, 156)

Adhering rigidly to a plan you made in the beginning may not work. Revising requires an ability to be flexible. When I am teaching my course, this week is when students will make some of the most drastic changes to their work: moving paragraphs, cutting cases, throwing out whole sections. Your structure can improve dramatically if you are willing to entertain the possibilities for revising deep structure.

Unfortunately, since many of us write on computers, it can be easy to lose the thread, a sense for the whole. Seeing just part of a paragraph doesn't help you keep the overall structure in mind. That's why you may need to develop some techniques to keep your grasp of the whole and ensure the parts of your text are properly linked.

TYPES OF STRUCTURES

Article structure occurs both at the level of the whole article and within each paragraph. Studying these different structures—micro and macro—may aid you in thinking about your article's best structure.

Micro Structure

Scholars argue that there are five basic organizational structures and that journal articles use them in combination (Meyer et al. 1989, 115–116; Meyer, Brandt, and Bluth 1980, 16, 72–103). When they train students to recognize these basic structures, their reading and retention improves, so they can aid us in understanding paragraph structure. The structures are:

Description. A structure organized by information about a topic (e.g., introduction section; who, what, where, when). Signals of this structure are "for example," "such as," or "that is."

Sequence. A structure organized by sequential order, most often chronological or procedural (e.g., background section, histories, experiments). Signals of this structure are "before," "after," or "more recently."

Causation. A structure organized by cause and effect relationships (e.g., results section). Signals of this structure are "because," "thus," or "therefore."

Problem/solution. A structure organized by a problem and a solution, it asks a question and answers it (e.g., discussion section). Signals of this structure are "argues that," "proposes," "responds."

Comparison. A structure organized by the differences and similarities among things (e.g., literature review). Signals of this structure are "in contrast," "instead," "on the other hand."

Knowing these structural types doesn't necessarily help you to know which organizational principle you should use when, however. Some principles that scholars recommend when structuring information are:

- Go from what your readers know to what they don't know. That is, start with the familiar.

- Go from the simple to the complex. Get your reader comfortable before introducing the difficult.

- Go from the uncontested to the more contested. Readers who have been convinced to believe one thing may more easily believe the next.

- Go from the general to the particular. Start with the large picture and then focus in on details.

- Go chronologically from the past to the present. (This common structure is not always the best one for your particular argument and evidence.)

- Go spatially through a succession of linked objects, as if on a guided tour. This works particular well for art history, geography, and so on.

But what about the macro structure of the journal article? What comes first and then second usually? How do journal articles usually end?

Macro Structure

The journal article has some rhetorical features that have persisted for thousands of years. The Greeks long ago contended that you should start a public speech with an introduction that attracts the audience (called an exordium) and follow this with background on the topic or issue. You then should propose your claim or argument, provide evidence for your argument, and refute potential criticisms of your argument. Finally, you should articulate a moving conclusion, often some kind of call to arms (called a peroration).

This ancient structure persists in the topic, thesis, evidence, and conclusion structure of most scientific articles. It also persists in the essay that many undergraduates are taught to write: set the context (who, what, where, when); introduce your argument (why, how); provide three proofs; and conclude and/or recommend.

In the humanities, a slight variation on this structure is proposing and proving successive arguments through the article. The article depends on making a series of arguments, each argument enabled by proving the previous argument.

In nonscientific writing, there have been some real alterations to the Greek structure. Since you are unconsciously aware of the conventions of these structures, they may cause you some problems in the structuring of your article. For instance, a classic newspaper article does not circle round or wrap up. It starts with a lead that answers at least one of the six basic journalistic questions: who, what, where, when, why, or how. For instance, "Former President Clinton [who] told one of the nation's largest Latino civil rights groups [where] Saturday [when] that the conservative wing of the Republican Party is using the immigration issue to divide Congress and the nation [what]" (Rabin 2006). Such an article then proceeds with a pyramid structure, in which the most important information appears first and the least important information last. (For instance, the Clinton article ended with comments by the California governor Arnold Schwarzenegger, comments that were related to Clinton's speech but not from it.) This pyramid structure emerges from a past technological limitation. Before publishers had computers, such a structure allowed editors to cut the article from the bottom up and fit it into the space that was available.

Another variant structure from the Greek model is in magazine article writing, which has a type of article called a "feature." Such articles start with a "billboard," an anecdotal narrative that captures the reader's attention, about one to three paragraphs long. This anecdote is followed by a "lede," a sentence that announces the articles' argument. This sentence is the pivot of the article, guiding readers in reading the rest of the article. The conclusion then refers back to the billboard. For instance, a feature will start with a story about Johnny, whose mother noticed that he was gaining weight and urinating more than usual. When she took him to the doctor, she found out that he had juvenile diabetes. The lede will then state that millions of children have undiagnosed juvenile diabetes, the argument that the anecdote illustrates. Often the feature will conclude with a return to the anecdote, in this case that Johnny is feeling better.

In addition to these common structures, we experience new forms every day. For instance, blogs have particular structures, often loose in style but chronological. Knowing the multiplicity of writing structures can help you write better journal articles, since it helps you prevent other structures from creeping into your academic writing.

Returning to journal article structure, some disciplines have more rigorous structures than others. The sciences have absolute formulas, the humanities have quite loose ones. Those in the sciences sometimes wish that their discipline's structural requirements were less rigid; those in the humanities sometimes wish that they had simple formulaic structures they could follow. The good news is that you can improve your writing by knowing the structuring principles of journal articles in various disciplines.

ARTICLE STRUCTURES IN THE SOCIAL SCIENCES AND HUMANITIES

Let's start with social science article structures and then move on to humanities article structures. Each of the three kinds of social science articles—quantitative, qualitative, and interpretive—has a different typical structure. Quantitative articles are the most scientific in their structure. Qualitative articles can have the same structure as quantitative articles, but they often don't. Interpretive social science articles are similar to humanities articles.

Quantitative Social Science Article Structure

Quantitative articles often follow what is called IMRD, an acronym for the order of the article's sections: Introduction, Methods, Results, and Discussion. This type of article moves from why and how the scholars got the results to what the results mean. Each section has specific formats organized around the research question. Here is a bit more detail on that structure.

Section One—pyramid structure, general to specific
- Introduction—general subject of investigation (often a problem)
- Review of the literature—literature on the subject of investigation (gaps and lacks)
- Statement of the hypothesis—your argument in the context of other work

Section Two—Description of study, all information needed to replicate study
- Methods
- Procedures
- Materials and Instruments
- Experiment
- Context and Setting
- Population

Section Three—inverse pyramid structure, specific to general
- Results—report on findings
- Discussion—comment on validity of methods and findings
- Conclusions—place research into the context of other work

Works Cited

Below is an example of the structure of an actual quantitative article, selected precisely because it is ordinary rather than spectacular. The article was about 3,000 words.

Sleep Habits, Prevalence, and Burden of Sleep Disturbances Among Japanese Graduate Students (Pallos et al 2004)

  I. Abstract

 II. Introduction (2 paragraphs, no subheads)

    A. Sleep disorder is a common problem.

    B. Sleep disorder among graduate students is rarely studied.

    C. The purpose of this study is to:

      1. estimate rates of sleep disturbance among graduate students in Japan

      2. determine if these sleep disturbances have an adverse affect

      3. find if affected students seek help from physicians

III. Methods (5 paragraphs, 3 subheads)

    A. Study design and subjects

      1. dates of study

      2. setting of study

        3. population studied

        4. survey implementation and analysis

    B. Questionnaires

        1. their use of the Pittsburgh Sleep Quality Index (PSQI)

        2. the questions they asked about sleep

        3. the questions they asked about demographics

        4. the questions they asked about attitudes and consequences

    C. Statistical analysis

IV. Results (4 paragraphs, 4 subheads)

    A. Sample characteristics

        1. states the number of respondents and their gender

    B. Prevalence rates of sleep disturbances and hypnotic medication use

        1. table of rates

        2. rate findings

        3. no significant differences in rates found between the genders

    C. Sleeping characteristics of graduate students

        1. table of characteristics

        2. findings

        3. no significant differences in characteristics found between the genders

    D. Consultation rate and the adverse consequences of sleep problems

        1. rate findings

        2. consequences findings

V. Discussion (6 paragraphs, no subheads)

    A. The purpose of the study was to learn the rate of sleep disturbances among Japanese graduate students.

    B. Why were these students less sleepy than others their age?

        1. prevalence rates were similar to what other researchers found

        2. except regarding gender (speculation on why that might be)

        3. perhaps students were less sleepy than other young adults because they might be taking naps

    C. Why aren't these students consulting doctors about sleep disturbance?

        1. sleep medications were not used much, perhaps because students did not consult doctors about the problem

        2. why didn't students consult doctors?

        3. further research should investigate this lack of consultation

    D. Literature review of related studies

        1. literature review of studies on undergraduate students' sleep habits shows similar findings to these findings on graduate students

        2. limitations of the study

        3. conclusion: hypothesis rejected: graduate students do not suffer more frequently from sleep disturbances than does the general Japanese young adult population.

Qualitative Social Science Article Structure

Qualitative article structure can vary quite a bit. Only dedicated study of articles in your own field can reveal typical article structures.

One of my students who studied linguistics articles found some standardization among articles in her field, which tended to be thirty to thirty-five pages in length with abstracts of 150–250 words. They had short introductions followed by literature reviews of three to five pages reviewing approximately forty to fifty citations. After a short methods section, they proceeded to the analysis or discussion, which typically took up about 75 percent of the article and was organized around the debate announced in the literature review. Another student did the same for articles in her field of anthropology. She found that, contrary to my advice, articles in her field devoted half their space to reviewing the literature and related theories. Most had literature reviews at least eight pages long and reviewed several different bodies of literature. Many of the articles also had about two paragraphs of background on the field site and population. Just as she did, you should test my advice by studying the norms of articles in your particular field.

Two scholars have formally studied articles in applied linguistics, finding that they often stray from the IMRD structure. For instance, they often include sections after the introduction that address the theoretical background, the related literature, or background information (Ruiying and Allison 2004). Applied linguistics articles also often had a section before the conclusion on the pedagogical implications of the research. The body of applied linguistics articles were taken up with argumentation, but of three different types. One body type was oriented toward theory, pursuing a series of sub-arguments. Another type had a problem-solution format. The last type had a problem-solution format but added a component on the application of the solution. I mention these variations in applied linguistics as just one example of variation from the ostensibly universal rules for social science articles.

Below is an example of the structure of an actual qualitative article. It demonstrates that no article follows the typical structure exactly—it must be altered to accommodate the particular data and findings. Something this article does brilliantly is organize the results or findings by theme, rather than dumping a stream of data on readers. Identifying patterns in the data and then creating and presenting a typology is a helpful way to organize a results or discussion section.

Changing Women: An Ethnographic Study of Homeless Mothers and Popular Education (Rivera 2003)

    I. Introduction (3 paragraphs)

        A. Context

            1. Who, what, where when. "Between 1995 and 1998, I studied the impact of popular education on a group of fifty homeless and formerly homeless mothers who participated in a shelter-based adult literacy program located in one of Boston's poorest neighborhoods."

            2. Background. "The popular education classes . . . were . . ."

B. Argument
    1. "The purpose of this article is to examine how the homeless mothers were affected by their participation in the popular education program at the Family Shelter. Based on my observations, I argue that the Family Shelter's popular education philosophy and the provision of comprehensive social services addressed the women's personal, academic, and community needs. I argue that popular education had a positive impact on the lives of the homeless mothers that extended beyond learning important reading and numeracy skills."

II. Methodology (how and when data collected) (2 paragraphs)
III. Profile of Sample (description of women in the study) (3 paragraphs)
IV. Theoretical Framework
    A. What is Popular Education? (7 paragraphs)
        1. History in U.S.
        2. Roots in Brazil
        3. Review of Freire's thought
        4. History of the specific shelter in this study
    B. Studies on the Impact of Popular Education (2 paragraphs)
        1. Literature review
        2. How her research relates to the literature

V. Findings
    A. First question: "Why do the Women Return to School?" (9 paragraphs)
    B. Second question: "What Are the Benefits of Popular Education?" (narratives about women and quotes from them)
        1. "I Have More Self-Esteem" that is, "participation in adult literacy education has a positive impact on adult learners' self-esteem" (3 paragraphs)
        2. "So You Teach Somebody Else" that is, the women "began to develop a community of support within the context of their popular education classes" (8 paragraphs)
        3. "It Gave Me a Backbone" that is, the women "increased [their desire] to address the root causes of problems and they often talked about changing 'the system'" (4 paragraphs)
        4. "We Sit Down and Do Homework. They Do Theirs, I Do Mine" that is, "Popular education strengthened the women's ability to advocate for their children's education" (5 paragraphs)

VI. Outcomes (what happened to the women later?) (5 paragraphs)
VII. Implications of the Study (4 paragraphs)
    A. Positive change. "Through a process of collective sharing and reflection, the homeless mothers in this study began to 'act upon the world,' challenging their internalized oppressions and understanding how structural forces shaped and constrained their lives"

    B. Possible problems. "The impact of 'work-first' welfare reform legislation on popular education programs"
    C. Policy implications. "As Congress prepares to reauthorize the Personal Responsibility and Work Opportunity Act, it should increase access to education . . . Indeed, the time is ripe for change."

Humanities Article Structure

Precisely because the structure of humanities articles can vary so much, it is difficult to give specific advice about how to structure such an article. Humanities articles proceed differently than in the social sciences, in that discussion occurs continuously, not just at the end of the article. The author presents a piece of evidence (usually a quote or observation about the text), interprets that evidence, suggests how that evidence supports the argument, and repeats this process until satisfied that the argument is convincing. Humanities articles start with an introduction to the subject or problem, discuss critical approaches, apply the approach to the subject, speculate on the implications, and conclude that the subject or approach has been validated. Here is a bit more detail on that structure.

I. Introduction
    A. Vivid context: who, what, why, where, when
    B. Review of the scholarly debate and/or general perception of the text
    C. Statement of author's argument relevant to context, debate, and perceptions (your new insight)
    D. Claim for the significance of the subject, approach, or argument
    E. Summary of article structure and points

II. Body
    A. Background (e.g., description, history)
    B. Analysis 1
        1. Subject of analysis 1 (e.g., book, artwork, event)
        2. Subject subjected to argument
        3. What was discovered, found, concluded
    C. Analysis 2
        1. Subject of analysis 2
        2. Subject subjected to argument
        3. What was discovered, found, concluded
    D. Analysis 3
        1. Subject of analysis 3
        2. Subject subjected to argument
        3. What was discovered, found, concluded

III. Summary (how all subjects, discoveries, and argument relate)

IV. Conclusion
    A. Why these discoveries are fascinating
    B. Why this article is a contribution to the scholarly debate and/or a contribution to the field

Below is an example of the structure of an actual humanities article. It follows the classic writing advice to detail an example (in this case a text) and then analyze and interpret the example. One strength of this article is the way it moves forward and summarizes at the same time, with regular reminders to the reader of what is at stake and what has been found so far.

'Indians': Textualism, Morality, and the Problem of History (Tompkins 1986)

I. Introduction (3 pages)
  A. Anecdote
  C. Problem: how to teach a nonracist history?
  D. Primary sources announced
  E. Theory being tested (poststructuralism)
  F. Problem with the theory
  G. Argument suggested
II. Body: Textual Analysis/Close Reading
  A. Modern history books
    1. Perry Miller's book analyzed (1964) (2 pages)
    2. Alden Vaughan's book analyzed (2 pages)
    3. Francis Jennings's book analyzed
    4. Summary sentence of analysis so far
    5. Calvin Martin's book analyzed (2 pages)
    6. Charles Hudson's book analyzed (2 pages)
    7. Summary of analysis so far
    8. Problem restated in relation to what has been found
  B. Captivity narratives and their analysis
    1. James Axtell's book analyzed
    2. Norman Heard's book analyzed
    3. Mary Rowlandson's book analyzed
    4. Summary of analysis so far
    5. Problem restated in relation to what has been found
  C. Seventeenth-century histories
    1. William Wood's book analyzed
    2. Alexander Whitaker's book analyzed
    3. Robert Berkhofer's book analyzed
    4. Karen Kuperman's book analyzed
    5. Summary of analysis so far
III. Results/Summary
  A. What to do with these conflicting accounts?
  B. Summary of analysis
  C. The problem restated in relation to what has been found
IV. Discussion/Solution
  A. The original problem was not formulated properly.
  B. This failure is due to the failure of poststructuralism.

C.   Argument stated: That facts are embedded in particular ways of seeing the world is not an argument against facts.

D.   Solution for teaching history: "If the accounts don't fit together neatly, that is not a reason for rejecting them all in favor of a metadiscourse about epistemology."

Synaptic Article Structure

Over the years that I have taught my writing workshop, a contingent of students has argued against rigid article structures. They insist that some published articles are not so argument driven but instead pose a question, move through a process of discovery, and reveal an answer only in the conclusion (if then). Such articles proceed with merely the promise of an answer or with only a provisional argument that cannot be understood until the piece has been read through. Argument is not a structure but a plot, these students say, a seductive puzzle that foments critical desire and depends on a perhaps endlessly deferred closure. I call such articles "synaptic," since they proceed by sparking readers' imaginations, lighting synapses up like fireworks with a series of epiphanies. Synaptic articles are often highly theoretical; Homi Bhaba and Judith Butler are masters of the form. The Tompkins article outlined above borders on synaptic, since it only fully announces the argument, or finding, in the final paragraphs. However, her article is extremely clear, while most synaptic articles revel in obscurity.

In warning students against writing endless plot summary, rehearsing others' theory, or stringing together tiny insights without any organizing principle, perhaps I *am* prohibiting the development of more sophisticated, intuitive, and open articles. It's worth discussing synaptic articles with those in your field to find out how such articles do in the peer-review process and whether they can be successful. They are certainly more difficult to write well. The Achilles heel of the synaptic article is organization; it is easy for readers to get lost in the maze or miss the payoff. If you are dedicated to this style, study the best examples of the type.

SOLVING STRUCTURAL PROBLEMS

The literary scholar Richard D. Altick once said that the sentences and paragraphs of your article "should fit as tightly as the teeth of a zipper" (1963, 188). This is a useful image. Each sentence is connected to the next— non sequitors and digressions are absent. Such sentence connections aid the whole article in being more unified and coherent. So do logical connections between paragraphs. What can you do to improve the structure of your article at the paragraph and article level?

Use subheads. Subheads help you the author, and your reader. One study showed that teaching college students to use descriptive headings in their writing resulted in a "marked improvement" in their article's organization, source use, and argument (Murphy 1998; Moore 2006). Other studies have found that readers do better when a text is organized and that organization is clearly signaled (Meyer 2003). Some useful signals of structure are headings and subheadings. Visible cues to structure are particularly helpful in getting reviewers to look on your article favorably. That is, even if you haven't succeeded in doing what you set out to do, your general project comes across more clearly, and they can push you to do what you promised rather than rejecting you.

Could I use more subheads? Where?	

Use summary. Peter Elbow advises writers to make "lots of summings up" (Elbow 1973, 35). He's right. Studies have found that preview statements, summary statements, and pointer words are useful signals of structure that aid the reader (Meyer 2003). If you don't like summaries, then you may have been reading bad ones. Good summaries move the article forward by articulating the argument and providing strong links between what has been said and what will be said. Good summaries are not simplistic, verbatim restatements.

Could I use more summarizing? Where?	

Do not use a discovery structure. Just because your precious insights took forever to arrive at, doesn't mean you should force us through your process. Only rarely will an article structured by the order in which you discovered the evidence provide a strong and satisfying structure. An order derived from the order in which you retrieved evidence from memory is unlikely to work well either. Such orders will most likely seem random to the reader. That's why it is best to start in the data collection stage to organize your notes and evidence by theme and topic. Then your structure can emerge from the beginning.

Do not use the mystery novel structure. Many students love the mystery novel format. They believe that readers will stop reading if told the argument too early, so they withhold it. Such students want to reach the last sentence of their article and then reveal, "the butler did it." Yet, readers are far more likely to read your article if they have a good sense of where it is going. Further, an article that announces the argument early and summarizes what is coming is more democratic and less controlling. Knowing the destination, the reader follows the evidence more carefully, evaluating at each stage if the evidence supports the argument. Such a structure enables the reader to be a fellow investigator instead of a passive observer waiting for the mystery to be solved. Most of all, students who withhold their article's purpose, import, or conclusions until the end of the article often have very tortured structures. They have to avoid being clear so that the mystery is sustained. Nothing is more likely to help you structure your article properly than to avoid mystery. If you are committed to the mystery structure, remember that the best mysteries give lots of clues so that the revelation is not a surprise.

Do I use a discovery or mystery structure? If so, what better structure could I use?	

Present evidence second. Many problems with structure arise from the author's failure to relate the particular, usually evidence or proofs, to the general, usually the theory or argument. We should learn no fact without knowing how it relates to your argument. Present codifying information first, evidence second. Don't give a close reading without making clear why you are doing the close reading. Don't provide a paragraph in the conclusion that shows us for the first time the meaning of everything that came before. As the late Guillermo E. Hernández used to say to me, "Remember, you don't eat a cake the way you make a cake." When you make a cake, the frosting arrives last; when you eat a cake, the frosting arrives first. We, the readers, want the richest part first.

Do I introduce evidence properly?	

Organize around your argument. Unlike a book or chapter, your article must be carefully organized around a single significant idea. Make sure each section and paragraph relates to your single significant idea. If it doesn't, delete it. Align your insights around your main point. Don't fall into the trap of letting your data organize your article. We should get a sense for your argument in the title, see it clearly in the abstract, again in the introduction, at least once in each section of the article, and clearly in the conclusion. If you can do this organically, simply by logical flow, great. If not, feel free to provide lots of road signs.

Stay on topic. Everyone knows that you shouldn't digress, but not everyone is ruthless about identifying what is relevant and what isn't. For instance, an article about drug use among homeless teenagers should not have long passages about teen pregnancy. Teen pregnancy is indirectly, not directly, related. Likewise, if your article is on mining metaphors in a certain body of literary texts and the word "mining" does not appear in nearly every paragraph, the article is not staying on topic.

Does my main topic or argument appear in every paragraph? If not, should I include it more?	

Develop the examples evenly. The article should be balanced between sections. Case studies don't have to be exactly the same length, but they need to be balanced. Your examples are not evenly developed if, for instance, in an article about drug use among homeless teenagers, you (1) address heroin use at length, detailing its use among homeless teens, its impact, and their comments about heroin, and then (2) include very little about ecstasy, but (3) proceed to discuss the history of marijuana in the Unites States as well as its use and impact among homeless teens. You have covered the first example more carefully, more in depth than the second. Heroin, ecstasy, and marijuana use among homeless teenagers should be covered with the same depth. The last example is not about drug use at all. You may need to cut some sections entirely if you cannot develop them to the same level as the others.

Could I develop my examples more evenly? Where?	

REVISING YOUR STRUCTURE

Day 1: Reading the Workbook

On the first day of your writing week, you should read the workbook up to this page and answer all the questions posed in the workbook up to this point.

Day 2: Outlining a Model Article

Return to the model article you examined in Week 1—the article that does well what you want to do in your article. Using the outline examples above, make an outline of the model article. Underline the subheadings and topic sentences that you find. Write up a summarizing sentence next to each paragraph. What do you find about how the article is put together? Are there parts that surprised you by being shorter or longer than you thought they would be? Are there more or less citations then you thought there would be? What are the implications of the model article for yours? If you have the time, study the structure of a number of articles in your field. You only have to do this once and it will help you for years.

Day 3: Outlining Your Article

Using the examples of outlines above, make an outline of your article as it stands. Many students have found this the most useful exercise in my whole course, so don't skip it. One way to do this is to print out your article, underline the subheadings and topic sentences that you find, and then use those to start constructing an outline. Another way is to write a summary phrase or sentence next to each paragraph, and then use those to construct an outline. When creating the outline, use numbered headings so that you can show the relationship among the various parts of your article.

Once you put an outline together, read through it. Do the parts follow logically? Does one paragraph lead to the next? Did you digress? Did you say enough on a topic? Have some of your methods wandered into the results section? If you find this outlining difficult to do, it may be because your article lacks a structure. If paragraphs are poorly constructed and contain discordant ideas, they are hard to outline.

The post-outline, as I call this, is a good step to do any time you feel like you are starting to lose control of the article. If you start to feel frustrated by the article, outlining it can help you feel calmer, more certain about the way forward.

If you are more visual than verbal, you might want to draw a map of your article. You can use words or symbols to represent the ideas in your article and their relationships to each other. This can help you to identify your topic or narrow it, especially if you feel like language sometimes traps you. You can also do a traditional outline, but the map can be more flexible, allowing you to see in more directions and notice omitted material.

If you found a number of problems in making the outline of your article, start a new outline of the article as you would like it to be. Revise the outline so that it reflects the article you would like to write. Indicate where you would add codifying information, subtract digressions, or move argument up.

Days 4 and 5: Restructuring Your Article

Now that you have a new outline, start restructuring your article around that new outline. If your article already had a solid structure, make whatever few changes are necessary.

DOCUMENTING YOUR WRITING TIME AND TASKS

On the following weekly plan, please graph when you expect to write and what tasks you hope to accomplish this week. Then keep track of what you actually did. Remember, you are to allot fifteen minutes to one hour every day to writing. At the end of the week, take pride in your accomplishments and evaluate whether any patterns need changing.

Time	Monday	Tuesday	Wednesday	Thursday	Friday	Saturday	Sunday
Week 6 Calendar							
5:00 a.m.							
6:00							
7:00							
8:00							
9:00							
10:00							
11:00							
12:00 p.m.							
1:00							
2:00							
3:00							
4:00							
5:00							
6:00							
7:00							
8:00							
9:00							
10:00							
11:00							
12:00 a.m.							
1:00							
2:00							
3:00							
4:00							
Total Minutes Actually Worked							
Tasks Completed							

Week 7

Presenting Your Evidence

Day to Do Task	Week 7 Daily Writing Tasks	Estimated Task Time
Day 1 (Monday?)	Read through page 199 and fill in the boxes on those pages; start documenting your time (page 200)	30 minutes
Day 2 (Tuesday?)	Discuss evidence with colleagues (page 199)	60 minutes
Day 3 (Wednesday?)	Revisit your evidence (page 199)	60 minutes
Day 4 (Thursday?)	Shape your evidence around your argument (page 199)	60 minutes
Day 5 (Friday?)	Shape your evidence around your argument (page 199)	60 minutes

Above are the tasks for your seventh week. Keep track of how long each task takes you on the weekly calendar provided at the end of the chapter.

SIXTH WEEK IN REVIEW

You have now spent six weeks working on your article. You have reached the halfway mark! It isn't easy doing such concentrated work, so congratulate yourself.

As Arthur L. Stinchcombe noted years ago, "The crucial peculiarity of research is that one has to choose an objective for oneself, and motivate oneself by that objective alone. . . . This means that only a person's own conviction that the result will be worthwhile is available as a motivation. [This] . . . is a weak reed to sustain . . . drudgery" (Stinchcombe 1986, 271–281).

In response to this drudgery, one of the readers of my monthly micro newsletter *Flourish* came up with an incentive system she called the "sexy dress fund." She e-mailed me that,

> Now that I am writing all the time, I'm feeling very unsexy because
> all I wear is sweats. So the idea of ever wearing a dress again, let

alone a sexy one, feels like a nice thing. Every day before I officially begin my writing, I break my work for the day into a series of smaller tasks. They are generally tasks I think I can accomplish within 30 to 60 minutes, or 90 at the most. For example, 'read a section of my chapter draft and make editorial notes.' Or, if I have the notes done, then, 'rewrite a section.'

I then estimate the amount of time it should take and set a kitchen timer (I occasionally cheat and add in an extra one or two minutes as a cushion). If I finish within the allotted time, I give myself a dollar. I have a beautiful wood antique box, and I physically put the dollar in each time I meet my deadline. I still belt out a cheer every time I make it. While the money I have now will only buy me a Barbie doll size dress, I anticipate that the fund will grow over time (even though I did not earn a single dollar today!)

One of the big benefits of this system is that it forces me to gain a more accurate understanding of how much time I need for certain tasks. It has convinced me that I have been working as fast as I possibly can, which is *very slow*. But this system has convinced me that this slowness is an integral part of how my mind works—and so I'm more willing to accept that now. I would previously beat myself up for being slow. And of course, the anxiety about my slowness made me even slower. I think that by accepting my slowness, I have actually become quicker!

So, if you are still searching for your incentive, now may be the time to think up a fund that might work for you.

TYPES OF EVIDENCE

This week I will give you the least amount of advice and the most amount of work. That's because it is easier to advise you how to have an argument and structure your article around your argument than advise you on how to select and present the evidence for your argument. The main body of research articles, where you present your evidence, varies tremendously by discipline, argument, writing style, and personality. Forms of proof in the humanities and social sciences are so different as to be impossible to discuss together. No universal rules exist.

Therefore, this week I am going to direct you to do some research on types of evidence in your particular discipline and field. Call some friends or drop by professors' offices, and ask the big question, "What constitutes evidence in our discipline?" You should have some fascinating and fruitful metadiscussions. We benefit from having such discussions more often; turning our critical eye on our own process aids us in making more sophisticated arguments. If you still need more advice than I give here, I recommend some books below that provide detailed instructions on writing up evidence by type and discipline.

What types of evidence do scholars bring to bear in convincing others of their arguments? Below are some of the more common types of data, which authors sift and select depending on their explanatory power regarding their particular arguments.

Qualitative evidence. Data on human behavior collected in the field through direct observation, in-depth interviews, and written documents; in other words, through ethnographic research. Excellent books exist on writing up qualitative evidence in a variety of social science fields. If you regularly do field research, you should own the *SAGE Handbook of Qualitative Research* (2005), which some consider the best on the topic.

Quantitative evidence. Data collected using standardized instruments that yield statistical information. For information on writing up quantitative evidence, see *Best Practices in Quantitative Methods* (Osborne 2007), which describes options for data analysis, or *Statistics for People Who (Think They) Hate Statistics* (Salkind 2007). Such data is frequently used in education, medicine, sociology, political science, psychology, and economics.

Historical evidence. Data collected through an examination of time and the relationship of people to particular periods and events. Such data is used in all disciplines and often collected from archives of primary materials.

Geographic evidence. Data collected through an examination of space and the relationship of people to particular places and environments. Archeological evidence is a form of geographic evidence.

Textual evidence. Data collected from texts like diaries, novels, poems, ship's logs, histories, sacred books, court testimonies, and so on. The humanities depends almost entirely on this type of evidence. The information collected and analyzed has to do with the work's form (e.g., genre, length, point of view, tone, characters, plot, scenes, setting, images, title), language (e.g., rhyme, rhythm, pace, diction, rhetoric), purpose (e.g., message, function), meaning (e.g., symbolism, theme, motif, subject matter, allusions, metaphors, figures of speech), and milieu (e.g., sources, influences, nation, culture, conflict, race, gender, identity, author).

Artistic evidence. Data collected from images like paintings, photographs, sculptures, maps, films, videos, television, and architecture, as well as from live performances like ballet, soccer, and demonstrations. The information collected and analyzed has to do with the work's physical properties (e.g., size, scale, material, form, medium, color, contrast, location, composition, sound, style, technique, date), purpose (e.g., message, function, title), meaning (e.g., symbolism, theme, motif, subject matter, category), and milieu (e.g., sources, influences, nation, culture, conflict, race, gender, identity, creator).

What type of evidence am I using?	

WRITING UP EVIDENCE
IN THE SOCIAL SCIENCES

Since quantitative and qualitative social science articles have standard forms, it is possible to give some information about writing up evidence in the social sciences according to each section of the article. My assumption, as always in this workbook, is that you have already conducted your experiment and are trying to find the best way to interpret and present your data.

Methods

In this section, you detail the methods you used to get your quantitative or qualitative data. In some ways, this is an easy section to write—you just describe what you did. Do so in enough detail that someone else could repeat your experiment and test your results. At the same time, although they seem simple, some typical problems plague methods or methodology sections. Here are some rules for writing a good methods section.

Identify your methodology. Your methodology is usually clear if you do the following correctly.

Describe your sample and sampling procedure. Who or what did you study? How did you pick your subjects? How many did you study? What were their characteristics? Are there any possible problems with your sample or procedures (e.g., not random, no control group)?

Describe your measurement instrument. What did you do to measure the findings (e.g., unstructured interview, closed questionnaire)? What did you measure? Who did the measuring? How long did you measure? Are there any possible problems with your instrument (e.g., observer effects, statistical problems)?

Describe your research context. Where did you do the study? Which people and events were key? Are there any possible problems with your test setting (e.g., context effects)?

Describe your variables. What are your independent variables? What are your dependent variables? What are your control variables?

Write in the past tense. This isn't difficult to remember if you did the study in the past. If you are still conducting research, you may have to work to describe the study as if it is over. Alternately, if you are using your study proposal to draft the methods section, don't let any future tense creep in (e.g., "this study will").

Don't give a statistics tutorial. Your aim is to describe the statistics you used, not to teach others how to do statistical analysis. Most statistical methods can be described very briefly. It's true that you may need to defend some statistical approaches, but that can usually be done quickly with citations to studies that defend those approaches.

Don't mix in your results. This is one of the most frequent mistakes that students make. The methods section is for describing how you did the study, not what you found. Be sure to check the last paragraph of your methods section for any results that have crept in.

Match methods' subheads to results' subheads. Some debate this advice; others think it is useful to structure your methodology section similarly to your results and discussion sections to help your reader keep track of the findings. Often the methods will be too short for subheads, but if you have them it is worth correlating them with the results.

Watch repetition. If you order your methods section chronologically—first you did x, then you did y—you may find yourself repeating a lot of information. Try to find an order that keeps repetition at a minimum.

Check your journal for instructions. Some journals prefer the methods section to be written in a particular way; that information is good to find out early.

Watch passive voice and dangling phrases. Because the social sciences often frown on the use of "I" or "we," most authors write their methods sections with passive voice (e.g., "the data were collected"). Just be sure to keep track in your own head of who is doing what. Sentences that start with gerunds (words ending in "ing") and use the passive voice are often incorrect. They reference the wrong actor (a grammatical error called dangling).

- *Passive and dangling.* Having chosen a regression method, the data were simplified. [This is incorrect because the data did not choose the method.]

- *Passive but correct.* The data were simplified once a regression method was chosen.

- *Active and correct.* Choosing a regression method helped simplify the data.

Keep it short. It is a real gift to give all the methods detail needed and yet be brief. The descriptive nature of the section tempts wordiness. Study any examples of short methods sections that you find in the literature in your field. You will learn much from them.

Now, go through your methods and check each of the points above. If you find any problems, correct them. Below, write some general instructions to yourself for improving the methods section.

How could I improve my methods section?	

Results

In the results or findings section, you describe what you found, the quantitative or qualitative data you collected, and the new information you have to offer.

Be choosy. Any study has more results than can be presented in one article. Don't use the results section as a data dump. Present only those results that relate to your argument or hypothesis.

Use tables and graphs. Information that is difficult to read in paragraph form becomes easily readable once in a table. Use only as many tables as necessary—remembering the point above about not dumping data. Just be sure to standardize tables so they appear the same way throughout.

Use rich tables and graphs. The purpose of a table or graph is to represent information that would be difficult to grasp in prose. Thus, it defeats the purpose if a table has only three or four bits of information. These bits could be more easily presented in the body of the text. Use a table only if the complexity of the data warrants it.

Design tables and graphs properly. Bad tables or graphs are worse than none at all. The expert on presenting data and information effectively is Edward Tufte, referred to as the "Galileo of graphics." See any of his books including *Beautiful Evidence, Visual Explanations,* and *The Visual Display of Quantitative Information.* He has the website www.edwardtufte.com, which includes some examples.

Title tables properly. The title should describe the variables that appear in the table as well as the type of data that is being presented. For example, "Attitudes Toward Racial Integration by Residential Neighborhood by Race." If you have dates, those are excellent to give as well. If your table title has only three or four words, it probably is not comprehensive enough.

Don't repeat the tables. Another frequent problem that students have is writing in great detail about information that appears in the tables. Don't pack a sentence with a list of percentages. Let the tables work for you; that is what they are there for. Use the text to point out trends in the tables or highlight the significance of some of the most interesting data; do not repeat the data. At the same time, make sure to mention all the tables in the text.

Don't organize your results by discovery. The chronology in which you discovered your information is usually irrelevant. Remember the advice to write like a lawyer, not a detective (see Week 3). We don't want to know how you came across each result. We are reading your article precisely because we want to save time.

Organize your results around your argument. If you are asking whether identity is a function of variable A, variable B, or variable C, organize your results section around variable A then B then C. If you are asking how homeless women's coursework is helping them, organize your results section by the types of benefits the women are receiving. If you are investigating the progression of multiracial identity, organize your results section by the stages of that progression. If you are examining how socialites participate in groups, organize your results section by types of participation.

Identify respondents. If you are quoting study participants, it may be helpful to include identifying information at the end of block quotes (e.g., male, 43, fourth-grade teacher).

Don't mix in your methods. This is a frequent mistake. Be sure to check the first paragraph of your results section for any methods. If you find them, move them back to their section.

Write in the past tense. You found your results in the past, describe them as such.

Keep it short. Unless you are combining your results section with your discussion section, this section should be short.

Now, go through your Results and check each of the points above. If you find any problems, correct them. Below, write some general instructions to yourself for improving the results section.

How could I improve my results section?	

Discussion

This is the most difficult section to write and yet the most important. How you write this section can determine your article's rejection or acceptance. Even if you have great data, your article can get rejected for poor or incorrect interpretation. Structuring your discussion around your argument will best enable readers to understand the significance of your study for their own research and the field.

State whether you confirmed your hypothesis. It is useful to start your discussion by stating your argument or conclusion. That is, what you thought would happen, what did happen, and why you think it happened. Many will have skipped reading your methodology and your results, so it is good to reiterate your findings and hypothesis here.

Link results. Identify the relationships among the results. That is, show which variables correlated and which didn't.

Relate results to previous research. State whether your findings confirmed other studies or contradicted them. Discuss why contradictions might exist.

List some implications. What do your findings suggest? What can we conjecture about the world based on your results? Should policy change?

Claim significance. Don't let readers walk away thinking "so what?" Spell out the significance of the results for them. Just be careful in claims about causality, as they are the trickiest to prove. What is novel about the findings?

Question the findings. Evaluate the evidence for the hypothesis: its relevance, contradictions, mechanisms, explanatory power. What degree of certainty does the evidence enable? Is causality shown or just correlation? Are there alternative explanations for the findings? Are there anomalies in the data? What could explain the differences in findings (e.g., gender)? Anticipate rebuttals and note unresolved questions and possible biases.

Note the limitations. All studies have some limitations. It is best to acknowledge the more important of these. Sometimes you can mention how you would do the study differently next time. Just be careful not to overemphasize or apologize for your study's limitations.

Suggest future research. You don't actually have to suggest future research, and some experts even advise against it as clichéd, but it used to be a typical part of many articles. If you have some suggestions, give them.

Discuss the results, don't repeat them. Since the discussion depends on the results, it can be tough to keep them separate. Still, you do want to discuss the results' meaning, not simply list the results.

Focus. Although this is often the longest section, be careful that it is not too long. It is easy to use this section to brainstorm about all the possible meanings of the data. Don't overanalyze. Before writing the discussion, spend some time categorizing and recategorizing your data, then linking it in different ways, so that you don't use the discussion section to brainstorm.

Now, go through your Discussion and check each of the points above. If you find any problems, correct them. Below, write some general instructions to yourself for improving the discussion section.

How could I improve my discussion section?	

WRITING UP EVIDENCE IN THE HUMANITIES

In the humanities, instruction abounds on such micro-writing issues as shortening your sentences, improving your diction, and correcting your grammar. Instruction on such macro-writing issues as marshalling and presenting evidence in a humanities article is much rarer. Few say much beyond noting that you should have evidence to support an argument. Rather than attempt to provide recommendations for a series of disciplines, I've selected just one and focused on it below.

Evidence in Literary Articles

The bodies of humanities' articles often consist of interpreting or analyzing texts. The approach to the text depends deeply on the author's theoretical approach. In literary criticism, two theoretical modes are common: interpretive new criticism (also called close reading) and analytical cultural studies. In the 1990s, these two modes were infrequently paired; now you often see them together. I continue to separate them out here so as to discuss the strengths and pitfalls of each.

Close Readings

In literary criticism articles that focus on "close reading"—an interpretative practice forwarded in the early twentieth century by the New Critics—the scholar focuses on discrete parts of the text, digging into the meanings of individual words and tropes in order to reveal the text's truths and beauties. The scholar interprets the text's poetic or aesthetic meaning, rather than analyzing its cultural context or complicity. Many wonderful articles have been published using this mode, but it can pose certain challenges. As a graduate student once said to me, "It's a lot more fun to write close readings than it is to read them." To present evidence fruitfully through close reading, remember the following.

Quote meaningfully. A close reading is not an excuse to pack your article with dozens of beautiful quotes from the text. You are to interpret the text, not replicate it. Be selective. Don't quote when you can paraphrase, don't quote material irrelevant to your argument, and don't quote at length unless your argument fails without that quote. The more famous the text, the less you should quote it and the more you should paraphrase. Always introduce quotes and interpret them, rather than letting them stand as ciphers.

Summarize briefly. Classroom papers often devote many pages to summarizing the plot of texts or describing texts. If any part of your article seems to move chapter by chapter through the text, you are probably not being argumentative enough.

Select carefully. Don't try to analyze every part of the text. Select only a few parts for analysis. To help you do this, ask "why" or "how" of the text not "what." For instance, "why is this particular rhyme scheme used?" rather than "what is the rhyme scheme?"

Reference the larger picture. Classroom papers often stop at simply discovering a particular theme, symbolism, or fact in the text. You must go beyond discovery and use what you discover to make an argument. Further, you must make that argument in the context of your critical approach, whether feminist, psychoanalytic, postcolonial, queer theory, cultural studies, and so on. Make sure to make the connections.

Limit notes. More and more humanities journals are limiting the number and type of footnotes or endnotes that authors are allowed. Some allow notes only for sources (documentary notes), and some allow only a few notes for defenses or explanations (substantive notes). Almost none allow them for digressions.

Cultural Studies

In literary criticism articles that focus on analyzing texts as a symptom of society, the evidence is not in close reading the themes, imagery, or diction of a text, but in asking questions of the social and political location of the text. The evidence in such articles will consist of exploring how the text reproduces the conflicts of its period or culture, participates in constructing particular knowledge systems, or highlights social or political contradictions. For instance, which characters get to speak when and to whom? How does the rhetoric, narrative, or language of the text enable relationships of power? How can understanding this text better enable us to create a more just society?

Avoid discussing intentionality. Classroom papers often focus on what the author or creator intended, or might have intended. In this mode of criticism, it is more typical to focus on the text and your reading of it, not the author. If you want to discuss intentionality, find a recent article in your field that does so, and study how the author successfully makes this analysis.

Avoid biography. Classroom papers often focus on how the life experiences of authors or creators shaped their creation. Again, in the cultural analysis mode it is better to focus on the text itself. If you feel that biography is important, find a recent article in your field that does such analysis well.

Avoid simple politicizing. Classroom papers often vulgarize cultural studies arguments by misusing its terms to bludgeon texts or peoples. The essence of sophisticated cultural studies criticism is an acknowledgement that it is difficult to know anything for certain, and that we all (strong and weak) participate in creating the world we live in, whether we are perpetuating or resisting its injustices. Be careful to nuance your argument.

Deploy theory; don't replicate it. Classroom papers often bog down in presenting literary theory rather than using it. Don't spend long sections of your paper explaining feminist theory, for instance; rather, make a feminist analysis of your text.

REVISING YOUR EVIDENCE

Day 1: Reading the Workbook

On the first day of your writing week, you should read the workbook up to this page and answer all the questions posed in the workbook up to this point. Then work on any tasks remaining from previous weeks or on your own list of tasks to accomplish.

Day 2: Discussing Evidence in Your Field

Make some appointments with colleagues to discuss what constitutes evidence in your field. This can be a good task to do in the library with access to journal volumes, so that you can study how those in your field present evidence. Then write up your notes about what you have found, send it to other colleagues, and ask them what they think. It's important to think about the meta aspects of writing in your field.

Day 3: Revisiting Your Evidence

Print out a copy of your article and pick up a pen. Using the instruction above, review each paragraph of the body of your article to determine whether your evidence is clear, and whether your interpretation of that evidence progresses logically and has explanatory power. If it doesn't, note in the margin how it could be improved. Use the information you gathered yesterday to aid you in this review.

Day 4 and 5:
Shaping Your Evidence Around Your Argument

Using the same print out, review each paragraph of the body of your article to determine if the evidence is supporting your argument. If it doesn't, note in the margin how you could refocus the paragraph around your argument or delete it. Once you are done with this second evaluation, go through and revise the body of your article accordingly.

DOCUMENTING YOUR
WRITING TIME AND TASKS

On the following weekly plan, please graph when you expect to write and what tasks you hope to accomplish this week. Then keep track of what you actually did. Remember, you are to allot fifteen minutes to one hour every day to writing. At the end of the week, take pride in your accomplishments and evaluate whether any patterns need changing.

Week 7 Calendar

Time	Monday	Tuesday	Wednesday	Thursday	Friday	Saturday	Sunday
5:00 a.m.							
6:00							
7:00							
8:00							
9:00							
10:00							
11:00							
12:00 p.m.							
1:00							
2:00							
3:00							
4:00							
5:00							
6:00							
7:00							
8:00							
9:00							
10:00							
11:00							
12:00 a.m.							
1:00							
2:00							
3:00							
4:00							
Total Minutes Actually Worked							
Tasks Completed							

Week 8

Opening and Concluding Your Article

Day to Do Task	Week 8 Daily Writing Tasks	Estimated Task Time
Day 1 (Monday?)	Read through page 209 and discuss and revise your title; start documenting your time (page 219)	30 minutes
Day 2 (Tuesday?)	Revise your introduction (pages 209–216)	60 minutes
Day 3 (Wednesday?)	Revise your introduction (pages 209–216)	60 minutes
Day 4 (Thursday?)	Revisit your abstract, related literature review, and author order (pages 216–217)	60 minutes
Day 5 (Friday?)	Revise your conclusion (pages 217–218)	60 minutes

Above are the tasks for your eighth week. Some articles will need a lot of revising at this point; other articles will be fine. Schedule when you will write and then track the time that you actually spend writing.

SEVENTH WEEK IN REVIEW

You have now spent seven weeks working on your article. You have sharpened your argument and structured your article around your argument, and are now more than halfway to the finish line. Congratulations! So, don't stop now. You'd only be joining the crowd. After all, 43 percent of U.S. faculty have not published any journal articles in the past two years and 26 percent spent no time at all writing and doing research (Lindholm et al 2005, 35). The rate in your particular field may be even higher. Why not keep going by turning to this week's tasks of revising the opening and conclusion of your article?

ON THE IMPORTANCE OF OPENINGS

First impressions are vital. We live amidst a barrage of media in which loud, bright, sexy, violent images work constantly to capture our consumer attention. Sophisticated delivery systems, which depend on consumers' ever more refined ability to read content in fractions of a second, remain the context of our writing. The expectation created by advertisements, talk shows, web pages, text messages, and so on, is that meaning can be communicated with tremendous brevity. Although the journal article is not competing with billboards or sitcoms for attention, it is shaped by such expectations and the dense commercial context of the United States. However quiet and unassuming, the twentieth-first century journal article is under pressure to prove its value quickly. And not just once, but twice.

For an article to get published, it must first do well in the peer-review process. U.S. peer reviewers can find an article frustrating if it fails to give certain information up front or meanders for several pages before getting to the point. In contrast, if your project, argument, approach, sources, contribution, and relevance are clearly stated in the first two or three pages, your article will tend to do better in peer review. Sometimes students tell me that such efficiency is less expected in their discipline, usually in the humanities. But when I ask them to give me an article they consider to be a model of good writing in the field, it almost always has a clear, pointed introduction. Starting strong will aid your article in making it through peer review regardless of field.

Second, any article you publish is competing for scholars' attention with the multitude of other academic articles published in each field every year. With at least 200,000 academic articles and 12,000 academic books published every year in the United States alone (Bowker 2004), skimming has become a way of life. Scholars read past the first page only if the value of the article has made itself apparent. Only two moves establish an article's value quickly: the reputation of the author(s) or the opening. Since none of us are famous (yet!) we must focus on the latter. Articles with strong titles, solid abstracts, and compelling introductions are more likely to be accepted for publication, more likely to be read, and more likely to be cited.

REVISING YOUR
OPENING AND CONCLUSION

Most of us need no convincing that starting strong is smart. How do you quickly and clearly establish the value of your article? In the following pages, I give the main ingredients for starting and ending strong. You can certainly cook without some of them, but you will have a poor concoction with none of them.

Day 1: Revising Your Title

Your title is the highway billboard of your article, the only part of your article most readers will ever see and even that, only briefly, as they whip by to other destinations. It is an announcement meant to draw readers to your work. As such, your title must be a direct, clear invitation to a particular conversation. Like an advertisement, your title will have a life of its own independent from your article: it will appear by itself on your curriculum vitae, in tables of contents, and on electronic databases. It is often the only part of your article provided to potential peer reviewers, who on its power will make a decision about whether to review your article. So be sure that your title clearly describes your article. The best title clearly communicates your article's topic. It aids scholars using electronic search engines to find your work easily by employing common keywords. It suggests your argument and any policy implications. It avoids distracting creative or allusive openings. Revisit your current title and use the following advice to consider if it could be improved.

My current title is:	

Avoid broad titles that would serve better for entire books or series. It is always tempting to suggest the importance of your article by giving it a grand title. But you only annoy your reader if it doesn't match the content. It is no fun to traipse to the library to locate "Twentieth-Century American Cultural Dynamics" only to find that the article should have been titled "Inventing Northern California Counterculture in the 1960s." Be honest in your title. Think about how often you have looked up an article only to find that it was much narrower than the title suggested. Further, many table of contents services use only the first part of article titles in their e-mailed announcements, another reason to ensure the first part communicates. Below are examples of titles that were revised to match the article's more specific content (underline highlights the change made).

Humanities Titles:

- **Original**: Reinterpreting the Cidian Cycle
  Revision: Gendering the <u>Spanish</u> Cidian Cycle: <u>Nineteenth-Century British</u> Writer <u>Felicia Hemans's</u> *The Siege of Valencia*[1]

- **Original**: Constructing West Hollywood
  Revision: Performing an Un-<u>Queer</u> City: West Hollywood's Image Creation Campaign, <u>1984–2000</u>[2]

- **Original**: The Mystery of the Missing Letters
  Revision: Forging the <u>Armenian</u> Past: Questionable Translations of Abstract Expressionist <u>Arshile Gorky's</u> Missing Letters[3]

Social Science Titles:

- **Original**: Mitigating Apprehension About Section 8
  Revision: Mitigating Apprehension about Section 8 Vouchers: The Positive Role of <u>Housing Specialists</u> in Search and Placement[4]

- **Original**: Tradition and the Spread of AIDS in Malawi
  Revision: Risky Traditional Practices Associated with the Spread of HIV/AIDS Among <u>Pregnant Women</u> in the <u>Blantyre</u> and <u>Lilongwe</u> Districts of Malawi[5]

Is my title too broad? If so, what would a more specific title be?	

Avoid strings of vague terms. First drafts of titles often start with three or four words strung together to give a sense for the broad import of the article. But 10,000 words is rarely going to measure up to those concepts, so it's better to leave them out. They frequently mean more to you than the average reader will understand on a quick read anyway.

Humanities Titles:

- **Original**: Consciousness, Controversy, and Comedy: How Dave Chappelle Made Us Think
  Revision: Squeezing <u>Racial Stereotypes</u> on <u>Showtime Television</u>: Dave Chappelle's Conscious Comedy[6]

Social Science Titles:

- **Original**: Revolution, Change, and Transition: Television in the Twenty-First Century
  Revision: <u>Primetime</u> Television Challenges to the Movie Industry: The Rise of <u>Reality Programming</u> in the 2000s

Do I use too many vague terms in my title? How can I make it more specific?	

Name your subjects. It is odd how many times quite specific articles do not name their topics in the title. If your article is about a particular author or text, name that author or text in the title. If it is about a particular city, region, or country, name that geography. If it is about a particular population—women, Latinos, students—name the group. It may seem obvious to you, but nothing is obvious to a search engine. Below are some student revisions to titles.

Humanities Titles:

- **Original:** Grotesque Readings: The Language of Violence in Cervantes
  Revision: Grotesque Readings: The Language of Violence in Cervantes' <u>*Don Quixote*</u>[7]

- **Original:** The Electoral Ethnic Bandwagon in New Democracies
  Revision: <u>Getting on</u> the Ethnic Bandwagon in New Democracies: Electoral Relationships between <u>Political Elites</u> and <u>Voters of Their Ethnicity</u>[8]

Social Science Titles:

- **Original:** Socially Organized Initiations, Responses, and Evaluations in an Elementary School Classroom
  Revision: Socially Organized <u>Questions</u> and <u>Answers: Student-Teacher Interaction</u> in an Elementary School <u>Science</u> Classroom[9]

- **Original:** Effect of Social Support on Pain and Depression
  Revision: Effect of Social Support on Pain and Depression among <u>Rheumatoid Arthritis Patients</u>[10]

Have I named my subjects in the title? If not, what should I add?	

Suggest your argument if possible. Rarely can you give a sense for your argument in the title, but if you can, you should. Below are examples of student revisions to good titles to make them even stronger by suggesting the article's argument.

Humanities Titles:

- **Original:** Grave Matters: The Representation of Women in Funerary Offerings in Pre-Columbian West Mexico
  Revision: Grave Matters: <u>Reexamining</u> the Representation of Women in Funerary Offerings in Pre-Columbian West Mexico[11]

- **Original:** Sources for the Fourteenth-Century Ethiopian *Kebra Negast* in Biblical and Koranic Texts
  Revision: <u>Rewriting</u> Biblical and Koranic Texts in the Fourteenth-Century Ethiopian *Kebra Negast*

Social Science Titles:

- **Original:** Exposure to Immigrant Culture and Dropping out of School among Asian and Latino Youths[12]
  Revision: The <u>Benefits of Biculturalism:</u> Exposure to Immigrant Culture and School Drop-Outs among Asian and Latino Youths

- **Original:** The Theory of and Evidence for the Role of Apology in the Criminal Justice Setting
  Revision: Evidence for the <u>Effectiveness</u> of Apology in the Criminal Justice Setting[13]

Have I suggested my argument in the title? If not, could I?	

Embed your title with searchable keywords. Given that many articles are only read or cited because they have been found through an electronic search, make sure to include common keywords in your title. This may mean being slightly repetitive.

For instance, consider the strong title "Gender-Based Violence, Relationship Power, and Risk of HIV Infection in Women Attending Antenatal Clinics in South Africa."[14] This title provides a tremendous amount of information in a short space. The authors name the country (South Africa), the problem (violence and HIV), and the location of the research (antenatal clinics). The word antenatal is communicating twice, because it suggests that the focus of the article is on violence against child-bearing women. Note that the authors also manage to fit in the similiar keywords "gender" and "women" so that their article will be found by researchers using either word.

In the example below, the student expanded the title to include important keywords that better signaled the gender and race component of her research, enabling like-minded researchers to find her work. For instance, it is easier to find an article with "African-American" in the title than to find an article with "Black" in the title. Black appears in many titles that have nothing to do with race.

- **Original:** Black Faculty Salary Differentials
  Revision: The Black <u>Professoriate:</u> Explaining the Salary <u>Gap</u> for <u>African-American Female</u> Faculty[15]

In the example below, the student added the term "genetic genealogy," which is a more searchable term than DNA, and a signal of the argument.

- **Original:** DNA and the Future of Diaspora Studies
  Revision: <u>Genetic Genealogy</u> and the Future of Diaspora Studies: A Caution[16]

In the example below, the student decided to translate her novel's title into English, since the article will appear in English.

- **Original:** From the Theater of Identity to the Arcane Production of Nationality: Goethe's *Wilhelm Meisters Lehrjahre*

Revision: From the Theater of Identity to the Arcane Production of Nationality: Reconsidering Goethe's _Wilhelm Meister's Apprenticeship_ as a Bildungsroman[17]

Have I given all the important keywords in the title? If not, what should I add?	

Avoid overly dense titles. Since my advice usually results in quite long titles, make sure you have not gone too far in that direction. Sometimes a title gets too bloated to read. Avoid creating titles that are nothing more than strings of nouns. Below are examples of revisions to titles to make them less dense and more readable.

- **Original:** Degas's Modistes, Chic Consumers, and Fashionable Commodities
  Revision: Fashionable Consumption: Women as Consumers and Clerks in the French Impressionist Painting of Degas[18]

- **Original:** John Powell, Somatic Acoustics, Racial Difference, and Symphonic Music
  Revision: The Somatic Acoustics of Racial Difference in the Symphonic Music of John Powell[19]

- **Original:** _The George Lopez Show_: An American Family Sitcom Redefining Latinidad on Prime Time Through the Logic of Consumer Capitalism and Individualism
  Revision: Redefining Latinidad on Prime Time Network Television: Consumer Capitalism and the American Family Sitcom _The George Lopez Show_[20]

Is my title too dense? If so, what should I add or cut?	

Include a verb if possible. Long titles that include only nouns and adjectives are difficult to absorb. See how much easier it is to read the revised title below?

- **Draft:** Processes of Landscape Change: A Comparative Historical Study of Driving Forces and Neighbourhoods in Stølsheimen and Sjodalen, Norway

Revision: Why <u>Do</u> Landscapes Change? A Comparative Historical Study of Driving Forces and Neighbourhoods in Stølsheimen and Sjodalen, Norway[21]

Do I have a verb in my title? If not, can I insert one?	

Avoid using your title to prove how witty or well-read you are. This rule is a matter of some debate and does depend a bit on your field. I am still going to argue that you should eschew cute titles. You have the whole article to prove your smarts. Using quotes, puns, double entendres, or allusions in titles is a time-honored tradition in the humanities, and most editors won't stop you, but such titles rarely serve you well in our electronic age. If your title is an obscure, exclusionary in-joke not entirely related to your topic and which can only be understood after reading the whole article word-for-word, reconsider. If, when questioned about the title, you find yourself saying "get it?!" reconsider.

Your title is not the place to compete with your literary subjects in creativity. If you must play with language, do so in your introduction where it is less distracting and there is adequate space to develop an idea. If you doubt the wisdom of what I'm saying, just go online and do a search in an academic article database for titles riffing on Blake's quote "burning bright" or Melville's quote "call me Ishmael" to see how quickly literary gymnastics start to seem hollow.

Below is an example of a title so generic, it is impossible to find electronically. But the author was attached to the musical pun in the title and wouldn't relinquish it. The revised title would have been a wiser choice.

- **Published**: Research Note[22]
  Revision: <u>A Song for My Father: Honoring the Family Roots of Research</u>

Below is an example of a published article with a title that is a play on the popular 1990s expression "shit happens." While some might find this cute, the title "Shift Happens" does not adequately reflect the content of the article. I think the title should have been revised.

- **Published**: Shift Happens: Spanish and English Transmission Between Parents and Their Children[23]
  Revision: <u>Latino Linguistic Diversity: Evidence for Bilingualism</u> and Spanish to English Language Shift among <u>Chicano</u> Children

Below is an example of one student's revision of a social science title to delete an unclear quote. Although the original is not bad—the quote does indicate something about the content—the revision is clearer and gives a better sense for the importance of the article.

- **Original:** "It's Not Abuse When. . . .": Situational Definitions of Child Abuse by Marginalized Parents
  Revision: <u>When Prevention Fails: The Role of Context in Persistent</u> Child Abuse[24]

If you remain unconvinced, and still really want to use a quote in your title, let's look at an example of one that works. In the following title, the quote is a full sentence, not an unreadable fragment, and it directly relates to the rest of the title. After reading the title twice, we can see that the author means to suggest that certain forms of masculinity are an American myth. On reading the title three times, we are not so sure; perhaps she means that something masculinist like Manifest Destiny is the most blatant of American myths. While creating this doubt is clever, is it helpful to the reader?

- **Published:** "The Most Blatant of All Our American Myths": Masculinity, Male Bonding, and the Wilderness in Sinclair Lewis's *Mantrap*.[25]

Finalizing the Title

Now try to put this together and create a stronger title. A great exercise for arriving at a better title is gathering a group of scholarly friends together with a blackboard to brainstorm. You can often see quite spectacular improvements under these conditions.

My new and improved title is:	

Days 2 and 3: Revising Your Introduction

If you have provided a strong title and a solid abstract, you may feel like there is little else you can do in your introduction. Never fear, much can be done in your introduction that can't be done elsewhere and must be done early. The main purpose of the introduction is to provide enough information for the reader to be able to understand your argument and its stakes.

Introductions have some standard features in common. Alex Henry and Robert L. Roseberry (1997) analyzed the introductions and conclusions of articles and found that most shared three "moves." All article introductions stated the central idea (what I am calling the argument in this workbook). Many also introduced the general topic and then narrowed the focus to the specific topic. Statements of the topic often included an example, a general history, a prediction, or a quote. Narrowing the focus often included statistics, dates, examples, background information, or rationales for the argument. Statements of the central idea often included stating a fact, a problem, or a solution. You might want to evaluate whether your article makes these moves.

You can also make your introduction stronger by starting with a telling anecdote, striking depiction of your subject, aggressive summary of the literature, or solid claim about the significance of your topic. Below are some strong openings of published articles, demonstrating the variations possible.

> **Anecdotal opening.** When I was growing up in New York City, my parents used to take me to an event in Inwood Park at which Indians—real American Indians dressed in feathers and blankets—could be seen and touched by children like me. This event was always a disappointment.[26] (For an article analyzing U.S. textbooks' presentation of American Indians' role in U.S. history.)

> **Subject opening.** Samuel Johnson was a person with multiple disabilities. He was blind in one eye and had poor vision in the other. He was also deaf in one ear.[27] (For an article discussing the absence of a discourse of disability in eighteenth-century England.)

> **Critical opening.** Historians have been much more concerned with explaining questions surrounding how Africans produced, transported, and sold captives than with exploring African strategies against the slave trade.[28] (For an article on Guinea Bissauans' strategies of resisting the slave trade.)

> **Significance opening.** Few children's movies can rival the success of *The Lion King* or the controversy that has surrounded it since it was first shown commercially in 1994.[29] (For an article on Latina/o immigration to the United States as the anxious subtext of a Disney film.)

> **Historical opening.** In the 1970s and 1980s, amid concerns over the negative effects of concentrated urban poverty and suburban resistance to the encroachment of public housing, the U.S. Department of Housing and Urban Development (HUD) slowed the construction of new large-scale public housing projects and increased the use of Section 8 certificates and vouchers to subsidize low-income households in the private rental market.[30] (For an article on tactics that community workers used to help low-income families gain housing when landlords were suspicious of Section 8 vouchers.)

> **Argumentative opening.** Civic education is important.[31] (For an article arguing that civic education is essential to a functioning democracy.)

What type of opening do I have? How could it be improved?	

Start with a gripping first sentence. There is nothing like a vivid first sentence to get your introduction off to a good start, especially in the humanities (the opening examples above are also first sentences). Unfortunately, many published journal articles do not start off strong. One typical humanities opening is analyzing a quote by someone else, which I have yet to see be really compelling. Others start with a series of unanswered questions, which I find frustrating. I have enough unanswered questions of my own! Of course, this is my taste, so when you read articles, identify what you find compelling in others' writing so you can craft compelling first sentences yourself.

Could my first sentence be more gripping? If so, how could I accomplish that?	

Give basic information about your subject. It is surprising how often introductions do not properly introduce the subject. "Often inexperienced or young writers don't have a sense of how much the reader needs to know: the writers has a complete image in mind . . . and they are surprised that their writing didn't convey the whole thing to the reader" (Willis 1993, 64). If you have not given the who, what, why, where, and how of the topic, you have not introduced it. Keep in mind two truths. When you are writing for publication, you are usually writing for people who know less than you do on the topic. And prose lasts. What appears perfectly clear right now—such as "9/11"—may be less so twenty years from now. So if you are discussing an event, give the dates; a place, give its geopolitical context; a new term, define it; a noncanonical text, give the author, date of publication, a summary, and its claim to importance.

Do not make the mistake of thinking that such basic information must be given in full sentences or long paragraphs. Such information can often be given quite quickly, in clauses. Indeed, when introducing case studies for which you have hundreds of pages of detail, you need to avoid giving too much information. Below are some examples of basic information in published articles.

> **Person**. Zora Neale Hurston, a black novelist and anthropologist, . . . [wrote] a book-length collection of folktales, songs, and hoodoo practices entitled *Mules and Men*.[32]

> **Text**. Among Europe's experimental films from the 1920s and 30s, perhaps none offers a more fascinating conjunction of psychoanalysis and representations of race than *Borderline*, the expressionist, interracial melodrama produced by the POOL group and directed by Kenneth Macpherson.[33]

> **Place**. With a focus on the Guinea-Bissau region of the Upper Guinea coast, an area that sat on the slaving frontiers of the powerful

interior state of Kaabu and the smaller coastal state of Casamance, this chapter will begin to answer these questions.[34]

Movement. The New Journalism—that genre-blurred mélange of ethnography, investigative reportage, and fiction—is widely and rightly considered to be *the* characteristic genre of the sixties.[35]

Theory. I focus here on Herman Witkin . . . the first researcher to extend the study of psychological sex differences into the area of human perception.[36]

Term. In this article, prosody refers collectively to variations in pitch, tempo, and rhythm.[37]

Do I give basic information about my subject? What else is needed?	

State your argument and, if possible, your findings. See Week 2 of this workbook for information on crafting an argument and stating it concisely. Remember that an argument is a statement to which you can coherently respond "I agree" or "I disagree." It should relate to research done by others. Note how the published examples below weave the argument together with claims for significance, basic information, and findings.

Humanities Openings:

- The focus of this essay is the device of the bloody handkerchief popularized by Thomas Kyd's spectacularly successful *The Spanish Tragedy* (1582–92). . . . By analyzing Kyd's subversion of a long tradition linking holy cloths and sacred blood in medieval drama, I wish to demonstrate that the bloody napkin is a ghostly palimpsest that absorbs meaning through intertextual borrowing as well as through fresh symbolic resonance. Further, I wish to argue that Kyd's appropriation of the handkerchief was not didactic, as has been argued by recent scholars of Reformation drama, but an opportunistic bid to recast the late medieval "contract of transformation" embodied by bloody cloth as an addictive "contract of sensation."[38]

- My purpose in this essay is to describe and define the ways in which Afro-American women intellectuals, in the last decade of the nineteenth century, theorized about the possibilities and limits of patriarchal power through its manipulation of racialized and gendered social categories and practices. . . . I hope that a discussion of Cooper, Wells, and Hopkins in the context of the black women's movement will direct readers to consider more seriously how black feminists conceptualized the possibilities for resisting sexual oppression.[39]

- Ecofeminists . . . contend that ecological destruction is, at its base, misogynist, and the inevitable result of the masculine drive to control and dominate the female. . . . This [article] challenges as biased and banal some of the ecofeminist assertions. . . . The discussion suggests alternative strategies for transcending some of the divisive ideological "isms and schisms" that present the major obstacle to realizing a more humane society for both women and men.[40]

Social Science Quantitative:

- Young people with high academic ability who excel during their elementary and secondary school years are not necessarily guaranteed similar success in their university experiences, [especially] students who represent the first [from their families] to pursue higher education.[41]

- [Some have] argued that the social construction of science as "masculine" discourages girls from participating in science by posing the risk of undermining their gender identity: girl scientists may be seen—and may thus be under pressure to see themselves—as more masculine and less feminine than their peers. However, the gendered image of science and scientists may be more flexible than appears from the above.[42]

Do I state my argument and findings? If not, what should I add and where?	

Identify your position vis-à-vis the previous research. As discussed in Week 5, your research must be demonstrably related to what has been written before. An important part of an introduction is nnouncing your entry point; that is, how your argument relates to previous arguments about your topic. So make sure you do this in your introduction.

What's my entry point? Do I state it clearly? Do I show how my research relates?	

Articulate the significance of your subject. Make sure that your reader knows the importance of the person, text, group, question, or problem you have taken as your subject. Do not assume that they know why it is important or how important. Even if the reader does know why, part of pulling readers into an article is your stating the case in a particularly clear or powerful way. This is part of how you demonstrate your authority to speak on the topic and what the reader will gain from reading your article.

What makes a subject significant? In the United States, being at an extreme—the first or the last, the best or the worst, the largest or the smallest—is a time-honored mark of significance. A traditional claim for significance is stating how the article contributes in important ways to our knowledge. In the opening sentences of the published articles excerpted below, the authors effectively claim the significance of their topics by establishing the tremendous impact of their subjects or the events associated with them. In this way, they also quickly contextualize their subjects, painting the larger picture that makes their question and argument important.

- The terrorist attacks of September 11, 2001, on New York City (NYC) were the largest human-made intentional disaster in U.S. history. The sheer scope of the attacks, the level of property destruction, the financial repercussions, and the continuing level of anxiety suggested that these attacks might have mental health consequences both for direct victims of the attacks and for the population at large.[43] (For an article on children's poor access to mental health services after 9/11.)

- In 1997 and 1998, Asia was hit with a severe economic crisis. Most countries in the region were faced with massive currency fluctuations, banking crises, and plummeting stock markets. Economic problems were compounded by political turmoil. Given past experiences in Asia of massive financial difficulties coupled with political upheaval—specifically in Thailand, South Korea, Indonesia, and Malaysia—I begin with a broad question: What is the relationship between economic crises and political change, specifically democratization?[44]

- Dolly Parton has achieved broad popularity over the past twentyyears as an exceptional country musician who successfully "crossed over" into pop music and is now perceived as one of the industry's most respected and prolific singer/songwriters. . . . As a fluent and savvy promoter of "Dolly," Parton provides a fascinating case study in the construction of a star image, specifically one that mediates the often contradictory ideals of gender, region, and class.[45]

Another traditional claim for significance is stating that the popular understandings of a subject are erroneous.

- Enshrined in the Bill of Rights in 1789, the grand jury has been praised as the greatest instrument of freedom known to democratic government and a bulwark against oppression. At the same time, the grand jury remains one of the most controversial and least understood aspects of the criminal justice system, and has been abolished in many states and in England.[46] (For an article about Latino participation on U.S. grand juries.)

- From the earliest accounts in New Spain to Hollywood's Golden Age, few items are as central to their tradition-bound popular image as Native Americans' bows and arrows. Yet archeologists believe that the earliest Americans did not use them.[47] (For an article about stone bifaces in American antiquity.)

What is the significance of my topic? Do I articulate it?	

Provide a road map of your article. Summarizing the structure of your article in your introduction makes it easier for the reader to follow your progress. Below are some sample summaries from published articles.

- Motivated by the need for a thorough investigation on convenience yield dynamics and its determinants, and in the light of the recent theoretical and empirical contributions in the literature, I analyze the daily convenience yield behavior for six commodity markets: crude oil, heating oil, gasoline, wheat, corn, and copper. I first evaluate whether option pricing can be used in statistically explaining daily convenience yield variations. Next, I question the appropriateness of the standard call option as the choice for option valuation framework and contrast it with another option, that is, the exchange option. Finally, I empirically test the two hypotheses on convenience yield behavior by Heinkel, Howe, and Hughes (1990).[48]

- In exploring the issue of how group size relates to exclusivist or inclusionist identification strategies, I begin with an overview of my basic theory of group size. I then consider the rhetorical strategies deployed in the recruitment of allies in a perspective which is inspired by action theory. Next, I turn to the conceptual tool kit of discourses on exclusion and inclusion. I then return to economic reasoning, often taken as the underlying cause of identity politics, and of politics in general.[49]

Do I summarize my article? Should I?	

Avoid the following clichés.

Don't start with a dictionary definition. Indeed, do not devote whole paragraphs anywhere in your article to various dictionary definitions of your main terms, unless your article is etymologically driven. Dictionaries are not sacred objects to be consulted as oracles.

Don't start with Wikipedia. Indeed, citing Wikipedia or any other encyclopedia in your article is often considered a sign of poor scholarship, unless you are citing them as primary sources you intend to analyze critically.

Don't start with vast claims. Claiming that something has been true "for all time" or "for all of human history" or "in all cultures" or "for all peoples" or "around the globe" will mark your article as unsophisticated. Almost nothing has always or everywhere been true.

Example of an Efficient Introduction

As an example, I have reproduced below the entire introduction to one article, accomplished in just over 200 words. Not every introduction has to be this efficient, and the first sentence of this one could be more gripping, but I want to show how little space it can take to give basic information, make a claim for significance, identify your position vis-à-vis the previous research, summarize the structure, and even list findings.

- Scholars in the fields of both sociology and political science have neglected the political importance of local feminist activists who organize in pursuit of electing women to public office. Such activists have remained mostly invisible to scholars due in large part to a disciplinary division of labor that treats social movement activity and electoral politics as two separate fields (. . .). I argue that the confines of these disciplinary traditions have also affected feminist research on women and politics, resulting in little if any research on community organizing as related to women's bids for elective office. To address this gap in the literature, I begin by reviewing the work of prominent researchers in the fields of electoral participation, community activism, and feminist work on women in politics. I then investigate the work and lives of members of a local chapter of the National Women's Political Caucus (NWPC), suggesting how the efforts of local feminist activists might add to our understanding of political and social change. In particular, a focus on local NWPC activists (1) refines our understanding of "being political," (2) suggests the importance of a local activist infrastructure for electoral change, and (3) makes visible the significance of local activism within a candidate-centered context.[50]

Day 4: Revisiting Your Abstract, Related Literature Review, and Author Order

You may be expected to provide an abstract when you submit your article. If your title is the highway billboard ad, your abstract is the full-page magazine ad. Many readers will decide whether to read your article based on your abstract. In fact, more than one person may cite your article on the basis of reading your abstract alone. A good abstract is an extremely important part of getting into publication and disseminating your research, so if you have not had a chance to finalize it yet, do so now. Follow the advice in Week 2, keeping in mind the changes you have made to the argument, related literature review, evidence, and structure. You can also revisit it in later weeks when you are closer to sending your article to a journal.

A good related literature review is an important part of a good journal article introduction. This was covered in Week 5, so feel free to turn back to that week if you feel it could still use some work.

A final issue to determine regarding your opening is relevant only to those writing articles with coauthors; in which case you must make final decisions about whose name goes first on the article and whose second, and so on. This is a vital issue that cannot be addressed properly here. Most associations now have detailed guidelines on authorship order, and some journals require authors to answer a series of questions about who conceived the hypothesis, who designed the experiment, who managed the laboratory, who collected the data, who analyzed the data, who drafted the article, and who revised the article so that editors can accurately determine authorship. Nevertheless, conflict over authorship of articles is common. I will only say here, make a written agreement with the other authors before you even start drafting. Hammer out what constitutes the duties of a first author, second author, and so on. If you haven't done that in advance, or no longer believe the agreement is fair, you have your work cut out for you now. Just remember that in the social sciences, many graduate students never get their names first on articles, and many scholars in their field wouldn't expect it. Even if a student wrote every draft of an article, it will be perceived as quite fair in many fields for the student not to appear as first author if he or she did not collect the data or arrive at the hypothesis. If it is any comfort, the more authors on an article, the higher its chances of acceptance and of being cited subsequently (Weller 2001, 128–129).

Do I have any coauthor issues? If so, how should I proceed?	

Day 5: Revising Your Conclusion

A good conclusion is one that summarizes your argument and its significance in a powerful way. The conclusion should restate the article's relevance to the scholarly literature and debate. Although the conclusion does not introduce new arguments, it does point beyond the article to the larger context or the more general case. It does not merely repeat the introduction, but takes a step back, out to the bigger picture and states why the argument matters in the larger scheme of things.

One survey found that all argumentative articles included conclusions (Hyland 1990). Another found that two moves were generally present: the authors made a claim about the strength of the argument and its supporting evidence and then linked that argument to the wider context (Henry & Roseberry 1997, 485). That is, they stated how the internal outcome of the article (the success of the argument) can lead to an external outcome (a change in the world or the way that we think about the world). Thus, conclusions were usually marked by an expansion from the argument through evaluation and implications. They also found that article conclusions tended to evaluate or reaffirm the argument, but also could include predictions, admonishments, consequences, solutions, or personal reactions.

Social science conclusions also sometimes include remarks about possible directions for future research and reservations about the argument. Humanities conclusions are often more eloquent than the rest of the article, with an elevation in language and lyricism. As the scholars Stevens and Stewart observed, humanities scholars tend to begin their articles by declaring the significance of their argument and conclude them by declaring the significance of their texts (e.g., the poem, score, or painting they analyzed) (Stevens and Stewart 1987, 110).

By the time you reach the conclusion, you may feel that you have no language left. If you are finding the conclusion difficult to write, ask your colleagues to read your article and tell you what they understand the article to be about and why it is important. They can often give you new language and slightly different ways of saying the same thing.

What are some useful sentences or words from my reviewer's summary of my article?	

DOCUMENTING YOUR WRITING TIME AND TASKS

On the following weekly plan, please graph when you expect to write and what tasks you hope to accomplish this week. Then keep track of what you actually did. Remember, you are to allot fifteen minutes to one hour every day to writing. At the end of the week, take pride in your accomplishments and evaluate whether any patterns need changing.

Time	Monday	Tuesday	Wednesday	Thursday	Friday	Saturday	Sunday
Week 8 Calendar							
5:00 a.m.							
6:00							
7:00							
8:00							
9:00							
10:00							
11:00							
12:00 p.m.							
1:00							
2:00							
3:00							
4:00							
5:00							
6:00							
7:00							
8:00							
9:00							
10:00							
11:00							
12:00 a.m.							
1:00							
2:00							
3:00							
4:00							
Total Minutes Actually Worked							
Tasks Completed							

Week 9

Giving, Getting, and
Using Others' Feedback

Day to Do Task	Week 9 Daily Writing Tasks	Estimated Task Time
Day 1 (Monday?)	Read through page 229; start documenting your time (page 233)	30 minutes
Day 2 (Tuesday?)	Share your article and get feedback (pages 229–230)	60 minutes
Day 3 (Wednesday?)	Make a list of tasks that remain to be done (page 230)	60 minutes
Day 4 (Thursday?)	Revise your article according to feedback (pages 230–231)	60 minutes
Day 5 (Friday?)	Revise your article according to feedback (pages 230–231)	60 minutes

Above are the tasks for your ninth week. It may take quite a bit longer to get feedback than you had anticipated, so you may need to move on to the next chapter while you are waiting to hear back from your readers. Make sure to start this week by scheduling when you will write and then tracking the time that you actually spend writing.

EIGHTH WEEK IN REVIEW

You have now spent eight weeks working on the most important tasks involved in revising an article for publication: designing a plan, selecting a text for revision, writing an abstract, organizing your article around your argument, searching for and picking the right journal, reading and writing up the scholarly literature, restructuring your article, and revising your title, introduction, and conclusion. It's an excellent time to get others' opinions on your article, while change is still possible.

With all this work done, you would think basic questions about the article's worth would not arise, but something about handing over your writing to another human being tends to inspire such questions. Is the article worth the time you are spending on it? Should you keep working on this particular article? If you are feeling good about the article, you can skip the following.

If you are feeling bad about your article, I hope your readers this week can reinvigorate your commitment to it. At this late stage, others can see your work more positively than you do, and you should trust them. If you are starting to wonder if the article is worth working on at all, ask yourself if the main reason you want to stop is because you are scared, tired, or bored. If so, push on! Those feelings will pass. As Bolker says, "Just as it's okay to be scared, it's also okay to be tired and bored, just so long as you keep working anyway" (Bolker 1998, 124). Don't be like Frodo in *Lord of the Rings* who spends his whole life making it to the volcano at Mount Doom only to decide not to throw the ring in (Lee 2005).

If, however, the reason you want to stop is because you have slowly discovered some fatal flaw in your article, and have confirmation from a trusted reader that the article cannot be salvaged, you have some decisions to make. If you are not going to work on this article, which one will you work on? You cannot simply stop writing; as an academic; you must always be working toward publication. You have two choices. You can select another article for revision and start work on it right away. Or, now that you have learned many of the principles for writing a publishable article, you can start from scratch on a brand new article.

If you make the decision to abandon the article and move on to another, don't feel you have wasted your time. Rather, you have learned something important about your own writing through the revising process. In my course, quite a few students do significant revising and then decide that the paper they chose was too flawed to revise into publishable quality. But many write to me later to say that the process of revising their own work taught them more than drafting articles from scratch ever had and that subsequent writing was much easier. Further, nothing confirms that you are a true writer more than having the courage to set writing aside and begin again.

TYPES OF FEEDBACK

This week is not about engaging in a formal peer review process, like that at journals, but about asking for the feedback of your colleagues, class-mates, or advisors. Receiving and using such feedback is an essential part of becoming a good writer.

Unfortunately, one of the occupational hazards of being in academia is that our critical faculties wax and our supportive faculties wane. By the time we get out of graduate school we are a lot better at pointing out what people are doing wrong than in enabling people to do better. While there is a place for pure critique, the informal activities of this chapter are about getting feedback that can help you improve your article, not abandon it.

In this section, then, are instructions for giving feedback, not receiving it. One of the best ways to improve your writing is to learn to give good feedback and be supportive of others' struggles. So, how do we learn to use our critical faculties to enable others to write better and, eventually, ourselves? You can learn to avoid the five obsessions of bad readers and to embrace the practices of good readers. You can also have potential readers read the following advice, so that they approach your writing with the same spirit in which you will approach theirs.

What Not To Do When You Are Giving Feedback

The following obsessions prevent us from giving good feedback to our friends and colleagues.

Do not obsess about the author's bibliographic sources. A good reader does not simply name five, ten, or fifty additional books that the author should have consulted and cited. Your job is to focus on what the author does with what they have read. In a thirty-page article, no one can possibly cite everything on a topic. An article is not meant to be exhaustive.

Recommending reading can be a substitute for actually engaging with the content of the article and how the author has gone about putting his or her ideas together. Don't use others' research as a leaping off point to think through your own ideas. Stay engaged with their project and their aims. If you read a thirty-page article with twenty to sixty citations, don't let your only feedback be a long list of titles. Don't develop the nervous tic of academia to rattle off only loosely related titles. People have written amazing articles without citing more than three or four other texts.

"But, but, but," you say, "are you really saying we should never recommend texts? What if the author really has left out an important text? What if I just happen to know a text that would provide them with a perfect proof? I love it when my professor tells me what to read!" You can recommend reading, but don't gild the lily. Ask yourself if, given the size of the article, the author has a fair number of references to literature in the field. If he or she does, really work to resist the impulse to recommend texts. Learn to accept that no article will ever cite everything relevant. If he or she doesn't seem to engage with their field—remember the author must say something new about something old—then you can make some kind of blanket comment about this. "I don't think you have enough about what other social scientists say about motivation" or "There's a fair amount of scholarship on Ngugi wa Thiong'o's theory, you might want to cite some of it."

And, if you read someone's article and you get this excited feeling that you can really help him or her by recommending a particular text, go for it. If you get this sinking feeling the longer you read and you find yourself repeatedly thinking, "How can they possibly write on this topic without mentioning so and so," then mention that text. If you feel that some sources are needed to back a particular argument, say that. You don't have to suggest which ones unless you really know which ones.

Do not obsess about what is not in the article. It is your job to focus on improving what is in the article, not to insist that the author include what isn't in the article. A thirty-page article can only do so much; by definition, it will have huge gaps. No author can cover every possible approach to the topic in such a limited space. It is perfectly acceptable to write an article about racism in middle schools without addressing gender; to write about nineteenth-century British thought without mentioning eighteenth-century British thought; to write about Southern California without mentioning Northern California; to write about African authors without mentioning Nadine Gordimer; to write about German art without mentioning surrealism. To make a general comment saying that the omission of race or classical thought raises serious questions is okay, but again, it shouldn't be the majority of your comments. Don't ask for additional research or experimentation; instead, comment on what the author managed to do with the data collected. If it isn't convincing, then say it isn't convincing. Good readers pay attention to what is there.

Do not obsess about fixing the article. Because most of us have more experience writing than reviewing, we tend to approach other people's articles as writers. That is, as if the article was our own writing. We don't separate ourselves enough from the text in front of us, and we think it is our job to rewrite it.

Two problems result from not setting enough distance from others' work. First, you often start to feel overwhelmed. It's a huge job to go into someone else's writing and solve it. You start to experience mistakes in an author's work as an offense: "How dare they ask me to read something that is so confused? Don't they know I'm busy? How am I supposed to help them when they need so much help?" You feel anxious because you are not sure how to fix the writing. This leads to the second problem. Since you don't feel adequate to the job and, since this feeling of inadequacy is unbearable, you sometimes take it out on the author. The review is then delivered in anger and frustration, which is almost always useless to the author, who can't hear the advice because of the emotional way that it is being delivered, which sparks his or her own anxieties. That's why I recommend that you not focus on fixing others' work, but on giving a response. It is not your job to fix other people's articles; it is your job to give them your reading of it.

Do not obsess about judging the work. You need not consider yourself an expert on anyone else's writing. You are simply a reader. One subjective, slightly tired, slightly distracted reader. So, don't see your own position as all-knowing.

In practice, what this means specifically is, don't be harsh. Be kind when you are reading others' work and your own. You shouldn't, of course, praise everything but you should avoid phrasing your criticisms in ways that are harsh and unhelpful. I mean such words as "sloppy," "incoherent," "nonsense," "ridiculous," "boring"—and I cite here just a few of the words I have seen on the margins of my own papers over the years.

Students have told me that professors have written on their papers "hackneyed," "rubbish," "tedious," "hokey," "fake," and (I don't know why I find this so shocking after all the rest) "shit." Such comments simply aren't helpful. Remember not to judge the article (it isn't a contest), but to give feedback according to your own subjective views.

It can be particularly difficult to avoid being a judge when you do not agree politically with the content of someone else's article. If you find someone else's work disturbing, you can always excuse yourself. "I just don't think I would be a good reader for your article deconstructing the poetry of this openly racist writer." That's all you need to say, and there is no reason for either side to feel bad. You are not obligated to read disturbing things. If you can't give feedback on an article at this initial stage without prejudice or emotion, best to leave it to others. If, however, you really disagree with the author's topic or approach and want to take it on, make a concerted effort to remember that you are not a judge and that it is your job to provide a response. Every argument has flaws; point out where the argument is not working on the author's own terms. Lee Bowie, a logic professor of mine, used to say, "It is difficult to convince individuals that their premises are wrong. It is easier to show them how their premises do not lead to their conclusions."

What To Do When You Are Giving Feedback

So, if those are the rules on how to avoid being a bad reader, how do you go about being a good one?

Start with the positive. A little bit of sugar makes the medicine go down. A student once told the class that she had two advisors. One she liked and did everything she recommended; the other she disliked and resisted everything she recommended. Why? The student commented,

> I realized that the reason I liked the one and disliked the other had nothing to do with the criticism itself. In fact, the one I disliked tended to have fewer critical things to say than the other. But the advisor I liked always started off enthusiastically, she always loved the paper, thought it was a great project, was sure it would be published, and then would give me a long list of what was wrong with it. But because she had "bought in," because I felt like she had signaled she was on my side, I listened to her and I walked away feeling encouraged. The other advisor always started off with the problems. It just felt so discouraging, "well, you've really got to work on your structure and you didn't cite these three people I told you to cite and you really should learn APA style better." At the end, she would say, "But, it's a very solid project and I think you are doing good work." By then, it just seemed like a kiss off, like bribery, like I was a little kid who could be bought off.

But why would she feel this way when the second advisor's criticisms weren't as wholesale as the first advisor? The student said, "What made the difference was that the first advisor always started off positive. And what's funny is that, even knowing this was the difference didn't help; I just never could quite hear the second advisor as well as I could the first." I have found this to be true for many people. One of the biggest steps you can make toward being a useful reader is to start off with the positive.

Be specific. However, when starting with the positive, make sure it's specific. Vague praise such as "Good paper!" is not enough. Most authors in the position of getting feedback are like patients waiting for the doctor to give them the results of their health test. As soon as the doctor walks into the room, the patient is trying to read her expression and her words for catastrophic news. For some reason, generalities inspire fear: "She just said that I'm looking good, that means I have something fatal!" Starting with a specific positive—I really like your argument about x, I thought your conclusion was really strong—lets the author know that you are being sincere, not just placating them until you get around to delivering the bad news that "you should never pick up a pen again."

If you feel that you do have a solution, that you do know something specific that would improve the article, be clear about it. Nothing is worse than someone who reads your work and tells you something is wrong with it but they aren't sure what it is. "I mean, it's a really good article, but, I don't know, something about it doesn't quite hang together, you know?" Likewise, don't tell someone, "Your writing style needs a lot of work," as this is vague and unhelpful. Say instead, "You might think about working on making your sentences more active and less passive." In delivering criticism, be purposeful and clear. This is the great balancing act of reviewing, humble but firm, respectful but sharp.

Focus on giving a response. The writing research says that the most helpful review you can give another writer is to tell them what you understood their article to say (Elbow 1973; McMurry 2004). You don't have to tell them what's wrong with it or how it should be changed to be correct. You only have to tell them: "I understood this, I didn't understand this, it seemed like your argument was this, you seemed to say that your article is a contribution because of this." If you focus on giving a response rather than on offering solutions, it will help you to be respectful of the author's person and intent. They are not you; they do not put things the way you would. And they do not have to agree with you or accept what you are saying to them.

Continuing on this theme, I believe that what is helpful for an author is not so much telling them what is wrong and how to fix it, but marking what made you stop. In other words, ideally, what a reader offers is a marker of what they have noticed, what stood out. What they say about what they noticed can sometimes be less important than the fact that they have identified a section to be addressed. Where did you have to reread the sentence or paragraph several times? Or, where did you stop because you thought, wow, that's really good! Just letting the author know these moments is helpful. For instance, sometimes it is exactly what someone praises that needs to go. That is, because you marked it the author realized that it sticks out, it is not like the rest, or it's over the top. Sometimes you mark where you stumbled and the author will realize that actually nothing is wrong there, it is the paragraph before that is the problem. In summary, this is the response approach to feedback, where you are not attempting to solve problems, but merely to identify where you as a reader had problems.

Always suggest. If you feel that you do have a solution, that you do know something specific that would improve the article, something that goes beyond response, frame it as a suggestion. Again, the work is not your own, you are not the expert on it, so all you can do is make suggestions. Admit your limitations and don't invent advice on material that is beyond your knowledge.

Copyeditors are trained to ask the author questions instead of telling them what to do. The difference between "Redundant." and "Redundant?" may not seem like a big difference, but that little question mark can prevent the criticism from making such a large dent in the author's ego. The period places you as the authority; the question mark places the author as the authority. "Sentence fragment. Rewrite?" or "Relevance?" suggests that it is possible that this is not an error but a choice on the part of the author, which it may be. All we can offer is our opinion on what works for us and what doesn't.

Focus on the macro. Most readers get distracted by the small stuff. You will become known as a good reviewer if you can stay focused on the big stuff. Does the article have an argument? Is that threaded throughout? Just focusing on the structure of the article can be extremely helpful to authors. Three solid observations about macro aspects of the article—its argument, evidence, structure, findings, or methods—are often worth dozens of smaller observations about grammar and punctuation. In these early stages, try to think about the whole and the logical flow of the piece. Most people can't absorb a number of comments at one time.

Spend the time. It takes two to five hours to read and comment on another's article thoroughly. If you haven't done much commenting before, it can take as many as eight to twelve hours.

What to Do When You Are Getting Feedback

Now let's leap over to the other side. How does one go about being a good recipient of feedback? How does one survive the process?

Give instructions. When you hand your article to another, let that reader know what kind of feedback you need. If you are about to send the article to a journal, you can say that you are looking just for a last check for typos or egregious errors; you aren't at a place where you can absorb much else. If you are having trouble with your methods section, ask them to focus on that section. Feel free to say that you are not currently looking for line editing, spelling and grammar correction, but attention to more macro issues. Or, vice versa.

Separate the delivery from the message. Many people are bad at giving criticism—they don't start with the positive, they get angry, they get frustrated. Try to ignore the emotion with which comments or suggestions are delivered. If you can stay calm and refuse to take any comments personally, you will be better able to evaluate the criticisms on their own merits. Criticism delivered in a hostile manner can still be correct; criticism delivered in a kind manner can still be wrong. You have to learn to sift the useful from the useless without reference to its delivery method. "Remember that the same person can be absolutely right about certain aspects of a piece and dead wrong about others" (Edelstein 1991, 13).

Listen, don't talk. A good practice when receiving criticism of your writing is to be silent. Just listen and take careful notes. Later you can decide which criticisms are useful or not; for now, just make sure that you understand clearly what the criticism is. It's easy to get swept up in defending your work instead of listening. But even if you orally convince others of your point, your defense still isn't on the page, which is where it needs to be. In fact, some writing groups have a rule that those being critiqued cannot speak until everyone has given their opinion. You don't have to go this far, but you should be listening more than you are talking. If you are working in a group, this allows you to have the wonderful experience of hearing others defending your work for you.

Take advantage. Every criticism is an opportunity for you as to explain your ideas more clearly. So, don't think, "What an idiot! Anyone smart would get that sentence." If your reader stumbles, use that feedback to clarify your writing.

You are the final authority on your own writing. You don't have to do anything anyone tells you to do, no matter how hard he or she pushes. Only make changes that you understand and that make sense to you. Once you really believe that you are the final judge of your writing, you can be more open to others' comments and suggestions.

Interestingly, the more famous you get, the less feedback you get. A student in one of my classes told us a story about her participation in a graduate student journal. They reviewed submissions anonymously and as a group. Everyone read all the articles, they then debated their strengths and weaknesses, and had someone draft a letter with the various recommendations. Only after doing so did they look at the names. On one occasion, they found that a submission was from an extremely famous scholar. The article was quite problematic, however, clearly a first draft. The students debated what to do and then decided, courageously, to proceed as they normally did and send off the recommendations. The scholar wrote back to them almost immediately, saying that it had been years since he had received detailed feedback and he was very grateful to them! He revised the article as suggested and resubmitted it. So, be glad that you are in a place where people still critique your work!

EXCHANGING YOUR ARTICLES

This week we are going to focus on giving and getting feedback. It's important to do both this week because in the process of giving feedback, you learn something about revising your own work. The tools you will learn can be used on your own writing.

Day 1: Reading the Workbook

On the first day of your writing week, you should read the workbook up to this page and answer all the questions posed in the workbook up to this point. Then work on any tasks remaining from previous weeks or on your own list of tasks to accomplish.

Day 2: Sharing Your Article and Getting Feedback

Sharing with professors. If possible, you want to have someone in your field read the article as it stands. If a professor recommended you pursue publication, you should ask him or her to read the article. As noted in the earlier section about picking a paper, a faculty member can save you tremendous amounts of time and put you way ahead of the game with a few good reading recommendations and some suggestions on structure and argument. If you feel anxious about presenting yourself as someone aspiring to publication, tell the professor that you are meeting merely to get advice on revising. You do not have to tell the professor that you have an eye on publication. Then, if the meeting goes well, you can relate your intention.

Sharing with colleagues. Find someone who is willing to do an article exchange with you. Exchange reviews are better than solo reviews because those who are about to be critiqued tend to be kinder in their own critiques. Then, get together in a place where you won't be interrupted and hand each other your article for reading right then. When you give an article to someone to read while alone, it can be difficult for him or her to get around to reading it, so why not make it social and read the article when together?

Once you have exchanged articles, then follow the reading process below. The reason for this particular process is to train readers to keep some distance from the article and not get too wrapped up in it. The reader's job is to identify problems, not try to solve them.

- Tell each other what kind of feedback you each need at this point in the writing process.

- Taking up the other's article, read it through once without a pen in your hand. Do not make any marks on the article, just familiarize yourself with it. Don't get distracted by the small stuff, you are trying to keep the whole in mind. (30–60 minutes)

- Then, go back to the beginning and pick up your pen. Go through the whole article putting a check mark next to whatever is good, clear, vivid, or compelling. You can put a check next to a whole paragraph, a sentence, a word, an example, a heading, whatever you think is good. If you want, you can write down next to the check what you liked about that part. (20 minutes)

- Then, go back to the beginning and circle the unclear, what you do not understand fully, would you would like to know more about, what could be improved. (30 minutes)

- Then, turn over the article and on the back page write a summary of what you understood the article to be about. (5 minutes)

- Then, go over your marks with the author. First, describe what you liked about the article in general. Starting with the positive is essential. Then, go over your checks and circles and explain what you liked or what caused you to stumble. If the author wants to work through possible solutions with you, that's fine, but don't feel you need to have solutions. Be sure to give your summary to the author so they can see what you took away from the article. This allows them to adjust it accordingly.

- If the author starts explaining aspects of the article, try to take notes as the author talks. These notes can help the author later.

Sharing with students. Don't assume that someone has to be an expert to help you. The research shows that even inexperienced writers can catch problems with tense, transitions, spelling, facts, and so on (Willis 1993, 56). Although professional editors are great, take advantage of the (free) resources you have.

On the next page is a form you can use if you want to be sure that your reader comments on all relevant aspects of your article.

Day 3: Making a List of Remaining Tasks

If you must wait for your readers to get back to you with their comments, this is a good time to take stock of where you are in the process of revising the article and what remains to be done. If you haven't sent out your query letter yet (see the advice in Week 4), now is a good time to do so.

Days 4 and 5: Revising Your Article According to Feedback

Follow the advice earlier in the chapter about using feedback and consult the relevant chapters in the workbook as you revise in response to the feedback you have received.

Feedback Form

These questions will help you to comment on the article you are reviewing. Your answers should give the author a guide in revising his or her work. You may not find all the questions relevant to reviewing the article that you are reading; use what is useful. The General series of questions are mine; the rest, which are more evaluative, are direct from a form that the journal *Cultural Anthropology* gives to its reviewers.

General

- What are the strengths of this article?

- Does the author state the article's topic?

- What is the topic of the article in three or four words?

- Does the author state the argument of the article early and clearly?

- What is the argument of the article (so far as you understand it)?

- Who is the audience?

Content

- Does the first sentence draw the reader in? If not, what might make it better?

- Does the author establish the significance or relevance of the article? If not, where might this be done?

- Does the author raise questions that go unanswered? If so, specify one.

- Were any parts of the article redundant or not relevant? If so, specify where.

Flow

- Does the ending circle back to the beginning? If not, specify what might tie it together.

- Are there any unclear or missing transitions? If so, specify one.

- Was there any section where you lost interest? If so, specify what might have held your interest better there.

Other

- Did you feel the structure of the article could be clearer or stronger? If so, specify how.

- Could the author's argument be better supported? If so, specify where.

- Does the article have any blind spots? If it does, specify one.

- Did you notice any errors in sources, dates, quotations, facts, or proper names? If so, note them on the article.

- What did you find most intriguing about this article?

DOCUMENTING YOUR WRITING TIME AND TASKS

On the following weekly plan, please graph when you expect to write and what tasks you hope to accomplish this week. Then keep track of what you actually did. Remember, you are to allot fifteen minutes to one hour every day to writing. At the end of the week, take pride in your accomplishments and evaluate whether any patterns need changing.

Week 9 Calendar							
Time	Monday	Tuesday	Wednesday	Thursday	Friday	Saturday	Sunday
5:00 a.m.							
6:00							
7:00							
8:00							
9:00							
10:00							
11:00							
12:00 p.m.							
1:00							
2:00							
3:00							
4:00							
5:00							
6:00							
7:00							
8:00							
9:00							
10:00							
11:00							
12:00 a.m.							
1:00							
2:00							
3:00							
4:00							
Total Minutes Actually Worked							
Tasks Completed							

Week 10

Editing Your Sentences

Day to Do Task	Week 10 Daily Writing Tasks	Estimated Task Time
Day 1 (Monday?)	Read through page 253; start documenting your time (page 266)	30 minutes
Day 2 (Tuesday?)	Run diagnostic test (pages 253–258)	60 minutes
Day 3 (Wednesday?)	Revise your article using the diagnostic test (pages 258–262)	60 minutes
Day 4 (Thursday?)	Revise your article using the diagnostic test (pages 258–262)	60 minutes
Day 5 (Friday?)	Correct other types of problem sentences (pages 262–265)	60 minutes

Above are the tasks for your tenth week. To increase your article's chances of publication, you should improve word choices, prune deadwood, add clarifying material, and straighten sentence structures. Make sure to start this week by scheduling when you will write and then tracking the time that you actually spend writing.

ON TAKING THE TIME

Years ago, when my family was living in Ethiopia, my father treated several patients who had diabetes. As a clinical researcher, he found the cases interesting since they were in stark contrast to those he had seen in North America. Unlike the great majority of American diabetics, who are middle-aged or older and overweight, these patients were teenagers and slender. They entered the hospital hyperventilating, dehydrated, and semicomatose.

So, he went to the medical college's library to see what he could find out about diabetes in Ethiopia. Fifteen years of the *Ethiopian Medical Journal* revealed no articles. An East African medical journal had only one small study on adult diabetes: they thought the pancreas was not producing enough insulin due to the patients' poor nutritional status. My father ended up doing a modified treatment, giving them some insulin but then turning to dietary restrictions and oral medications, based on his thought that these were intermediate cases, between adult onset and juvenile diabetes. The patients responded to his treatment and later could be treated with oral medications alone, unlike typical juvenile diabetics.

He mentioned the cases to my mother, who encouraged him to publish his thoughts. He demurred, saying he had only three cases and wasn't sure whether anybody outside of Ethiopia would be interested in them. Besides, he didn't think the findings were impressive enough to be publishable. My mother responded, "It's the first article on the topic; it doesn't have to be comprehensive, it just has to be written." Maybe later, he said, as it was very busy at the provincial hospital. "Later rarely comes," she wisely commented. So he took the time then and submitted a brief article to the *Ethiopian Medical Journal* on the cases he had seen. In 1969, it was published.

Thirty years later, in 1999, my father was walking toward his hotel in the capital Addis Ababa when he saw a sign for a medical clinic that had a lab. Curious, he decided to walk in. The clerk took him to meet the Ethiopian doctor in charge of the lab and they got to talking. The topic of diabetes came up, and my father mentioned that he had treated some patients years ago and written a little article on the topic. The Ethiopian doctor exclaimed, "That was you?! I know that article. Everyone knows that article. It was the first article published about diabetes in Ethiopia, one of the few articles to be written about rural medicine. It's wonderful to meet you."

When I commented to my father that it was a good thing he wrote the article, he nodded. "I didn't know then what I know now, that even little things can have a long-term impact. At the time, it always seemed like an imposition to spend so much time writing something so small. But years later, that small thing would still be making a contribution, long after everything else I was doing, which seemed so important at the time, had been forgotten."

Don't let life's trivialities stop you from creating something permanent. You are getting close to the finish line, so keep moving!

TYPES OF REVISING

Revising can be divided into two categories: macro and micro.

Macrostructure Revising

You have spent many weeks doing macrostructure revising: reviewing the literature, naming the debate, aiming for a particular journal, stating an argument early and clearly, and making sure you have a solid structure. Macrostructure revising involves big changes—moving paragraphs, adding examples, deleting sections, and rewriting pages.

The writing research shows that macrostructure revising is the most difficult kind of revising to do, the least likely to get done, and the most difficult to teach. Studies show that inexperienced writers tend to make surface changes to their prose, while experienced writers make deeper changes. As the scholar Meredith Sue Willis points out, when most of us first learned to write, we simply wrote down the words that came to mind.[1] Those words were largely others' words and we did not revise them. In one study, novice writers were shown to do very little revising. They made only 12 percent of their changes to meaning, while experienced writers made 34 percent of their changes to meaning (Faigley and Witte 1981). Surprising, isn't it? You would think that better writers would produce flawless drafts the first time around, that better writers would make fewer changes to their prose, but in fact, the opposite is true—good writers make more changes. They know that there is more than one way to say something and that they may not have hit the best way on their first try. So, if you have been making lots of big changes to your article, that is a sign of your skill, not your lack of it! Just know that many bad writers avoid macrostructure revising, and many good writers continue to struggle with it—that's why so much of this workbook is devoted to it.

Microstructure Revising

This week you will turn to the second category of revising: microstructure revising. Many people call this kind of revising "editing" or even "proofreading," in which you examine individual words and sentences for opportunities to address grammar, punctuation, spelling, and diction. When people talk about "good writing," they often mean that the piece is working at the microstructure level, without grammatical errors or infelicities of style.

Although I only spend one week on this type of revising, it is vital that you learn to edit your own writing. It can make a huge difference in the acceptability of your article. Good writing can (unfortunately) cover up bad research and bad ideas, but good research usually cannot carry a badly written article into publication. Further, good microstructure revising can lead to good macro revising. Sometimes improving a single word can help you to put your argument better and lead you back to macrostructure revising.

Once you have done the revising proposed in this chapter, you will be ready to finalize your article for submission.

THE RULES OF EDITING

Many excellent books have been published about how to improve academic writing. One of the best books is Joseph M. William's *Style: Ten Lessons in*

Clarity and Grace (now in its eighth edition). It is packed with quotes on writing, brief histories of right and wrong English style, hilarious explanations of why writers on English grammar are often such terrible writers (including himself), and plain advice. Williams has distilled much of his advice down to one principle. Look at every sentence in your writing and ask yourself a simple question: Does the sentence have a character (noun subject) and does that character act (verb)? Every sentence must tell a clear story, with both characters and actions. If the character and its actions emerge in the first seven or eight words of the sentence (excepting introductory clauses), great! If they don't, rewrite the sentence until both are clear. To understand exactly what a character and action are, how to detect them, and how to include them, you will need to read William's book. It's well worth it. He also gives good advice on such macrostructure issues as coherence and coordination, which few writing manuals address.

One of the easiest books to use is Bruce Ross-Larson's *Edit Yourself: A Manual for Everyone Who Works with Words*. He doesn't explain how to edit, he just provides hundreds of examples of poor word phrases and their better versions. He arranges the examples in alphabetical order based on various style manuals, including Skillin and Gay's *Words into Type* (1974), which started the practice of listing poor phrases and their replacements.

Another good book is *Common Mistakes in English* by T. J. Fitikides, which helps those for whom English is not a native language. This is the only book I know that starts from typical ESL errors, which helps if you are looking to push your grasp of English to the next level. Typical problems revolve around prepositions and articles—using the wrong one, omitting the right one, or including unnecessary ones—as well as using the wrong verb tense or number, placing adverbs incorrectly, and un-English expressions.

At this point in the article revising process, however, you may be sick of your article and just want to send it as quickly as possible! You may not be interested in learning all the fine points of grammar and when to use "who" or "whom," "that" or "which." I've designed this week's exercises with speed in mind. I identify some common academic writing errors and then give you a tool for diagnosing where your writing could be briefer, clearer, or stronger. Once you have diagnosed your writing for simple problems, you can work toward improving your word choice and sentence structure. While some will insist that you must know all the rules to be a good writer, our objective this week is publication not perfection. If you are not used to editing your own writing, starting with small, manageable tasks helps. The more proficient you get at these small corrections, the more skills you will bring to more complicated self-editing tasks.

To get you going, here are a few principles of American English academic style.

- Don't use two words when one will do.

- Don't use a noun when you can use a verb.

- Don't use an adjective or adverb unless you must.[2]

- Don't use a pronoun when a noun would be clearer.

- Don't use a general word when you can use a specific one.

- Don't use the passive voice unless the subject is unknown or unimportant.

For most of human history, the more flowery and elaborate your language, the more admired you were as a wordsmith. In the United States, with the exponential increase in print, however, value has come to inhere in brevity. Modern people want not just fast cars and fast food but fast texts.

You should remember one caveat, however. All this advice about brevity and clarity is prescriptive—it doesn't necessarily reflect what is happening in the pages of academic journals. Some research indicates that prestigious journals' articles tend to be less readable and more complex than those articles in less prestigious journals (Shelley and Schuh 2001). Some scholars have fulminated against the demand in U.S. education for clear writing, reminding scholars about "the uses of obscurity" and "the delights of jargon" (Lanham 2007). Further, Merriam-Webster's wonderful *Dictionary of English Usage* shows that many of the most sacrosanct writing "rules" are simply preferences. All the most famous English writers split infinitives, ended sentences with prepositions, and used "comprise" when they should have used "compose." If you are confused about what is correct, it is precisely because you have seen so many incorrect instances in print.

So why do instructors give this advice about clarity? Because you must be more skilled to pull off a complex sentence than a simple one. Maintaining links in a complex sentence is difficult and teaching how to write good complex sentences is even more difficult. In contrast, teaching how to write a simple sentence is straightforward. Thus, recommending clarity is the easiest advice to give those with poor prose. Once poor writers have learned to link material in simple ways, they can start attempting a more complex writing style.

The conclusion? Developing skills in writing clear sentences will help you become a better complex writer in the end. So, let's look at some ways of improving clarity.

THE BELCHER DIAGNOSTIC TEST

I have innovated a diagnostic test to help students determine where they could improve their word choice and sentence structure. I've based the test on the principle that certain words signal the possibility of certain problems. If you can focus your revising attention on these signal words and the words around them, you can improve your writing without having to memorize a lot of rules.

Some caveats. The test is not that helpful for nonnative speakers of English. The test is best at capturing the tics of those trained to write in North American or British schools. For nonnative speakers, I highly recommend any of the books by John M. Swales and Christine B. Feak, including *Academic Writing for Graduate Students* (1994) and *English in Today's Research World* (2000). Further, this diagnostic test cannot identify all the places where you could improve your prose. Only long experience reading in your field, studying style and grammar manuals, or taking composition classes can give you all the tools you need to identify poor prose and write correct prose.

Many students know that they should do something to improve their prose, but when they sit down with their entire article of 5,000 to 15,000 words, they feel overwhelmed. Where to start and how? My diagnostic test makes the task of line editing less daunting by identifying some straightforward problems and giving some simple solutions. It gives you a method for entering sentences and fixing problems. Then you will find it easier to solve the sentence's other problems. The test is also helpful for good self-editors who need a (fun) way to defamiliarize their prose for a last check. All writers have blind spots and this test can help you to detect them.

If the test seems overwhelming at first, remember that according to linguistic theory, there are only four categories of transformation: deletion, addition, substitution, and rearrangement. In other words, there are only four kinds of changes you can make to your prose. That seems manageable, right? Start with the simplest possible solution, and only if that doesn't work should you try something more complicated. I studied copyediting with a famous instructor in Washington D.C., Bita Lanys, who taught generations of copyeditors to train their steely eyes on turgid government prose. On the first day of class, she told us that any idiot could change a text 50 percent and improve it 50 percent. You were an editor, she said, when you could change a text 5 percent and improve it 50 percent.

Read the principles below to understand why the diagnostic test will focus on signal words.

Diagnostic Test Part I:
Words that Might Need to Be Cut

The following words signal possible deadwood (unneeded words). If you can rewrite the sentence without them, consider doing so. (Those of you familiar with Strunk and White's *Elements of Style* will notice that it has inspired quite a few of the examples below.)

Search for *and* and *or*. Either of these conjunctions can signal doubling (the use of two words where one will do). To improve a sentence with doubling, delete the signal word and one of the similar terms.

* Doubles: Yang **and** Yu argued **that** emotion **is** necessary **and** essential.
   Singles: Yang and Yu argued that emotion is necessary.
   Note: "Yang and Yu" is not a doubling—the two words do not mean the same thing—so you cannot cut either. But "necessary and essential" is a doubling; pick one of the words.

Either of these conjunctions can signal a list, which is fine if the list is not comprehensive. If you have listed all the subcategories, consider deleting the comprehensive list and using the category instead.

- List of subcategories: She asked the men, women, **and** children to stand.

   Category: She asked the congregation to stand.

   Note: Any list should have a parallel structure (more on this principle later).

Either of these conjunctions can signal a list, which is fine if you introduce it. Structure the sentence so that the list concept appears first and then the list.

- List concept last: The predominant sounds **of** the steel guitar **and** fiddle, vocal timbers **of** strain **in their** higher registers, regional accents, comparable ranges, **and** lyrics **that** address the pains **of** romance demonstrate **that** Wells **and** Williams sung about similar topics, such **as** infidelity, **in** comparable manners.

   List concept first: The music of Wells and Williams has in common the predominance of the steel guitar and fiddle, a strain in the higher vocal registers, distinct regional accents, and heart wrenching lyrics about infidelity and the other pains of romance.

Either of these conjunctions can signal a list, which is fine if the list is parallel. Structure the items in the list so that they appear in similar ways. Each item in the list should follow naturally from the words right before the list. The easiest way to make a list parallel is to start each item in the list with the word that appeared right before the list. Once every item starts with the same word, you know it is parallel and you can remove the word. In the example below, see how you could make the sentence parallel by adding the word "as" to each item.

- Not parallel: During the war, women **did** all sorts **of** new jobs, including acting **as** the police, truck driving, factory workers, **and** harvesting **and** planting.

   Parallel but awkward: During the war, women did all sorts **of** new jobs, including acting **as** the police, driving trucks, working **in** factories, **and** farming land.

   Parallel: During the war, women took on new jobs as police officers, truck drivers, factory workers, and farm laborers.[3]

   Note: In the first sentence, the items were a verb, a noun, a noun, and a verb—not parallel. In the second sentence, all were verbs but the first item was awkward. In the third sentence, all the items are nouns that followed naturally from "as."

Either of these conjunctions can signal a run-on sentence. If you can split a sentence into two, consider doing so.

- Run-on sentence: **In their** study **of** working-class youth, Skinitz **and** Sobmon contended **that** the tendency **of** women **and** working class youth to retain **and** make decisions **with** respect **to** relationships **is** often interpreted **by** social science researchers **as** constraining, rather than enabling, **their** development, reflecting a bias **that** emphasizes a predominant American "developmental vision" **of** heroic separation **from** past ties **to** move forward.

Strong sentences: In their study of working-class youth, Skinitz and Sobmon argued that women and working class youth tended to make decisions based on family ties and that social science researchers tended to interpret such decision making as constraining their subjects' individual growth. According to Skinitz and Sobmon, this interpretation reflects a bias toward heroic separation from past ties, a peculiarly American "developmental vision."

Search for *there* and *it*. Either of these pronouns can signal deadwood or weak verbs, particularly when paired with the verb *to be* and *that* or *which*. To improve a sentence with a cluster of these signal words, delete the signal words, delete the verb *to be*, bring in a stronger verb, and then move the subject up to the front of the sentence.

- Cluttered: **There were** a great number **of** test tubes lying **on** the counter.
  Better: A number **of** test tubes lay **on** the counter.
  Best: Test tubes covered the counter.

- Cluttered: **It was** clear **from** the high attendance **that there are** many **who** enjoy opera.
  Better: The high attendance clearly showed that many enjoy opera.
  Best: The high attendance demonstrated that many enjoy opera.
  Note: "There are" or "It was" can sometimes help your rhythm or transitions. So you don't have to delete them all, just examine each instance to see if you should cut it in particular.

The pronoun *it* often appears without a clear antecedent. Check every instance of *it* and make sure its antecedent is clear.

- Unclear pronoun: The experiment survived the power failure, due **to** the university's backup generator, but **it** soon grew overheated **and** then **it was** ruined.
  Clear pronoun: The experiment survived the power failure, due to the university's backup generator, but the generator soon overheated and the experiment was ruined.
  Best sentence: The university's backup generator saved the experiment when the power failed, but the generator soon overheated and the experiment was ruined.

Either of these pronouns can signal a dangling participle if they appear with the verb *to be* and after an introductory clause. Check every instance of these pronouns right after a comma.

- Dangling: **Having** completed the experiment, **there is** no reason **for** the students to stay.

Attached: Having completed the experiment, the students had no reason to stay.

Note: The experiment was not conducted by "there" but by "the students." You must change the sentence to avoid the introductory clause modifying the wrong word.

Search for *that* and *which* and *who*. Any of these relative pronouns often signals deadwood, especially when paired with the verb *to be* and *there* or *it*. When these words appear together, you can often delete them. For instance, "there are many who" can become "many." Or, "the man who is in the front office" can become "the receptionist." You can often transform a noun later in the sentence into an earlier modifier or verb. Just be careful—sometimes *that* or *which* is essential to the meaning of the sentence (especially right after a comma).

- Wordy: His fundamental belief **is that there is** a conflict between Sartre's philosophy **and** his ethics.
  Clear: He believes that Sartre's philosophy conflicts with his ethics.

- Wordy: Poor households pay more **for** the food **that** they buy because local merchants exploit them.
  Clean: Poor households pay more for their food because local merchants exploit them.

- Wordy: Government facilities can on**ly** spend funds **that are** available.
  Clean: Government facilities can only spend available funds.

- Wordy: **It** should **be** noted **that there are** several **who did not** agree **with** the verdict.
  Better: Several did **not** agree with the verdict.
  Clean: Several disagreed with the verdict.
  Note: See the section on "not" below for advice on how to do the second revision.

Search for prepositions like *by, of, to, for, toward, on, at, from, in, with,* and *as*. Any of these prepositions, especially when they appear in clusters, often signal unneeded phrases. You can improve the sentence in which these phrases appear by deleting the phrases or changing nouns into modifiers.

- Wordy: **In** order **to** pass the test **in** the field **of** sociology, you must study the textbook.
  Clean: To pass the sociology test, you must study the textbook.

- Wordy: **With** reference **to** democracy, we should encourage **it by** way **of** a free press.
  Clean: We should encourage democracy with a free press.

- Cluttered: **In** the case **of** a great number **of** developing countries, the volume **of** production rose over the course **of** the year far higher than the predictions **of** the economists.

Clean: The yearly production **of** many developing countries rose higher than economists predicted.

Best: The yearly production **of** many developing countries exceeded economists' predictions.

Clean: Many developing countries' yearly production exceeded economists' predictions.

Note: Some will feel that the third revision is going too far as the subject is now a string of five adjectives and nouns. You can stay with the second revision and avoid strings of nouns in a row.

Prepositions often signal verbs buried as nouns (called nominalizations), especially when paired with pronouns like *it*. If you can unbury the verb, consider doing so.

- Buried verbs: **In** the event **that** I forget to explain the purpose **of** the article, please send an e-mail **to** me **with** a reminder about **it**.

  Unburied verbs: If I forget to explain the article's purpose, please remind me in an e-mail.

Prepositions often signal wordy constructions, especially when paired with the verb *to be*. If you can replace the prepositional phrase with an adjective, consider doing so.

- Wordy: **It is a** question **of** some importance how Russians remember Stalin.

  Strong: An important question is how Russians remember Stalin.

Strings of prepositional phrases often signal awkward sentence constructions. Evaluate each sentence with three or more prepositions. If you can rewrite the sentence without some of them, consider doing so.

- Cluttered: **There had** been major changes **in** the presentation related **to** the data accumulated **as** a consequence **of** exhaustive study **of** the results **of** treatment in cancers **of** the head **and** neck, breast, **and** gynecological tract.

  Clean: The author changed her presentation after exhaustively studying the results of treated cancers of the head and neck, breast, and gynecological tract.

  Note: Not all prepositions were removed; some were needed. Avoid replacing strings of prepositions with strings of adjectives (e.g., see the "yearly production" example above).

Prepositions often signal cluttered writing, especially when paired with words like *fact, kind, sort, type, way, form, variety, range,* and so on. If you can rewrite the sentence without them, consider doing so.

- Wordy: Nkuku **was** the type **of** individual who could not make up his mind.

  Better: Nkuku was an individual **who** could **not** make up his mind.

  Better: Nkuku could **not** make up his mind.

  Clean: Nkuku was indecisive.

- Wordy: Due **to** the fact **that** I **have** to teach **at** that time, I will **not be** able **to** come **to** your talk.

  Better: I have to teach **at that** time, so I will **not be** able **to** attend your talk.

  Clean: I cannot attend your talk because I have to teach then.

  Note: Sometimes switching the sentence around can solve the problem.

- Wordy: The way **in which** the candidates conducted themselves **was** observed **by** the election observers.

  Better: The election observers observed how the candidates conducted themselves.

  Clean: The election observers monitored the candidates' conduct.

Diagnostic Test Part II: Words that Might Need to Be Added

Sometimes you need to add a few extra words, not cut a few. Look at your pronouns to see if you need to clarify their relationship to the noun. A pronoun is a word used in place of a noun. Sometimes, it is not clear which noun the pronoun is replacing—pronouns can easily drift from their antecedent and the reader must reread the sentence to understand it. Evaluate each pronoun to see if you could replace it with a noun or add a noun to it.

Search for *this* and *these* and *those*. These demonstrative pronouns often appear alone, leaving their meaning unclear. Evaluate each occurrence and consider placing the antecedent, a noun, after these pronouns. The farther the pronoun is from its noun, the more likely that you need to add a noun to the pronoun to make it clear.

- Unclear pronoun: **These** caused the problem.

  Clear noun: These manufacturers caused the problem.

- Unclear pronoun: **This** demonstrates the ways **in which** syntax **is** tied **to** public **and** visible processes **of** projection.

  Clear noun: This study demonstrates how syntax **is** tied to public **and** visible projection processes.

  Best sentence: This study demonstrates how syntax interacts with visible projection processes.

- Unclear pronoun: **Those in which** the variables **were** left undecided **were** few.

  Clear noun: Those studies **in which** the variables **were** left undecided **were** few.

  Best sentence: Few studies left the variables undecided.

Demonstrative pronouns can be used mistakenly, their placement referencing the wrong antecedent. Make sure that clauses and pronouns are working together, not dangling.

- Unclear: Using the multiple choice tests **and** essay questions, **these were** prepared **for** the registrar.

Dangling and passive: Using the multiple choice tests and essay questions, **these** class grades **were** prepared **for** the registrar.

Attached and active: Using the multiple choice tests and essay questions, I prepared the class grades for the registrar.

Note: The first and second versions are grammatically incorrect. The grades or the registrar did not use the tests and questions, the teacher did. Fixing the passive voice helped make this clear in the third version. Passive voice after an introductory clause often leads to dangling constructions.

Search for *they* and *them* and *their* and *its*. These pronouns (as well as *it*) can appear too distant from their correct antecedents or too close to the wrong antecedents. Evaluate each occurrence and consider replacing the pronoun with a noun. Other pronouns are *she/her/hers* and *he/him/his* and *we/us/ours*.

- Unclear pronouns: The students **were** supposed to compete against **their** lecturers **in** football but **they** waited **in** vain for **them** to show up.

  Clear nouns: The students were supposed to compete against their lecturers in football but the students waited **in** vain **for** the lecturers to show up.

  Best sentence: The students were supposed to compete against their lecturers in football but the lecturers never showed up.

  Note: In the first version, "they" appeared after "the lecturers" but referenced "the students." Replacing pronouns with nouns made who was doing what clear.

- Unclear pronouns: **They** cannot always **be** confident about **its** results.

  Clear nouns: The researchers cannot be confident of the test's results.

- Unclear pronouns: **It was not** always efficacious **for** all the patients, **they** told **them**.

  Clear nouns: The drug **was not** always efficacious **for** all the patients, the researchers told the company.

  Best sentence: The drug did not help all the patients, the researchers told the company.

The pronoun should not appear *before* its antecedent. If the pronoun appears before its noun antecedent, switch them so that the pronoun is not premature.

- Premature pronoun: If **she had** taken to heart all the criticism **of** her research, Margaret Mead might never **have** published.

  Clear: If Margaret Mead had taken to heart all the criticism of her research, she might never have published.

  Note: The verb *had* is necessary to the verb tense and shouldn't be deleted.

Diagnostic Test Part III:
Words that Might Need to Be Changed

Sometimes you can't cut words or add words; you need to change words. That is, you need to replace a weak word with a strong word. In particular, academic writing tends to bury verbs as nouns or to employ vague verbs instead of vivid verbs.

Search for forms of the verb *to be*, including *is, are, was, were, am, be, being,* and *been*. As has often been observed, the verb *to be* is the workhorse of English verbs. It is essential for the progressive tense (e.g., the dog was running), for copulas (e.g., Abena is tall), and for the passive voice. The verb *to be* will always be common in your writing; just make sure you have not used it when another verb or sentence construction would be stronger.

You can often replace the verb *to be* with a more vivid verb. Evaluate each occurrence of the verb *to be* in your writing. If you can rewrite the sentence without it, consider doing so.

- Weak verb: In the early twentieth century, "the Mexican Problem" **was** the phrase most often used **in** reference to Mexican American culture.
  Strong verbs: In the early twentieth century, scholars' frequent condemnation of "the Mexican Problem" denigrated Mexican American culture.

- Weak verb: Mohammed **is** a mountain climber **and** the designer **of** hiking boots.
  Strong verbs: Mohammed climbs mountains and designs hiking boots.
  Note: Often, as in this example, you can find a stronger verb in one of the sentence's nouns (e.g., "climber" becomes "climbs").

You can often delete the verb *to be* when followed closely by *and*.

- Cluttered: Human kind **is** a part **of** nature **and** shares **in** the phenomenon **that** applies **to** other animals.
  Clean: Human kind, a part of nature, shares in the phenomenon that applies to other animals.

The verb *to be* often signals passive construction (e.g., a sentence that buries the subject). If the subject of the sentence is delivering the action, it is in the active voice. If the subject is receiving the action, the sentence is in the passive voice.

- Passive: The ball [object] was hit by her [subject].
  Active: She [subject] hit the ball [object].

The signal of a passive sentence is a form of the verb *to be* followed by a verb in the past tense (often ending in "ed"). If you can rewrite the sentence as an active sentence, consider doing so.

- Passive: My first visit **to** a butcher shall always **be** remembered **by** me.
  Active: I shall always remember my first visit to a butcher.

- Passive: The new city hall **was** designed **by** my sister's architecture firm.
  Active: My sister's architecture firm designed the new city hall.

The verb *to be* in the passive voice is appropriate when the subject is unknown or unimportant or when the object has been the subject of the paragraph. Passive voice also may be appropriate to avoid putting a long list at the beginning of the sentence.

- Passive: My sister won several prizes for her architectural designs. Unfortunately, she has not been asked to join any architectural firm.
  Active: [Since "sister" is the subject of the first sentence, the passive voice in the second sentence is fine.]

- Passive: The paint must be carefully prepared before it can be used in the restoration process.
  Active: [Leaving this sentence in the passive voice may be appropriate. If the section in which the sentence appears is instructional, it may not be possible to introduce an anonymous subject like "the art restoration expert" or "you." The context may not support either an invented actor or the repetition of the subject.]

- Passive: The new bridge was completed in April.
  Active: [We may not need to know that the Los Angeles Department of Public Works completed the work. In some contexts, we may have little interest in who completed the bridge.]

- Passive: Peter was attacked outside the gym and suffered a knee injury.
  Active: [The impact of the action on the known "object" Peter may be more important than the unknown "subject," the attacker.]

Search for forms of the verb *to have*, including *had* and *has*. The verb *to have* is essential for the perfect tense (e.g., they have waited, they will have waited). But *to have* sometimes buries another verb as a noun, especially when paired with an article like *a* or *an*. If you can rewrite the sentence to unbury the verb, or without *to have* entirely, do so.

- Buried verb: The candidates **have** a tendency **to** exaggerate **their** accomplishments, **which is** indicative **of their** insecurity.
  Unburied verb: The candidates tend to exaggerate their accomplishments, indicating their insecurity.
  Strong sentence: The candidates' insecurity leads them to exaggerate their accomplishments.

- Weak verb: Poor scholarship also **has** problems with adequate research.
  Strong verb: Poor scholarship also suffers from inadequate research.

Search for forms of the verb *to do*, including *does* and *did*. The verb *to do* is essential for questions about actions (e.g., do you intend to go?). But *to do* can bury a verb as a noun, especially when paired with an article like *a* or *an* or the word *not*. If you can rewrite the sentence without this verb, do so.

- Buried verb: We would like to **do** a study **on** animal husbandry.
  Unburied verb: We would like to study animal husbandry.

- Cluttered: **It is** clear **that** the experim**ent that they did did not** succeed.
  Better: Their experiment did not succeed.
  Strong sentence: Their experiment failed.

Search for forms of the verb *to make, to provide, to perform, to get, to seem,* and *to serve*. These verbs can also bury a strong verb, especially when paired with an article like *a* or *an* and prepositions. If you can rewrite the sentence with a stronger verb, do so.

- Weak: **This** course will **provide an** introduc**tion to** animal husbandry **to** undergraduates.
  Strong: This course will introduce undergraduates to animal husbandry.

Search for words ending in *ent, ence, ion,* and *ize*. These endings often signal verbs buried as nouns (nominalizations), especially if they appear with a preposition. If you can rewrite the sentence to convert the noun back into a verb, consider doing so.

- Buried verb: I would like to draw **this inference from the sentence in** *Finnegan's Wake* that . . .
  Unburied verb: I infer from the sentence in *Finnegan's Wake* that . . .
  Note: Not all words ending in *ent* are buried verbs (e.g., spent, sentence). Such words do not need to be changed.

- Buried verbs: The state's **improvement was** due **to** the establish**ment of an** impartial judiciary.
  Unburied verb: The state's improvem**ent was** due to establishing an impartial judiciary.
  Unburied verbs: The state improved upon establishing an impartial judiciary.

You can convert almost any word with these endings when it is bracketed by *the* and *of* :

- Buried verb: Policymaking involves the developm**ent of** acceptable courses **of** action.
  Unburied verb: Policymaking involves developing acceptable courses of action.

Search for *not*. The word *not* can signal a weak noun, a weak adjective, or a problem with multiple negatives. Evaluate each occurrence of the word in your writing. If you can rewrite the sentence without it, consider doing so.

- Multiple negatives: **Not** only **does** Bosey's novel **not have** a well-defined plot, but **it** also **does not have** strong character development **or** interesting writing.
  Better but weak adjectives: Bosey's novel **does not have** a well-defined plot, strong character development, **or** interesting writing.

Best sentence: A murky plot, poor character development, **and** uninteresting writing mar Bosey's novel.

Note: The writer veiled the harsh criticism in the first version; it is on full display in the third version. Writers afraid of their arguments embrace *not* because it appears kinder, but sometimes it pays to be harsh and memorable rather than wimpy and forgettable.

Search for *very*. This adjective can often signal cluttered writing or weak verbs. Evaluate each occurrence of this word in your writing. If you can rewrite the sentence without it, consider doing so.

- Cluttered: **They were very** tired.
  Better: **They were** exhausted.
  Best: The project participants were exhausted.

- Weak verb: **This** article **on** irriga**tion is very** helpful **and** should serve **to** undercut the **very** intense fears **of** those involved **in** the project.
  Strong verb: This helpful article on irrigation should allay the fears of the project participants.

Search for words ending in *ly*. Such modifiers often signal weak verbs or are themselves weak. Evaluate each occurrence of these words in your writing. If you can rewrite the sentence without them, consider doing so.

- Weak adjectives: They **absolutely** believed that Epifania would **very successfully** complete her project.
  Strong: They were confident that Epifania would complete her project.

- Weak adjective: Memory **is** selective: **it** represses (**or** forgets) incidents **that are of** less interest **or that** reflect bad**ly upon** the individual.
  Strong: Memory is selective: individuals repress uninteresting or unflattering incidents.

- Wordy: Universalists might argue **that** what society accepts **is not** necessar**ily that which is** most ethical. **It seems to** me, however, **that** such a principle **for** determining what **is** ethical must **at** a minimum play a large role **in** the determina**tion of** what **is** right **and** wrong.
  Strong: Universalists might argue that the practices society accepts are not always ethical. I believe, however, that social acceptability must play a large role in determining right from wrong.

Diagnostic Test Principles Summarized

Given all these examples of signal words and what to do when you find them, what should you remember? Seeing any of these words in your prose does not automatically indicate a problem. Many instances of signal words will be perfectly acceptable. But clusters of signal words do indicate good places to consider revising.

Scrutinize Your Lists

Much that is wrong with poor academic writing involves lists. That is, items strung together with little more than a conjunction to support them. Sometimes journal articles seem to be nothing but lists! By searching for *and* and *or*, you will identify the lists in your writing and can pay particular attention to improving them.

False lists (or doublings). Don't use two words where one will do. Don't say, "the desires are blocked and obstructed." The last two words are similar; the reader needs only one to get your meaning. Use one and delete the other.[4] If you are not sure whether the list is a doubling, use Microsoft's Thesaurus to check if the words appear as synonyms.

All-inclusive lists. Don't allow your thought processes to stand unedited on the page. If you have named all the items in a category, delete the list and use the category. For instance, replace "American army, navy, and air force" with "U.S. Armed Forces" (which includes the U.S. Coast Guard and National Guard).

Disordered lists. Present list items in some kind of order. Alphabetical or chronological order will often do, but so can order by word length. Ross-Larson argues that words with few syllables should appear before those with many syllables (e.g., "arts and letters" not "letters and arts") and that phrases with few words should appear before phrases with many words (e.g., *Beowulf, Pilgrim's Progress,* and *Pride and Prejudice*).

Nonparallel lists. Present list items in parallel. To be parallel, each item in the list must follow naturally from the last word before the list. The easiest way to make a list parallel is to start each item in the list with the same word and then, once everything works with that same word, remove the word (see page 241).

Scrutinize Your Verbs

Much of what else is wrong with poor academic writing involves verbs. That is, the overuse of weak verbs and the underuse of strong verbs. If you pay attention to your verbs, you can improve your writing immensely. For great examples of commanding verbs in academic prose, see Mike Davis's book *City of Quartz* (1992).

Weak verbs. If you can use a stronger verb than *to be, do.* If you can avoid overused verbs like *to make, to do, to provide,* and so on, do so.

Buried verbs. Many verbs get buried as nouns. If you can dig them out, do. Why write the wordy, "she gave the explanation for" when you can write the vigorous, "she explained"?

Passive voice. Advice about the passive voice has varied over the years. Some insist that writers root it out of their writing. The active voice is more direct, more forceful, and more economical because it doesn't obscure the subject. And studies do show that readers find passive sentences more difficult to understand than active sentences. Others insist however, that the passive voice has long been useful and should continue to be embraced.

How can you tell when passive voice is appropriate? Passive sentences come in two forms: with the subject and without the subject. If your passive sentence is missing its subject entirely, this absence may suggest that the subject is not relevant. You can leave the sentence in passive voice. If your sentence has a named subject, this may suggest that you can easily convert it into active voice. Do not restructure a passive sentence to emphasize an unimportant or unknown subject.

The easiest way to check your sentences for passive voice is Microsoft Word's grammar check feature. Not everything the grammar check identifies as passive voice is passive, and not everything it skips isn't. But it helps you to address the most obvious examples of passive voice. Microsoft Word can also let you know what percentage of your sentences is in passive voice (just make "Show readability statistics" part of your grammar check). If you see your proportion of passive sentences drifting over 18 percent, consider converting some of the passive voice in your article into active voice.

Scrutinize Your Pronouns

Poor academic writing also suffers from pronouns with unclear antecedents or meanings. Focus on improving or deleting your pronouns.

Empty pronouns. You can often delete such pronouns as *it, there, that, which,* or *who* and transform some words around them into modifiers or verbs.

Unclear pronouns. If you use a noun in one sentence and then in the next refer to that noun with a pronoun, the connection may not always be clear. If the pronoun would be unclear alone, add nouns to pronouns like *this, these,* and *those.*

Distant pronouns. Prevent pronouns like *them, they, their,* or *its* drifting too far from their antecedents.

Premature pronouns. Use pronouns like *he, she,* or *they* after their antecedents, not before them.

Dangling pronouns. Pronouns combined with passive voice after an introductory clause are almost always dangling. Convert them into nouns and active voice to solve the problem.

Cut Unnecessary Words

Every writing instructor tells you to cut. If you cut as often as they told you to cut, you would have nothing left! Nevertheless, learning to cut is an important skill. You can cut certain consistent phrases and constructions without losing the meaning of your text.

Prepositional overload. Watch the number of prepositions in a sentence. If they start piling up, turn some of the nouns into adjectives and some of the nouns into verbs.

Negatives. Avoid using *not* to hide your real thoughts or arguments. Better to be criticized for being too strong than being wimpy.

Weak adjectives. You can do without many adjectives. Try looking at any use of *very* and any words ending in *ly* to see if you can delete them.

EDITING YOUR ARTICLE

It's time to take a closer look at your sentences and word choices. Let's go through this process step by step.

Day 1: Reading the Workbook

On the first day of your writing week, you should read the workbook up to this page and skim the following pages.

Also, look through any copyediting you may have received on previous articles. Maybe a professor told you to work on a particular aspect of grammar. Maybe you published something previously and possess the editor's corrections. If you are lucky enough to have a professional edit your writing, you should really study what he or she did to improve your prose. Most of us have certain consistent problems that we need to avoid—editors can help you identify yours.

What does the copyediting of my previous writing teach me about how I need to improve my writing?	

Day 2: Running the Belcher Diagnostic Test

Most academics read too quickly to see individual letters and words; this diagnostic test, which highlights signal words identified in the previous section, will help you to slow down and identify problem areas. You can perform the Belcher diagnostic test in either of two ways: by hand on a print out of your article *or* by using Microsoft Word's Find and Replace program on an electronic version of your article. If you are working by hand, print out a copy of your article and use colored pencils to highlight the signal words or phrases. If you don't have colored pencils, use other symbols to mark the signal words (e.g., circles, boxes, underscores, overscores, check marks).

Alternately, you can take advantage of Microsoft Word's powerful search options features, including its search for various forms of a word and its search for word patterns that uses wildcards. If you are not familiar with them, don't worry—you should be able to perform this test by following my instructions. Microsoft has Help features that explain Find and Replace, if you need assistance. If at any point the test is not performing as I indicated that it would, carefully check that you have selected the right options under Search options. It is easy to forget to set Use Wildcards, for instance, especially if you have stopped and restarted the test. It also may be easiest to run the test by hand.

Running the Diagnostic Test with Colored Pencils

Below is the list of signal words and their code color (or code symbol if you do not have colored pencils).

Cutting words

- Search for conjunctions *and* and *or* and highlight with **red** (or put a box around the word).

- Search for *there* and *it* and highlight with **blue** (or underscore it).

- Search for *that* and *which* and *who* and highlight with **blue** (or underscore it).

- Search for prepositions like *by, of, to, for, toward, on, at, from, in, with,* and *as* and highlight with **purple** (or circle it).

Adding words

- Search for *this* and *these* and *those* and highlight with **orange** (or underscore it).

- Search for *them, they, their,* and *its* and highlight with **orange** (or underscore it).

Changing words

- Search for forms of the verb *to be* and highlight it with **green** (or overscore it).

- Search for forms of the verb *to have* and highlight it with **green** (or overscore it).

- Search for forms of the verb *to do* and highlight it with **green** (or overscore it).

- Search for forms of the verb *to make* and highlight it with **green** (or overscore it).

- Search for forms of the verb *to provide* and highlight it with **green** (or overscore it).

- Search for forms of the verb *to perform* and highlight it with **green** (or overscore it).

- Search for forms of the verb *to get* and highlight it with **green** (or overscore it).

- Search for forms of the verb *to seem* and highlight it with **green** (or overscore it).

- Search for forms of the verb *to serve* and highlight it with **green** (or overscore it).

- Search for *not* and *n't* and highlight with **brown** (or put a checkmark above it).

- Search for *very* and highlight with **brown** (or put a checkmark above it).

- Search for words ending in *ent, ence, ion, ize, ed*, and highlight with **green** (or overscore it).

- Search for *ly* and highlight with **brown** (or put a checkmark above it).

Running the Diagnostic Test with Microsoft Word's Find and Replace Feature

If you have superior skills in Microsoft Word, you will find unnecessarily detailed the following instructions for using its Find and Replace feature to highlight signal words with various colors. Just skim the instructions above (with colored pencils) and extrapolate. If you are not so knowledgeable, do not be intimidated! Every step is detailed below and you will find that it is not half so complicated as it looks. Just follow each step.

- Open an electronic copy of your article in Microsoft Word, save it as a copy, and work in the copy (just in case anything goes wrong).

- Place your cursor before the first character in the document.

- Move your arrow to the TOOLBAR and click on the EDIT menu. In the dialog box that pops up, click REPLACE.

- In the dialog box that pops up, click on MORE.

- Under SEARCH OPTIONS, click on FIND WHOLE WORDS ONLY. Make sure no other options in SEARCH OPTIONS are selected.

- In the REPLACE WITH box, type ^&. The caret and the ampersand should be the only characters in the box—no quotation marks, periods, spaces, or words should ever be in the box throughout this exercise.

- Make sure your cursor is in the REPLACE WITH box, and then move your arrow down to select the button FORMAT.

- In the dialog box that pops up, select FONT and then click on the tiny scroll bar next to FONT COLOR. Pick the code color **red** and click OKAY. Under the REPLACE WITH box should now appear the words "Font Color: Red."

  If "Font Color: Red." appear in the FIND WHAT box, then you have made a mistake. Click NO FORMATTING or UNDO REPLACE ALL and make sure your cursor is in the REPLACE WITH box and try again. At any point, you can erase the formatting in the FIND WHAT or REPLACE WITH boxes by clicking on NO FORMATTING at the bottom of the Find and Replace dialog box. Doing so will revert the setting to default.

- In the FIND WHAT box, type the first word from the Signal Words List: *and*.

- Click the REPLACE ALL button and watch the red version of *and* replace the black versions of *and*. All appearances of the signal word should now be in red.

  If there is a problem, reread through steps 2 through 9 and make sure you have the right options selected.

- In the FIND WHAT box, type *or* and then click the REPLACE ALL button.

- Now change your font color. Move your cursor to the REPLACE WITH box. Move your arrow down to select the button FORMAT. In the dialog box that pops up, select FONT and FONT COLOR **blue** and click OKAY. Under the REPLACE WITH box should now appear the words "Font Color: Blue." (It doesn't matter what color blue you use.)

- In the FIND WHAT box, type *there* and click the REPLACE ALL button.

- Repeat the previous step with each of the following words: *it, that, which,* and *who*.

- Now change your FONT COLOR. Move your cursor to the REPLACE WITH box. Move your arrow down to select the button FORMAT. In the dialog box that pops up, select FONT and FONT COLOR **purple** and click OKAY. Under the REPLACE WITH box should now appear the words "Font Color: Purple."

- In the FIND WHAT box, type *by* and click the REPLACE ALL button.

- Repeat the previous step with each of the following words: *of, to, for, toward, on, at, from, in, with,* and *as*.

- Now change your FONT COLOR. Move your cursor to the REPLACE WITH box. Move your arrow down to select the button FORMAT. In the dialog box that pops up, select FONT and FONT COLOR **orange** and click OKAY. Under the REPLACE WITH box should now appear the words "Font Color: Orange."

- In the FIND WHAT box, type *this* and click the REPLACE ALL button.

- Repeat the previous step with each of the following words: *these, those, their, them, they,* and *its*.

- Now change the options. Under SEARCH OPTIONS in the Find and Replace dialog box, click off FIND WHOLE WORDS ONLY and click on FIND ALL WORD FORMS.

- Now change your FONT COLOR. Move your cursor to the REPLACE WITH box. Move your arrow down to select the button FORMAT. In the dialog box that pops up, select FONT and FONT COLOR **green** and click OKAY. Under the REPLACE WITH box should now appear the words "Font Color: Green."

- In the FIND WHAT box, type *is* and click the REPLACE ALL button. A dialog box will pop up with a warning about using REPLACE ALL with FIND ALL WORD FORMS. You want to ignore the warning, so click OKAY. Word will do a search for all forms of the verb *to be*, including *is, are, was, were, am, be, being,* and *been*.

- In the FIND WHAT box, type *have* and then click the REPLACE ALL button. Word will do a search for all forms of the verb *to have*, including *has, have, hasn't, haven't,* and *having*.

- In the FIND WHAT box, type *do* and then click the REPLACE ALL button. Word will do a search for all forms of the verb *to do*, including *did, does, don't,* and *doing*.

- In the FIND WHAT box, type *make* and then click the REPLACE ALL button. Word will do a search for all forms of the verb *to make*, including *made, makes,* and *making*.

- In the FIND WHAT box, type *provide* and then click the REPLACE ALL button.

- In the FIND WHAT box, type *perform* and then click the REPLACE ALL button.

- In the FIND WHAT box, type *get* and then click the REPLACE ALL button.

- In the FIND WHAT box, type *seem* and then click the REPLACE ALL button.

- In the FIND WHAT box, type *serve* and then click the REPLACE ALL button.

- Now change your FONT COLOR. Move your cursor to the REPLACE WITH box. Move your arrow down to select the button FORMAT. In the dialog box that pops up, select FONT and FONT COLOR **brown** and click OKAY. Under the REPLACE WITH box should now appear the words "Font Color: Brown."

- In the FIND WHAT box, type *not* and click the REPLACE ALL button.

- In the FIND WHAT box, type *very* and then click the REPLACE ALL button.

- Now change the options. Under SEARCH OPTIONS, click off FIND ALL WORD FORMS and click off FIND WHOLE WORDS ONLY (if it isn't off already). Do click on USE WILDCARDS. Wildcards allow you to search for patterns rather than specific characters. If you are not familiar with wildcards, read the Microsoft Word Help.

- Now change the FONT COLOR. Move your cursor to the REPLACE WITH box and move your arrow down to select the button FORMAT. In the dialog box that pops up, select FONT and FONT COLOR **green** and click OKAY. Under the REPLACE WITH box should now appear the words "Font Color: Green."

- In the FIND WHAT box, type *(ent)>*. Do include the parentheses and arrow so you find only those words that end in *ent* and do not start with *ent* (e.g., finds "referent" but not "enter"). Click the REPLACE ALL button.

- Repeat the previous step with each of the following: *(ence)>*, *(ion)>*, and *(ize)>*.

- In the FIND WHAT box, type *(ed)>*. Then click the REPLACE ALL button. This will find many verbs in the past tense, which will help you identify passive voice.

- Now change your FONT COLOR. Move your cursor to the REPLACE WITH box. Move your arrow down to select the button FORMAT. In the dialog box that pops up, select FONT and FONT COLOR **brown** and click OKAY. Under the REPLACE WITH box should now appear the words "Font Color: Brown."

- In the FIND WHAT box, type *(ly)>* and click REPLACE ALL.

- Save your file with all the changes, so you can work on it tomorrow.

Day 3–4: Revising Your Article with the Diagnostic Test

Now you should have quite a colorful article! How do you revise in response to all this color? Skim your article and look for color clusters. The more red, blue, purple, orange, brown, and green words that cluster in a sentence or paragraph, the more likely the prose there needs to be improved. Look back at pages 240–253 for examples of how to address the color clusters. You can also read through the summary on the next page and the list of poor phrases that follows. Some instances of the signal words will be quite correct; some will not be.

Red words: redundant doublings and lists. Starting from the beginning of the article, pick the first sentence with several red words. Look carefully at the black words on either side of the red. If they are a doubling, could you delete one of them? If they are a list, could you use a summarizing word instead? If you need the list, does it appear in the right place in the sentence, after being introduced? If it appears in the right place, do the items in the list appear in the correct order (e.g., alphabetically, chronologically)? If the signal words are a run-on sentence, can you correct it? Go through your article asking if the words before or after the red could be deleted or converted.

Blue words: unneeded pronouns. Go back to the beginning of your article and start looking at sentences with several blue words, especially when they appear near green words. Could you delete the blue words (vague pronouns)? Do you need "there are . . . that" or "it was . . . who" or "it is [word] to [word] that"? The verb "to be" used with "there" and "it" can often be cut.

Orange words: floating pronouns. Examine all orange words to make sure that their referent is clear. If *this* or *these* appear without a noun, consider adding one. If it is not clear whom *they* or *them* refers to, replace the unclear orange pronoun with its noun antecedent. Blue and orange words can often participate in forming dangling participles. If you see orange words close to green words, that may mean a problem with wordiness.

Purple words: unneeded prepositional phrases. Examine sentences with lots of purple (extra prepositions), especially when they appear with brown words. Look at the words around them. Could you convert them into verbs or modifiers? For instance, "a great number of" could become *many*. Purple and brown words often appear with empty words like *fact, kind, sort, type, way, form, variety, range,* and so on. Sometimes you need them, but delete all you can.

Brown words: empty words. Examine sentences with several brown words, which often are doing little but cluttering up the sentence. Are you using *not* to avoid saying something with strength? Then use the strong words instead. Does a sentence have several negatives? Are you using *very* to intensify a weak adverb instead of picking the right adverb? Use the strong adverb instead. Are words ending in *ly* (e.g., really, actually, definitely) weakening your prose? Delete them.

Green words: weak verbs and passive voice. Examine all green words (weak verbs), especially when they appear close to blue words, to see if they are verbs buried as nouns. If so, try to unbury them. Is that form of the verb *to be* or *to make* needed? What about that word ending in *ion*? If it is just adding clutter, convert it into a verb or delete it. For instance, "this theory is important and makes a contribution to our understanding" could become "this important theory contributes to our understanding." You can usually improve words with green endings when followed by "that the." Forms of the verb *to be* can also signal passive voice. Only use passive voice when the actor is not important or when the object of the sentence is the subject of the paragraph.

Some Quick Fixes for Weak Phrases	
Weak Phrase	**Improved Phrase**
Red signal words (and/or)	
are careful or cautious	are cautious
are short and brief	are brief
Blue signal words (that, it, who, there)	
due to the fact that	because
in the event that	if
it is those who build	builders
in which the cars	when the cars
the roads that are paved	the paved roads
the bread that they ate	their bread
the plane which flew fast	the fast plane
the people who ran	the runners
there are those who	they
Purple signal words (of, by, as, for)	
a small part of	some
a variety of	different
as a result of	from
as of	starting
as regards	on, for, about
as to whether	whether
at the end of	after
by means of	by
by way of pulling	to pull
for a period of	for
for the purpose of	for
from the standpoint of	for
in an effort to	to
in order to	to
in spite of the fact that	despite

Purple signal words (of, by, as, for) (continued)	
in terms of	by, in, of . . .
in the amount of	for
in the near future	soon
in the vicinity of	near, about
in view of	because
of the purpose of the paper	the paper's purpose
on the basis of	by, on . . .
on a regular basis	regularly
the number of	some
the type of	[delete]
the great number of	many
with respect to	on, for, about
with the exception of	except
Orange signal words (this, these, them)	
them	the parents
this is odd	this odd incident
this was unfortunate	unfortunately
these are vital bees	these vital bees
these kinds of trees	these trees
those who are rich	the rich
Green signal words (to be)	
is a cause of	causes
is a critic of	criticized
is a need for	must
is applicable to	applies
is indicative of	shows
it isn't always that	rarely
it is the case that all	all
it is unfortunate that	unfortunately
it is this which	this
there are tubes	the tubes cover
there are birds that	some birds
there are cars which	some cars
y was led by x	x led y
Green signal words (do, make, have)	
do a study of	study
had gotten arrested	was arrested
has the ability to	can

(Continued)

Green signal words (do, make, have) (Continued)	
has to balance	must balance
have a tendency to	tend to
make a practice of	habitually
make use of	use
perform a dance	danced
provide a loan	loaned
serve as an example	exemplifies
there have been many	many have
Green signal words (-ence/-ion)	
had an experience with	experienced
explanation of	explain
Brown signal words (not, very, -ly)	
basically	[delete]
not different	similar
not many	few
not often	rarely
not very hard	easy
obviously	[delete]
to repeatedly go	to go

Cleaning Up After Running the Diagnostic Test

When you are completely done with your revising process, you will want to turn the remaining colorful words back into black. To do that, move your arrow to the TOOLBAR and click on the EDIT menu, and then on SELECT ALL. This will highlight your whole document. Then move your arrow to the Toolbar, select FORMAT, and FONT, and change the FONT COLOR to **automatic**. That will return all your words to their original black color.

Day 5: Correcting Other Types of Problem Sentences

We cannot address some significant self-editing issues in this workbook. If you have a problem with verb tense, subject-verb agreement (or any other kind of agreement), possessives, conjunctions, sentence construction, dangling or misplaced modifiers, please study a text on grammar.

Many manuals and some editors also advise you to attend to other matters than we have addressed above. They will want you to correct your capitalization, italics, alignment, and so on. This is not so important in your initial submission, but if you are interested, some instructions follow.

Commas. Academic style requires a serial comma. That is, a comma after the last item in a list. Set Microsoft Word's grammar check on

"Comma required before last list item" to "always" and it will prompt you to change "Simon Cowell, Paula Abdul and Randy Jackson" to "Simon Cowell, Paula Abdul, and Randy Jackson." Not using a serial comma alerts an editor or reader to your status as a novice.

Quotation marks I. U.S. academic journals use "double" quote marks; British and commonwealth journals use 'single' quote marks. U.S. journals put punctuation inside the quotation marks; British journals put them outside. Set the grammar check on "punctuation required with quotes" to "inside" if it is a U.S. journal.

Quotation marks II. Do not put quotation marks around material in block quotes unless those quotation marks appeared in the original text. Separate any quote that is longer than four or five lines into a block quote.

Quotation marks III. Rarely put quotation marks around single words or phrases to indicate that they are problematic or that you are using them in an ironic way. You can do this once per phrase, but don't repeatedly put quotation marks around a particular word or phrase. If the term is problematic, find another; don't reproduce the problem. If you can't, then just use the term; don't constantly signal that it is a problem.

Exclamation marks. In the humanities, you can use one exclamation mark somewhere in your journal article, but that's pretty much it. In the social sciences, that is one exclamation mark too many. Let your sentence structure deliver the emphasis.

Capitalization. Almost all U.S. academic journals have what's called a "down style." That is, they rarely capitalize anything but proper nouns. It depends somewhat on the journal, but most will not capitalize the names of racial groups (e.g., white or black) or titles standing alone (e.g., the professor or the president). Using many capital letters is a bit like typing your e-mail in all capitals; it is considered "shouting." When running the grammar check, make sure you have selected CAPITALIZATION as something to be checked.

Italics and bold face. Most journals prefer that you use italics only for foreign words or titles of books, journals, periodicals, movies, and television programs. If you regularly use italics for emphasis, most editors will see this as a form of "shouting." If your sentence structure is clear, you shouldn't need italics for emphasis. The one exception is in block quotes, where you cannot restructure the sentence but may want to draw attention to parts of it. If you add italics to a block quote, always put at the end of the block quote the phrase "(italics added)." Never use bold face for emphasis; it is almost never seen in academic journals. Of course, you can use it for headings, but not to highlight the importance of a word or phrase.

Acronyms. Always spell out an acronym on its first appearance in the body of your article (e.g., United States Agency of International Development [USAID]). Thereafter, use the acronym not the full version of the name.

Proper names. Be careful not to refer to men and women differently; for example, calling men by their last name but women by their first name (e.g., McCain and Hillary). You should refer to all by their last name. In grammar check, select "gender specific words" to be checked. Give the full first name of any person on its first appearance in your article (e.g., Erich Auerbach, not just Auerbach.)

Hyphens and dashes. One easy thing you can do to make your writing look more professional is to use the correct symbols for hyphens and dashes. A hyphen is the well-known bar that appears in compound words. It appears on your keyboard and is the shortest horizontal line available to you. A dash is a break in thought and is the equivalent of three hyphens in a row. Editors call it an em-dash—a dash that is the width of an m. You can create it by clicking on INSERT in your TOOLBAR, then SYMBOL, SPECIAL CHARACTER, and EM DASH. It also is automatically generated in Microsoft Word if you type a word, leave no space, type two hyphens in a row, leave no space, and then type another word. There is one more kind of dash, called an en-dash, the width of an n, and it generally appears in number ranges (e.g., 35–45).

Spelling. Always run a spelling check before you send your document. A spelling check won't help you with proper nouns, unless you use the technique described on page 80. If you spell Mazeika as "Mazeika" in the text and as "Mazieka" in the bibliography, you will have to check the Microsoft dictionary to catch that error. Pay attention to authors' names and spell them the same throughout.

Running Grammar Check

To use Microsoft Word's grammar check, move your arrow to the TOOLBAR and click on TOOLS, then select SPELLING & GRAMMAR. In the dialog box that pops up, select CHECK GRAMMAR box. Then select the button to the right called OPTIONS. In the dialog box that pops up, select SETTINGS. In the dialog box, you will be able to set up the exact kind of grammar check you want to do. You should set it up to check everything and then run it on a sample of your writing. If you find that the grammar check is consistently prompting you to correct something that is perfectly fine, go ahead and turn it off. For instance, I don't find the grammar check very helpful regarding sentence fragments and run-on sentences, but the check on correct capitalization is good, as is the check on use of multiple negatives; number agreement (this is rarely right, but when it is, it's important); misuse of possessives; incorrect punctuation (will check for serial comma and placement of punctuation inside); subject-verb agreement (also rarely right, but when it is, it's important); incorrect verb tenses; gender-biased language; compound words; passive sentences; strings of prepositional phrases; and split infinitives. You can set it to catch number of spaces between sentences (one only) as well.

Editing Each Other's Writing

If you are struggling with revising your own writing, you might try meeting with a colleague and exchanging paragraphs. That is, each of you work on revising a paragraph of the other person's work. Focus on adding, deleting, substituting, and rearranging the words, whatever makes it sound better to you. Then discuss the paragraph revisions with each other. Don't insist that your way is better, it's up to the original author to decide what he or she wants to do, but this exercise can help you to see how many different ways there are of saying the same thing and what kinds of changes tend to improve a sentence. It can also help you to be a better editor; by dialoguing with the author you learn the article's possibilities and how to expand them.

When I am teaching the writing workshop, we do this exercise as a group. Gather a group of people who have run the diagnostic test on their writing. Have each person select a particularly problematic sentence and write it on the board or an overhead, or project it on a screen. Then, out loud, work together to improve the sentence, with the author of the sentence making the possible edits on the draft. We often found that together we could do a much better job of improving the sentence than by working alone.

DOCUMENTING YOUR WRITING TIME AND TASKS

On the following weekly plan, please graph when you expect to write and what tasks you hope to accomplish this week. Then keep track of what you actually did. Remember, you are to allot fifteen minutes to one hour every day to writing. At the end of the week, take pride in your accomplishments and evaluate whether any patterns need changing.

Time	Monday	Tuesday	Wednesday	Thursday	Friday	Saturday	Sunday
	Week 10 Calendar						
5:00 a.m.							
6:00							
7:00							
8:00							
9:00							
10:00							
11:00							
12:00 p.m.							
1:00							
2:00							
3:00							
4:00							
5:00							
6:00							
7:00							
8:00							
9:00							
10:00							
11:00							
12:00 a.m.							
1:00							
2:00							
3:00							
4:00							
Total Minutes Actually Worked							
Tasks Completed							

Week 11

Wrapping Up Your Article

Day to Do Task	Week 11 Daily Writing Tasks	Estimated Task Time
Day 1 (Monday?)	Read through page 268; start documenting your time (page 270)	30 minutes
Day 2 (Tuesday?)	Finalize your related literature review and bibliography (page 268)	60 minutes
Day 3 (Wednesday?)	Finalize your introduction (page 268)	60 minutes
Day 4 (Thursday?)	Finalize your evidence and structure (page 269)	60 minutes
Day 5 (Friday?)	Finalize your conclusion (and make sure you've chosen a journal) (page 269)	60 minutes

Above are the tasks for your eleventh week. It is time to start finalizing your article by wrapping up your revisions. Make sure to start this week by scheduling when you will write and then tracking the time that you actually spend writing.

ON THE PERILS OF PERFECTION

In the advertising world, they tell a story to encourage novice writers who are about to present a campaign to a client for the first time. During the Renaissance, an apprentice painter was assigned to paint a portrait of a son in the royal family. When the apprentice showed the completed painting to the master painter, the master said, "This is beautifully done, exquisite coloring, perfect in every detail. It won't do."

"What?" the puzzled apprentice asked.

"The problem is that when the prince looks at this painting," said the master, "he will find fault with the shape of his nose or the color of his hair. Things that you have rendered perfectly. That's why you have to include a green arm."

"Excuse me?"

"If you paint one arm a bit green, it will be the first thing that the prince sees and he will attack it. He will shout that he does not have a green arm and you will agree, apologize profusely, and correct the error with a couple of brush strokes. He will then think he has asserted his will, you have obeyed, and the painting is now perfected according to his wishes. Most important, he won't search for things to criticize simply to assert himself." The artist directs the client's critical energy with an obvious flaw.

The moral of the story is that there are diminishing returns to perfecting your work. After all, the peer reviewers must have something to criticize. So, if you are worried about your article not being perfect—about that source you never got to read or that conclusion you could make just a bit stronger— perhaps that's a plus. Perhaps your article's imperfections will function to draw critical fire. It's time to start distinguishing between all possible changes that could be made to your article and what changes you should prioritize now.

Your biggest enemy at this point is fear of finishing. As Joan Bolker notes, feelings of sadness accompany the completion of projects (Bolker 1998, 128). We start to slow down to prevent closure. We become aware of the huge gap between what we imagined our article would be and what it ended up being. But, you must learn to send your imperfect work out into the world. (It helps to realize that no text is perfect; even the valuable writing of giants like Noam Chomsky and Elaine Scarry has been attacked.) You are on a journey and your articles are way stations, not the destination.

FINALIZING YOUR ARTICLE

This week is devoted to completing your macro-revisions. It may take longer than a week to finalize these sections, especially if you are waiting for feedback from an advisor, but keep going until you are done. Let's go through it step by step.

Day 1: Finalizing Your Argument

Print out a hard copy of your article. Read through it and mark up what needs to be improved. Ask yourself if each change is essential to the article or a barrier to completing it. Then review the instructions in Week 3 of the workbook, on argument, and reread the article with an eye for improving the logical flow of your article's argument.

Day 2: Finalizing Your Related Literature Review

Review the instructions in Week 5 on related literature reviews, and reread your article with an eye for wrapping up your literature review and other citations. Is your bibliography clean? Have you cited what you need to?

Day 3: Finalizing Your Introduction

Review the instructions in Week 8 on openings, and reread your article with an eye for completing your introduction.

Day 4: Finalizing Your Evidence and Structure

Review the instructions in Week 6 and 7, and reread your article with an eye for finalizing the body of your article. Focus on improving not overhauling. Don't forget your journal's word limits, but if you are only one hundred words over the maximum, don't agonize. Most editors don't expect you to hit the mark exactly.

Devoting a three- or four-hour stretch of time to this task may be helpful as you get close to sending. As one author said, "I can write volumes in the midst of confusion and I can easily write on the run. But, I do need solitude to edit. It is hard for me to take the confusion out of my writing when I am surrounded by confusion" (Klauser 1987, xi).

Day 5: Finalizing Your Conclusion

Review the instructions in Week 8 on conclusions, and reread your article with an eye for completing your conclusion. The best conclusions are short, clear ones.

DOCUMENTING YOUR WRITING TIME AND TASKS

On the following weekly plan, please graph when you expect to write and what tasks you hope to accomplish this week. Then keep track of what you actually did. Remember, you are to allot fifteen minutes to one hour every day to writing. At the end of the week, take pride in your accomplishments and evaluate whether any patterns need changing.

Time	Monday	Tuesday	Wednesday	Thursday	Friday	Saturday	Sunday
5:00 a.m.							
6:00							
7:00							
8:00							
9:00							
10:00							
11:00							
12:00 p.m.							
1:00							
2:00							
3:00							
4:00							
5:00							
6:00							
7:00							
8:00							
9:00							
10:00							
11:00							
12:00 a.m.							
1:00							
2:00							
3:00							
4:00							
Total Minutes Actually Worked							
Tasks Completed							

Week 11 Calendar

Week 12

Sending Your Article!

Day to Do Task	Week 12 Daily Writing Tasks	Estimated Task Time
Day 1 (Monday?)	Start documenting your time (page 285); write the submission cover letter (pages 272–275)	30 minutes
Day 2 (Tuesday?)	Prepare the illustrations, if any (pages 275–276)	60 minutes
Day 3 (Wednesday?)	Put the article in the journal's style, paying particular attention to the bibliography and notes (pages 276–277)	60 minutes
Day 4 (Thursday?)	Prepare the final print or electronic version (pages 277–283)	60 minutes
Day 5 (Friday?)	Send and celebrate! (page 284)	60 minutes

Above are the final tasks for your twelfth week. It is time to send! Make sure to start this week by scheduling when you will write and then tracking the time that you actually spend writing.

ON THE IMPORTANCE OF FINISHING

The primary goals of this workbook have been to aid you in revising an article and actually sending it to the editor of a suitable journal. I have designed this workbook as an end run around our common tendency both to procrastinate (by not writing) and to perfect (by endlessly revising). To get published, you have to train yourself to get over both tendencies.

Let me put this another way. At a dinner party hosted by a fellow writer, I met an engineer who had published eight hundred articles. His publication list, in ten-point type, was thirty-two pages long.

"Eight hundred articles!" I exclaimed. I had never met someone who had published so much, although I knew that engineers tended to publish more than those in other scientific disciplines, and far more than those in the humanities. "You've got to tell me," I said, "what is the secret of your success?"

He replied with a smile, "You know, I have one."

I waited with bated breath and he said, smiling, "Beyond the scope of this article."

"What?" I said.

"I do a little research, I do a little typing, when I run through what I know and am up against something I don't, I simply type that such and such is 'beyond the scope of this article,' and I'm done. I print it out and send it off."

This may not seem like genius at first blush, but it is. He has learned how to abandon the posture of mastery in order to pursue the search for knowledge. This is the "secret" at the heart of his tremendous productivity. Like him, you need to decide what is beyond the scope of your article. Then you must take the most difficult step of all. Letting go.

GETTING THE SUBMISSION READY

Getting your article ready to send requires several last steps. Let's go through them step by step.

Day 1: Writing the Cover Letter

When submitting an article, authors often ignore the importance of crafting a good cover letter. A professional cover letter favorably disposes the editor toward you and your work. While some journals do not examine them very closely, other journals use your cover letter to decide whether to read the article at all or to pick peer reviewers. So, it is worthwhile to make sure your cover letter addresses everything it is supposed to and gets you through the first cut. Make sure to do the following:

Use letterhead. If you are affiliated with a university, use university letterhead. (It gives a better impression than your personal stationery.)

Name the editor. Address the letter to a specific person, not just "Editor." (Usually this information is online. It shows that you've done your research and are not randomly sending your work to any journal.)

Provide the title. Give the title of your article so that the editor has all the needed information in the letter.

Note if requested. If the article was solicited in any way, thank the editor for requesting that you submit it and remind the editor of where this request was made.

Include the abstract. Describe the article's contents. (It is fine to use part of your abstract to do this, but the abstract should be blended into the letter, not set apart as an abstract.)

Articulate the contribution. State the significance of work to the field. (This should be clear but not too self-aggrandizing. In other words, you don't need to state that the article is going to change the field; just that it is a contribution to our thinking or fills a gap.)

Describe the appeal to the readers. If possible, declare why you think this particular journal's subscribers might be interested in reading the article. (For instance, the article fits the journal's mandate or the journal has published previous articles on the topic, particularly if your article launches from those articles. If you cannot think of why these particular readers would be interested in your article, that may be a sign that you are sending it to the wrong journal. The appropriate question is not "where would I like my article to appear?" but "which journal's subscribers would be interested in reading my article?")

Mention the journal. State your reason for wanting your article to appear in this particular journal. (You should not be obsequious, but you can state that you would like to see your article in the pages of the journal because it is the journal of record in the field or has been publishing innovative scholarship on your topic.)

Offer warrants. Like many academic documents, the cover letter is becoming a legal document. Editors now use it to protect themselves. If true (and only if true), include the following warrants about your article:

Authorship. State that you are the "sole author" or "we are the sole authors." (If you are not the author, you should not be sending it to a publisher.)

Ownership. State that you "own the copyright." (Everyone owns their work from the time of its inception, so the only reason you would not own the copyright to your own work is if you signed over the copyright to a publisher. If you do not own the copyright, you should not be sending the article to a publisher.)

Publication. State that the article "has not been published before in any form." (This means that no part of the article has been published online or in print in any country. It is perfectly acceptable, even desirable, for you to have orally presented the paper at a conference, so having done so does not preclude you from making the statement above. You can make this claim even if you have published articles with similar arguments, so long as the exact wording of the articles are not the same. If a small section of the article proceeds in exactly the same way as a published article of yours—the same background information or methodology section, for instance—state instead that the article "has not been published before." Leave off the words "in any form." If more than 10 percent of the article has been published previously, you must ask the editor in advance by e-mail if it is okay for you to submit the article. Most editors will accept the paper for consideration if the argument and/or data are different.) Some other wording to use, if you cannot say that the article has not been published before, is:

- "This article has not been published in a peer-reviewed journal, but previously appeared as a working paper with [the name of the institute]."
- "This article has not been published in a peer-reviewed journal, but was posted online for [the name of conference] and is still available online" or "is no longer available online."

Submission. State that the article "is not currently under submission at any other journal or publisher." (If your article is under submission elsewhere, you should not be sending it to a publisher.)

Give the word count. Provide the total word count of the article, including notes and works cited. (This is particularly important if you have worked to meet the journal's word limit.)

Mention any permissions. State whether you are reproducing any copyright material in your article (e.g., maps, photographs, illustrations). If you are, state that you are currently requesting permission to reproduce copyrighted material (see section on permissions).

Mention any funding. State any corporate funding sources for your project. (Editors will want to know if there are any possible conflicts of interest.)

Include your full contact information. Note any changes you anticipate over the next six months. (Be sure to include information for your coauthors as well, and to indicate who the "corresponding" author is, that is, the author who will be the point person.)

Omit status. Do not mention that you are a graduate student or an independent scholar. (Your status should be irrelevant to the editor. If the editor is unethical, then better to protect yourself by not including it.)

Miscellaneous. You rarely see any of the following statements in cover letters, but if they happen to be true of you, you might want to consider including them.

Human Subjects. In the social sciences, you may need to state that all human subjects gave informed consent and that your Human Subjects Review board approved your application.

Conflicts. In the social sciences, you may need to state that you have no conflict of interests, financial or otherwise, regarding the content or data in the article.

Awards. Note any awards you received for the article itself (e.g., best graduate student paper, best paper in conference) or to fund its research (e.g., Fulbright fellowship).

Buzz. Mention any attention that the article has drawn, such as sparking a heated debate at a recent conference.

Supplementary. Some authors mention the name of the good journals in which any articles directly related to the submission have been published. Others think this is tacky.

Coauthorship. Some social science journals will ask you to fill out a form on the contribution that each coauthor made to the article. This will be made clear on the journal's website, where they often provide a form.

Reviewers. Some journals will ask you to suggest potential reviewers. Don't suggest any unless the editors or journal website ask you to do so (although you can offer to give suggestions of peer reviewers if they are interested). If you know for a fact that someone in your field cannot give you a fair review, you can tell the editors that you would prefer that they not select that person to review your article but I think this raises more problems than it solves. Nothing prevents an editor from asking this person for a review precisely because you named them. Better not to name them and take your chances. One method to get around this problem is to send the article to that critic in advance, and then mention in the cover letter that so-and-so has read the article already and so may not be a suitable reviewer. Again, nothing prevents the editor from picking this person exactly because you named them.

Sample Submission Cover Letter

Dear Dr. [Editor],

Thank you for encouraging me, at the [Conference Name], to submit the enclosed article, [Article Title], for possible publication in [Journal Name]. I think it is the kind of research that would interest your readers, since you regularly publish important scholarship on [Your Topic]. I am the sole author of this 8,000-word article, which has not been published before in any form and is not under submission to any other journal or publisher.

In this article, I argue that . . . While investigating . . ., I found that . . . Based on . . ., I identified . . . After discussing these issues . . ., I suggest how. . . .

I have included a photocopy of a possible illustration, which would be the only material for which I would need permission. I look forward to hearing from you.

Sincerely,

[Your Name]

Day 2: Preparing Illustrations

If you plan to include photographs or illustrations in your article, you will need to provide the journal publisher with print-quality versions. You don't need to include original illustrations in your initial submission; just a photocopy or scan of the illustration will do at this point. Since you will need the real thing eventually, however, make sure you have access to a version that will be of sufficient quality.

A frequent mistake that beginning authors make is assuming that an image that works on the web or in a newspaper can be used in a print journal or book. It can't. The amount of detail in a web image is thousands of times less than that needed for a print journal. For instance, a web image is often 70 to 700 kb, while a print image is often 7,000 to 30,000 kb. Almost never will an image taken from an ordinary website or scanned from a newspaper work for print. If you are scanning an original, be aware that the standard settings on most scanners will not be set high enough; a minimum of 300 dpi is usually required. Poor scans from books or from photocopies will rarely be accepted for publication.

Plan in advance to procure good versions of your images since they may not be available for photographing when you want them. Archival items, in particular, are sometimes in process, moving, lost, or lent out, and so cannot be photographed.

Day 3: Putting Your Article in the Journal's Style

Some editors require that initial submissions appear in their journal's style, some don't, but as one journal editor said to me, "When an article arrives in our style, it looks like something we would publish." It can't hurt to make sure that the style is correct. The easiest way to do this is to follow the instructions on the journal's website or consult the style manual they use, of which there are four or five.

Style manuals give detailed instructions for the preparation of academic materials. Each manual represents particular conventions of standardizing punctuation, spelling, foreign languages, capitalization, abbreviations, headings, quotations, numbers, names and terms, math, tables, figures, notes, and reference citations in text and references. Since authors and editors from around the world in various fields have different trainings and therefore present information in widely varied ways, style manuals are attempts to standardize these presentations. By setting rules on matters of taste and choice, style manuals ensure that all the articles in a journal or book are presented in a uniform manner. For instance, while everyone agrees that a period should appear at the end of a sentence, should a footnote number precede the period or follow it? What about a quotation mark? There is no right or wrong answer, but since regular patterns increase readability, it is helpful if the editor ensures that the number always appears in the same place throughout your article and the others in the volume.

Three of the most common style manuals are listed below.

American Psychological Association. 2001. *Publication Manual of the American Psychological Association.* 5th ed. Washington, D.C.: APA.

Commonly called the APA, this manual is the standard for those in the social sciences, not just psychology. It focuses on the preparation of journal articles, not books. It provides more advice for authors on writing than some style manuals as it was originally designed for first-time authors. In addition to technical matters of style, it addresses designing and reporting on research, structuring articles, writing clearly, following ethical standards, avoiding bias in language, and converting the dissertation into a journal article. APA has an excellent section on writing clear and useful abstracts. Online information about how to put articles into APA style is available at many websites.

Modern Language Association. 2008. *MLA Style Manual and Guide to Scholarly Publishing*. 3rd ed. New York: Modern Language Association of America.
Commonly called the MLA, this manual is the standard for those writing on literature or language. It can be used to prepare either articles or books. Like the APA, it is more addressed to authors than editors. In addition to technical matters of style, it addresses selecting a journal or publisher, wading through the swamp of copyright issues, and writing for a particular audience. Online information about how to put articles into MLA style is available at many websites.

University of Chicago Press. 2003. *The Chicago Manual of Style*. 15th ed. Chicago and London: University of Chicago Press.
Commonly called Chicago, this manual is the standard for the preparation of books. That is, it has a focus on books, rather than journal articles, and is oriented toward editors more than authors. It now gives more advice about writing than it used to, but is much more comprehensive than any other style manual about technical matters. It includes an entire section on printing issues, such as composition and binding. Online information about how to put articles into Chicago style is available at many websites.

Documentation Styles

Style manuals give important guidance on presenting your sources in the text and in the bibliography. If you do not have access to these style manuals, some of the most common document types and their styles appear on the next pages.

Day 4: Preparing the Final Print or Electronic Version

Always follow the journal's instructions to the letter. In the absence of clear instruction, follow the instructions below. You can place a check in the box when you have accomplished each one. Be especially sure to strip the article of anything that could aid the reviewers in identifying you—blank out your advisor's name, funding sources, or any previous publications. You can add them back in later. Your name should appear nowhere in the article, including the citations.

Chart of Documentation Styles					
Type of Document	Document Citation Placement	American Psychological Association (APA) Style	Chicago 1 (chap. 17) Social Science or Author-Date System	Chicago 2 (chap. 16) Humanities or Notes and Biblio System	Modern Language Association (MLA) Style
Book	When cited in the bibliography	Doniger, W. (1999). *Splitting the difference: Gender and myth in ancient Greece and India.* Chicago: University of Chicago Press.	Doniger, Wendy. 1999. *Splitting the difference: Gender and myth in ancient Greece and India.* Chicago: University of Chicago Press.	Doniger, Wendy. *Splitting the Difference: Gender and Myth in Ancient Greece and India.* Chicago: University of Chicago Press, 1999.	Doniger, Wendy. *Splitting the Difference: Gender and Myth in Ancient Greece and India.* Chicago: U. of Chicago Press, 1999. Print.
	When cited in the text or a note	(Doniger, 1999, p. 23)	(Doniger 1999, 23)	Wendy Doniger, *Splitting the Difference: Gender and Myth in Ancient Greece and India* (Chicago: University of Chicago Press, 1999).	(Doniger 23)
Article in a journal	When cited in the bibliography	Aguilar, L. (1993). Artist's statement. *Nueva Luz: A Photographic Journal, 4*(2), 22–40.	Aguilar, Laura. 1993. Artist's statement. *Nueva Luz: A Photographic Journal* 4, no. 2: 22–40.	Aguilar, Laura. "Artist's Statement." *Nueva Luz: A Photographic Journal* 4, no. 2 (1993): 22–40.	Aguilar, Laura. "Artist's Statement." *Nueva Luz: A Photographic Journal* 4.2 (1993): 22–40. Print.
	When cited in the text or a note	(Aguilar, 1993, p. 22)	(Aguilar 1993, 22)	Laura Aguilar, "Artist's Statement," *Nueva Luz: A Photographic Journal* 4, no. 2 (1993): 22.	(Aguilar 22)
Web document	When cited in the bibliography	Kurland, P. B., & Lerner, R. (Eds.). (2000). *The founders' Constitution.* Chicago: University of Chicago Press. Retrieved June 20, 2003, from http://press-pubs. uchicago.edu/ founders/	Kurland, Philip B., and Ralph Lerner, eds. 2000. *The founders' Constitution.* Chicago: University of Chicago Press. Also available online at http://press-pubs. uchicago.edu/ founders/.	Kurland, Philip B., and Ralph Lerner, eds. *The Founders' Constitution.* Chicago: University of Chicago Press, 2000. Also available online at http://press-pubs. uchicago.edu /founders/.	Kurland, Philip B., and Ralph Lerner, eds. *The Founders' Constitution.* Chicago: U. of Chicago Press, 2000. Web. 12 May 1997.
	When cited in the text or a note	(Kurland & Lerner, 2000)	(Kurland and Lerner 2000, chap. 9, doc. 3)	Philip B. Kurland and Ralph Lerner, eds., *The Founders' Constitution* (Chicago: University of Chicago Press, 2000), chap. 9, doc. 3, http://press-pubs.uchicago.edu/ founders	(Kurland and Lerner)

Type of Document	Document Citation Placement	American Psychological Association (APA) Style	Chicago 1 (chap. 17) Social Science or Author-Date System	Chicago 2 (chap. 16) Humanities or Notes and Biblio System	Modern Language Association (MLA) Style
Government document	When cited in the bibliography	Environmental Protection Agency. (1986). *Toxicology handbook* (2d ed.). Rockville, MD: Government Printing Office.	Environmental Protection Agency (EPA). 1986. *Toxicology handbook.* 2d ed. Rockville, MD: Government Printing Office.	Environmental Protection Agency (EPA). *Toxicology Handbook.* 2d ed. Rockville, MD: Government Printing Office, 1986.	Environmental Protection Agency (EPA). *Toxicology Handbook.* 2d ed. Rockville: GPO, 1986. Print.
	When cited in the text or a note	(Environmental Protection Agency, 1986, p. 101–114)	(EPA 1986, 101–114)	Environmental Protection Agency (EPA). *Toxicology Handbook.* 2d ed. (Rockville, MD: Government Institutes, 1986), 101–114.	(Environmental Protection Agency)
Book chapter	When cited in the bibliography	Fromson, O. (1990). Progressives in the late twentieth century. W. F. Turner (Ed.), *To left and right: Cycles in American politics* (pp. 627–42). Jackson, MS: Lighthouse Press.	Fromson, Orlando. 1990. Progressives in the late twentieth century. In *To left and right: Cycles in American politics,* ed. Wilmer F. Turner (Jackson, MS: Lighthouse Press).	Fromson, Orlando. "Progressives in the Late Twentieth Century." In *To Left and Right: Cycles in American Politics,* ed. Wilmer F. Turner, 627–42. Jackson, MS: Lighthouse Press, 1990.	Fromson, Orlando. "Progressives in the Late Twentieth Century." *To Left and Right: Cycles in American Politics.* Ed. Wilmer F. Turner. Jackson, MS: Lighthouse, 1990. 627–42. Print.
	When cited in the text or a note	(Fromson, 1990, p. 627)	(Fromson 1990, 627)	Orlando Fromson, "Progressives in the Late Twentieth Century," *To Left and Right: Cycles in American Politics,* ed. Wilmer F. Turner (Jackson, MS: Lighthouse Press, 1990), 627.	(Fromson 627)
Master's thesis or dissertation	When cited in the bibliography	Ontiveros, M. (1994). Circumscribing identities: Chicana muralists and the representation of Chicana subjectivity. (Unpublished master's thesis, University of California, Riverside).	Ontiveros, Mario. 1994. Circumscribing identities: Chicana muralists and the representation of Chicana subjectivity. Master's thesis, Department of Art History, University of California, Riverside.	Ontiveros, Mario. "Circumscribing Identities: Chicana Muralists and the Representation of Chicana Subjectivity." Master's thesis, Department of Art History, University of California, Riverside, 1994.	Ontiveros, Mario. 1994. "Circumscribing Identities: Chicana Muralists and the Representation of Chicana Subjectivity," Master's thesis, Department of Art History, University of California, Riverside.
	When cited in the text or a note	(Ontiveros, 1994, p. 44)	(Ontiveros 1994, 44)	Mario Ontiveros, "Circumscribing Identities: Chicana Muralists and the Representation of Chicana Subjectivity," (Master's thesis, Department of Art History, University of California, Riverside, 1994), 44.	(Ontiveros 44)

(Continued)

(Continued)

Type of Document	Document Citation Placement	American Psychological Association (APA) Style	Chicago 1 (chap. 17) Social Science or Author-Date System	Chicago 2 (chap. 16) Humanities or Notes and Biblio System	Modern Language Association (MLA) Style
Article from a database	When cited in the bibliography	Iwanowski, J. (1994). Goliath vs. Goliath: Best Buy battles Circuit City. *Business Week*, 54, 12. Retrieved May 9, 1997, from ABI/Inform database <http://proquest. umi.com>.	Iwanowski, James. 1994. Goliath vs. Goliath: Best Buy battles Circuit City. *Business Week* 54: 12. ABI/Inform database <http://proquest. umi.com>.	Iwanowski, James. "Goliath vs. Goliath: Best Buy Battles Circuit City." *Business Week* 54 (1994): 12. ABI/Inform database <http://proquest. umi.com>.	Iwanowski, James. "Goliath vs. Goliath: Best Buy Battles Circuit City." *Business Week* 54 (1994): 12. ABI/Inform database. Web. 9 May 1999.
	When cited in the text or a note	(Iwanowski, 1994, p. 12)	(Iwanowski 1994, 12)	James Iwanowski, "Goliath vs. Goliath: Best Buy Battles Circuit City," *Business Week* 54 (1994): 12. ABI/Inform database <http://proquest. umi.com>.	(Iwanowski)
Paper presentation	When cited in the bibliography	Speth, J. D., & Davis, D. D. (1975). *Seasonal variability in early hominid predation.* Paper presented at Conference on Archeology in Anthropology: Broadening Subject Matter, Flat Prairie, Illinois.	Speth, Jeff D., and Don D. Davis. 1975. Seasonal variability in early hominid predation. Paper presented at Conference on Archeology in Anthropology: Broadening Subject Matter, May 24–26, at Midland University, Flat Prairie, Illinois.	Speth, Jeff D., and Don D. Davis. "Seasonal Variability in Early Hominid Predation." Paper presented at Conference on Archeology in Anthropology: Broadening Subject Matter, Midland University, Flat Prairie, Illinois, May 24–26, 1975.	Speth, Jeff D., and Don D. Davis. 1975. "Seasonal Variability in Early Hominid Predation." Paper presented at Conference on Archeology in Anthropology: Broadening Subject Matter, 24–26 May, at Midland University, Flat Prairie, Illinois.
	When cited in the text or a note	(Speth & Davis, 1975, p. 31)	(Speth and Davis 1975, 31)	Jeff D. Speth and Don D. Davis, "Seasonal Variability in Early Hominid Predation" (paper presented at Conference on Archeology in Anthropology: Broadening Subject Matter, Midland University, Flat Prairie, Illinois, May 24–26, 1975), 31.	(Speth and Davis 31)

Preparing the Final Electronic Version

What Not to Do When Preparing the Electronic Version

❑ Never include headers or footers with your name on every page.

❑ Never include your own name in the Works Cited or the body of the text.

❑ Never put two spaces after a period, colon, or semicolon.

❑ Never use blank lines to separate paragraphs.

❑ Never use hard returns and single spaces to indicate indentation.

❑ Never use the space key rather than the tab key to indent.

❑ Never use a small font size or more than one font.

❑ Never use less than one-inch margins.

❑ Never put titles or subtitles in all capitals.

❑ Never use *foot*notes (notes that appear at the bottom of the page).

❑ Never place tables and figures within the text, put them at the end.

❑ Never skip the notes when doing a spelling check.

What to Do When Preparing the Electronic Version

❑ Turn off automatic justification or hyphenation.

❑ Create dashes with the em-dash symbol or use two hyphens without spaces.

❑ Indicate where illustrations are to be inserted by typing, for example "<table 5 here>" on a separate line.

❑ Reference any illustrations in the text "(see fig. 1)."

❑ Provide captions for all illustrations and sources for all tables and charts.

❑ Use *end*notes (notes that appear at the end of text).

❑ Check in-text references against the bibliography.

❑ Spell-check a manuscript, including the notes, before sending.

❑ Provide a complete bibliography in a consistent style.

❑ Check quoted matter against the original source one last time.

❑ Proofread one last time.

❑ Check that the editor can open documents you produced on your word processing software if it is other than Microsoft Word.

❑ Include your full contact information, your article's full title, and the date separately from the article, on a cover page.

❑ Record the exact day when you sent the article to the journal in the journal log form on page 284.

❑ Preserve a backup of the electronic copy (which should remain untouched so you have a version that is exactly the same as the editor's).

❑ Save all responses you get from the editor (every single one). Keep track of when material was sent and when responses came in.

Preparing the Final Print Version

What Not to Do When Preparing the Print Version

- ❑ Never staple the pages together.
- ❑ Never print on both sides of the paper.
- ❑ Never include your name on every page.
- ❑ Never include your own name in the Works Cited or the body of the text.
- ❑ Never use *foot*notes (notes that appear at the bottom of the page).
- ❑ Never use a small font size or more than two fonts.
- ❑ Never use less than one-inch margins.
- ❑ Never have more than two or three handwritten marks on the final manuscript.
- ❑ Never send original art for review.
- ❑ Never send difficult-to-read photocopies of your article.

What to Do When Preparing the Print Version

- ❑ Vertically double-space every part of the text (sometimes even the tables).
- ❑ Include a least two copies of the article.
- ❑ Provide page numbers, even for appendices (number separately).
- ❑ Turn off automatic justification or hyphenation.
- ❑ Place tables and figures at the end of the text.
- ❑ Indicate where illustrations are to be inserted by typing, for example "<table 5 here>" on a separate line.
- ❑ Reference any illustrations in the text "(see fig. 1)."
- ❑ Provide captions for all illustrations and sources for all tables and charts.
- ❑ Use *end*notes (notes that appear at the end of the text).
- ❑ Check in-text references against the bibliography.
- ❑ Spell-check the manuscript, including the notes, before sending.
- ❑ Provide a complete bibliography in a consistent style.
- ❑ Check quoted matter against the original source one last time.
- ❑ Proofread the hard copy one last time.
- ❑ Print the journal's address and your return address clearly on the envelope.
- ❑ Use the correct postage.
- ❑ Record the exact day when you sent the article to the journal in the journal log form on page 284.
- ❑ Keep a hard copy of the article and back up the electronic copy (which should remain untouched), along with your query letter and any responses you get from the editor.
- ❑ Keep an electronic file for any changes you think of before the article comes back.

Journal Submission Log

Article Title:		Journal Title:
Contact Name		
Date Queried		
Date Sent		
Date Acknowledged		
To Peer Review?		
Date Notified of Status		
Date Copyedited		
Date Proofread		
Date Published		

Article Title:		Journal Title:
Contact Name		
Date Queried		
Date Sent		
Date Acknowledged		
To Peer Review?		
Date Notified of Status		
Date Copyedited		
Date Proofread		
Date Published		

Article Title:		Journal Title:
Contact Name		
Date Queried		
Date Sent		
Date Acknowledged		
To Peer Review?		
Date Notified of Status		
Date Copyedited		
Date Proofread		
Date Published		

Day 5: Send and Celebrate!

Submit that electronic document online. Or, seal that envelope, walk it to the nearest post office, and drop it in the mailbox. Then go celebrate! You deserve it. You have just accomplished something many people dream of and never accomplish. You have joined those brave souls who have had the courage to send their writing to an actual publisher. Well done!

DOCUMENTING YOUR WRITING TIME AND TASKS

On the following weekly plan, please graph when you expect to write and what tasks you hope to accomplish this week. Then keep track of what you actually did. Remember, you are to allot fifteen minutes to one hour every day to writing. At the end of the week, take pride in your accomplishments and evaluate whether any patterns need changing.

Week 12 Calendar							
Time	**Monday**	**Tuesday**	**Wednesday**	**Thursday**	**Friday**	**Saturday**	**Sunday**
5:00 a.m.							
6:00							
7:00							
8:00							
9:00							
10:00							
11:00							
12:00 p.m.							
1:00							
2:00							
3:00							
4:00							
5:00							
6:00							
7:00							
8:00							
9:00							
10:00							
11:00							
12:00 a.m.							
1:00							
2:00							
3:00							
4:00							
Total Minutes Actually Worked							
Tasks Completed							

Week X

Responding to Journal Decisions

Day to Do Task	Week X Daily Writing Tasks	Estimated Task Time
	Read through page 298 and follow the instructions for reading the editors' letter and the reviewers' reports	60 minutes
	Identify which journal decision was made, and decide how you will proceed (pages 298–303)	60 minutes
	Prepare a list of recommended changes and how you plan to respond to them (pages 304–306)	60 minutes
	Revise article (pages 306–310)	?
	Draft your revision cover letter and send article back out (pages 310–314)	60 minutes
	Start the illustration permissions process, if any (pages 314–319)	30 minutes

Above are the tasks you will need to complete once a journal gives you a decision on your article. These tasks are not part of the twelve-week schedule for submitting an article to a journal, but they are the necessary last steps to achieving academic publishing success. Make sure to return to this workbook when you get the journal's decision so that you can make an appropriate plan for revising your article. Depending on the readers' reports, these tasks may take longer than a week.

AN EXHORTATION

How you respond to journal decisions about your submitted articles will determine your academic career. That may seem to be strong language, but it is true. If you take negative journal decisions as accurate assessments of your aptitude for scholarship, if you fail to revise when advised to do so, or if you abandon an article just because it was rejected, you will not do well in your chosen profession. Those who persevere despite abuse, dismissal, and rejection are those who succeed.

I met a wonderful example of this as I was completing this workbook. A graduate student asked if he could strategize with me about how to respond to four revise and resubmit notices that he had recently received from journals. It turned out that these multiple positive notices were the result of five years of awe-inspiring labor on his part. He had not only written six different articles over that time but also submitted them a total of seventeen times to peer-reviewed journals. Seventeen times! That means he had persevered despite eleven rejections. One of the articles had been rejected by five different journals. Another had been rejected by three. But every time an article of his was rejected, the graduate student revised the article (if the editor passed along any reviewers' comments), and sent it right back out. The fruit of his labor was that he had published two articles (one at the first journal to which he submitted, the other at the second), and now had four articles on the verge of being accepted for publication (including the one that had been rejected by five other journals). Clearly, he had learned much doing eleven revisions on six articles, because the last article he submitted was later accepted at the first journal to which he sent it—*PMLA*, widely regarded as the leading journal in a number of literary disciplines.

When I expressed my admiration for his ability to persevere despite so much rejection, he confessed that his classmates thought he was crazy, and he himself suspected that his persistence had partly to do with feelings of insecurity about his educational background. What kept him going was not confidence, he insisted, but a real desire to learn what others thought of his ideas and how to be a better writer. He was grateful to the reviewers and editors who had taken the time to review his work, even those who had profound reservations about his writing style and arguments. What a wonderful attitude! So, if you get one or two or ten rejections, remember the perseverance of this graduate student. He is neither crazy nor superhuman; he's just doing what it takes to get published. Persistence and hard work, not necessarily brilliance or divine intervention, is what garners attention from journals.

So, how exactly should you proceed through the post-submission process? Let's go through it step by step.

WAITING FOR THE JOURNAL'S DECISION

Although it is tough waiting to hear from the journal to which you submitted your article, the good news is that a little waiting is a good sign. Rejections often come very quickly: in as little as one day (if you submitted your article electronically and the journal has such a large backlog that it is temporarily rejecting everything), or one or two weeks (if the journal editors decide that the article is not worthy of peer review). So, a very quick response is not in your interest.

Usually, it will be at least three weeks before you receive a decision, often it will be about three months, and it can be as long as one year or more. The editors should tell you how long they anticipate the review process will take in their letters acknowledging receipt of your manuscript. Many good social science journals are now aiming for a two- to three-week review process and delivering decisions within a month; many good humanities journals are aiming for delivering decisions within three months. But many poorly staffed or poorly run journals continue to take six to nine months to return decisions. As you wait for a decision, several questions may occur to you.

When should I start asking how much longer it will take? As I mentioned in previous chapters, once your article has been with a journal for three months, you should start sending regular e-mails to the editor of the journal, politely inquiring about the status of your article. Editors know that authors deserve a timely decision, and they accept that it is your right to be persistent when they have exceeded three months.

Generally, it is not the editors' fault that they have been unable to give a decision, but the recalcitrant reviewers' fault. The editors cannot move forward until the reviewers have read and responded to your article. In fact, the editors may be as frustrated as you are with the slow review process and can even appreciate a persistent e-mail from you, because it reminds them to send a persistent e-mail to the reviewers asking them to submit their reviews.

In some cases, it is the editors' fault. They just aren't on the ball and never actually sent your article to any reviewers. Or the editors have alienated their staff, who are dragging their feet on doing their tasks. Or the editors have resigned, and no one even recorded your initial submission much less sent it for review. Or there is a war going on between the various editors and/or the editorial board and so the review process is at a standstill.

Since you cannot know what the real story is, your marker for the viability of the journal's review process must be the editors' responsiveness to the e-mail inquiries you start to send. If the editors respond with the information that they are working to extract reviews from the reviewers, that's a good sign. Just keep waiting.

If the editors do not respond to your e-mails, you should make your e-mail inquiries more frequent: once a month starting at the three month mark, once every two weeks starting at the four month mark, once a week starting at the fifth month, and once a day starting in the sixth month (if you still feel like hanging in there). If you are getting no response, the e-mail should never change, it should never escalate in tone, it should be the exact same wording: "I'm just e-mailing to inquire about the status of my article titled such-and-such, which I submitted to your journal such-and-such on such-and-such date." If you have had interest from other parties (e.g., if someone asked if he or she could include your article in an edited volume), you should include that information in the e-mail.

Should I ever withdraw my article? If a journal is not responding to e-mail inquiries about the status of your article, you are always within your rights to withdraw your article from their consideration. Submission is not a contract, you have not signed over anything to them, and you still own the copyright. Just make sure that you have clearly notified them in writing that you are withdrawing the piece; sending the message both by e-mail and post is a good idea.

Generally, however, I recommend withdrawing only if the journal never responded to you or has stopped responding despite repeated inquiries. If the editors regularly respond to your inquiries and say that they are working to get the reviews, stick it out. If you have sent more than four e-mails to various e-mail addresses over the fourth and fifth month of review and have heard nothing, I recommend withdrawing your piece. If you want to be more cautious, that's fine, but if the editors are not responding into the six month, it's time to think seriously about moving on.

An additional reason to withdraw an article after five or six months is that, statistically, your chances of getting a positive decision are dwindling. Most peer reviewers take longer to reject an article than to accept it. In a study of peer reviewer types, a scholar identified one as the "procrastinator," those reviewers who took the longest to review a piece. Such reviewers, the scholar claimed, always had only negative comments, so you can anticipate little reward for hanging in there (Fagan 1990). Good reviewers take about two to three hours to review an article and return those reviews in an average of four to twenty weeks, depending on discipline.[1]

An interesting new trend among some savvy journals is to ask authors to promise that the editors have exclusive consideration of your article for fourth months. If the editors have not delivered a decision in that period, they allow you automatically to submit the article to another journal. It is one way of lightening the onerous rule against simultaneous or multiple submission.

What should I do while I am waiting for the review? You should continue working on other projects and preparing other material for submission. Some people in the social sciences say you should always have three articles in progress at any given time: an article under development, an article under submission to a journal, and an article under revision for a journal. This is a good rule of thumb because the process can take such a long time and one article can stall out, or be repeatedly rejected, while another sails through. Placing your eggs all in one article basket may lead to significant delays.

READING THE JOURNAL'S DECISION

In the humanities, journal decisions usually arrive by post. I recommend that you avoid opening the letter if you are just about to teach or enter a meeting. Try to save the letter for a time when you can emotionally absorb its contents on your own. If you get the decision by e-mail and reading it is unavoidable, you can read the e-mail itself but wait to read the reviewers' reports, which often come as attachments, until you have some real time. Even positive decisions usually arrive with some critical comments, so it is better to wait until you have the emotional space to cope.

Once you are in a place where you can absorb the contents, take a deep breath and remind yourself that all reviews are subjective and that academic reviewers do not see their purpose as affirming your brilliance but as critiquing your shortcomings. Studies have shown that peer reviewers always have more negative comments than positive comments (Bakanic, McPhail, Simon 1989). Remember that detailed reviewers' reports are not just rare, but a compliment—few scholars take the time to rake over an article they do not consider worthwhile. Then, open the letter. Some scholars prefer to skim the letter as quickly as possible to get the general gist and then set it aside for a day or two. When you return to reading it, you are more able to absorb the recommendations or decision. For some reason, letting the decision settle for a few days can help you to take on the specifics of the news more easily.

Years ago, an author brilliantly explained why it is so important to give yourself time over several days, to absorb the journal's decision:

> The rejection of my own manuscripts has a sordid aftermath: (a) one day of depression; (b) one day of utter contempt for the editor and his accomplices; (c) one day of decrying the conspiracy against letting Truth be published; (d) one day of fretful ideas about changing my profession; (e) one day of re-evaluating the manuscript in view of the editors [sic] comments followed by the conclusion that I was lucky it wasn't accepted! (Underwood 1957, 87)

This emotional journey is one that published authors are very familiar with—allow yourself the time and space for the whole journey.

Another truth is that you don't have enough evidence to evaluate the reviewers' recommendations until you have completed the actual revision process. Many authors have ranted about the journal's decision and the reviewers' comments until they get started on revising the article. Then authors tend to realize that, no matter the wisdom or idiocy of the comments themselves, the very process of revising always produces a stronger article.

The chance of the comments being problematic is high. For instance, one study found that 25 percent of reviews were very poor in quality (McKenzie 1995). Another study found that over 40 percent had comments indicating bias and prejudice (Spencer, Hartnett, and Mahoney 1986). Many studies have shown that given the exact same article to review, reviewers will have a range of responses, some rejecting, some accepting it, with agreement between the reviewers ranging from a low of 40 percent to only as high as 70 percent.[2]

At the same time, studies have repeatedly shown that peer review improved the quality of articles, especially in the discussion of the study's limitations, the generalization of the findings, the tone of the conclusion, and general readability.[3] Maybe that's why the lengthier the peer reviewers' comments, the more likely the article is to be cited in the future (Laband 1990). So, don't dismiss the peer-review process and insist that it's all about who you know. While some studies have found that editors have a bias toward former graduate students, friends, and prestigious institutions, many other studies found no significant correlation between higher acceptance rates and editors' relationships with authors or authors' institutional affiliations.[4] Whatever its faults, the peer-review process has a proven record of enabling authors to produce stronger articles.

TYPES OF JOURNAL DECISIONS

Once you have absorbed the letter emotionally, your first task is to interpret the journal's decision. Surprisingly, it can be difficult to determine just what the journal is telling you. Sometimes this is due to poor wording or editorial inexperience, but most often, it is due to editorial avoidance. They are unclear because they don't want to be devastating. Unfortunately, there is no standard language and no agreed-upon formula for delivering the verdict on publication.

To aid you in parsing the letter, keep the following in mind. Editorial decisions fall into three broad categories: editors can accept your article, ask you to revise and resubmit your article, or reject your article. The most room for interpretation comes with the revision and rejection decisions. That's why you need to decide which of the six decisions listed below has been made about your article because it affects how you proceed from this point. If you aren't sure which decision it is, it is always appropriate to ask the editors to clarify their decision. I will address later how to respond to each of these decisions.

Forms of Editorial Acceptance

Pure accept. This almost never happens. In my eleven years as a managing editor of a peer-reviewed journal, we never once "accepted as is" an article at our journal. An editor at another journal states that "for the more than 250 manuscripts received while I have been assisting with JLR, not one first draft has been accepted unconditionally, and very few have been conditionally accepted pending minor revisions" (Holschuh 1998). I have sometimes seen my students receive such decisions, but usually the editor expresses astonishment that the reviewers loved the piece and had only grammatical or style recommendations to make. In other words, don't expect any journal to "accept" your initial submission; this is not the reality of how journals work. The best-case scenario is really one of the following two decisions.

Revise minor problems and resubmit. Receiving a decision like this, sometimes called a "warm R&R," is a cause for celebration. Articles in this category have been conditionally accepted, pending minor revisions specified by the reviewers in their attached reports. Although many inexperienced authors assume that any criticism is a bad sign, it's not. You can only get this kind of decision if all the peer reviewers and the editors liked your article. The journal has taken your article seriously, given you a few recommendations for improvement, and asked you to resubmit the article once you have revised it accordingly. Therefore, your chances of publication are now very high.

So, if you have received such a decision, drop everything, make the revisions, and resubmit it. Usually, the original reviewers do not see the article again, it just goes back to the editors, who check to make sure that you made the changes recommended. If you have, the journal publishes your article. When students tell me that they have been sitting for one or two years on a warm R&R, I can't help but start chiding. Such a journal decision should be treated as just a stage, like copyediting, in the publishing process. You must make the revisions but then you are published. All submitted articles require some rewriting. Should the editor ask you to make minor revisions, do it!

The only problem with this journal decision is detecting it. That is, the editors do not always make clear that the article has been accepted. They may simply ask you to make the revisions and resubmit it. Some signs that the article is conditionally accepted is the editor urging you to resubmit the article by a certain date or suggesting that, if you get the revision back by a certain date, the article will appear in a certain issue. Another sign that the article is conditionally accepted is the recommendation of only minor changes, such as rewriting the abstract, expanding the methodology section, adding a few references, developing the conclusion, or defining some terms.

Revise major problems and resubmit. This is also an excellent decision to receive and still considered a "warm" response. Articles in this category have been conditionally accepted, pending major revisions specified by the reviewers in their attached reports. You usually get this kind of decision when the reviewers and editors liked the piece but at least one had substantial suggestions for improvement. Sometimes you will get this decision even if one of the reviewers had major reservations, but only if the editors did not agree that the identified problems were serious or difficult to fix.

This journal decision often results in a different review process for your article than the previous decision. At some journals, all articles that have gone through major revisions must go back to the original reviewers for vetting. The reviewers conduct a second review to see if you have responded to their recommendations. If they believe that you have appropriately corrected the problems, then the article will be published. However, many journals hate to trouble their reviewers and so the editors (or editorial assistants) review the article to see if you have made the reviewers' recommended changes. Thus, it is important for you to know whether the same reviewers will read your revision, since editors are more likely to be lenient about how closely you followed specific reviewer suggestions than the actual reviewers. You can ask the editors for this information.

Whether reviewers or editors review your changes, the chances of rejection, while generally lower, are higher than with the "pending minor revisions" decision above. Everyone agrees on how to make minor revisions, but there can be wide disagreement about how to make major changes. If you do not revise the article sufficiently, or in the ways they had hoped, then the editors can respond by saying that the article was not appropriately revised and so must be revised again or rejected. Sometimes editors will give you another chance at revision. Most of the time, however, the editors will reject such an article on the second round since you did not perform the revision to their satisfaction.

This type of decision is the most difficult to detect. Editors delivering this kind of decision often won't mention that the article is conditionally accepted, but instead will make confusingly discouraging or encouraging remarks. Below are two different letters that reveal the language the editors might use:

- **Editors' letter 1.** Enclosed please find the reviewers' reports on your essay. One reviewer has minor recommendations for revision, the other has fairly substantial recommendations. Although their reports are very positive about your essay, they also include helpful suggestions for improving the essay, especially regarding [some revisable element, most often the argument or the related literature]. Given the reviewers' concerns, I cannot accept the essay in its present form. I can offer, however, to send a revised version of the essay back to the second reviewer, should you wish to rework your argument substantially in line with these reports and resubmit the essay to us. I am sorry to have to convey what I know must be disappointing news, but I do feel strongly that with careful revision this essay could be accepted for publication in our journal.

- **Editors' letter 2.** I am sorry to have to return your manuscript because it falls outside our guidelines. However, we would like to invite you to resubmit your article. In order to conform to our guidelines, you would need to reformulate your article to clarify your thesis and re-situate the piece within a more scholarly background. Thank you for considering our journal and we look forward to hearing from you.

Another problem with interpreting this decision is that sometimes editors suggest that revisions are major, when in fact they are minor; or that they are minor when they are major. To me, major revisions are rewriting sections of the essay, restructuring the essay, reviewing a whole new body of literature, refining the argument throughout, significantly shortening or lengthening the article, or (the most difficult task) repairing theoretical or methodological flaws. Make your own decision about how difficult and substantive the changes must be.

If you get this decision, you are not obligated to revise and resubmit your article to the journal, but if you think the reviewers' comments were helpful and that you can address them without starting from scratch, or reading fifty books, it is always in your interest to revise and resubmit the article. Your chances of publication are much higher on resubmission to any journal than on initial submission. Unless you can't stomach most of the changes they are recommending, you should revise and resubmit.

Forms of Editorial Rejection

Rejected but will entertain a resubmit. This is not a great decision to receive, but it is far from the worst decision you can get. This decision means you still have a chance of getting your article published with the journal. Articles in this category have been rejected, but the editor indicates a willingness to see a revision, thus the decision is still a form of "revise and resubmit," in this case, a "cool R&R." Reviewers' reports always accompany this form of rejection, and usually all the reviewers have substantial suggestions for improving the essay.

If you decide to go ahead and revise and resubmit this article, it will go through the review process again. Depending on the journal, it may go back to the original reviewers or to brand new reviewers. Some editors will even helpfully specify that the article will be treated as a new submission. It is a better sign for you if the editors say that the article will go back to the original reviewers.

The difference between this decision and the acceptance decisions above can be extremely difficult to detect. The decision may even be delivered in the exact same language as cited above. Some language the editor might use:

- **Editors' letter 3.** Enclosed please find the reviewers' reports on your essay. They agree that you have a very promising idea, but that serious revision is necessary. In particular, they would like to see [some major improvement like a better grasp of the chosen theoretical approach, or a more organized line of argumentation, etc.]. Given their concerns, I cannot accept the essay for publication in its current form. Should you feel able to address their concerns and submit a substantially revised version of the essay, I would be glad to ask the reviewers to read the essay again.

- **Editors' letter 4.** Given the reviewers' reports, we cannot accept your essay for publication. Should you choose to revise the essay thoroughly according to the reviewers' substantial recommendations and submit it again to us, we will send it to new reviewers.

- **Editors' letter 5.** Although the reviewers thought the article was [some positive word like "strong" or "thought-provoking"], they have noted some serious flaws that must be addressed before the article is publishable. Please see the attached for the reviewers' suggestions.

Search for such keywords in the editors' letter as "not publishable in its current form" or "not yet ready." This suggests that they might welcome it in another form. The difference between this journal decision and the previous decision lies mainly, then, in the editors' confidence in your ability to pull off the scale of the revision. If the editors think you can do the recommended revisions, you get the conditional acceptance described in the previous section; if they think you can't do it, you get this conditional rejection.

Editors give this decision for several reasons. Sometimes they don't have the heart to say that they have rejected the article, so this is their attempt to be encouraging. At my journal, I know we have sometimes been surprised to see an article resubmitted that we thought we had rejected, but when we reread our decision letter we can see how the (hopeful) author might have read into it more than we intended. The editor must tread a fine line between clarity and cruelty. Most of the time, however, editors give this decision because they thought the article was strong but fatally flawed in some way. Since the article was interesting, the editors don't want to close off the unlikely possibility that you will come up with some brilliant solution for its problems.

The decision about whether to revise and resubmit the article to the same journal is up to you (see below for more comments on revising if you decide to resubmit). If you feel that the reviewers did a wonderful job and you are happy to follow their suggestions, then it might be good to resubmit it. But most journal editors don't really expect to see again an article that received this decision, believing that you will probably move on to another journal for a more positive response.

Rejected and dismissed. This is an absolute rejection, with reviewers' reports attached to back up the editors' claim that the article "is not publishable" or "is not ready for publication" or "cannot be published at this time" or "does not meet our standards for publication" or "is not right for us." Some other language the editor might use:

- **Editors' letter 6.** I am sorry to return your article, but our submissions guidelines require that articles reveal something new and demonstrate a thorough grasp of previous criticism on the topic. Your submission lacks this dimension, and therefore we cannot consider it further at this time.

- **Editors' letter 7.** Thank you for offering us your manuscript. We have read it with interest and regret that we cannot accept it for publication. . . . We hope that the attached readers' report proves helpful to you as you revise the essay for publication in another journal.

Rarely will the editors be so clear. And none will directly say "we have rejected your article" or "please don't resubmit this article." Indeed, editorial politeness causes a number of problems for the recipients of such letters, especially if they are not native speakers of English. Can the editors be rejecting the article if their letter is encouraging and includes suggestions for improving the article? Yes. Although the editors may include some positive language (e.g., "the reviewers appreciated your line of thought") and may even seem to suggest that you continue working on the essay (e.g., "we hope that you will find the reviewers' reports helpful as you continue to work on these interesting ideas"), it is not a revise and resubmit notice unless they mention resubmission. If you can't tell whether your article has been rejected or not, it is always acceptable to e-mail the editor and ask: "Thank you for sending me your decision on my article. I just wanted to make sure that I understand it properly: Are you requesting that I revise and resubmit this essay or do you not expect to see it again?"

Some authors are deceived into thinking that the mere presence of reviewers' reports with concrete suggestions is a positive sign. This is not the case if the decision letter itself mentions nothing about resubmission. As one editor explained to me, "when I send along a reader's report saying that the central premise is flawed, I think it's pretty clear that the article probably needs to be gutted with maybe a few parts recycled into a brand new article, not that it should be prettied up and sent back." Thus, the editors attach the reviewers' reports because you might find their remarks helpful or simply because the reports exist and should not go to waste.

If the editors' negative decision seems to contrast with the reviewers' more positive suggestions, it may be that the editors didn't like your essay or didn't include the most critical parts of the reviewers' reports. Many journals now ask for separate reports—a review that goes straight to the author and a decision that goes only to the editor. In such a situation, the reviewer may choose to be encouraging in the report to the author but more direct about its problems to the editor. Also, reports connected to these kinds of decisions can be brutal, and the editor may want to spare you the most direct comments if they are couched in personal or universal terms (e.g., "how did this person get through graduate school with such a poor grasp of history/grammar/my work/etc."?) Removing the vindictive is an important part of the editors' job; let them do it.

If you can use the reports to revise the article for another journal, good for you. Sometimes the editors will even suggest that that you think about submitting the article to another journal because that other journal is better suited to your topic or argument. (You will sometimes get this decision after the peer-review process, as a kind of consolation, but a good editor will not allow an inappropriate article to go through the review process.) If the comments aren't helpful, then just move on.

Surprisingly, this decision is not the worst decision you can receive. Any time an article of yours makes it to peer review, you should consider it a triumph (since so many editors now reject articles without sending them to peer review). The opposite of love is not hate, but indifference. If the reviewers really hated what you were doing, maybe you are on to something!

Rejected by editor. This an absolute rejection without any reviewers' reports. The lack of reports is one of the clearest signs of rejection, as is the appearance anywhere in the decision letter of the phrase "best of luck!" That phrase means the editor considers your exchange now closed and is expecting you to move on to try your luck elsewhere.

The difficulty, in this case, is knowing why you were rejected, since there are no reviewers' reports. Usually, the lack of reports indicates that the article never went through the peer-review process, and reports don't exist. The editors made the decision alone. This is especially true if you get this letter fairly quickly. As mentioned, more and more journal editors are rejecting articles *before* they go through peer review if they think that the article is unlikely to be accepted. Peer reviewers' time is valuable and they can get cranky if they regularly receive articles that are not publishable. So, such a rejection may have to do with the article's quality.

But the lack of reports could indicate that the editors are rejecting your article because of its topic. The editors may have accepted too many articles on your author, period, theory, population, country, etc., and may need to return yours without reading it. For instance, our journal once had to return a good article to the author because we had just published an article on that very topic. Unfortunately for us, the second article was better than the published article, but those are the breaks. We were hardly going to say as much in the rejection letter.

If the article did go through the peer-review process, maybe the reviewers' reports were too hostile to be passed along, or too brief, saying in effect, "Why did you bother me with this article? I'm too busy to write a detailed report listing all the many reasons it should be rejected!" It's also possible that the editors sent your article for review but never could get the reviewers to respond and just decided to reject the article rather than explain their failure.

Thus, your main problem with this decision is that it can mean your article is truly terrible or that no one took the time to find out. If the editors mention the reports and yet do not attach them, you can ask for them but I don't generally recommend it. The editor is usually trying to protect you from unhelpful reports or they don't exist. Lots of scholars get this kind of unexplained rejection; just move on to your second-choice journal.

What decision did my article receive from the journal 's editors?	

If there is any doubt in your mind about what the decision was, contact the editors and find out.

RESPONDING TO JOURNAL DECISIONS

It's time to strategize how you are going to respond to the editor's letter and reviewer's comments on your work. Let's go through this process step by step.

Task 1: Reading the Workbook

On the first day of your writing week, you should read the workbook up to this page and answer all the questions posed in the workbook up to this point.

Task 2: Evaluating and Responding to the Journal Decision

Read the review and put it away for several days. What seems shocking and rude on the first day may seem much more manageable by the third day. Getting some distance on the comments is useful for strategizing on how you are going to respond. Once you have done that, make sure you are clear on what decision you have received. You will have to proceed differently depending on whether the journal has rejected your article or asked you to revise and resubmit it.

Responding to a Journal's Decision to Reject

Let's say that your article gets savaged and rejected. First, remember that almost all scholars have had their work rejected at one point or another—between 85 and 90 percent of prominent authors admit to having their work rejected (Gans and Shepherd 1994). Second, allow yourself to feel angry and depressed. You are only human!

Third, after allowing yourself to feel down for a week or two, revisit the letter and its recommendations, if there are any. It is time to make a decision about how you are going to proceed. Your options upon rejection are (1) to abandon the article, (2) to send the article without a single change to another journal, (3) to revise the article and send it to another journal, or (4) to protest or appeal the decision and try to resubmit the article to the rejecting journal. Let's go through these choices.

Should I abandon the article? Studies conducted several decades ago on the publication experiences of those in the physical and social sciences found that one-third of the authors who had an article rejected, abandoned not only the article but also the entire line of research on which it was based (Garvey, Lin, and Tomita 1972). Don't let that be you! If your article is rejected the first time you send it to a journal, you should definitely send it to a second journal. About 85 percent of scholars now send their rejected articles to another journal (Rotton, Foos, Van Meek 1995). If three or more journals have rejected the article, it may be time to think about giving up on it, but remember the story that started this chapter. Further, a political science professor recently told a student of mine that an article of his had been rejected eight times before being published. The main reason to abandon an article is if reviewers raise objections to your methodology, theoretical approach, or argument so serious that you believe, upon long reflection, that they are unsolvable. Another reason is if the peer reviewers regularly agree on what is wrong with the article. Research shows that peer reviewers tend to agree with each other when an article is poor, but tend to disagree when an article is strong.[5] In other words, if you are getting split reviews, that's a good sign.

Should I resubmit the article elsewhere without revising it? Some scholars insist that they never revise an article until it has been rejected by three different journals. As one author put it, "Once it's clear the editor is not interested, I'm not that interested in what the reviewers had to say [because] . . . one reviewer may argue strongly that you change x to y, another may argue equally strongly that you change y to x. Authors should be wary of being drawn into this morass until they find an interested editor. When that happens, then you pay extremely close attention to the reviewers' comments" (Welch 2006). Given the subjectivity of reviewing, this is not a bad plan. In the humanities, such scholars prepare three envelopes, each to different journals, so that if the article comes back from the first or second journal, they can send it right back out that day. If these authors get three rejections, only then do they sit down and really read the reviewers' comments, see whether there is any agreement among them, and then revise accordingly. One study shows that about half of rejected articles that were resubmitted to other journals were not revised (Yankauer 1985). However, and this is important, revising an article increases the chances of a second journal accepting it (Bakanic, McPhail, and Simon 1987).

Should I revise and resubmit the article elsewhere? Most scholars try to use the recommendations to revise the article each time it is rejected so that they can send an improved article to the next journal. You can't go wrong with this practice, so long as you do not spend too much time on revising and you only respond to critiques with which you agree. You should take care of any factual errors or real mistakes. The purpose of peer review is to provide you with sound recommendations for improving your article; you might as well use them.

Although three-quarters of authors felt that peer reviewers had some recommendations that were based on "whim, bias, or personal preference," about as many authors also felt that the process of peer review improved their articles (Bradley 1981). It seems that authors must live with two contradictory truths: peer review is a subjective, biased process rife with problems AND peer review is a process that definitely improves articles. The editors' review of the reviewers' reports can be particularly helpful in deciding how to proceed.

Should I resubmit my article to a better journal? Deciding which journal to resend your article to is another important decision. A question students frequently ask me is: Should I send my rejected but revised article to a better journal than the one that rejected it or a worse one?

According to several studies, scholars traditionally send their rejected articles to less prestigious journals. But other studies show that many scholars send their rejected articles to equivalent journals and some send them to better journals.[6] I think it depends on how you feel about your revision. If you got excellent comments the first time around and have substantially strengthened the article, you may want to pick a better journal. If you want to resubmit the article without revising it, you may want to pick an equivalent journal, or a lower tiered one.

Your resubmission strategy depends on your initial strategy, as well. Some authors start off by sending the article to a tough, disciplinary journal known for rejecting articles but giving useful reviewers' reports that they can use to improve their article. If this process leads to the article getting into the first, highly-ranked journal, all the better; if it doesn't, such authors feel that the first journal's reviewers' reports are improving their chances of getting into their second choice. Given the subjectivity of reviewing, I'm not sure this is a brilliant strategy. Reviewers at disciplinary journals may ask for the kinds of changes that would not improve your chances at an interdisciplinary journal. As Robert Heinlein said years ago, "don't rewrite unless someone who can buy it tells you to" (Pournelle and Pournelle 1996). If the journal is not going to "buy" it, why revise for them? But there is some evidence for this start-at-the-top strategy: studies suggest that a high percentage of articles rejected by prestigious journals are published elsewhere.[7] For instance, 72 percent of the articles rejected by the *American Journal of Public Health* were subsequently published in other journals (Koch-Weser and Yankauer 1993).

Other authors start by sending their article to their second-choice journal first and if their article is not accepted there, but they get useful reviewers' reports that lead them to make a strong revision, they then move up the chain and send the improved article to a better journal. (Yes, you are under no obligation to send your work to the journal that led to that improvement. You have not signed any agreement.)

What's the upshot? If you revise and resubmit your article to another journal, you increase your chances of getting published. Several studies suggest that at least 20 percent of published articles were first rejected by another journal.[8] An older study found that about 1 percent of published articles were rejected by four or more journals before being accepted (Garvey, Lin, and Tomita 1972). As the librarian Ann C. Weller concludes in her review of this research, "studies have shown that indeed, a good percentage of rejected manuscripts do become a part of the published literature" (Weller 2001, 70).

Should I protest the decision? Sometimes, even after allowing yourself time and space, you perceive the reviewers' or editors' comments as cruel, unfair, or outrageous. In these situations, is it worthwhile or effective to complain to the journal editors (the very people who delivered the decision)? On the one hand, everyone has the right to speak truth to power and if you want to exercise that right, go ahead. All editors have received one or two rants from authors about their decisions or their reviewers' reports—yours won't be the first or the last. Just make sure that your protest letter does not commit the same sins that inspired it: Do not be insulting. Since we often lose impartiality in such situations, let someone edit your protest letter before you send it.

On the other hand, the plain truth is that writing such letters won't change anything. Recently, an interviewer asked a well-published faculty member if he ever protested journal decisions. The author answered with one word, "Yes." The interviewer then asked if protesting ever worked. The author again answered with one word, "No" (Welch 2006, 2). Journal editors are well aware that the process is flawed; thus, they tend to think that the real problem is authors' expectation that it be otherwise:

> People have a great many fantasies about peer review, and one of the most powerful is that it is a highly objective, reliable, and consistent process. . . . If I ask people to rank painters like Titian, Tintoretto, Bellini, Carpaccio, and Veronese, I would never expect them to come up with the same order. A scientific study submitted

to a medical journal may not be as complex a work as a Tintoretto altarpiece, but it is complex. Inevitably people will take different views on its strengths, weaknesses, and importance. (Smith 2006)

Most important, however, is that protesting has very low returns. Writing a protest letter takes up valuable time that you could spend sending your work to another, more receptive journal. Why try to improve the universe and its fairness quotient when you can focus on getting published? Further, if you send a protest to the journal editor, you may feel awkward submitting work to that journal in future, and you don't want to feel awkward submitting work to any journal.

Fortunately, the desire to protest journal decisions tends to wane as you get more experience with submitting articles. You come to understand that plenty of articles are successfully published that have received harsh treatment at the hands of others and you learn to move on. So, if you feel like protesting your first or second journal decision, resist the impulse. You don't know enough yet about how it all works. Get some more experience under your belt.

If it is any comfort, in eleven years as an editor reading reports by reviewers I knew, I began to sense that there was a correlation between niceness and productivity. I can't prove it, but it seemed to me that the kinder and more constructive reviewers were more likely to be productive writers themselves. The harsher and less helpful reviewers were more likely to be unproductive writers. We give others the messages we give ourselves.

Are silence and ineffective protest your only options? No. Another option, if you ever deign to submit work to that journal again, is to mention in your cover letter that you thought you received an "unhelpful" review (use that exact word, not anything stronger) the previous time and would prefer, if possible, to have a different reviewer this time. I'm not sure I recommend this tactic, but some editors will respect this request.

What you definitely should not do is insist that you know who the unkind reviewer was and that that person has a personal vendetta against you. Some authors find it difficult to refrain from trying to guess who the reviewers are. All I can say is that your chances of being right are low. In my years as an editor, I have never had an author guess correctly. And I have seen more than one relationship fail because the author was wrongly convinced about the identity of a negative reviewer. Don't waste time on this game.

Should I appeal the decision? Some large disciplinary journals have formal appeal processes, with independent boards. Many scholars have recommended over the years that more journals institute better appeal processes and provide authors and reviewers with more chances to dialog—but this sea change does not seem to be coming any time soon (Epstein 1995). A study of author appeals to *American Sociological Review* found that only 13 percent of appeals were successful (Simon, Bakanic, and McPhail 1986). Your chances of publication are higher, I think, if you move on to another journal.

Should I ask for additional reviewers? You can sometimes convince an editor who has rejected your article to send it to new reviewers. Only the most dispassionate of appeals, based on evidence not rhetoric, will win the day. For instance, a professor in one of my courses explained how he converted a journal editor's decision to reject an article into a request for a revision. When this author got the editor's negative decision with the reviewers' reports, he wrote to the editor commenting that both reviewers had paid no attention to the content of his article but only to its methodology. The author thought he could solve the methodological problems they identified, so he wrote to the editor and asked, "if I revise the article as the reviewers suggest, would you be able to send it to new reviewers who would comment on the content?" The editor responded that he would do so if the author truly addressed the first reviewers' comments. The professor revised, the editor agreed that the methodological problems had been solved and sent the revision to two new reviewers. They liked the article and it was published. An important key to this author's success was the very professional tone that he maintained throughout, never insulting the reviewers, accepting that their concerns were valid, and being willing to go through a second review process. Persistence was key.

On very rare occasions, editors may change their decision. At our interdisciplinary journal, we once gave a negative decision to an author with whose subject matter we were not familiar and who received one favorable report and one very negative report. The author responded to the negative reviewer's report with an eight-page, single-spaced defense. The tone of the defense was never insulting, but very focused, providing a swath of data to disprove the reviewer's objections and laying out how the author's and the reviewer's differences reflected a much larger debate going on in the field. The author insisted that the reviewer had not given the article a fair hearing. Since we liked controversial work and found the defense convincing, we asked the author to include much of that defense in the article itself and we published it. So, although protests can't carry the day, professional responses directly addressing the reviewers' critiques sometimes can.

Of course, I don't recommend that you spend time writing eight-page defenses, especially to journals that have sent unkind or unhelpful remarks. If you receive a definitive rejection, it is best to move on to the next journal.

How will I proceed now that my article has been rejected?	

Responding to a Revise and Resubmit Notice

Let's say, alternatively, that your article receives some kind of revise and resubmit notice. You should, of course, revise and resubmit your essay. Remember that your chances of publication increase substantially on a revised and resubmitted article (by some estimates to 60 percent). But, how exactly should you undertake that process?

Task 3: Planning Your Revision

On first getting a recommendation to revise, it is easy to feel that the revision is going to take a long time and that you should wait until you have more time to do the revision. Resist this impulse! Often, a revision will take less time than you anticipate. The article will seem at a distance, since you last worked on it several months ago, but it will become familiar within a few hours of your working on it. So, within two weeks of receiving a revise and resubmit notice, make sure to open the article, reread it, and make at least one change to the article. Return it to the front burner. Aim for getting the article back to the journal within a month or two, unless the journal requests it be returned more quickly. Although most editors will not give you a deadline for when to send the article back, new articles are always coming through and you don't want to be scooped. Also, the longer you wait, the more likely it is that you will have to do your related literature review again. So, get on it!

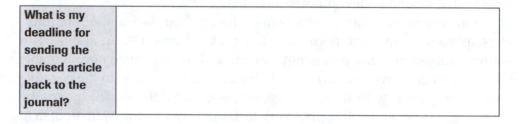

What is my deadline for sending the revised article back to the journal?	

Get any needed clarifications from the editor. It is not always clear how the editor wants you to revise. For instance, if the reviewers make opposing recommendations, which do you do? If the editor says that the article needs to be shortened, and both reviewers are making recommendations that lengthen it, whose directions should you follow? If you are not sure what you want to do, you can e-mail the editor asking for clarification on which changes to make. If you do know what changes you want to make, then don't ask the editor, just make the changes that make the most sense to you. In other words, don't ask for advice you are unwilling to take.

Do I need to contact the editor for clarification?	

Start a revision cover letter. Standard practice in the social sciences, and increasingly in the humanities, is for authors to submit, along with their revised article, a letter stating exactly how they revised the article according to the reviewers' recommendations. It is always in your best interest to write such a letter to guide the editor in interpreting your responsiveness. With such a letter, you can signal your obedience to the editors' requests, but also explain any choices you made not to follow reviewers' recommendations for revising. Also, since it is easy to forget what you have done to improve an article, creating an electronic file for the revision cover letter allows you to keep track of improvements (see Task 5 for more instructions).

Reviewer's Recommended Change	Reviewer 1, 2, or 3?	Valid Recommendation?	Level of Revision?	Revision Made?	Notes

Perform triage on the reviewers' recommendations. Just as it can be difficult to detect what decision an editor has made about your piece, it can be difficult to understand or keep track of what exactly the reviewers want you to do. Use the form on the previous page to identify and track changes.

If there are many changes, it is better to create your own spreadsheet with a line for each reviewer-recommended change, along with information on which reviewer made the recommendation, the validity of the recommendation, the level of revision it requires (none, small, medium, large), and the revisions planned to address the recommendation. If you don't want to be so formal, photocopy the reviewers' reports and mark them up. Whatever you do, don't treat their comments lightly. Make sure you understand them and that you brainstorm various ways of addressing them. Also, be sure that you cross reference the editors' letter with the reviewers' reports in case the editor has disagreed with or underscored any points.

Task 4: Revising Your Article

If the recommended changes are not substantial, you can start by fixing the smallest problems: spelling, syntax, missing information. This is a great way to get back into the article and usually won't take long. If the recommended changes are substantial, however, you might as well start tackling the largest problems first since you may be deleting sections with the smaller problems.

I think that the biggest mistake authors make when asked to revise and resubmit an article is planning to do too much in response to the reviewers' recommendations. Even serious objections to your work can often be solved in straightforward ways. Don't make the mistake of thinking that the more serious the objection, the more time, effort, and suffering you must invest. Sometimes this is true; many times it isn't. So, don't start off by planning a massive overhaul of your article.

Start off by making the smallest possible changes you can make to solve the largest objections. If the car doesn't start, don't take out the carburetor. Trying filling up the gas tank first. If making small changes leads you to make larger, more substantive changes, good for you. Any article can be improved. But it is best to start off with very targeted revisions. That way you won't get overwhelmed and you will be more likely to resubmit the article. This approach doesn't prevent you from doing more, but it does prevent you from doing too much.

Revising citations. The reviewer's report that does not recommend additional citations is rare. Almost all recommend that you cite one or twenty books or articles that you have not read. You can, of course, go and read this important literature. That makes you a good scholar. It does not necessarily make you a published author. I recommend that you first try to include suggested citations in your article before reading them. Revising an article for publication does not require that you know those books and articles by heart. In fact, reading those books and articles may make completing your revision more difficult. Inexperienced authors, in particular, imagine that other authors have put concepts more cogently and so begin to lard their article with quotes that cause more problems than they solve. Instead, start by identifying where you would discuss those citations in your article and draft a sentence or two referring to those citations based on what you already know. Then, and only then, read book reviews and abstracts on that additional work to see if you need to read any further. If you do, then, and only then, read the literature that is being recommended. If you already have twenty to fifty solid citations, then be wary of spending a lot of time carefully reading new material and adding whole paragraphs on new citations. A sentence here and there will usually suffice.

In my experience as an editor, recommended citations are rarely essential to the article. They are the books that popped into the reviewers' heads, either because they recently read them or wrote them. If your initial response to the reviewers' recommendations is planning on reading ten new books and incorporating a paragraph on each of them, the editor is not going to be happy with how bloated your article has become. You are doing too much in response to the recommendation.

There is one exception to my advice. Sometimes reviewers will state that it is odd that you do not cite so-and-so's article on your topic since you seem to be making very similar arguments or directly contradictory arguments. You will need to read that work carefully, particularly if that scholar is a seminal figure in your field. It will be important to differentiate what you are doing from what that scholar is doing. Otherwise, most reviewers are not expecting to see you engage their recommended citations at length.

Revising literature reviews. Re-read Week 5 of the workbook. Sometimes the reviewers will state that you have not discussed a whole body of scholarship or the relationship of your argument to it. If the body of scholarship is not on your topic, you may not need to address the objection. That is, it may not be necessary to cite recent work on biostatistics in Brazil if you are addressing biostatics in Morocco. But if the reviewers' recommendations cite a body of scholarship that is relevant, such a comment must be taken seriously. This is particularly true if the reviewer suggests that you are unaware of a new stream in the research on your exact topic, or if the reviewer notes that you haven't cited anything published in the last five to ten years. Not engaging the previous literature is a frequent error of inexperienced authors, and you should be grateful to a reviewer who merely asks you to revise an article that makes this mistake. Not only have they saved you from embarrassment, but their recommendations enable you to appear better versed than you are and to make your article stronger and smarter. Revising your article to address such problems will take more time but will improve it.

As you revise your article in response to that scholarship, remember that no publishable article can include many pages summarizing new research. Try to find a review essay that helps you think about that body of scholarship as a whole and your argument vis-à-vis it. Likewise, as you read the most useful works, think carefully about how your argument relates to their arguments. It is vastly more important for you to state how your work relates to that scholarship than for you to summarize it in any detail.

A case may be illustrative here. In an article our journal once received, the author had stated that there was no published research on the topic of her article and that her work filled this gap. One of the reviewers scribbled the word "nonsense" next to that claim and penciled in five titles published in the last few years that dealt with exactly that topic. Since the article was based on careful fieldwork and strong findings, we did not reject it, but we did ask that the article be better situated in the related literature. When the article came back, the author had simply switched the claim for significance, taking out the sentence about the gap and inserting a sentence about the exciting new research being done on the topic. She then placed a footnote at the end of that sentence and listed the five recommended books. Two of the books came up briefly later in the discussion, but the article was not significantly revised on the basis of that literature. Some editors would reject such a revision as insufficient. Others would concentrate on whether the article was an original contribution. We thought hers was and we published it. My own instinct as an author would have been to take more advantage of that previous research. But my point here is to convince you that briefly addressing the direct problem can work.

Revising terms and definitions. Many reviewers ask you to define your terms more carefully. Often this is lazy reviewing, but it certainly can't hurt your article for you to be clearer. Just do not take up much time or space adding definitions. It is easy to go overboard. Usually, adding five to ten words upon the first mention of the term can clarify matters perfectly. If you think further clarification is really necessary, use the footnotes to give a one- or two-sentence definition, either your own or someone else's. If the reviewers have major objections to the term, citing someone else's definition can be a good tack.

For instance, let's say that your reference to an "Irish diaspora" enraged one respondent, who insisted that the term diaspora could not be used to refer to the Irish and that the entire piece was vitiated by the regular reference to such. Despite the reviewer's strong response, the other reviewers don't even mention the term. You could attempt an overhaul, but if you believe in the term, the best response would be to include a footnote the first time you use the term. In it, cite the term's use by other academics: "My use of the term 'Irish diaspora' follows that of so-an-so and such-and-such and should be understood as referring to . . ." Remember that, in academia as in law, the best defense is precedent. If a reviewer challenges your use of a term, find another scholar who uses it in the same way. If you look at published articles, you will often find this kind of footnote, especially on terminology. You can, of course, also decide that the reviewer is correct and revise your use of the term.

Revising to shorten. These days it is almost axiomatic for editors to ask authors to shorten their work. Journal articles are getting shorter and shorter. Brevity can work for research that doesn't challenge the status quo, but poses problems for research that does. But let's say that your editor insists. Which of your precious jewels should be cut?

If you need to get the word count down significantly, start by cutting out block quotes, footnotes, long summaries of others' research, and additional cases. In the humanities, it is usually safer to delete evidence—some close readings, some historical analysis—than articulations of your argument or contribution. Then, start at the beginning of the article and examine each sentence for ways to make it shorter. If you work your way through your article taking out dead wood (e.g., unnecessary words), you will definitely improve it as a piece of prose (re-read Week 10). Also, if you remove just two words per sentence in a 7,500 word article, you can reduce your count by over 600 words. If your article is far too long, twice the allowed length, perhaps it is time to think about how it could be split into two different articles. This is especially successful if you can revise the two articles so that each would appeal to a different type of journal or even discipline.

Revising to lengthen. Reviewers tend to ask authors to expand and elucidate. I recently heard of a professor whose review of others' work consisted entirely of scrawling the word "More!" next to sentences and paragraphs. Apparently, the professor was never in need of less. Unfortunately, editors almost always are. Since so many journals are run by corporations, which impose exact page limits to keep paper costs down, editors wanting to have enough articles to make the journal interesting must limit their authors to fewer words each.

These contradictory instructions—shorten! lengthen!—create one of the main dilemmas facing authors. Whose instructions to follow? Fortunately, you can use this contradiction to your advantage. If the reviewers have asked for more on an issue you know little about or see as irrelevant, you can use the word limit to explain your failure to address their concerns. If the editor agrees that the recommendations were not essential, this will work. If the editor thinks they are important, it won't work. Thus, you cannot use word limits to defend your failure to make the work clearer, more theoretically sophisticated, or more significant. It can only be used as a polite way to decline a recommendation to add more on tangential topics. If the reviewers have asked for more on a topic that you do think is relevant, then you can ask the editor if you can have extra words to insert that now required material.

Revising theoretical or methodological approaches. If the reviewers have major objections to your theory or method, there are no short cuts. If you think the reviewers are wrong, move on to a new journal. If you think they are right, embark on a serious overhaul. Sometimes you can directly address the objection by stating in the article that the problem is a limitation or shortcoming of your research and allowing that further research is needed.

Revising argument. Re-read the advice in Week 3 of this workbook. A frequent comment of reviewers and editors is that the argument could be clearer or better defended. This always represents an opportunity to make your contribution more lucid. One easy fix is bringing material from your conclusion to your introduction (since we tend to get clearer as we go along). Make sure that you announce your argument clearly and early and reference it throughout your article. You can also add subheads to direct the reader. Another fix is to make sure that you do not vary your main terms too much. Avoid repetition when it comes to adjectives and verbs; increase it for your main nouns.

Revising structure. Re-read Week 6 of the workbook.

Revising grammar and style. Re-read Week 10 of the workbook. If the editor says that your writing needs real improvement (especially for ESL problems), consider hiring a copyeditor. A copyeditor will cost you anywhere from $250 to $1,000. A copyeditor charges $25 to $60 an hour and can copyedit one to four pages an hour. While this may seem like a lot of money, if lack of a published article is preventing you from getting a tenure-track job, or tenure itself, hiring a copyeditor is an important investment in your future earnings. Copyeditors can be found at the Editorial Freelancers Association website www.the-efa.org. Emeriti professors are sometimes interested in helping junior scholars as well.

Revising documentation. When requesting that you revise and resubmit an essay, the editors will generally ask that you ensure the documentation is correct. Even if the editors don't ask for this, do it. Follow the journal's directions and be meticulous. If you are using author-date documentation style, make sure that the authors' names and dates in the text match the names and dates in the bibliography. Little is more annoying to an editor than an author who has been sloppy about the in-text references or bibliography. If you are sloppy enough, it can get your essay returned to you.

Share. Once you have made your changes, you might want to think about sharing your revised essay with a writing group. You can let them know the reviewers' concerns and ask the group if they think you have addressed the concerns adequately.

Consult with coauthors. If you have coauthors but are responsible for making the changes, don't forget to run the revised version of the article by them.

Task 5: Drafting Your Revision Cover Letter

Since many revised articles are not read very carefully, a detailed revision cover letter is your best weapon in getting a revised article accepted. If the letter is professional and indicates a deep commitment to revision, the editor may take you at your word and do little more than skim the article to see if you have made the recommended changes. It is best to arrange the letter as a series of bullet points with the reviewers' critiques listed individually or grouped by category and then the alteration you made to solve the problem. This helps you stay organized and is easier for the editor to follow. It is also best to start the revision cover letter with all the changes you made in response to the reviewers' recommendations and only at the end to list your reasons for not addressing some of their recommendations.

In my course, a regular question arises: Do I have to do everything the reviewers or editors tell me to do? Absolutely not. In fact, few editors expect you to do all the recommended changes. What you must do, however, is take all recommendations seriously and address them in the body of the article or your cover letter. Further, you must be able to offer an academic reason for not making recommended changes. No matter how accurate, the given reasons cannot be: "The reviewer is an idiot," "The reviewer is a sexist pig," "The reviewer clearly hasn't read anything written in the last five years," "I don't think the reviewer actually read my article," or "I have a good idea who this reviewer is and he has always hated me."

Here are the kinds of defenses you can give in your revision cover letter:

- **Dates.** Reviewer 1 has disputed my dating of [some event]. I stand by my dating, but have added a footnote explaining how I arrived at the dates and providing some additional sources.

- **Analysis.** Reviewer 2 disagrees with my list of the causes of [some crisis]. Although I think my list is correct, there is a debate in the literature on the causes, so I have added a reference to that debate in the text.

- **Argument.** Reviewer 1 seems to have misread the premise of my article, which was [premise]. I thought I was clear, but I have taken the opportunity to clarify this premise so it is less easily misread.

- **Data.** Although the comment of Reviewer 1 on the relevance of my argument about child psychiatry to pet therapy was intriguing, I could not add material on that topic and still meet the word limit.

- **Data.** I thought the second reviewer's comment regarding the relevance of [such-and-such] was astute, but after several attempts, I could not frame this in the text in a brief enough space. Instead, I have inserted a general note.

- **Cases.** Since the reviewers were in conflict on the treatment of the second case (one recommending that I say more about it and the other recommending that I cut it), I have chosen to follow the second reviewer and cut that discussion.

- **Title.** I did keep more of the title than one reviewer recommended, as I think it better suggests the argument, but I have added more specificity so it will more accurately show up in online searches.

- **Citation.** The second reviewer recommended that I address [such-and-such], but there just wasn't space for it and [famous author] addresses this at length, so I just added an endnote referencing that reading.

- **Term.** One reviewer thought my use of the word [word] was too obscure, but I have found it used in this way more than a dozen times in academic texts in the field, so I have chosen to keep it. I can provide you with those citations if you wish.

- **Additional.** Once I started revising in response to the peer reviewers' helpful comments, I saw some other problems and revised several sections so that they were tighter and more to the point. I also changed my text/case in the second section from [text/case 1] to [text/case 2], since it supports my point better.

Note the even tone of these responses. Don't attack the reviewers; rather, explain how their recommendations have enabled you to improve the article even if you have not done what they told you to do. As editors, we assume that the reviewers stumbled for a reason. Their solution may not be right, but they are always right about indicating a problem, which often requires you to clarify and defend your meaning. As one editor advises,

> If a reader misinterprets something you wrote, there must be an improvement that will help . . . Try not to become so invested in the organization or the prose of the work that you are unwilling to make major changes if they are suggested and seem appropriate. There is nearly always a better way to present a finding or express a thought. (Rothman 1995)

If the editor sends the article back to the reviewers, they will undoubtedly get your revision cover letter as well. Thus, if your letter is sent as a hard copy, you may want to separate your point-by-point response from the letter so that the editor does not have to disguise your name from the reviewers.

Some suggest you list page numbers for each change you made, but page numbers change, so you must decide how useful this will be.

If you do make additional changes to the article, beyond what the reviewers suggested, do mention this in the cover letter. That you spent extra time to improve the article will usually impress editors, but they will also want to check to make sure you haven't worsened the article.

Sample Revision Letter 1

Dear [Editor's Name]:

Enclosed please find the revised version of my article titled [title]. I am grateful for the thorough reading of the reviewers and have addressed their concerns in the following ways.

Errors. I added the missing . . . and corrected the . . . .

Significance. One of the reviewers thought I should make my contribution clearer, so I have . . .

Introduction. I have tightened the introduction but have also provided examples of . . . so my subject is clearer and clarified the meaning of my main term. . . .

Theoretical framework. I shortened the theoretical section but also added material on so-and-so's work, as the second reviewer requested, so it is now a bit longer. The recommendation meant I was also able to address the first reviewer's concern about . . . so the increased length seems warranted.

Terms. I have abandoned the problematic classification of . . .

Section 1. In the section on . . ., I have incorporated the texts that the second reviewer recommended . . .

Section 2. For reasons of length, I have eliminated much of . . .

Section 3. I have developed the section as recommended . . .

Conclusion. I have focused on arguing more strongly from the rest of the article, providing more provocative conclusions from my analysis.

Length. By adding the recommended texts, defining my subject more clearly, expanding the readings with references to each other and the theoretical texts, and threading my argument throughout, the essay expanded beyond the word limit. To get it back down, I radically cut the notes, works cited, block quotes, and textual examples. This meant that many careful notes had to be dropped. It also meant that any secondary literature not directly related to the texts had to be sacrificed, such as all the references in the introduction and theoretical section. The essay is now just under the word limit.

I believe these revisions have radically improved the essay's argument and clarity—thanks to the editors' and reviewers' thoughtful recommendations. Please let me know if there is anything further I can do; in particular, I can return deleted material to the text for clarity.

Sincerely,

[Your Name]

Sample Revision Letter 2

Dear [Editor's Name]:

Thank you for considering my article [give title and journal's number for the article] for [journal title]. I appreciate the comments I received and am resubmitting this manuscript for your consideration. In this letter, I detail how I addressed the reviewers' comments.

The first reviewer's comments and my revisions were as follows:

"I would be curious to know if gender affected . . ."
My Revisions:

- While, as this reviewer noted, this is hard to determine because of the size of my sample (n=9), I revisited and re-analyzed the data. There appeared to be no significant differences in how men and women viewed. . . .

- At the beginning of the "Results" section, I added a phrase that notes that there were few differences in responses across gender and socioeconomic status.

- When addressing the limitations of this study in the "Implications" section, I added a sentence that suggests that the small sample size limits my ability to determine whether there are differences between men and women in . . .

"I also wonder how [variable] may have changed over time . . ."
My Revisions:

- On page 24, I added that longitudinal study of [variable] and how it changed over time, especially focusing on how . . . is necessary to further our understanding of this population.

- On page 26, I highlighted as a limitation of this study that it is not longitudinal.

Thank you very much for your time and consideration. If you have any questions about the manuscript or changes that I have made, please do not hesitate to be in touch. I can be reached by e-mail at . . .

Sincerely,

[Your Name]

Task 6: Requesting Permissions

If you plan to reproduce a significant portion of someone else's creation in your article, you will need to provide the journal publishers with permission from the copyright owner of the work. It is your responsibility, not the journal's, to arrange all copyright permissions and to pay any permission fees, so it's best to start this process even before your article is finally accepted for publication, since it can take many months for permissions to come through. Copyright owners often require six to eight weeks to process requests. A word to the wise: the permissions process is so complicated, many authors decide not to include any material that requires permissions.

What should I include in my submission? You don't need to include your letters of permission or original illustrations in your revision submission. But you should include a photocopy of the illustrations you plan to use with the submission. You will need the real versions if the article is accepted.

What is copyright? Copyright acts in Canada, the United States, Britain, and the European Union assert the exclusive rights of a creator to reproduce and distribute his or her own work. No one else has that right unless the creator signs over the rights. The creator does not have to register the work with the Copyright Office in order for the work to be copyrighted; any artwork is copyrighted by the creator from conception. Therefore, if you want to reproduce and distribute someone else's work, you have to get their permission. Most journals are very alert to copyright considerations so you cannot ignore this step.

What material most often requires permission? Images are the materials most commonly needing permission to reproduce in journals.

- Any photograph, map, cartoon, painting, sculpture, film, video, or other form of visual illustration requires permission to reproduce. The more creative the work, the more likely that you will need to ask permission. The only visual material that you do not have to ask permission to reproduce are advertisements, such as movie stills.

- Any table, graph, or chart produced by someone else.

- Any close adaptation of a previously published image, table, or graph.

- Any photographs of living people, especially children, must be accompanied by signed releases showing that they have agreed to let their image be used in this context. The ethnocentric exception is photographs of people from outside of Europe or North America. Most journals will not require signed releases from such subjects.

Do I need permission to reproduce words? Almost all of you writing journal articles are citing others' published texts in "fair use" ways and do not need to ask for permission. But just to make sure the terms are clear, you do not need to ask for permission to reproduce text under the following conditions:

- If you are reproducing only a fraction of the text (whether it be a creative poem, short story, novel, or nonfiction pamphlet, article, or book), you do not need to ask for permission. In the United States, you are generally allowed to quote up to a total of 400 words from a book, or fifty words or less from an article or chapter in an anthology. If you reproduce more than that, you may need to ask for permission. (Since the trend is away from block quotes in journal articles, you should not have a problem staying under this minimum.)

- If the text was first published in the United States seventy-five or more years ago, you do not need to ask for permission. Such works are considered in the public domain; that is, as belonging to the public. Thus, anyone can reproduce Shakespeare's plays as they originally were written long ago.

- If the text is part of any U.S. government publication, you do not need to ask for permission (these are published for public use).

- If the text is not artistic or intellectual (e.g., the phonebook), you do not need to ask for permission. Copyright law protects expression, not ideas or facts.

- If you created the text yourself and have not signed away the copyright to that text, you do not need to ask for permission.

When must I ask permission to reproduce words? Unpublished texts are strongly protected. You will need to ask permission of the creator or owner (usually an archive or museum) to reproduce correspondence (electronic or postal), diaries, memos, interviews, and so on. Also, if you want to reproduce all of a work of your own for which you have signed away copyright, you will need to ask permission.

When can I run into trouble reproducing words? You are not likely to run into the following problems writing a journal article, but it is good to be aware of them.

- If you reproduce the heart of a text, that is not "fair use." For instance, if you list the seven habits of the highly successful in seven sentences in your journal article, you might get in trouble with the author of the book on that topic because the owner can say that potential buyers feel they no longer need to buy the book.

- If you reproduce a significant percentage of an original text, that is not "fair use." For instance, if you cite both lines of a two-line poem. Even though your quote is short, it constitutes the entirety of the poem. Most courts, however, have allowed more leeway for textual analysis, so if you are including the whole poem for the purposes of close reading, you don't need permission. But, if you are including the whole poem just as an epigraph, without analysis, you may not be protected.

- Lyrics for popular songs are strongly protected in the United States. Again, if you are carefully analyzing them, you are probably protected, but if you are just mentioning them, you may need to ask for permission to reproduce even one or two lines.

Who do I ask for permission? Authors and artists often sign over the copyright to their work in order to get it published. Thus, the copyright owner is often a publisher. One of your first tasks, then, is to find out who owns the copyright. The source of illustrations are sometimes given in the figure caption or in the acknowledgements. If you aren't sure who owns the copyright, it is easiest to start with the publisher, since they can forward you to the artist if needed.

What do I say in the permission letter? The *Chicago Manual of Style* has an excellent section on permission requests, and it is a good idea to follow their advice. If you don't have access to the manual, be sure to include explicit information in the letter about the material you want permission to use and the journal you might be reproducing the material in. You cannot set a deadline for their reply, although you can urge them to reply soon.

What if the copyright owner does not respond? This is a common problem. Copyright owners change addresses, and ownership may move from one publisher to another or revert to the author. Fortunately, you are only obligated to make a reasonable effort to contact the copyright owner and if this fails, you can proceed with publication without the permission. It's important, therefore, for you to keep a record of all your correspondence as proof that you have attempted to gain permission to use the material. If you have made several efforts, you can then publish the work with the following notice, "Every effort has been made to trace copyright holders and to obtain their permission for the use of copyright material. The publisher apologizes for any errors or omissions in the above list and would be grateful if notified of any corrections that should be incorporated in future reprints or editions of this book."

What if the copyright owner denies the request? This is within their rights; you have little recourse but the courts.

What if the copyright owner insists that I pay stiff fees for the permission to reprint? Unfortunately, this is common, even when you are asking permission to reproduce an illustration in an obscure journal with few readers. I once had an art history student who was told by the museum owner that it would cost $2,000 for her to include in her dissertation each of the dozens of paintings she discussed. As a result, her dissertation included not one of the paintings that were its subject. You can beg the owner to reduce their fees, but you can do little more. Some institutions have funds for the costs of photography and permissions, so if the cost won't come down, find out if your institution will subsidize the cost.

How should I submit the permission to the journal editors when it comes? Most journal editors will require a copy by post of the request letter and/or forms with the original signatures. Faxes, photocopies, and e-mail communications will not usually be accepted, and some journals will postpone or refuse publication if all permissions have not been secured by copyediting. If asked, you should provide captions that include the permission language that the copyright owner specified.

Should I err on the safe side when asking for permissions? The *Chicago Manual of Style* says:

> The right of fair use is a valuable one to scholarship, and it should not be allowed to decay through the failure of scholars to employ it boldly. Furthermore, excessive caution can be dangerous if the copyright owner proves uncooperative. Far from establishing good faith and protecting the author from suit or unreasonable demands, a permission request may have just the opposite effect. The act of seeking permission establishes that the author feels permission is needed, and the tacit admission may be damaging to the author's cause. (1993, 148)

Regarding this last point, the U.S. Supreme Court disagrees: "If the use is otherwise fair, then no permission need be sought or granted. Thus being denied permission to use the work does not weigh against the finding of fair use."[9] Likewise, "The 'permission' system established by the publishers is irrelevant to a determination of fair use."[10]

And that's it! That is what you need to think about when preparing an article for resubmission.

ON THE IMPORTANCE OF PERSEVERING

In the 1960s, a first-year assistant professor wrote an article based on some techniques in his dissertation. He spent many evenings talking over the ideas in his article with a colleague, then worked to make the article readable, gave it a fun title, and sent it off to the big journal in his field. The editors rejected it, responding that the article was interesting but "trivial," according to the scholar's own report. The scholar then sent the article back out to a second-tier journal, whose editors rejected it for the opposite reason, stating that the article was too "general" to be published. The scholar began to think that his entire line of research was problematic. Still, he sent the article back out to a third-tier journal, whose editors also rejected it, saying that it was too "trivial" again. By now, the scholar was feeling quite discouraged, and he let the article sit around on his desk for some time.

After a trip to India that resparked his interest, he finally managed to revise the article and sent it off to a fourth journal, quite small and, to his amazement, they accepted it, four years after he first sent the article out. Since he felt "lucky" that he had gotten the article published anywhere, he moved on to other research interests. By then, his department was concerned about his productivity and refused to promote him because he had not published enough. Soon after, he fell sick and was diagnosed with clinical depression. So, it was a surprise to the professor when, not long after his thrice-rejected article was published, strangers started to approach him at conferences to say that they found his article fascinating.

Thirty years later, Berkeley professor George Akerlof won the Nobel Prize in economics for the research in that landmark article. It is one of the most highly cited articles ever to be published in any field, and the thoughts that he first articulated there have profoundly changed the real worlds of insurance, markets, and the law.

The title of his article is "The Market for 'Lemons': Quality, Uncertainty, and the Market Mechanism." By lemons, Akerlof did not mean the citrus fruit; he was talking about used cars. Not incidentally, Akerlof's own theory about why the article was rejected so many times is that it was not "solemn" enough. A friend who is an economist has another theory: "The reason that it got rejected is because it is remarkably clear and well written . . . He made it all seem so simple and obvious, which in a way it was." In other words, the very reason that people still read Akerlof's article today—because it is clear and readable—is the reason that it took so long to get published.

Akerlof's experience is not anomalous, according to the author of an article titled "Have Referees Rejected Some of the Most-Cited Articles of All Time?" (Campanario 1995). The author examined the cases of eight scholars who eventually earned Nobel Prizes for ideas that were initially rejected by reviewers and editors. According to other studies, as many as one in five of field-changing articles were initially rejected (Campanario 1996, Gans and Shepherd 1994).

Three important lessons can be learned from Akerlof's story. First, just because an article is rejected—one, two, even three times—does not mean that it is a bad article. Second, it may take thirty years for the Nobel Prize committee to recognize your genius . . . so hang in there! Third, you may have to go through hell to get a good article published. Fortunately, you will be in good company.

End Notes

Week 1: Designing Your Plan for Writing

1. Like almost all authors of books about professional academic writing written in the last decade, I have based this chapter on the faculty productivity research by Robert Boice, who did more to explain academics to themselves than perhaps any other scholar. His work (see my Works Cited and Recommended Reading for a list) informs almost every paragraph of this chapter. Over his long career, Boice innovated many solutions for academic writers, ones that I have found work. I am particularly grateful for his early encouragement of my own teaching. His former student, emeriti assistant vice chancellor Jim Turner, used many of Boice's precepts to transform graduate education at UCLA from 1996 to 2006.

2. "Writer's block is a modern notion. . . . Before, writers regarded what they did as a rational, purposeful activity, which they controlled. By contrast, the early Romantics came to see poetry as something externally, and magically, conferred. . . . In terms of getting up in the morning and sitting down to work, a crueler theory can hardly be imagined" (Acocella 2004).

3. Robert Boice has conducted much of this research on scholarly writing productivity (1982, 1983, 1989, 1990, 1992, 1997a, 1997b, 2000), but others have confirmed his findings (Krashen 2002). The general research on procrastination and productivity also supports the conclusion that short bursts can accomplish much and is a common pattern among very productive individuals. For instance, John Grisham wrote his first novel by arriving at his office at 5:30 a.m., five days a week, and writing until his full-time job as a state representative started (Pringle 2007, 21).

Week 2: Starting Your Article

1. "The art of concealing your source" Franklin P. Jones; "Undetected plagiarism" William R. Inge; "The fine art of remembering what you hear but forgetting where you heard it" Laurence J. Peter; "Nothing but judicious imitation. The most original writers borrowed one from the other" Voltaire; all from Brussell (1988).

2. The stylized masks of the Kwele, Fang, and Kota peoples from Gabon and of the Songye people from the Democratic Republic of the Congo inspired such twentieth-century artists as Picasso and Juan Gris. See the Walt Disney-Tishman African Art Collection at the Smithsonian's National Museum of African Art and the work of Simon Gikandi (2006).

3. The important scholar Suresh Canagarajah has written an award-winning book on this topic (2002), describing the publication experiences of Sri Lankan scholars, including himself, and analyzing the restricting conventions of mainstream journals.

4. Based on Elin Skaar's research.

5. Based on Chon A. Noriega's research.

6. This paper was later published; note how the title and abstract changed from the earlier version cited in this paper. When published:
Feliciano, Cynthia. 2001. "The Benefits of Biculturalism: Exposure to Immigrant Culture and Dropping out of School among Asian and Latino Youths." *Social Science Quarterly* 82, no. 4: 865–879. This study examines how retaining an immigrant culture affects school dropout rates among Vietnamese, Koreans, Chinese, Filipinos, Japanese, Mexicans, Puerto Ricans, and Cubans. *Methods*. I use 1990 Census data to analyze how language use, household language, and presence of immigrants in the household affect dropping out of school. *Results*. Overall, I found that these measures have similar effects on these diverse groups: Bilingual students are less likely to drop out than English-only speakers, students in bilingual households are less likely to drop out than those in English-dominant or English-limited households, and students in immigrant households are less likely to drop out than those in nonimmigrant households. *Conclusions*. These findings suggest that those who enjoy the greatest educational success are not those who have abandoned their ethnic cultures and are most acculturated. Rather, bicultural youths who can draw resources from both the immigrant community and mainstream society are best situated to enjoy educational success.

Week 3: Advancing Your Argument

1. For instance, see the research on legal writing, which found that judges and attorneys tend to skip block quotations (Robbins 2004).

2. Kelly 1998.

3. See Patrick Scott's work on problems with the "right way" to analyze texts for the British A-Level exams, and Eagleston's thoughts on "theme-hunting" based on Scott's work, in Eaglestone 2000, 31.

Week 4: Selecting a Journal

1. An electronic search at *Ulrich's International Periodicals Directory* on March 5, 2008, for "active," "academic/scholarly," and "refereed" journals returned 23,991 hits.

2. If we take statistics from *The Chronicle of Higher Education* Almanac Issue 2001–2 (August 31, 2001), which states that there are 996,417 full- and part-time faculty members in the United States and approximately 41,000 graduate students receiving their doctorate each year, we can estimate that there are 1,037,417 scholars active in the United States in any given year. If we take the statistics from the HERI survey cited in the first chapter, which estimates that less than 25 percent of faculty are active in publishing, that suggests that fewer than 259,104 scholars submit an article each year to a journal. Since there were 7,314 academic journals published in the United States in 2001, that's an average of 35 articles submitted per journal per year in the United States. If each journal publishes an average of 15 articles a year, then the average rejection rate is 42 percent, or 3 out of 7 submitted manuscripts are accepted. That's a lot of ifs, but even if we assume a more competitive environment, in which twice as many scholars are sending articles, we still get a rejection rate of 80 percent, not the generally assumed rejection rate of 90 percent.

3. For a review of the literature on this topic, see Weller 2001, 59–69.

4. Simultaneous submission is a matter of ongoing debate among scholars, with opinion pieces on the topic appearing in the *Chronicle of Higher Education*, *PMLA*, and other journals.

5. For histories of journal publishing, see Meadows 1980.

6. If you are a graduate student editor and are reading my comments here with dismay, apologies! Serving as an editor is a great experience that undoubtedly will help you in your career. As someone who has worked on graduate student journals, I will only add that if you have worked hard enough on the journal to carry it beyond their usual misfortunes, congratulations. Now resign. To make a success of a journal requires more time than any graduate student has. If you are making a journal a going concern, you are probably ignoring your studies. Remember, helping others get published should never be a substitute for getting published yourself. The best-run student journal I know, *Mester*, limits editors to one-year appointments and pays them a full salary.

7. Interestingly, according to statistics from *Ulrich's International Periodicals Directory*, the number of electronic-only academic journals may have declined from this peak in 2000. Ulrich's lists 2,345 academic journals that are online only. See its chart "Online-Only Titles Analysis by Serials Subtype" at www.ulrichsweb.com.

8. An electronic search at *Ulrich's International Periodicals Directory* on March 5, 2008, found that of the 23,991 active peer-reviewed journals, 7,883 are based in the United States and 4,585 are based in the United Kingdom.

9. E-mail correspondence June 21, 2004, with MLA Publications.

10. *Journal Citation Reports* is available online through ISI Web of Knowledge.

11. Studies show that professors' opinions of what constitutes the leading journals in their field are more similar than their opinions of mid- or low-level journals (Weller 2001, 58).

12. See, for instance, Miller 1999.

13. One study found, from 1948 to 1968, that 61 percent of almost 300 editors and editorial board members of the *American Sociological Review* were professors from Chicago, Columbia, or Harvard (Yoels 1971). Yoels' study of other disciplines supported his finding that professors from the universities producing the most doctorates in that discipline dominated editorial boards (Yoels 1974). Yoels argued that this domination supported a "vicious circle" in which graduates of certain universities became editors and peer reviewers of prestigious journals, and then accepted the work of graduates from those same schools, increasing their prestige (Yoels 1974). Another study found that two-thirds of editorial board members of a particular journal had published in that journal in the past two years (Gibbons 1990).

Week 5: Reviewing the Related Literature

1. Even fifty years ago, scholars were complaining about the "staggering" number of articles and books published every year (Altick 1963, 129).

2. Adapted from Kathryn Riley's research, cited in Parker and Riley 1995, 84–85.

3. Sciubba 2006.

4. Adapted from Kathryn Riley's research as cited in Parker and Riley 1995, 87.

5. Cynthia Feliciano's research (2001).

6. Ortiz and Gonzales 2000.

7. Hamilton 2001.

8. Albert, Gunton, and Day 2003.

9. Henderson 1990.

10. Gabriel 1989.

11. Sharpe 1991.

12. Guo and Yao 2005.

13. Tagoe et al 2005.
14. Williams 1989.
15. Flores 1995 [1954].
16. Hale 2004.
17. Livingston 1989, 220.
18. Morris 1988.
19. Wilding 2003.
20. Griffin 2006.
21. As one sixteenth-century author put it, do not fatten your writing with others' works. "They lard their lean books with the fat of others' works." Robert Burton, cited in Altick 1963, 185.

Week 8: Opening and Concluding Your Article

1. Pilar Asensio's research.
2. Renia Ehrenfeucht's research.
3. Ramela Grigorian's research.
4. Matthew D. Marr's research (2005).
5. Lily Kumbani's research.
6. Vanessa Ochoa's research.
7. Alvaro Molina's research.
8. Jean Tompihé's research.
9. Carleen A. Curley's research.
10. Shana B. Traina's research.
11. Angelica Afanador's research.
12. Cynthia Feliciano's research (2001).
13. Carrie Petrucci's research (2002).
14. Dunkle, Jewkes, Brown, Gray, McIntryre, Harlow 2004.
15. Elizabeth Guillory's research (2001).
16. Matthew S. Hopper's research.
17. Charlton Payne's research.
18. Ruth E. Iskin's research (2006).
19. Lester Feder's research (forthcoming).
20. Maria Munoz's research.
21. Sebastian Eiter and Kerstin Potthoff's research.
22. Noriega 2002.
23. Hurtado and Vega 2004.
24. Saskia Subramanian's research.
25. Town 2004.
26. Tompkins 1986.
27. Davis 2000.
28. Hawthorne 2003.
29. Martín-Rodríguez 2000.
30. Marr 2005.
31. Blair 2003.
32. Johnson 1985.
33. Walton 1997.
34. Hawthorne 2003.

35. Staub 1997.
36. Haaken 1988.
37. Hardison 2004.
38. Sofer 2000.
39. Carby 1985.
40. Chingono 2001.
41. Olenchak and Hébert 2002.
42. Breakwell, Vignoles, Robertson 2003.
43. Fairbrother, Stuber, Galea, Pfefferbaum, and Fleischman 2004.
44. Freedman 2004.
45. Wilson 1998.
46. Fukurai 2001.
47. Shott 1997.
48. Kocagil 2004.
49. Schlee 2004.
50. Marshall 2002.

Week 10: Editing Your Sentences

1. Willis cites the author Ron Padgett on this topic. He says that, as a child, "I assumed I had to accept whatever words came into my head . . . my writing mode was passive . . . I had almost no control over the entire process" (Willis 1993, 2).

2. The memorable quote on this American desire for vigor: "Write with nouns and verbs, not with adjectives and adverbs. The adjective hasn't been built that can pull a weak or inaccurate noun out of a tight place" (Strunk and White 1979, 71). For an argument against Strunk and White, see Pullum 2004.

3. The correct sentence is in Hubbuch 1992.

4. I am not sure who first said it, but for years now government writers have been told that "Doublings satisfy a yearning for symmetry . . . [but] whatever differences the writer may see between such synonyms, they are lost on readers. Choose one." The reason that we like doublings is that they are very common in spoken English and older English. The King James Version of the Bible is full of them. So, something about a doubling just feels right; "this and this" preserves rhythm. Williams points out that writers got in the habit of pairing an English word with a French or Latinate word to sound more learned, which suggests why doubling is a problem now, when such fancying up is frowned upon.

Week X: Responding to Journal Decisions

1. For a review of these studies, see Weller 2001, chapter five, "The Role of Reviewers." In this chapter, I am indebted to Weller's book compiling and evaluating the studies conducted between 1945 and 1997 on peer review.

2. For a review of these studies, see Weller 2001, chapter six, "Reviewer Agreement."

3. See, for instance, Roberts, Fletcher, and Fletcher 1994. For a review of this issue, see Weller 2001, chapter four, "The Authorship Problem."

4. For a review of these studies, see Weller 2001, chapter three, "Editors and Editorial Boards: Who They Are and What They Do."

5. For a review of these studies, see Weller 2001, 193–197.

6. For a review of these studies, see Weller 2001, chapter two, "The Rejected Manuscript," especially p. 68.

7. See the chart summarizing the research about the "Final Publication Outcome of Rejected Manuscripts," in Weller 2001, 66.

8. See the chart summarizing the research about the "Final Publication Outcome of Rejected Manuscripts," in Weller 2001, 66.

9. *Princeton University Press v. Michigan Document Services,* 1996 FED App. 0357P, 99 F.3d 1381 (6th Cir. 1996).

10. *Luther R. Campbell AKA Luke Skyywalker, et al., Petitioners V. Acuff Rose Music, Inc.* See at www.law.cornell.edu/supct/html/92-1292.ZO.html

Works Cited

Acocella, Joan. 2004. "Blocked: Why Do Writers Stop Writing?" *New Yorker* (June 14–21).

Akerlof, George. 1970. "The Market for 'Lemons': Quality, Uncertainty, and the Market Mechanism." *Quarterly Journal of Economics* 84, no. 3 (August): 488–500.

Albert, Karin H. and Thomas I. Gunton, and J. C. Day. 2003. "Achieving Effective Implementation: An Evaluation of a Collaborative Land Use Planning Process." *Environments* 31, no. 3 (December): 51–69.

ALPSP (Association of Learned and Professional Society Publishers). 2000. "Current Practice in Peer Review: Results of a Survey Conducted during Oct/Nov 2000." ALPSP. Accessed November 1, 2008, at www.alpsp.org

Altick, Richard D. 1963. *The Art of Literary Research*. New York: W. W. Norton & Co.

American Library Association. 1983. *The ALA Glossary of Library & Information Science*, ed. Heartsill Young. Chicago: ALA.

American Psychological Association. 2001. *Publication Manual of the American Psychological Association*. 5th ed. Washington, DC: American Psychological Association.

Asquith, P.J. 1996. "Japanese Science and Western Hegemonies: Primatology and the Limits Set to Questions." In *Naked Science: Anthropological Inquiry into Boundaries, Power and Knowledge*, ed. Laura Nader, 239–256. New York: Routledge.

Association of Research Libraries. 2000. *Directory of Scholarly Electronic Journals and Academic Discussion Lists*. Washington, DC: ALA. Accessed June 20, 2004, at dsej.arl.org/dsej/2000/foreword.html

Auerbach, Erich. 1953. *Mimesis: The Representation of Reality in Western Literature*, trans. Willard R. Trask. Princeton: Princeton University Press.

Autorino, Riccardo, Giuseppe Quarto, Giuseppe Di Lorenzo, Marco De Sio, and Rocco Damiano. 2007. "Are Abstracts Presented at the EAU Meeting Followed by Publication in Peer-Reviewed Journals? A Critical Analysis." *European Urology* 51, no. 3 (March): 833–840.

Bakanic, V., C. McPhail, and R. J. Simon. 1989. "Mixed Messages: Referees' Comments on the Manuscripts They Review." *Sociological Quarterly* 30, no. 4 (Winter): 639–654.

Bakanic, V., C. McPhail, and R. J. Simon. 1987. "The Manuscript Review and Decision-Making Process." *American Sociological Review* 52, no. 5 (October): 631.

Baker, Nicholson. 1991. *U and I: A True Story*. New York: Random House.

Bartlett, Thomas, and Scott Smallwood. 2004. "Special Report: Plagiarism." *Chronicle of Higher Education* (December 17) 51, no. 17.

Becker, Howard S. 1986. *Writing for Social Scientists: How to Start and Finish Your Thesis, Book, or Article*. Chicago: University of Chicago Press.

Belcher, Wendy. 1987. *Street Beat: The Art of the Street*. Washington, DC: Potter's House Press.

Belcher, Wendy. 1999. "The Prisoner: Pramoedya Ananta Toer, Indonesia's Leading Writer, Out on Tour." *LA Weekly* (June 4–10, 1999): 45.

Berg, Charles Ramírez. 2003. "Colonialism and Movies in Southern California, 1910–1934." *Aztlán: A Journal of Chicano Studies* 28, no. 1 (Spring): 75–96.

Blackburn-Munro, G., and R. E. Blackburn-Munro. 2001. "Chronic Pain, Chronic Stress and Depression: Coincidence or Consequence?" *Journal of Neuroendocrinology* (December) 13, no. 12: 1009–1023.

Blair, H. 2003. "Jump-Starting Democracy: Adult Civic Education and Democratic Participation in Three Countries." *Democratization* 10, no. 1 (Spring): 53–76.

Boice, Robert. 1982. "Increasing the Writing Productivity of 'Blocked' Academicians." *Behaviour Research & Therapy* 20, no. 3: 197–207.

Boice, Robert. 1983. "Contingency Management in Writing and the Appearance of Creative Ideas: Implications for the Treatment of Writing Blocks." *Behaviour Research & Therapy* 21, no. 5: 537–543.

Boice, Robert. 1989. "Procrastination, Busyness, and Bingeing." *Behaviour Research & Therapy* 27, no. 6: 605–611.

Boice, Robert. 1990. *Professors as Writers*. Stillwater, OK: New Forums Press.

Boice, Robert. 1992. *The New Faculty Member: Supporting and Fostering Professional Development*. San Francisco: Jossey-Bass.

Boice, Robert. 1997a. "Strategies for Enhancing Scholarly Productivity." In *Writing and Publishing for Academic Authors*, ed. Joseph M. Moxley and Todd Taylor, 19–34. Lanham, MD: Rowman & Littlefield.

Boice, Robert. 1997b. "Which Is More Productive, Writing in Binge Patterns of Creative Illness or in Moderation?" *Written Communications* 14, no. 4: 435–460.

Boice, Robert. 2000. *Advice for New Faculty Members: Nihil Nimus*. Boston: Allyn & Bacon.

Bolker, Joan. 1998. *Writing Your Dissertation in Fifteen Minutes a Day: A Guide to Starting, Revising, and Finishing Your Doctoral Thesis*. New York: Henry Holt & Co.

Booth, Wayne C., Gregory G. Colomb, and Joseph M. Williams. 1995. *The Craft of Research*. Chicago: University of Chicago Press.

Boswell, James. 1793. *Life of Samuel Johnson, LL.D.*, ed. G. B. Hill and L. F. Powell. Oxford: Clarendon Press, 1934–1964.

Bowker, R. R. 2008. "Bowker Reports U.S. Book Production Flat in 2007." Bowker Press Release. New Providence, NJ: Bowker, May 28. Accessed August 30, 2008 at www.bowker.com/index.php/press-releases

Bradley, J. V. 1981. "Pernicious Publication Practices." *Bulletin of the Psychonomic Society* 18, no. 1 (January): 31–34.

Breakwell, Glynis M., Vivian L. Vignoles, Toby Robertson. 2003. "Stereotypes and Crossed-Category Evaluations: The Case of Gender and Science Education." *British Journal of Psychology* 94, no. 4 (November): 437–456.

Brussell, Eugene E., ed. 1988. *Webster's New World Dictionary of Quotable Definitions*, 2nd ed. Englewood Cliffs, NJ: Prentice Hall.

Burns, David D. 1999. *Feeling Good: The New Mood Therapy*, New York: Avon, (William Morrow, 1980).

Campanario, J. M. 1995. "On Influential Books and Journal Articles Initially Rejected because of Negative Referee's Evaluation." *Science Communication* 16, no. 3 (March): 304–325.

Campanario, J. M. 1996. "Have Referees Rejected Some of the Most-Cited Articles of All Times." *Journal of the American Society for Information Science* 47, no. 4 (April): 302–310.

Canagarajah, A. Suresh. 2002. *A Geopolitics of Academic Writing.* Pittsburg, PA: University of Pittsburgh Press.

Carby, Hazel. 1985. "'On the Threshold of Woman's Era': Lynching, Empire, and Sexuality in Black Feminist Theory," *Critical Inquiry* 12, no. 1 (Autumn): 21–37.

Chingono, Mark. 2001. "Women, Knowledge, and Power in Environmental and Social Change." In *African Women and Children: Crisis and Response*, ed. Apollo Rwomire. Westport, CT: Praeger Publishers.

Collett-White, Mike. "'Da Vinci Code' Key? Dan Brown's Wife: Blythe Brown Helped Her Husband Research Ideas for the Novel." (*Reuters*, March 16, 2006).

Davis, Lennard J. 2000. "Dr. Johnson, Amelia, and the Discourse of Disability in the Eighteenth Century." In *"Defects": Engendering the Modern Body*, ed. Helen Deutsch and Felicity Nussbaum. Ann Arbor: University of Michigan Press.

Davis, Mike. 1992. *The City of Quartz. Excavating the Future in Los Angeles.* New York: Vintage Books.

Davis, Robert, and Mark Shadle. 2000. "'Building a Mystery': Alternative Research Writing and the Academic Art of Seeking." *College Composition & Communication* 51, no. 3 (February): 417–446.

Denzin, Norman K., and Yvonna S. Lincoln. 2005. *The SAGE Handbook of Qualitative Research*, 3rd ed. Thousand Oaks, CA: Sage.

Disraeli, Benjamin. 1870. *Lothair.* New York: D. Appleton and Co.

Dunkle, Kristin L., Rachel K. Jewkes, Heather C. Brown, Glenda E. Gray, James A. McIntryre, Sioban D. Harlow. 2004. "Gender-Based Violence, Relationship Power, and Risk of HIV Infection in Women Attending Antenatal Clinics in South Africa." *Lancet* 363 (May): 1415–1435.

Eaglestone, Robert. 2000. *Doing English: A Guide for Literature Students.* London: Routledge.

Edelstein, Scott. 1991. *1,818 Ways to Write Better and Get Published.* Cincinnati, OH: Writer's Digest Books.

Edwards, Brian T. 2007. "Marock in Morocco: Reading Moroccan Films in the Age of Circulation." *Journal of North African Studies* 12, no. 3 (Fall): 287–307.

Elbow, Peter. 1973. *Writing Without Teachers.* Oxford: Oxford University Press.

Epstein, S. 1995. "What Can Be Done to Improve the Journal Review Process." *American Psychologist* 50, no. 9 (October): 883–885.

Fagan, W. T. 1990. "To Accept or Reject: Peer Review." *Journal of Educational Thought* 24, no. 2 (August): 103–113.

Faigley, Lester, and Stephen Witte. 1981. "Analyzing Revision." *College Composition & Communication* 32, no. 4: 400–414.

Fairbrother, Gerry, Jennifer Stuber, Sandro Galea, Betty Pfefferbaum, and Alan R. Fleischman. 2004. "Unmet Need for Counseling Services By Children in New York City After the September 11th Attacks on the World Trade Center: Implications For Pediatricians." *Pediatrics* 113. no. 5 (May): 1367–1375.

Feak, Christine B., and John M. Swales. 1997. *Academic Writing for Graduate Students : Essential Tasks and Skills : A Course for Nonnative Speakers of English* (English for Specific Purposes). Ann Arbor: University of Michigan Press.

Feder, Lester. Forthcoming. "Unequal Temperament: The Somatic Acoustics of Racial Difference in. the Symphonic Music of John Powell." *Musical Quarterly.*

Feliciano, Cynthia. 2001. "The Benefits of Biculturalism: Exposure to Immigrant Culture and Dropping out of School among Asian and Latino Youths." *Social Science Quarterly*, 82, no. 4: 865–879.

Finifter, Ada. W. 1997. "Report of the. Managing Editor of the *American Political. Science Review.*" *PS: Political Science & Politics* 29: 755–768.

Fitikides, T. J. 2000. *Common Mistakes in English*. 6th ed. London: Longman.

Flores, Angel. 1995. "Magical Realism in Spanish American Fiction." In *Magical Realism: Theory, History, Community*, ed. Lois Parkinson Zamora and Wendy B. Faris, 109–118. Durham, NC: Duke University Press. [Original pub., 1954].

Fong, Colleen, and Judy Yung. 1996. "In Search of the Right Spouse: Interracial Marriage among Chinese and Japanese Americans." *Amerasia Journal* 21, no. 3: 77–97.

Freedman, Amy L. 2004. "Economic Crises and Political Change: Indonesia, South Korea, and Malaysia." *World Affairs* 166, no. 4 (Spring): 185–197.

Fukurai, Hiroshi. 2001. "Critical Evaluations of Hispanic Participation on the Grand Jury: Key-man Selection, Jurymandering, Language, and Representative Quotas." *Texas Hispanic Journal of Law & Policy* 5, no. 1 (Spring): 7–40.

Fulkerson, Richard. 1996. *Teaching the Argument in Writing*. Urbana, IL: National Council of Teachers of English.

Gabriel, Teshome H. 1989. "Towards a Critical Theory of Third World Films." In *Questions of Third World Cinema*, ed. Jim Pines and Paul Willeman, 30–52. London: British Film Institute.

Gans, Joshua S., and George B. Shepherd. 1994. "How Are the Mighty Fallen: Rejected Classic Articles by Leading Economists." *Journal of Economic Perspectives* 8, no. 1 (Winter): 165–179.

Garvey, W. D., N. Lin, and K. Tomita. 1972. "Research Studies in Patterns of Scientific Communication: III. Information-exchange Processes Associated with the Production of Journal Articles." *Information Storage & Retrieval* 8, no. 5 (October): 207–211.

Geertz, Clifford. 1973. "Thick Description: Toward an Interpretive Theory of Culture." In *The Interpretation of Cultures*. New York: Basic Books.

Gibbons, J. D. 1990. "U.S. Institutional Representation on Editorial Boards of U.S. Statistics Journals." *American Statistician* 44, 3 (August): 210–213.

Gikandi, Simon. 2006. "Picasso, Africa, and the Schemata of Difference." In *Beautiful-ugly: African and Diaspora Aesthetics*, ed. Sarah Nuttall, 30–59. Durham, NC: Duke University Press.

Giroux, Henry. 2003. Interview in *Critical Intellectuals on Writing*, ed. Gary A. Olson and Lynn Worsham. New York: SUNY Press.

Graff, Gerald, and Cathy Birkenstein. 2005. *They Say/ I Say: The Moves That Matter in Academic Writing*. New York: W. W. Norton.

Griffin, Kimberly A. 2006. "Striving for Success: A Qualitative Exploration of Competing Theories of High-Achieving Black College Students' Academic Motivation." *Journal of College Student Development* 47, no. 4 (July–August): 384–400.

Guillory, Elizabeth. 2001. "The Black Professoriate: Explaining the Salary Gap for African-American Female Professors." *Race Ethnicity & Education* 4, no. 3 (September): 129–148.

Haaken, Janice. 1988. "Field Dependence Research: A Historical Analysis of a Psychological Construct." *Signs: Journal of Women in Culture & Society* 13, no. 2: 311–330.

Hale, Henry E. 2004. "Explaining Ethnicity." *Comparative Political Studies* 37; no. 4 (May): 458–485.

Hamilton, Susan. 2001. "Making History with Frances Power Cobbe: Victorian Feminism, Domestic Violence, and the Language of Imperialism." *Victorian Studies* 43, no. 3 (Spring): 437–460.

Hardison, Debra M. 2004. "Generalization of Computer-Assisted Prosody Training: Quantitative and Qualitative Findings." *Language, Learning & Technology* 8, no. 1 (January): 34–52.

Hawthorne, Walter. 2003. "Strategies of the Decentralized: Defending Communities from Slave Raiders in Coastal Guinea-Bissau, 1450–1815." *Fighting the Slave Trade: West African Strategies,* ed. Sylviane A. Diof. Oxford: James Currey Press.

Henderson, Bill. 1998. *Pushcart's Complete Rotten Reviews and Rejections*: New York: Pushcart Press.

Henderson, Mae Gwendolyn. 1990. "Speaking in Tongues: Dialogics, Dialectics and the Black Woman Writer's Literary Tradition." In *Reading Black, Reading Feminist: A Critical Anthology.* New York: Meridian Press.

Henige, David. 2001. "Miss/Adventures in Mis/Quoting." *Journal of Scholarly Publishing* 32, no. 3 (April): 123–135.

Henry, A., and R. L. Roseberry. 1997. "An Investigation of the Functions, Strategies, and Linguistic Features of the Introductions and Conclusions of Essays." *System* 25: 479–495.

Henson, Kenneth T. 1995. "Writing for Publication: Messages from Editors." *Phi Delta Kappan* 76, no. 10: 801–804.

Henson, Kenneth T. 1995. *The Art of Writing for Publication.* Boston: Allyn & Bacon.

Holschuh, Jodi. 1998. "Editorial: Why Manuscripts Get Rejected and What Can Be Done about It: Understanding the Editorial Process from an Insider's Perspective." *Journal of Literacy Research* 30, no. 1, (1998): 1–7.

Hubbuch, Susan M. 1992. *Writing Research Papers Across the Curriculum.* 3rd ed. New York: Holt, Rinehart, & Winston.

Hurtado, Aida, and Luis A. Vega. 2004. "Shift Happens: Spanish and English Transmission between Parents and Their Children." *Journal of Social Issues* 60, no. 1 (Spring): 137–155.

Hyland, Ken. 1990. "A Genre Description of the Argumentative Essay." *RELC Journal* 21, no. 1: 66–78.

Hyland, Ken. 2004. *Disciplinary Discourses: Social Interactions in Academic Writing.* Michigan Classics Edition. Ann Arbor: University of Michigan Press.

Iskin, Ruth. 2007. *Modern Women and Parisian Consumer Culture in Impressionist Painting.* New York: Cambridge University Press.

Johnson, Barbara. 1985. "Thresholds of Difference: Structures of Address in Zora Neale Hurston." *Critical Inquiry* 12, no. 1 (Autumn): 317–328.

Johnson, Samuel. 1751 [1969.] *The Rambler,* ed W. J. Bate and Albrecht B. Strauss, v 39. New Haven: Yale University Press.

Guo, Kai, and Yang Yao. 2005. "Causes of Privatization in China." SO: *The Economics of Transition* 13, no. 2: 211–238.

Kelly, Jeffrey A. 1998. "Group Psychotherapy for Persons with HIV and AIDS-Related Illnesses." *International Journal of Group Psychotherapy* (April) 48, no. 2: 143–162.

Kershaw, Alex. 1997. *Jack London: A Life.* New York: St. Martin's Press.

Ketcham-Van Orsdel, Lee, and Kathleen Born. 1999. "Serials Publishing in Flux." *Library Journal* 124, no. 7 (April 15): 48–53.

Keynes, John Maynard. 1936. *The General Theory of Employment, Interest and Money.* Cambridge: Cambridge University Press, for Royal Economic Society.

Klauser, Henriette Anne. 1987. *Writing on Both Sides of the Brain: Breaththrough Techniques for People Who Write.* San Francisco: Harper and Row.

Kocagil, Ahmet E. 2004. "Optionality and Daily Dynamics of Convenience Yield Behavior: An Empirical Analysis." *Journal of Financial Research* 27, no. 1 (Spring): 143–159.

Koch-Weser, D., and A. Yankauer. 1993. "The Authorship and Fate of International Health Papers Submitted to the American Journal of Public Health." *American Journal of Public Health* 83, no. 11 (November): 1618–1620.

Krashen, Stephen. 2002. "Optimal Levels of Writing Management: A Re-Analysis of Boice (1983)." *Education* 122, no. 3: 605–608.

Laband, D. N. 1990. "Is There Value-added from the Review Process in Economics? Preliminary Evidence from Authors." *Quarterly Journal of Economics* 105, no. 2 (May): 341–352.

Lanham, Richard A. 2007. *Style: An Anti-Textbook.* 2nd ed. Philadelphia, PA: Paul Dry Books.

Lee, Susie J. 2005. "Frodo Baggins, A.B.D." *Chronicle of Higher Education* (August 28).

Lindholm, Jennifer A., Katalin Szelényi, Sylvia Hurtado, and William S. Korn. 2005. *The American College Teacher: National Norms for the 2004–2005 HERI Faculty Survey.* Los Angeles: UCLA Higher Education Research Institute.

Livingston, Chella C. 1989. "Johnson and the Independent Woman: A Reading of Irene." *The Age of Johnson*, ed. P. J. Korshin. New York: AMS Press.

Lunsford, Andrea A., and John J. Ruszkiewicz. 2003. *Everything's an Argument.* 3rd edition. New York: Bedford, St. Martin's.

Luther R. Campbell Aka Luke Skyywalker, Et Al., Petitioners V. Acuff Rose Music, Inc. Accessed November 1, 2008, at supct.law.cornell.edu/supct/html/92-1292.ZO.html

Marr, Matthew D. 2005. "Mitigating Apprehension about Section 8 Vouchers: The Positive Role of Housing Specialists in Search and Placement." *Housing Policy Debate* 16, no. 1: 85–111.

Marshall, Ann. 2002. "Organizing Across the Divide: Local Feminist Activism, Everyday Life, and the Election of Women to Public Office." *Social Science Quarterly* 83, no. 3 (September): 707–726.

Martín-Rodríguez, Manuel M. 2000. "Hyenas in the Pride Lands: Latinos/as and Immigration in Disney's *The Lion King*." *Aztlán: A Journal of Chicano Studies* 25, no. 1 (Spring): 47–66.

McKenzie, S. 1995. "Reviewing Scientific Papers." *Archives of Disease in Childhood* 72, no. 6 (June): 539–540.

McMurry, Alison Irvine. 2004. "Preparing Students for Peer Review." M.A. Thesis, Brigham Young University.

Meadows, A. Jack. 1980. *Development of Science Publishing in Europe.* Amsterdam: Elsevier.

Merriam-Webster. 1994. *Merriam-Webster's Dictionary of English Usage.* Springfield, MA: Merriam-Webster.

Meyer, Bonnie J.F., D. M. Brandt, and G. J. Bluth. 1980. "Use of the Top-level Structure in Text: Key for Reading Comprehension of Ninth-grade Students." *Reading Research Quarterly* 16: 72–103.

Meyer, Bonnie J. F. 2003. "Text Coherence and Readability." *Topics in Language Disorders* 23, no. 3 (July–September): 204–225.

Meyer, Bonnie J. F., Carole J. Young, and Brendan J. Bartlett. 1989. *Memory Improved: Reading and Memory Enhancement across the Life Span through Strategic Text Structures*. Hillsdale, NJ: Lawrence Erlbaum Associates.

Miller, D. W. 1999. "Sociologists Debate How to Broaden Scholarship in Their Flagship Journal." *Chronicle of Higher Education* 46, no. 2 (3 September). A24–A25.

Modern Language Association. 2008. *MLA Style Manual and Guide to Scholarly Publishing*. 3rd ed. New York: Modern Language Association of America.

Moore, N. A. J. 2006. "Aligning Theme and Information Structure to Improve the Readability of Technical Writing." *Journal of Technical Writing & Communication* 36, no. 1 (Winter): 43–57.

Morison, Samuel Eliot. 1953. *Land and by Sea: Essays and Addresses*. New York: Knopf.

Morris, Meaghan. 1988. "A-mazing Grace: Notes on Mary Daly's Poetics." In *The Pirate's Fiancée: Feminism, Reading Postmodernism*. New York: Verso.

Morton, Herbert C., and Anne J. Price, with Robert Cameron Mitchell. 1989. *The ACLS Survey of Scholars: Final Report of Views on Publications, Computers, and Libraries*. Washington, DC: University Press of America for the American Council of Learned Societies.

Moxley, Joseph M., and Todd Taylor. 1997. *Writing and Publishing for Academic Authors*. 2nd ed. Lanham, MD: Rowman & Littlefield.

Murphy, Eamon. 1998. "Using Descriptive Headings to Improve First Year Student Writing." In *Teaching and Learning in Changing Times*, ed. B. Black and N. Stanley. Proceedings of the 7th Annual Teaching Learning Forum, The University of Western Australia, February 1998. Perth: University of Western Australia.

National Science Foundation, Division of Science Resources Statistics. 2004. *Gender Differences in the Careers of Academic Scientists and Engineers*. NSF 04-323, Project Officer, Alan I. Rapoport. Arlington, VA: National Science Foundation.

Nietzsche, Friedrich. 1989 [1907]. *Beyond Good and Evil*, trans. Helen Zimmern. Buffalo, NY: Prometheus Books.

Nixon, Rob. 2000. "Please Don't Email Me about This Article." *Chronicle of Higher Education* (September 29): B20.

Noriega, Chon A. 2002. "Research Note." *Aztlán: A Journal of Chicano Studies* 27, no. 2 (Fall): 1–8.

Olenchak, F. Richard, and Thomas P. Hébert. 2002. "Endangered Academic Talent: Lessons Learned from Gifted First-Generation College Males." *Journal of College Student Development* 43, no. 2 (March/April): 195–212.

Olson, Gary A. 1997. "Publishing Scholarship in the Humanistic Disciplines: Joining the Conversation." In *Writing and Publishing for Academic Authors*, ed. Joseph M. Moxley and Todd Taylor, 51–69. Lanham, MD: Rowman & Littlefield.

Ortiz, Flora Ida, and Rosa Gonzales. 2000. "Latino High School Students' Pursuit of Higher Education." *Aztlán: A Journal of Chicano Studies* 25, no. 1 (Spring): 67–107.

Osborne, Jason W. 2007. *Best Practices in Quantitative Methods*. Thousand Oaks, CA: Sage.

Pallos, Henrik, Naoto Yamada, Yuriko Doi, Masako Okawa. 2004. "Sleep Habits, Prevalence and Burden of Sleep Disturbances Among Japanese Graduate Students." *Sleep & Biological Rhythms* 2, no. 1: 37–42.

Parker, Frank, and Kathryn Riley. 1995. *Writing for Academic Publication: A Guide to Getting Started.* Superior, WI: Parlay Enterprises.

Petrucci, Carrie. 2002. "Apology in the Criminal Justice Setting: Evidence for Including Apology as an Additional Component in the Legal System." *Behavioral Sciences & the Law* 20: 1–26.

Posusta, Steven. 1996. *Don't Panic: The Procrastinator's Guide to Writing an Effective Term Paper (You Know Who You Are).* Santa Barbara, CA: Bandanna Books.

Pournelle, Jerry, and Alex Pournelle. 1996. "Modern Letters." *Internet World* (February): 102.

Pringle, Mary Beth. 2007. *Revisiting John Grisham: A Critical Companion.* Westport, CT: Greenwood Press.

Pullinger, David J. 1996. "Economics and Organisation of Primary Scientific Publication." Paper presented at Joint ICSU Press/UNESCO Expert Conference on Electronic Publishing In Science in Paris, February 19–23. Accessed November 1, 2008, at www.library.uiuc.edu/icsu/pullin~1.htm

Pullum, Geoffrey K. 2004. "Omit Stupid Grammar Teaching." (May 31). Accessed November 1, 2008, at itre.cis.upenn.edu/~myl/languagelog/archives/000994.html

Rabin, Jeffrey L. 2006. "Clinton Speaks Out on Illegal Workers." *Los Angeles Times* (July 9).

Ringle, Ken. 1998. "The Big Questions Come Naturally; Pulitzer Prize-Winning Sociobiologist Edward O. Wilson Casts His Lofty Gaze on the Global Anthill and Says Humanity Can Do Better." *Los Angeles Times* (July 5): 3.

Rivera, Lorna. 2003. "Changing Women: An Ethnographic Study of Homeless Mothers and Popular Education." *Journal of Sociology & Social Welfare* 30, no. 2 (June): 31–52.

Robbins, Ruth Anne. 2004. "Painting With Print: Incorporating Concepts of Typographic and Layout Design into the Text of Legal Writing Documents." *Journal of the Association of Legal Writing Directors* (Fall): 108–123.

Roberts, John C., Robert H. Fletcher, and Suzanne W. Fletcher 1994. "Effects of Peer Review and Editing on the Readability of Articles Published in Annals of Internal Medicine." *JAMA: Journal of the American Medical Association* 272, no. 2 (July 13): 119–121.

Rochon, Gurwitz, Cheung, Hayes & Chalmers. 1994. "Evaluating the Quality of Articles Published in Journal Supplements Compared with the Quality of Those Published in the Parent Journal." *JAMA: The Journal of the American Medical Association* (July 13) 272, no. 2: 108–113.

Ross-Larson, Bruce. 1982. *Edit Yourself: A Manual for Everyone Who Works with Words.* New York: W. W. Norton & Co.

Rothman, Kenneth J. "Writing for Epidemiology." *Epidemiology* 9, no. 3 (May 1995): 333–337.

Rotton, J. P. Foos, L. Van Meek. 1995. "Publication Practices and the File Drawer Problem: A Survey of Published Authors." *Journal of Social Behavior & Personality* 10, no. 1: 1–13.

Rowling, J. K. 1998. *Harry Potter and the Chamber of Secrets.* New York: Scholastic Books.

Ruiying, Yang, and Desmond Allison. 2004. "Research Articles in Applied Linguistics: Moving from Results to Conclusions." *English for Specific Purposes* 22, no. 4 (2003): 365–385.

Salkind, Neil J. 2007. *Statistics for People Who (Think They) Hate Statistics.* Thousand Oaks, CA: Sage.

Sax, Linda J., Linda Serra Hagedorn, Marisol Arredondo, and Frank A. Dicrisi III. 2002. "Faculty Research Productivity: Exploring the Role of Gender and Family-Related Factors." *Research in Higher Education* 43, no. 4 (August): 423–446.

Schlee, Gunther. 2004. "Taking Sides and Constructing Identities: Reflections on Conflict Theory." *Journal of the Royal Anthropological Institute* 10, no. 1 (March): 135–157.

Sciubba, Emanuela. 2006. "The Evolution of Portfolio Rules and the Capital Asset Pricing Model." *Economic Theory* 29: 123–150.

Sharpe, Jenny. 1991. "The Unspeakable Limits of Rape: Colonial Violence and Counter-Insurgency." *Genders* 10 (Spring): 25–46.

Shelley II, Mack C., and John H. Schuh. 2001. "Are the Best Higher Education Journals Really the Best? A Meta-Analysis of Writing Quality and Readability Journal of Scholarly Publishing." *Journal of Scholarly Publishing* (October) 33, no. 1: 11–22.

Shott, Michael J. 1997. "Stones and Shafts Redux: The Metric Discrimination of Chipped-Stone Dart and Arrow Points." *American Antiquity* 62, no. 1: 86–101.

Sigelman, Lee. 2005. "Report of the Editor of the American Political Science Review, 2003–2004." *PSOnline* (January). Accessed November 1, 2008, at www.apsanet.org

Silverman, Robert J., and Eric L. Collins. 1975. "Publishing Relationships in Higher Education." *Research In Higher Education* 3, no. 4 (December): 365–382.

Simon, Patrick. 2003. "France and the Unknown Second Generation: Preliminary Results on Social Mobility." *International Migration Review* 37, no. 4 (Winter): 1091–1120.

Simon, Rita J., Von Bakanic, and Clark McPhail. 1986. "Who Complains to Journal Editors and What Happens." *Sociological Inquiry* 56, no. 2: 259–271.

Simonton, D K. 1988. *Scientific Genius*. New York: Cambridge University Press.

Skillin, Marjorie E. and Robert Malcolm Gay. 1974. *Words into Type*. 3rd ed. New York: Prentice Hall.

Smith, Richard. 2006. "Peer Review: A Flawed Process at the Heart of Science Journals." *Journal of the Royal Society of Medicine* 99, no. 4 (April): 178–182.

Sofer, Andrew. 2000. "Absorbing Interests: Kyd's Bloody Handkerchief As Palimpsest." *Comparative Drama* 34, no. 12 (Summer): 127–153.

Spencer, N. J., J. Hartnett, and J. Mahoney. 1986. "Problems with Reviews in the Standard Editorial Practice." *Journal of Social Behavior & Personality* 1, no. 1 (January): 21–26.

Staub, Michael E. 1997. "Black Panthers, New Journalism, and the Rewriting of the Sixties." *Representations* 57 (Winter): 53–72.

Stevens, Bonnie Klomp, and Larry L. Stewart. 1987. *A Guide to Literary Criticism and Research*. New York: Holt, Rinehart, & Winston.

Stinchcombe, Arthur L. 1986. "On Getting 'Hung Up' and Other Assorted Illnesses: A Discourse Concerning Researchers, Wherein the Nature of Their Mental Health Problems Is Discussed and Illustrated." In *Stratification and Organization: Selected Papers*, ed. by A. L. Stinchcombe. Cambridge: Cambridge University Press.

Strunk, W., Jr., and E. B. White. 1979. *The Elements of Style*. 3rd ed. New York: Macmillan.

Swales, John M., and Christine B. Feak. 1994. *Academic Writing for Gradate Students: Essential Tasks and Skills, A Course for Nonnative Speakers of English*. Ann Arbor: University of Michigan Press.

Swales, John M., and Christine B. Feak. 2000. *English in Today's Research World: A Writing Guide*. Ann Arbor: University of Michigan Press.

Tagoe, Noel, Ernest Nyarko, and Ebenezer Anuwa-Amarh. 2005. "Financial Challenges Facing Urban SMES Under Financial Sector Liberalization in Ghana (Small and Medium-Sized Enterprises)." *Journal of Small Business Management* 43, no. 3 (July): 331–344.

Tompkins, Jane. 1986. "'Indians': Textualism, Morality, and the Problem of History." *Critical Inquiry* 13, no. 1 (Autumn): 59–77.

Town, Caren J. 2004. "'The Most Blatant of All Our American Myths': Masculinity, Male Bonding, and the Wilderness in Sinclair Lewis's *Mantrap*." *Journal of Men's Studies* 12, no. 3 (Spring): 193–206.

Tufte, Edward. 2006. *Beautiful Evidence*. Cheshire, CT: Graphics Press.

Underwood, B. J. 1957. *Psychological Research*. New York: Appleton Century-Crofts.

University of Chicago. 2003. *Chicago Manual of Style: The Essential Guide for Writers, Editors, and Publishers*, 15th edition. Chicago, IL: University of Chicago Press.

Van Orsdel, Lee C. and Kathleen Born. 2007. "Periodicals Price Survey 2007: Serial Wars: As open access gains ground, STM publishers change tactics, and librarians ask hard questions." *Library Journal* (April 15). Accessed November 1, 2008, at www.libraryjournal.com/article/CA6431958.html.

Walton, Jean. 1997. "'Nightmare of the Uncoordinated White-Folk': Race, Psychoanalysis, and Borderline." *Discourse* 19, no. 2 (Winter): 88–109.

Welch, H. Gilbert. 2006. "Ask the Expert: How to Handle Rejection." *Society of General Internal Medicine Forum* 29, no. 7 (July): 2, 8.

Weller, Ann C. 2001. *Editorial Peer Review: Its Strengths and Weaknesses*. Medford, NJ: Information Today Inc for American Society for Information Science and Technology.

Wilding, Raelene. 2003. "Romantic Love and 'Getting Married': Narratives of the Wedding in and Out of Cinema Texts." *Journal of Sociology* 39, no. 4 (December): 373–390.

Wiley, Mark. 2000. "The Popularity of Formulaic Writing (And Why We Need to Resist)." *English Journal* 90, no. 1 (September): 61–67.

Williams, Joseph M. 1997. *Style: Ten Lessons in Clarity and Grace*. 5th ed. New York: Longman.

Williams, Patrick. 1989. "*Kim* and Orientalism." *Kipling Considered*, ed. P. Mallet. London: Macmillan.

Willis, Meredith Sue. 1993. *Deep Revision: A Guide for Teachers, Students, and Other Writers*. New York: Teachers and Writers Collaborative.

Wilson, Pamela. 1998. "Mountains of Contradictions: Gender Class, and Region in the Star Image of Dolly Parton." *Reading Country Music: Steel Guitars, Opry Stars, and Honky-Tonk Bars*, ed. Cecelia Tichi. Durham, NC: Duke University Press.

Yankauer, A. 1985. "Peering at Peer Review." *CBE Views* 8, no. 2 (Summer): 7–10.

Yoels, W. C. 1971. "Destiny or Dynasty: Doctoral Origins and Appointments Patterns of Editors of the *American Sociological Review*, 1948–68." *American Sociologist* 6, no. 2: 134–139.

Yoels, W. C. 1974. "The Structure of Scientific Fields and the Allocation of Editorships on Scientific Journals: Some Observations on the Politics of Knowledge." *Sociological Quarterly* 15, no. 2: 264–276.

Žižek, Slavoj. 2003. "Interview." *Critical Intellectuals on Writing*, ed. Gary A. Olson and Lynn Worsham, 192–200. New York: State University of New York Press.

Recommended Reading

SCHOLARLY WRITING FOR PUBLICATION

Cantor, Jeffrey A. 1993. *A Guide to Academic Writing*. Westport, CT: Greenwood Publishing Group.

Useful focus on publishing strategies rather than writing. Includes chapter on writing for professional journals. Advises on writing conference papers and grants. Deals at length with book publication, including contracts, prospectuses, and textbooks.

Day, Robert A., and Barbara Gastel. 2006. *How to Write and Publish a Scientific Paper*. 6th ed. New York: Greenwood Press.

Specifically for those in the sciences. Amazon.com says "each edition of this witty and practical guide to writing, organizing, illustrating, and submitting scientific research for publication in a scholarly scientific journal has become an instant bestseller."

Germano, William. 2001. *Getting It Published: A Guide for Scholars and Anyone Else Serious about Serious Books*. Chicago: University of Chicago Press.

Written by the former publishing director of Routledge, this long-time academic editor details why editors choose some books and decline others, how the publishing process works regarding books, how to read a contract, and other details of publishing a book.

Huff, Anne Sigismund. 1998. *Writing for Scholarly Publication*. Thousand Oaks, CA: Sage.

Not focused on journal articles and devoted largely to prewriting.

Luey, Beth. 2002. *Handbook for Academic Authors*. 4th ed. Cambridge: Cambridge University Press.

A comprehensive book on academic publishing. Includes only twenty pages on writing for journals. Includes a useful chapter on revising a dissertation into a book. Discusses at length how to work with publishers. Addresses submission mechanics.

Matkin, Ralph E. and T. F. Riggar. 1991. *Persist and Publish: Helpful Hints for Academic Writing and Publishing*. Boulder: University Press of Colorado.

General methods for increasing "productivity and achievement in the publish-or-perish academic world." Many useful figures and tables. Includes twenty pages on writing for journals.

Moxley, Joseph M., and Todd Taylor. 1997. *Writing and Publishing for Academic Authors*. 2nd ed. Lanham, MD: Rowman & Littlefield.

Collected volume of essays by various authors. Broad book on academic publishing. Little on journal article publishing.

Parker, Frank, and Kathryn Riley. 1996. *Writing for Academic Publication: A Guide to Getting Started.* Superior, WI: Parlay Enterprises.
Broad advice on writing academic reviews, book reviews, abstracts, conference papers, and articles.

Silverman, Franklin H. 1999. *Publishing for Tenure and Beyond.* New York: Praeger.
"Provides graduate students who intend to pursue a career in academia and tenure-track junior faculty with candid information about developing an adequate publication record . . . [and how to] maximize the likelihood of having their articles accepted for publication by peer-reviewed professional, scientific, and scholarly journals." For graduate students and junior faculty, it focuses on journal article publication and the large picture—what content is selling today.

ON STAYING MOTIVATED AND SANE

Becker, Howard S. 2007. *Writing for Social Scientists: How to Start and Finish Your Thesis, Book, or Article.* 2nd ed. Chicago: University of Chicago Press.
Originally published in 1985, this book represents an insightful analysis of why most academic writing is so terrible and a personal reflection on the task of writing well on meaningful topics. Motivational but never sentimental.

Boice, Robert. 2000. *Advice for New Faculty Members: Nihil Nimus.* Boston: Allyn & Bacon.
The best work by the best scholar on academic writing. "Nihil Nimus" means "nothing in excess." This advice is based on Boice's finding that moderation is the single most reliable predictor of success in academic life. The book is full of practical rules for combining teaching, socializing, and brief, daily sessions of writing. "It is the first guidebook to move beyond anecdotes and surmises for its directives, based on the author's extensive experience and solid research in the areas of staff and faculty development," says an Amazon.com review.

Boice, Robert. 1992. *The New Faculty Member: Supporting and Fostering Professional Development.* San Francisco: Jossey-Bass.
An earlier excellent text by the leading authority on academic writing.

Boice, Robert. 1990. *Professors as Writers: A Self-Help Guide to Productive Writing.* Stillwater, OK: New Forums Press.
An extremely helpful, practical guide by the leading authority on academic writing. Includes an extensive diagnostic questionnaire. See especially Chapter 1: "Why Professors Don't Write."

Bolker, Joan. 1998. *Writing Your Dissertation in Fifteen Minutes a Day: A Guide to Starting, Revising, and Finishing Your Doctoral Thesis.* New York: Henry Holt & Co.
Excellent and very popular text on the psychological aspects of writing your dissertation. For writing a dissertation, not journal articles. Focuses on the emotional management of graduate school writing. Well written and to the point. She is a clinical psychologist who has spent the past two decades helping blocked dissertation writers, so it is not surprising that she brings real skill to her task.

Caplan, Paula J. 1994. *Lifting a Ton of Feathers: A Woman's Guide to Surviving in the Academic World.* Toronto: University of Toronto Press.
A useful book for anyone, male or female, in the academy about its "unwritten rules," twenty-seven "myths," and fifteen "catch-22s." Gives some general principles for coping with these myths and gives specific suggestions on dealing with specific challenges. Extensive bibliography of guides for non-dominant groups in the academy.

Fiore, Neil. 2007. *The Now Habit: A Strategic Program for Overcoming Procrastination and Enjoying Guilt-Free Play.* Rev. ed. New York: Tarcher.
First published in 1988, this book is recommended by many of my students.

Goldsmith, John A., John Komlos, and Penny Schine Gold. 2001. *The Chicago Guide to Your Academic Career: A Portable Mentor for Scholars from Graduate School through Tenure.* Chicago: University of Chicago Press.
Gives advice on how to manage graduate school—working with mentors, writing a dissertation, and landing a job—as well as how to handle being an assistant professor, teaching and doing research, getting tenure, and how to combine work and your personal life. Written as a conversation among the three authors.

Peterson, Karen E. 1996. *The Tomorrow Trap: Unlocking the Secrets of the Procrastination-Protection Syndrome.* Deerfield Beach, FL: Health Communications.
Explains that procrastination is caused by emotional protectiveness not laziness. Uses exercises to aid students in recognizing the causes of procrastination and overcoming them.

Peterson, Karen E. 2006. *Write: 10 Days to Overcome Writer's Block. Period.* Cincinnati, OH: Adams Media.
This psychologist and writing instructor bases the book on her research on writer's block and procrastination.

Zerubavel, Eviatar. 1999. *The Clockwork Muse: A Practical Guide to Writing Theses, Dissertations, and Books.* Cambridge: Harvard University Press.
Focused on time management of long projects.

GUIDES FOR NONNATIVE SPEAKERS OF ENGLISH

Feak, Christine B., and John M. Swales. 1997. *Academic Writing for Graduate Students: Essential Tasks and Skills: A Course for Nonnative Speakers of English (English for Specific Purposes).* Ann Arbor: University of Michigan Press.
Another useful book for anyone seeking extremely specific advice about how to write graduate-level research papers. Aimed at students for whom English is a second language, this guide is useful for anyone not entirely sure about what is expected in various parts of an academic paper.

Oshima, Alice. 2006. *Writing Academic English; A Writing and Sentence Structure Handbook for International Students.* 4th ed.: Reading, MA: Addison Wesley Longman, Inc.

Swales, John M., and Christine B. Feak. 2000. *English in Today's Research World: A Writing Guide.* Ann Arbor: University of Michigan Press.
For ESL students with superior skills. Focuses on dissertations, conference abstracts, research articles, fellowship applications, recommendations.

ON WRITING

Lanham, Richard A. 1992. *Revising Prose.* 3rd ed. New York: Macmillan.

Lunsford, Andrea S., and John J. Ruszkiewicz. 2003. *Everything's an Argument,* 3rd ed. Boston: Bedford/St. Martins.
An informal guide for undergraduates written from a more radical perspective on argument.

Ross-Larson, Bruce. 1982. *Edit Yourself: A Manual for Everyone Who Works with Words.* New York: W. W. Norton & Co.
Provides hundreds of examples of poor phrasing and their improvements.

Strunk, W., Jr., and E. B. White. 1979. *The Elements of Style.* 3rd ed. New York: Macmillan.

Williams, Joseph M. 2005. *Style: Ten Lessons in Clarity and Grace.* 6th ed. New York: Longman.
The long-time favorite of writing instructors. Advises that each sentence should have a character and action.

Williams, Joseph M. and Gregory G. Colomb. 2001. *The Craft of Argument.* New York: Longman.
A formal guide for undergraduates written from a traditional perspective on argument.

DICTIONARIES

Merriam-Webster. 2003. *Merriam-Webster's Collegiate Dictionary.* 11th ed. Springfield, MA: Merriam-Webster.
Some dictionaries are more equal than others. Webster's is the standard dictionary for academic writing and is particularly recommended for use with the *Chicago Manual of Style*.

Schwartz, Marilyn. 1995. *Guidelines for Bias-Free Writing.* Bloomington, IN: Indiana University Press. Findings of the Task Force on Bias-Free Language of the Association of American University Presses.
Gives clear advice on how to avoid disparaging, exclusive, or otherwise incorrect usage.

OTHER

Both Sage and the University of Chicago have excellent book series in which experts explain how to perform various professorial tasks, including writing grants, finishing book projects, writing up qualitative research, running statistics, and designing research. See, respectively, www.sagepub.com and www.press.uchicago.edu/Subjects/virtual_guide.html for titles.

Index

About the Author

Wendy Laura Belcher is an award-winning author, academic editor, international lecturer, and professor. She designed one of the first publication-focused writing courses for graduate students and junior faculty in the nation, and for ten years has conducted such courses at the University of California, Los Angeles, and in research institutions around the world, including those in Norway, Malawi, Sudan, and Egypt. These popular workshops are based on her twenty years of experience as an academic editor, including eleven years managing an ethnic studies press and the peer-reviewed journal of record in the field, *Aztlan: A Journal of Chicano Studies*, as well as her two master's degrees in the social sciences and a doctorate in the humanities. She is also a published nonfiction author, whose memoir about her childhood in Ethiopia and Ghana, *Honey from the Lion: An African Journey,* won a Washington State Governor's Writers Award and honorable mention in the Martha Albrand/PEN Society Award for first book of nonfiction. She is now an assistant professor of African literature in the Princeton University Department of Comparative Literature and the Center for African American Studies. For more information, see www.wendybelcher.com.

Supporting researchers for more than 40 years

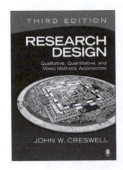
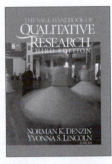

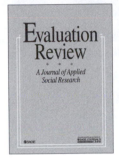

Research methods have always been at the core of SAGE's publishing. Founder Sara Miller McCune founded SAGE in 1965, and soon after, she published SAGE's first methods book, *Public Policy Evaluation*. A few years later, she launched the *Quantitative Applications in the Social Sciences* series—affectionately known as the "little green books."

Always at the forefront of developing and supporting new approaches in methods, SAGE published early groundbreaking texts and journals in the fields of qualitative methods and evaluation.

Today, more than 40 years and two million little green books later, SAGE continues to push the boundaries with a growing list of more than 1,200 research methods books, journals, and reference works across the social, behavioral, and health sciences.

From qualitative, quantitative, and mixed methods to evaluation, SAGE is the essential resource for academics and practitioners looking for the latest methods by leading scholars.

www.sagepub.com